WOODROFFE & LOWE CONSUMER LAW AND PRACTICE

Tenth Edition

By

GEOFFREY WOODROFFE, M.A. (Cantab.)
*Solicitor, Formerly Professor and Director of the
Centre for Consumer and Commercial Law Research,
Brunel University*

CHRISTIAN TWIGG-FLESNER
*Professor of Commercial Law
University of Hull*

CHRIS WILLETT
*Professor of Commercial Law
University of Essex*

*with Precedents by
District Judge Paul Middleton-Roy*

THOMSON REUTERS   **SWEET & MAXWELL**

First Edition 1980
Second Edition 1985
Third Edition 1991
Reprinted 1993
Fourth Edition 1995
Reprinted 1996
Fifth Edition 1999
Reprinted 2000
Sixth Edition 2004
Seventh Edition 2007
Eighth Edition 2010
Ninth Edition 2013
Tenth Edition 2016

Published in 2016 by Thomson Reuters (Professional) UK Limited,
trading as Sweet & Maxwell, Friars House, 160 Blackfriars Road,
London, SE1 8EZ (Registered in England & Wales,
Company No.1679046. Registered Office and address for service:
2nd floor, 1 Mark Square, Leonard Street, London, EC2A 4EG).

For further information on our products and services, visit
www.sweetandmaxwell.co.uk

Typeset by Servis Filmsetting Ltd, Stockport, Cheshire
Printed and bound in Great Britain by T.J. International Ltd, Padstow, Cornwall

No natural forests were destroyed to make this product; only
farmed timber was used and replanted

A CIP catalogue record for this book is available from the
British Library

ISBN 9780414056121

Thomson Reuters and the Thomson Reuters logo are trademarks of Thomson
Reuters. Sweet & Maxwell ™ is a registered trademark of Thomson Reuters
(Professional) UK Limited.

For Robert Lowe
Solicitor, Lecturer and Author
1932–2016

PREFACE TO THE TENTH EDITION

The major changes in consumer law since the Ninth Edition in 2013 emanate from the Consumer Rights Act 2015 (the CRA 2015). The most important provisions appear in Parts 1 and 2 of the CRA 2015. Although it is in essence a consolidating statute, so that the familiar terms such as satisfactory quality, fitness for purpose and unfair terms remain, many detailed amendments have been made to such terms and to consumers' remedies. A brief outline of these changes is given at the end of Chapter One. They are explained in detail in Chapters Two to Five and Eight to Ten.

Another significant change results from the implementation of the EU Directive 2011/83/EU on consumer rights. The Consumer Contracts (Information, Cancellation and Additional Charges) Regulations 2013 consolidate and amend the Doorstep Selling and Distance Selling Regulations and are analysed in Chapter Six.

Of course, case law figures extensively. For example, in Chapter Five *Hufford v Samsung Electronics (UK) Ltd* is a product liability case about a fridge/freezer. In Chapter Seven we relate three claims against airlines: two are Court of Appeal cases—*Jet2.Com Ltd v Huzar* about delay and extraordinary circumstances and *Dawson v Thomson Airways Ltd* about the interrelation between the Montreal Convention and EU Regulation 261/2004—and the third, *Hook v British Airways Plc*, is a Supreme Court decision on the same interrelation. Two cases on the Consumer Credit Act 1974 also reached the Supreme Court: *Durkin v DSG Retail Ltd,* an appeal from Scotland on s.75, is discussed in Chapter Twenty-Four and *Plevin v Paragon Finance Ltd* in Chapter Twenty-Six concerns a PPI policy and unfair relationships under s.140.

As usual Approved Codes of Practice are covered in Chapter Eleven. Since the Chartered Trading Standards Institute succeeded to the OFT's role the pace of approval has quickened with eight achieving Stage Two in three years and six more en route at Stage One.

My thanks again go to the BIS staff, especially Victoria Griffiths, and to Jacqui Guerreiro of the Chartered Trading Standards Institute for their helpful advice. As always Nicola Thurlow and her editorial colleagues deserve our thanks having done their best to cope with the peripatetic life styles of the co-authors; in the end we all managed to ensure publication before the start of the academic year. The same goal was shared by my dear wife, who as a Scottish solicitor was able to help in the detailed task of preparing new material and checking it and the proofs—many thanks, Rosemary.

Special thanks go to Stephen Gerlis who has been our judicial companion and friend on this literary journey from the beginning until the Ninth Edition. He will now, I hope, enjoy a long and happy retirement by the sea. The judicial role of keeping up to date the procedural details of litigation in Chapter Twelve and the practical County Court Precedents in Appendix One has been generously taken over by Judge Paul Middleton-Roy.

I have now decided to share the load by asking two friends and respected consumer law experts to become co-authors. Professors Christian Twigg-Flesner and Chris Willett have worked with me as collaborator in the Journal of Consumer Policy, colleague or co-researcher for many years and I was delighted when they both agreed to join me.

The first six editions—from 1980 to 2004—were written by Robert Lowe and me. The Preface to the First Edition, reprinted below, explains the aims which we had in mind in 1976 when as colleagues at the College of Law (now the University of Law) we conceived the idea, which we proposed to Sweet and Maxwell, of a book on consumer law with a practical approach. Robert Lowe retired from this joint role in 2004 and I carried the baton for the next three editions.

I now have the sad duty of reporting that Robert died recently and so did not see the publication of the Tenth Edition on the fortieth anniversary of the book's conception. This edition is dedicated to my ebullient and larger-than-life friend Robert Lowe.

We have tried to state the law as at 30 April 2016.

Geoffrey Woodroffe

PREFACE TO THE FIRST EDITION

There are many ways of writing a book on consumer protection. One can trace the historical development; one can analyse the economic and social effects; one can deal with the subject from a comparative point of view. In this book we have decided to concentrate on practical problems and remedies. The book is written primarily for law students and for those who are called upon to advise on consumer problems, whether legal or para-legal practitioners. We hope that it will also be useful to persons in industry and their legal advisers as an indication of the growing battery of controls—civil, criminal and administrative—which the law now imposes on business activity. With this aim in mind we have tried to adopt a very practical approach.

A further problem for writers on this subject is that of selection. The term "consumer protection" has no precise definition and it could quite properly be given an immensely wide meaning. Thus every citizen of this country is a consumer, or potential consumer, of welfare benefits, public utilities, health services, educational services and so on. Then again it can be argued that the term "consumer protection" should include the law relating to the supply of housing. Another relevant area is the law of competition which has an underlying consumer protection philosophy. Finally, we have had Government regulation of business activity and in particular we have had price control. In view of our basic approach outlined above we have decided not to deal in any detail with these wide areas. Indeed, we shall concentrate on the types of problem most likely to arise where an individual consumer orders goods or services from a supplier who then proceeds to render defective performance or no performance at all.

Our remedies-based approach has influenced the structure of this book. Part I is entitled "The Consumer and the Civil Law" and deals with such matters as defective performance of contracts to supply goods or services, product liability, the remedies available to the consumer, attempts to exclude them and finally the all-important question of how the remedies can be enforced. Special attention is given to the methods of extra-legal enforcement provided by the growing number of voluntary Codes of Practice. Part II of the book is entitled "The Consumer and the Criminal Law"; special consideration is given to the Trade Descriptions Act 1968 and there is also a chapter dealing with compensation orders. Part III of the book describes the most significant development of consumer protection—administrative control under the Fair Trading Act 1973. Part IV contains nine chapters dealing with "Consumer Protection in Credit Transactions". The book ends with a chapter entitled "The EEC Dimension".

This is a new venture and we would welcome suggestions for improvement. In the meantime we would like to thank the many people who took the trouble to read parts of the typescript and to answer our questions. Special thanks are due to a number of individuals at the Office of Fair Trading, Department of Trade, National Consumer Council, Society of Motor Manufacturers and Traders, Motor Agents Association and the Manchester Arbitration Scheme. The views which they expressed are necessarily personal ones but nevertheless we have found them of great value. We would also like to thank Bill Thomas (solicitor), Valerie Chiswell (consumer adviser), Malcolm Leder (Senior Lecturer at Middlesex Polytechnic), and Peter Chiswell, Peter Hawkins, Tony King, and Chris Whitehouse (all at the College of Law). All of them made very helpful suggestions and assisted in the tiresome task of proof reading.

At the time of going to press there is a Bill before Parliament entitled the Sale of Goods Bill. This is a pure consolidation measure which does not make any changes in the law. The future of the London Small Claims Court, which is discussed in Chapter 9, is still in the balance; we understand that a grant of £5,000 will enable it to survive.

We have tried to state the law as at October 1, 1979.

Robert Lowe
Geoffrey Woodroffe

CONTENTS

PART II: THE CONSUMER AND THE CRIMINAL LAW

PART III: ADMINISTRATIVE CONTROL

PART IV: CREDIT TRANSACTIONS

TABLE OF CASES

TABLE OF STATUTES

TABLE OF STATUTORY INSTRUMENTS

TABLE OF EU DIRECTIVES

INTRODUCTION

"The coffee at McDonald's was too hot"
"The central heating isn't working"
"The holiday was ruined"
"The car has been off the road for a month"
"The salesman wouldn't go away until I signed"
"There was a snail in the ginger beer"

1. HISTORICAL PERSPECTIVE

This book is concerned with complaints which consumers may have against a **1.01** supplier of goods, services or credit and with the remedies available to them. It is a vast subject and it is necessary to curtail it.

In the words of the Molony Committee on Consumer Protection (1961) "the consumer, unlike some classes with claims on public bounty, is everybody all the time". In the present book, however, the word "consumer" will be used to describe a customer who buys for personal use and not for business purposes.

A number of learned writers, e.g. Borrie and Diamond in their excellent book *The Consumer, Society and the Law*, have traced the history of the subject and have shown that, although the subject is comparatively new, its roots are old. Thus the law has imposed duties on persons exercising certain callings for many centuries, e.g. inn-keepers and carriers. Nevertheless, the explosion of interest in consumer matters was very much a creature of the second half of the 20th century. We can see this simply by looking at the dates of some of the principal reforming legislation:

Hire-Purchase Acts 1954 and 1964 **1.02**

Trade Descriptions Act 1968

Fair Trading Act 1973

Supply of Goods (Implied Terms) Act 1973

Consumer Credit Act 1974

Unfair Contract Terms Act 1977

Consumer Safety Act 1978

Supply of Goods and Services Act 1982

Consumer Protection Act 1987

Sale and Supply of Goods Act 1994

Unfair Terms in Consumer Contracts Regulations 1999

Sale and Supply of Goods to Consumers Regulations 2002

Enterprise Act 2002

Consumer Protection from Unfair Trading Regulations 2008

Consumer Rights Act 2015

What is the reason for this tremendous upsurge of activity? The answer is two-fold—a combination of new business methods and changing social attitudes. The key factors on business methods are to be found in the complexity of the goods themselves and in the changing forms of advertising, marketing and distribution. To quote again from the Molony Report (p.31):

> [The last half century] has seen a growing tendency for manufacturers ... to appeal directly to the public by forceful national advertising and other promotional methods ... a further influence during the same period has been the development of a mass market for extremely complex mechanical and electrical goods. ... Their performance cannot in some cases be accurately established by a short trial; shortcomings of design are not apparent to the inexpert eye; inherent faults may only come to light when the article breaks down after a period of use.

In other words, the need for what is called consumer protection has become far greater because consumers are no longer in a position to rely on their own judgment when buying a complex article.

The second motivating force is the general move from individualism to collectivism. The 20th century saw not only consumer protection but also the Rent Acts, the Financial Services and Markets Act, the massive volume of legislation protecting employees and, of course, the welfare state. The extent to which some of these measures hamper business activity is, of course, a matter of keen and continual political debate.

1.03   A government White Paper "modern markets; confident consumers" was published as our Fifth Edition went to press in July 1999. Welcoming the decision to place consumers at the heart of government policy the Director General of Fair Trading pointed out that

> consumer complaints are now running at 900,000 a year and these are the tip of the iceberg—I believe that tens of millions of transactions for goods or services cause problems for the consumers. Rightly UK consumers expect better service and better quality and that demand is going to get stronger. (OFT Press Notice 22 July 1999)

In the following year research carried out by the Office of Fair Trading (OFT) estimated that "defective goods, substandard service and poor information cost consumers £83 billion—with those on lower incomes particularly badly hit" (OFT Press Notices 11/00 and 12/00). Obviously the scale of the problem is even higher now.

The international dimension

It is clear that the judiciary of the United States has been a long way ahead of **1.04** this country in recognising and dealing with consumer problems. In particular, the American courts have increased the manufacturer's liability in two respects: (1) by moving from negligence liability to strict liability; and (2) by breaking the shackles of the privity of contract rule. In the UK these changes have been left to Parliament.[1]

The subject of consumer protection is also very much alive in the EU and most UK legislation in the last 30 years derives from EU Directives.

The original Rome Treaty did not refer specifically to consumer protection but now, under the Maastricht amendments, art.3(r) specifies "a contribution to the strengthening of consumer protection" as one of the key activities of the Community. The previous editions of this book highlighted a number of major EU initiatives which have become part of English law—product liability, misleading advertisements, doorstep selling, package holidays, unfair contract terms, distance selling, consumer remedies and unfair commercial practices. A list of consumer protection Directives and their implementation into domestic law can be found in the Enterprise Act 2002 (Pt 8 Community Infringements Specified UK Laws) Order 2003 (SI 2003/1374).

2. CONSUMER PROTECTION ORGANISATIONS

There is a very large number of bodies concerned with consumer protec- **1.05** tion matters and they can be divided into Government Departments, Government-sponsored bodies, local authorities and voluntary bodies.

Government departments

The Department for Business Innovation and Skills

The Department for Business Innovation and Skills (BIS, formerly DTI **1.06** and, briefly, BERR) seeks to improve consumer protection both directly (through consumer protection legislation and advice) and indirectly (through competition law). A speech given by a previous Minister (Dr Howells) to the Yorkshire Fiscal Group contains the following passage:

> "To prosper, companies need satisfied customers, but the expectations of customers are growing. Well-informed consumers, able to make discerning choices, put pressure on businesses to provide better goods and services, tailored to the needs of their customers and sold at competitive prices ... The revolution in shopping via the Internet and digital highways will enable consumers to compare prices and product quality not only against those available in the other Member States of the European Union but elsewhere in the world including the US. I

---

[1] See para.4.06 below.

have no doubt that this will change forever the ways we judge whether and if we are getting a good deal . . . We are also working on proposals to ensure that consumer law is consistently enforced and that traders who cheat consumers are quickly stopped."

He also referred to the Competition Act 1998 which brought about a long-awaited reform of competition law and gave the OFT much-needed, sweeping new powers to take action against "firms and cartels which try to restrict competition or rig prices ripping off the consumer". These powers were further increased by the Enterprise Act 2002 which, for the first time, imposed criminal liability on cartels.

Among its principal duties BIS makes Regulations under the Consumer Credit Act 1974 and the Pt II of the Consumer Protection Act 1987. It also issues a large number of Press Releases and offers a great deal of business information and advice on issues ranging from pyramid selling ("if an offer seems too good to be true it probably is") to e-shopping, consumer credit and how to complain. These can be viewed on its website *http://www.bis.gov.uk*.

Office of Fair Trading

1.07 Closely linked to BIS was the Office of Fair Trading (OFT), a statutory body set up under the Fair Trading Act 1973. After 40 years its licensing functions were taken over in April 2014 by the Financial Conduct Authority (FCA) and its enforcement role by the Competition and Markets Authority (CMA).

Its duties included promoting good practice in the carrying out of activities which might affect the economic interests of consumers and, until April 2013, approving Codes of Practice. It issued a large number of press releases setting out warnings and details of enforcement action and also publications containing advice in everyday language (a guide aimed at students was entitled "wake up, wise up, speak up, don't get stuffed").

One of the OFT's main functions was the licensing of credit businesses under the Consumer Credit Act 1974. It was also involved closely in monitoring unfair terms: it had running battles with the banks, estate agents and health and fitness clubs.

The OFT's support of codes of practice, latterly under the umbrella of the Consumer Codes Approval Scheme, was a valuable contribution to consumer protection and should not be overlooked when considering the conciliation and resolution of consumer complaints.

In spite of the OFT's success the Government decided in 2014 to bring the OFT's 40 years of consumer protection to an end. Its codes' functions were transferred to the Chartered Institute of Trading Standards (see Chapter Eleven).

Financial Conduct Authority

1.08 The vital regulation of credit was allotted to the newly created FCA and CMA. The FCA was set up under the Financial Services Act 2012 in the wake of the financial crisis. It took over the responsibilities of banking supervision from the Financial Services Authority and the licensing of credit and financial services firms from the OFT. We explain briefly in Chapter Twenty-One the FCA authorisation process.

Government-sponsored bodies

A number of bodies now have the power to apply for a court injunction to restrain the continued use of unfair terms in consumer contracts. This topic is considered in Chapter Ten. **1.09**

National Consumer Council and Citizens Advice

The National Consumer Council (NCC) had been in operation as a company since 1974 and in recent years was branded as Consumer Focus. It was an independent, publicly-funded body acting as a watchdog and pressure group to protect consumer interests. **1.10**

As part of the reorganisation of consumer bodies—we have just mentioned the demise of the OFT—in April 2013 the NCC was restructured to become the Regulated Industries Unit (RIU) with responsibility for postal services and energy in Great Britain; in 2014 the RIU transferred to Citizens Advice (CA). Its general advocacy and education roles moved directly to CA in April 2013, and the advice line Consumer Direct was also replaced by the Citizens Advice Consumer Helpline then.

The NCC was created after the abolition of the Consumer Council in 1971 and had a fine record of lobbying and promoting consumer legislation. For example, it was responsible for the birth of the Supply of Goods and Services Act 1982 as a Private Members' Bill.

Unhappily we say goodbye to both the OFT and NCC. Their activities have been of immense value to consumers for four decades.

British Standards Institute

BIS also makes a grant to the British Standards Institute (BSI). This voluntary body has been in existence since 1901. One of its functions is to lay down uniform specifications for certain products. If a product bears a BSI "kite mark" this means that it has been tested by BSI. Regular spot checks will follow and the mark will be withdrawn if these prove unsatisfactory. It can be seen on products worldwide—from manhole covers and Christmas lights to lawnmowers and cricket balls—enabling manufacturers to achieve product differentiation. **1.11**

Local authorities

The county councils and the London boroughs make three major contributions to consumer protection. First they employ trading standards inspectors (their former name was weights and measures inspectors) who have extensive responsibilities in the enforcement of legislation including the Consumer Credit Act 1974. They also have enforcement powers under the Consumer Rights Act 2015 (see Chapter Ten). Secondly, Environmental Health Departments are responsible for the enforcement of legislation on **1.12** a number of matters including noise, pollution, waste disposal and bad housing.

Voluntary bodies

1.13   Which? (formerly the Consumers' Association) is widely known for its comparative testing of goods and services. The results are published in *Which?* magazine and are clearly of great value to prospective consumers. Which? is very active in promoting legislation dealing with consumer affairs (including consumer awareness of legal remedies).

There is also a number of consumer groups at local level; their main function is to carry out research into the quality of local services and to publish the results of these surveys to their members. There is a central co-ordinating body formerly known as the National Federation of Consumer Groups; it became the National Consumer Federation in 2002 when it amalgamated with Consumer Congress after the Department of Trade and Industry withdrew the funding of both organisations.

Another body working in a closely related field is the Money Advice Trust which is an umbrella organisation formed in 1991 to bring together a large number of money advice bodies. Back in 1999, the Chairman Robert Colville stated that "over a million people every year seek help from money advisers and demand for their services is exceeding supply".

Trade Association Codes

1.14   We should mention trade and professional associations (e.g. the Association of British Travel Agents and the Finance and Leasing Association). These are in no sense consumer protection agencies but many of them operate voluntary conciliation and arbitration procedures. A consumer with a complaint may well find that an approach to the relevant association will produce a more satisfactory outcome than embarking on the hazards of litigation. The codes of practice and complaints procedures operated by a number of associations under the Consumer Codes Approval Scheme are examined in Chapter Eleven of this book.

Ombudsmen

1.15   One important aspect of the voluntary procedures referred to above has been the creation of an "Ombudsman" for particular business activities. The Insurance Ombudsman's Bureau was set up, on a voluntary basis, in 1981. Similar bodies were set up in relation to other sectors such as banking, building societies, funerals, estate agents, pensions and unit trusts. Many of them were brought together as a "one stop shop" by the Financial Ombudsman Service. They are discussed in Chapter Eleven.

Part I

THE CONSUMER AND THE CIVIL LAW

1. SCHEME OF CHAPTERS TWO – TWELVE

The civil law assists the consumer by imposing certain obligations on manu-   **1.16**
facturers and suppliers of goods and services and by restricting attempts to
exclude or cut down these obligations or the remedies available on breach.

In Chapters Two to Four we shall consider the consumer's rights against
the *immediate supplier* of goods for failure to pass title, to deliver the goods
contracted for or to deliver goods of the right quality and fitness. Then in
Chapter Five we shall discuss the rights against the *manufacturer (and other
suppliers in the distribution chain)* both under the general law and under Pt
I of the Consumer Protection Act 1987. Chapters Six and Seven deal with a
number of common consumer problems including defective performance,
late delivery, distance selling, disputes about the price and holidays. In
Chapter Eight we shall analyse and explain the remedies available to the consumer. This will be followed in Chapters Nine and Ten by an examination of
unfair terms and exemption clauses.

The last two chapters in this Part deal with questions of enforcement.
In Chapter Eleven we shall describe ways in which the consumer can seek
redress without going to court—including codes of practice and ombudsmen. Finally Chapter Twelve is entitled "What happens if I go to court?"; it
describes the conduct of cases under the Civil Procedure Rules.

2. CONSUMER RIGHTS ACT 2015—AN INTRODUCTION

The main purpose of the Consumer Rights Act 2015 (CRA 2015) was to   **1.17**
make the law less complex and more accessible to consumers by consolidating the various statutes into one Act. Most of them covered consumers'
contractual rights and business-to-business agreements too. They continue
to apply to business contracts and to contracts between consumers. We give
below a brief outline of the main changes.

Goods and Services

Generally where possible the language of the earlier statutes has been   **1.18**
retained—see, for example, ss.9 and 10 which replicate the satisfactory

quality and fitness for purpose provisions in s.14(2) and (3) of the Sale of Goods Act 1979 (1979 Act).

The opportunity was taken to clarify the previous language in places. Thus in s.17 "property"—the word used in s.12(1) of the 1979 Act—has been replaced by "ownership", defined in s.4(1) as "the general property in goods"; however, s.4(2) does not deal with the rules on "when ownership is transferred", but instead refers to the "property" rules in ss.16–20 of the 1979 Act. Thus consolidation is not quite complete and the 1979 Act on this and some other aspects continues to apply to both business *and* consumer contracts.[1]

The statutes relating to supplies of goods and services which have been consolidated (mainly the provisions about implied terms and remedies) are:

- The Supply of Goods (Implied Terms) Act 1973
- The Sale of Goods Act 1979
- The Supply of Goods and Services Act 1982.

One new implied term about goods has been added. Section 14 provides that where the consumer has seen a model of the goods, they must match the model.

Supplies of goods are now covered by Part 1, Chapter 2, of the CRA 2015 and supplies of services by Part 1, Chapter 4.

Digital content

1.19   Contracts to supply digital content were not specifically dealt with in the previous Acts or Regulations. They are now covered by Part 1, Chapter 3, of the CRA 2015 which contains implied terms similar to those relating to goods.

Unfair terms

1.20   A related area, which was unduly complex because of the interrelation and overlap between two sets of provisions, concerns unfair terms:

- The Unfair Contract Terms Act 1977
- The Unfair Terms in Consumer Contracts Regulations 1999

The Act affected exclusion and limitation clauses in both consumer and business contracts. The Regulations were confined, as their title states, to consumer contracts.

Both sets of statutory provisions have now been amalgamated in Part 3 of the CRA 2015.

---

[1]   i.e. sales by consumers to other consumers or to traders.

Key Definitions

Part 1, Chapter 1, of the CRA 2015 contains two sections. Section 1 briefly **1.21**
describes which chapters of Part 1 cover which types of contract; we explained
these earlier. Section 2 contains "Key definitions":

Trader

By s.2(2): **1.22**

> "Trader" means a person acting for purposes relating to that person's trade,
> business, craft or profession . . .

Consumer

By s.2(3): **1.23**

> "Consumer" means an individual acting for purposes that are wholly or mainly
> outside that individual's trade, business, craft or profession.

By s.2(4) a trader claiming that this is not the case must prove it.

Goods

By s.2(8): **1.24**

> "Goods" means any tangible moveable items.

This includes water, gas or electricity, if supplied in a limited volume or set
quantity.

Digital content

By s.2(9): **1.25**

> "Digital content" means data which are produced and supplied in digital form.

CHAPTER TWO

"THEY SAY IT ISN'T MINE"

(1) A owns a diamond ring. B steals it and sells it to C who sells it to D. The **2.01**
police have now traced the ring and have seized it from D's home.
(2) E takes his car to F, a car dealer, and says "Find me a buyer but don't sell
for less than £5,000." F sells to G for £3,000 and disappears.
(3) H, a finance house, supplies a car to I on hire purchase. Before completing
her payments I sells the car to J, a motor dealer, who lets the car out to K on a
fresh hire-purchase agreement. H now claim from K the unpaid balance due
on the original agreement.

These problems all concern the transfer of "ownership", which is defined in **2.02**
s.4(1) of the CRA 2015 as "the general property in goods". "Ownership" is the
word chosen in the CRA 2015 to describe what the 1979 Act calls "property".
This word needs to be borne in mind too, if only because the rules about the
transfer of ownership from seller to buyer are still to be found in the 1979 Act:
s.4(2) of the CRA 2015 specifically cross-refers to them. To confuse matters
further the word "title" is often used instead in discussing problems of this type
and in drafting commercial contracts (e.g. reservation of title clauses).

In unravelling this type of problem three closely connected principles must **2.03**
be distinguished:

(1) Does any buyer acquire title to the goods?

(2) What are the rights as between each buyer and seller? This question will
usually only be relevant in advising a buyer who has not acquired title.

(3) What are the rights of a buyer who has spent money on improving
the goods?

In this chapter it is proposed to deal separately with these three questions.

The first question will almost always concern a contract for the sale of
goods. "A sales contract" is one of the various types of "contracts to supply
goods" covered by Chapter 2 of the CRA 2015. They are listed in s.3 and
defined separately in ss.5 to 8.

Section 5 defines "Sales contracts" as follows: **2.04**

(1) A contract is a sales contract if under it—

(a) the trader transfers or agrees to transfer ownership of goods to the consumer, and

(b) the consumer pays or agrees to pay the price.

(2) A contract is a sales contract (whether or not it would be one under subsection (1)) if under the contract—

(a) goods are to be manufactured or produced and the trader agrees to supply them to the consumer,
(b) on being supplied, the goods will be owned by the consumer, and
(c) the consumer pays or agrees to pay the price.

(3) A sales contract may be conditional (see section 3(5)), but in this Part "conditional sales contract" means a sales contract under which—

(a) the price for the goods or part of it is payable by instalments, and
(b) the trader retains ownership of the goods until the conditions specified in the contract (for the payment of instalments or otherwise) are met;

and it makes no difference whether or not the consumer possesses the goods.

Its two essential elements are set out in s.5(1): the trader's transfer of ownership to the consumer and the consumer's payment of the price.

(This is very similar to the wording of s.2(1) of the 1979 Act.)

A sales contract must be distinguished from other contracts for the supply of goods—hire, hire-purchase, work and materials, exchange—although the law is similar in many key areas. Hire and hire-purchase are not sales because the contract does not "transfer ownership of goods" to the other party, who merely has a right to the use and possession of the goods and, in the case of hire-purchase,[1] an option to purchase them too. Work and materials contracts are not sales because of the presence of services as well. Finally, an exchange of goods is not a sale as no "price" is paid.

1. Does the Buyer get Title?

2.05   Where goods are sold by a non-owner the law is faced with a clear policy choice. Lord Denning MR has described it as follows[2]:

> "In the development of our law two principles have striven for mastery. The first is for the protection of property; no one can give a better title than he himself possesses.[3] The second is for the protection of commercial transactions; the person who takes in good faith and for value without notice[4] should get a good title."

Faced with this choice the law has developed in a piecemeal and haphazard way with a basic rule protecting property and a number of exceptions protecting commercial transactions. The Crowther Committee on Consumer Credit described the rules as "arbitrary and capricious" and pointed out that their application depended "not on principles of equity or justice but on fine technicalities which have little rhyme and less reason".[5]

---

[1] *Helby v Matthews* [1895] A.C. 471. See CRA 2015 ss.6, 7.
[2] *Bishopsgate Motor Finance Corp Ltd v Transport Brakes Ltd* [1949] 1 K.B. 322 at 336–337.
[3] This is commonly referred to as the *"nemo dat"* rule, i.e. *nemo dat quod non habet*.
[4] See *Gray v Smith* [2013] EWHC 4136 (Comm).
[5] Report, p.178.

There has been only one small step to bring this area of the law into line with modern commercial life. The rules of "market overt", dating back to the 16th century, enabled a buyer in certain types of market to acquire a good title from a non-owner (e.g. a thief). This ancient rule was enshrined in s.22(1) of the 1979 Act but it was finally abolished by the Sale of Goods (Amendment) Act 1994.

The nemo dat rule

With this warning we can examine the relevant provisions. The cornerstone is **2.06** to be found in s.21(1) of the 1979 Act. It reads:

> Subject to this Act, where the goods are sold[6] by a person who is not their owner, and who does not sell them under the authority or with the consent of the owner, the buyer acquires no better title to the goods than the seller had, unless the owner of the goods is by his conduct precluded from denying the seller's authority to sell.

If we revert to our three examples, the effect of s.21(1) is that the goods will still belong to A, E and H unless someone along the line acquired title under one of the exceptions to the basic rule. We must now consider the scope and extent of these exceptions.

Does an exception apply?

Let us first list the nine principal exceptions: **2.07**

Sale under order of court

Sale under a common law or statutory power

Sale with the owner's consent

Sale where the owner is precluded from denying the seller's right to sell ("estoppel")

Disposition by a mercantile agent

Sale under a voidable title

Disposition by a seller in possession

Disposition by a buyer in possession

Disposition of a motor vehicle under Pt III of the Hire-Purchase Act 1964

It is now proposed to examine six of the more important of these exceptions. Nearly all of the examples chosen relate to cars; this is clearly the area where the consumer is most likely to buy goods which do not belong to the

---

[6] "Sold" does not cover an agreement to sell by the intermediate seller: *Shaw v Commissioner of Police of the Metropolis* [1987] 1 W.L.R. 1332 CA.

seller. There is substantial overlap between these provisions and it is often advisable to plead more than one.

(a) Estoppel

2.08   Section 21(1) itself displaces the basic *nemo dat* rule where the owner, by his conduct, is precluded from denying the seller's right to sell. The courts have construed this provision in a fairly narrow way. In the words of Lord Wilberforce:

> "English law has generally taken the robust line that the man who owns property is not under a general duty to safeguard it and that he may sue for its recovery any person into whose hands it has come."[7]

2.09   In *Central Newbury Car Auctions Ltd v Unity Finance Ltd*[8]:

> A distinguished looking swindler wished to acquire a car from Central Newbury Car Auctions on hire purchase terms and intimated that he was prepared to leave his own car in part exchange. He filled in an application form for a hire purchase agreement. If the deal went through the dealer would sell to a finance company who would let the car to him on hire purchase. Central Newbury allowed him to take the new car and its registration book away. Within a very short time it was discovered that (i) he had given a false name, address and employer; (ii) the car which he had left in part exchange did not belong to him; and (iii) he had sold the new car to Unity Finance. Central Newbury sued Unity Finance for the return of the car.

It was the classic situation; which of two innocent parties should suffer for the fraud of a third? Many people would agree with Lord Denning that the loss should fall on Central Newbury in view of their carelessness in parting with the car. Nevertheless this was a minority view; the majority in the Court of Appeal applied what Lord Wilberforce has described as the "robust" view.[9] All that Central Newbury had done was to hand over physical possession; that was not conduct which precluded them from setting up their ownership; the car was still theirs. The only right of Unity Finance would be an action against the swindler under s.17(1) of the CRA 2015[10] and this would almost certainly be worthless.

2.10   In the later case of *Moorgate Mercantile Co v Twitchings*[11]:

> Finance companies set up a company called HPI and 98 per cent of all finance companies belonged to it. The object was to register subsisting hire purchase agreements—some four-and-a-half million—and to pass on information to motor dealers who were associated members. Any dealer who was considering buying a car could contact HPI to find out whether a hire purchase agreement relating to that car was registered. Several thousand inquiries were

---

[7] *Moorgate Mercantile Co v Twitchings* [1977] A.C. 890 at 902.
[8] [1957] 1 Q.B. 371.
[9] See above.
[10] See para.2.27 below.
[11] [1977] A.C. 890.

made each day. The M. Finance Co. entered into a hire purchase agreement, but for some unexplained reason they failed to register it with HPI. The hirer offered to sell the car to T, a dealer. T contacted HPI and was told that nothing had been registered. He then bought the car from the hirer. M. Finance Co. claimed that the car was still theirs. The House of Lords, by a majority, upheld this claim.

The case was fought on two grounds—estoppel and negligence. As to estoppel the question was two-fold: (i) were HPI the agents of the finance companies? (ii) did their answers amount to a representation that no finance company had an interest in the car? By a majority of four to one (Lord Salmon dissenting) the House of Lords gave a negative answer to both of these questions. The other argument was negligence—the M. Finance Co owed a legal duty of care to dealers and were in breach of that duty. This argument was accepted by the Court of Appeal and by Lords Salmon and Wilberforce but the majority of the House of Lords rejected it. One of the main reasons which influenced the majority was the fact that (i) membership of HPI was voluntary, and (ii) there was no duty to register agreements. Neither of these arguments appears totally convincing but they indicate that the owner of goods will seldom lose his ownership by reason of carelessness, even though this causes serious loss to an innocent buyer. We shall see later that HPI can also be used by a prospective private buyer.[12]

The only type of case where owners may be estopped is where they make a positive representation that the seller owns the goods[13] or where they sign a document which clearly conveys that impression.[14]

Not surprisingly a document signed at gunpoint during an armed robbery does not create an estoppel.[15]

(b) Disposition by a mercantile agent

We have seen that the mere delivery of possession does not preclude the owner from setting up his ownership. There is, however, one statutory exception. The basic effect of s.2 of the Factors Act 1889 (the 1889 Act) is that if the owner transfers possession to a "mercantile agent", this may amount to a representation that the agent has authority to sell. If the agent then sells in the ordinary course of business, the owner may lose his ownership even though the agent went beyond his instructions.

2.11

The 1889 Act starts by defining a mercantile agent. By s.1:

2.12

'Mercantile agent' shall mean a mercantile agent having in the customary course of his business as such agent authority to sell goods, or to consign goods for the purpose of sale, or to buy goods, or to raise money on the security of goods.

---

[12] See para.2.25 below.
[13] See *Henderson v Williams* [1895] 1 Q.B. 521.
[14] See *Eastern Distributors v Goldring* [1957] 2 Q.B. 600.
[15] *Debs v Sibec Developments* [1990] R.T.R. 91.

Then comes the key provision. By s.2(1):

> Where a mercantile agent is, with the consent of the owner, in the possession of goods . . . any sale, pledge or other disposition of the goods, made by him when acting in the ordinary course of business of a mercantile agent, shall . . . be as valid as if he were expressly authorised by the owner of the goods to make the same; provided that the person taking under the disposition acts in good faith, and has not at the time of the disposition notice that the person making the disposition has not authority to make the same.

This section could apply to the second example at the beginning of this chapter.[16] If the agent receives instructions not to sell for less than £5,000 or if he is merely instructed to take offers, the buyer will usually not be aware of these restrictions and will get a good title under s.2 even though the agent exceeded his authority.

The sale by the agent must be in the ordinary course of business and the buyer must have no notice of the restrictions on the agent's authority. In practice these points are unlikely to give rise to difficulty. There are, however, three other points which could defeat the buyer's claim. Thus:

(1) The section will apply only if the agent was in possession *in his capacity of mercantile agent*. It would not apply if, for example, a garage which happened to be a mercantile agent received a car for servicing or repair and then sold it.[17]

(2) The agent must have received possession of the goods with the owner's consent. The mere fact that consent was obtained by fraud[18] or that consent has ended[19] does not affect the buyer unless he knows of this—an obviously sensible rule. On the other hand, the owner may decide to keep the registration document and/or the ignition key. What happens if he accidentally leaves them with the dealer or in the car? In *Pearson v Rose and Young*[20]:

> The owner of a car instructed a dealer to obtain offers. He never intended to hand over the registration book but by mistake he left it in the dealer's showroom. The dealer sold the car with its registration book to a buyer. The Court of Appeal held that (i) in the case of a second-hand car the words 'goods' included the registration book and the consent of the owner must extend to the registration book as well as to the car itself; (ii) there had been no consent to the handing over of the book; (iii) the dealer must therefore be treated as if he had sold the car without the book; (iv) such a sale would not be in the ordinary course of business; (v) consequently the buyer obtained no title under section 2.[21]

---

[16] See para.2.01 above.

[17] See, e.g. *Belvoir Finance Co Ltd v Harold G. Cole & Co Ltd* [1969] 1 W.L.R. 1877.

[18] *Folkes v King* [1923] 1 K.B. 282; but perhaps the position would be different if the owner was under a fundamental mistake as to the agent's identity.

[19] The 1889 Act s.2(2).

[20] [1951] 1 K.B. 275.

[21] See also *Stadium Finance Ltd v Robbins* [1962] 2 Q.B. 664 CA (log book accidentally left in car; key not handed over at all; buyer from agent not protected).

(3) The buyer must act in good faith. In *Summers v Havard*[22]:

> The appellant H, a motor dealer, bought 36 cars from another dealer X. H knew that X was in financial trouble and up to skulduggery and that some of the cars in X's possession did not belong to X.

The Court of Appeal held that H was not acting in good faith. "If a person deliberately refrained from making enquiries he was not acting in good faith" (per Arden LJ at para.17).

(c) Seller with a voidable title

Where a contract is voidable (e.g. for misrepresentation) it is a valid contract until the innocent party takes steps to set it aside, i.e. rescinds the contract. The remedy of rescission is an equitable one and in certain cases it will not be possible to rescind. One such case is concerned with third party rights—once a third party has acquired rights under the voidable contract it will be too late to rescind it. This principle now appears in s.23 of the 1979 Act as follows: **2.13**

> When the seller of goods has a voidable title to them, but his title has not been avoided at the time of the sale, the buyer acquires a good title to the goods, provided that he buys them in good faith and without notice of the seller's defect of title.

In virtually all the reported cases under this section the goods were obtained as a result of a fraudulent misrepresentation. The position of the ultimate buyer depends on a highly technical rule—was the title of the fraudulent buyer *voidable* for misrepresentation or *void* for mistake? In the well-known case of *Ingram v Little*[23]:

> Three ladies agreed to sell a car to a man who called himself 'Hutchinson'. They were reluctant to take a cheque from him but he gave them the initials and address of a real Hutchinson. After checking in the telephone directory they let him take the car away in return for a cheque. He sold the car to a buyer; the cheque was dishonoured. The Court of Appeal held that (i) the offer to sell was made to the real Hutchinson and could not be accepted by anyone else; (ii) consequently the contract with the rogue was void for unilateral mistake; (iii) consequently section 23 did not apply and the buyer acquired no title.

Some years ago, the Law Reform Committee recommended that the fraudulent person should always be treated as having a *voidable* title, so that the ultimate buyer would be protected. No such legislation has been enacted but the courts have, in effect, achieved this result. In the later case of *Lewis v Averay* **2.14**

---

[22] [2011] EWCA Civ 764.
[23] [1961] 1 Q.B. 31. For a more recent case with the same result see *Shogun Finance Ltd v Hudson* [2001] EWCA 1000 which is discussed in [2002] 23(2) B.L.R. 288–290.

(No.1)[24] the facts were somewhat similar to those in *Ingram v Little* but the decision went the other way. In that case:

> A rogue calling himself Richard Green—a well-known television actor—induced the owner of a car to sell it to him in return for a cheque. He resold the car to a buyer. The cheque was dishonoured.

The Court of Appeal held that the rogue had a voidable title, with the result that s.23 protected the buyer. They treated *Ingram v Little* as a case turning on very special facts and laid down the broad principle that where the parties were face-to-face, the seller would normally be treated as intending to deal with the actual person in front of him. If this intention was brought about by fraud or by a trick, this would make the transaction voidable but not void.

2.15   Section 23 does not apply if the owner has avoided the contract *before* the resale takes place. In general the innocent party must give notice of rescission and this can raise a practical problem, since not all fraudulent buyers supply their sellers with a correct address. In *Car and Universal Finance Co v Caldwell*[25] the Court of Appeal held that avoidance was possible in this type of case without notifying the fraudulent buyer. In that case the seller reported the matter to the police and the AA as soon as the cheque was dishonoured and asked them to trace the car. It was held that his conduct did amount to an avoidance of contract. The practical effect of this case has however been largely undermined by the later case of *Newtons of Wembley Ltd v Williams* which is considered later in this chapter.[26] The onus is on the ultimate buyer to prove that title passed before the contract was avoided.[27]

(d) Seller in possession after a previous sale

2.16   We have seen that the owner of goods may lose his ownership if he transfers possession to a mercantile agent who disposes of them in the ordinary course of business.[28] We now meet two further cases where ownership and possession are split. The first concerns a sale where the buyer becomes the owner but the seller retains possession. Let us assume that X, an antique dealer, agrees to sell to Y an antique vase. Y agrees to collect it on the following day. By mistake the dealer sells the same vase to Z who pays for it and takes it away. On these facts the first sale may have initially passed the ownership to Y[29] but nevertheless the second sale, coupled with delivery, may have then passed the ownership to Z. The authority for this is s.24 of the 1979 Act which reads as follows:

---

[24] [1972] 1 Q.B. 198.
[25] [1965] 1 Q.B. 525.
[26] See para.2.19 below.
[27] *Thomas v Heelas* [1988] C.L.Y. 3175.
[28] See para.2.11 above.
[29] The 1979 Act s.18, r.1.

Where a person having sold goods continues or is in possession of the goods . . . the delivery or transfer by that person or by a mercantile agent acting for him of the goods . . . under any sale, pledge or other disposition thereof to any person receiving the same in good faith and without notice of the previous sale, has the same effect as if the person making the delivery or transfer were expressly authorised by the owner of the goods to make the same.

Thus in advising Z one would start by claiming that X was still the owner at the time of the sale to him. If this is not so (see above) Z may acquire title under s.24, provided that the sale to him was coupled with delivery. After earlier doubts it now seems clear that the nature of X's possession is immaterial—he may be in possession as seller, as repairer, as warehouseman or in any other capacity.

As already stated[30] these rules are highly technical. Consider the following **2.17** problem:

X sells a car to Y as a result of a fraudulent misrepresentation made by Y. Y pays by cheque. Y sells to Z and retains possession. When Y's cheque is dishonoured X comes to Y's premises. Y allows X to take the car back in return for a promise by X not to enforce the cheque.

The sale from Y to Z gave Z a title under s.23.[31] After that sale Y became a "seller in possession". The return of the car to X amounts to a delivery under a "sale, pledge *or other disposition*" within s.24. Consequently title is re-transferred to X.[32]

A modern example occurs where a seller raises finance by selling goods to a finance company and then leases them back. A situation can arise where a person (a) sells goods, (b) retains possession and then, (c) enters into a sale-and-lease-back operation with a finance company buyer. Where the seller acknowledges that he holds the goods on behalf of the finance company this can amount to a "delivery" to them. Consequently the sale-and-lease-back can confer a s.24 title on the finance company.[33]

(e) Sale by a buyer in possession

Section 25(1) is the exact converse of s.24. It is again concerned with a split **2.18** between ownership and possession but this time it is the seller who retains ownership and the buyer who obtains possession. There is, in fact, a very substantial overlap with s.23. Let us assume that B buys a car from A and pays by cheque. The contract provides that no property shall pass to B until the cheque is cleared. B obtains possession of the car with A's consent, and sells and delivers the car to C. B's cheque is dishonoured. Although C bought from a non-owner he may acquire title under s.25(1). The section reads as follows:

---

[30] See para.2.02 above.
[31] See para.2.13 above.
[32] See *Worcester Works Finance Ltd v Cooden Engineering Co Ltd* [1972] 1 Q.B. 210 CA.
[33] *Michael Gerson (Leasing) Ltd v Wilkinson* [2001] Q.B. 514 CA.

> Where a person having bought or agreed to buy goods obtains, with the consent of the seller, possession of the goods . . . the delivery or transfer by that person, or by a mercantile agent acting for him, of the goods . . . under any sale, pledge or other disposition thereof, to any person receiving the same in good faith and without notice of any lien or other right of the original seller in respect of the goods, shall have the same effect as if the person making the delivery or transfer were a mercantile agent in possession of the goods . . . with the consent of the owner.

2.19 This provision has been before the courts on a number of occasions and the following points emerge:

(a) The section applies only where a person has *bought or agreed to buy* goods. It does not apply where, for example, the goods have been let out on hire purchase[34] or stolen.[35] Similarly, a buyer under a conditional sale agreement within the Consumer Credit Act 1974 is *not* (for this purpose) a person who has "agreed to buy" so that a transfer by him will not enjoy the protection of the section.[36]

(b) The first buyer must obtain possession with the *consent* of the seller; this includes consent obtained by fraud.[37]

(c) The section can apply even where the first buyer has obtained a voidable title and even if the disposition by him takes place *after* his title has been avoided (see below).

(d) What is the meaning of the obscure words "shall have the same effect as if the person making the delivery or transfer were a mercantile agent in possession . . . with the consent of the owner"? In *Newtons of Wembley Ltd v Williams*[38] the Court of Appeal reached the conclusion that the disposition by the first buyer must be in the ordinary course of business of a mercantile agent—even though that buyer is not such an agent! In that case:

A agreed to buy a Sunbeam Rapier car from Newtons of Wembley. The contract provided that no property should pass to the buyer until his cheque was cleared. When the cheque was dishonoured Newtons took steps to trace the car and recover it. A then sold it to B in an open-air market in Warren Street. B resold it to Williams. A pleaded guilty to obtaining the car by false pretences

---

[34] *Helby v Matthews* [1895] A.C. 471. It is not a sale because the hirer has an option, not an obligation, to purchase. Note however that the label used by the parties is not conclusive. If therefore a "hire purchase" agreement contains a binding obligation to pay all future instalments (and a provision that the property *will* pass when the final instalment is paid) the section *will* apply: *Forthright Finance Ltd v Carlyle Finance Ltd* [1997] C.C.L.R. 84. For a further illustration of the distinction see *Close Asset Finance v Case Graphics Machinery Ltd* [2000] C.C.L.R. 43 QB.

[35] *National Employers' Mutual General Insurance Association v Jones* [1990] 1 A.C. 24 HL. Lord Goff's judgment contains a clear, historical analysis of this and related statutory exceptions.

[36] See Consumer Credit Act 1974 Sch.4.

[37] *Du Jardin v Beadman Bros* [1952] 2 Q.B. 712.

[38] [1965] 1 Q.B. 560. See *Angara Maritime Ltd v Oceanconnect UK Ltd* [2010] EWHC 619 (QB): a shipping case on the sale of fuel bunkers.

and Newtons of Wembley sued Williams for the return of the car. The claim was unsuccessful.

The Court of Appeal held that A was a buyer in possession; even though he was not a mercantile agent the sale to B was in the ordinary course of business of a mercantile agent; B took in good faith; accordingly B acquired a good title which he could pass on to Williams. **2.20**

It will be appreciated that the first transferee from the original buyer must take "in good faith". This condition was satisfied in this case but not in the earlier case of *Car and Universal Finance Co Ltd v Caldwell*.[39] The effect of the *Newton* decision is to restrict severely the practical consequences of the original seller avoiding a voidable title acquired by the fraudulent buyer. The original seller may, however, recover his goods from the sub-buyer if (a) the original sale and sub-sale both reserved ownership until payment, and (b) payment has not been made.[40]

(f) Disposition of a motor vehicle held on hire purchase

The problem here is caused by the fact that a hirer under a hire-purchase agreement has no title to the goods,[41] but a right to use and possession only. Thus if a consumer buys a car from such a hirer, the *nemo dat* rule applies. **2.21**

The final rule, which may protect such a consumer, was introduced by Part III of the Hire-Purchase Act 1964 (the 1964 Act) and verbal amendments were made to it by the Consumer Credit Act 1974.

The provision was introduced after an earlier proposal had been rejected, for administrative reasons, by the finance companies. This would have provided for the retention of the registration books by the finance companies and the issue of cards to the hirers.

One of the real problems in this area of law is that many people ignore the warning in the registration certificate that "THIS DOCUMENT IS NOT PROOF OF OWNERSHIP" and that the name is the name of the "registered keeper". **2.22**

Part III applies if the following conditions are satisfied:

(a) a motor vehicle is let out on hire purchase or agreed to be sold under a conditional sale agreement; and

(b) the hirer or buyer ("the debtor") disposes of it before the property has passed to him.[42]

---

[39] See para.2.15 above.
[40] See *Re Highway Foods International, The Times*, 1 November 1994.
[41] *Helby v Matthews* [1895] A.C. 471.
[42] Where a finance company lets out goods to two or more hirers, each of them can be treated as a "debtor"; consequently a disposition by one of them can confer title under Pt III: *Keeble v Combined Lease Finance Plc* [1996] C.C.L.R. 63 CA.

The section can apply even if the hire-purchase agreement is an oral one[43] and even though it fails to satisfy the formality requirements of the Consumer Credit Act 1974.[44] On the other hand, the section will not apply if the hire purchase agreement is void[45] or has not yet been made prior to the "disposition".[46]

2.23   The Act then makes a distinction between:

(a) a disposition to a *private purchaser*; and

(b) a disposition to a *trade or finance purchaser*.

In the former case the purchaser may get a good title. In the words of s.27 of the 1964 Act (in its amended form):

> Where the disposition . . . is to a private purchaser, and he is a purchaser of the motor vehicle in good faith without notice of the hire-purchase or conditional sale agreement (the 'relevant agreement') that disposition shall have effect as if the creditor's title to the vehicle had been vested in the debtor immediately before that disposition.

2.24   Two points should be noted. First, the private purchaser must have no actual notice of a subsisting hire-purchase or conditional sale-agreement.[47] Secondly, the "creditor's title" means the title of the person who was described as the creditor in the hire-purchase or conditional sale agreement (i.e. the person who made the relevant agreement as owner or seller).

> Suppose that X, a thief, sells a car to Y who lets it on hire-purchase to Z and Z sells it to A. Even if A takes in good faith he will only get the title which was vested in Y. Since Y had no title, the section does not protect A.

If we now assume that the hirer or buyer disposes of the vehicle to a trade or finance purchaser, that purchaser has no Pt III protection (presumably because he will be able to use the HPI facilities[48]) but if further dispositions take place the Act protects the *first private purchaser* if he takes in good faith and without notice.[49] It, therefore, becomes crucial to find out whether the original transferee was a trade or finance purchaser. A trade purchaser is defined by s.29(2) as a person who at the time of the disposition "carries on a business"[50] of buying motor vehicles for sale,[51] while a finance purchaser

---

[43] *Hitchens v General Guarantee Corp* [2001] EWCA Civ 359.

[44] As above.

[45] *Shogun Finance Ltd v Hudson* [2001] EWCA 1000 which is discussed in [2002] 23(2) B.L.R. 288–290 (forged signature). The law was criticised as unsatisfactory.

[46] *Rohit Kulkarni v Manor Credit (Davenham) Ltd* [2010] EWCA Civ 69.

[47] *Barker v Bell* [1971] 1 W.L.R. 983 CA.

[48] See para.2.10 above.

[49] The mere fact that the transaction should have aroused suspicion is not necessarily fatal (*Hall v Rover Financial Services (GB) Ltd* [2002] EWCA Civ 1514—buyer suffered from "moral blindness").

[50] This may be a part-time business: *Stevenson v Beverley Bentinck Ltd* [1976] 1 W.L.R. 483 CA. Section 29(2) also includes someone buying his first vehicles for stock for a new business venture: *GE Capital Bank Ltd v Rushton* [2006] All E.R. 865 CA.

[51] *Welcome Financial Services Ltd v Nine Regions Ltd (T/A Log Book Loans)* [2010] 2 Lloyd's Rep. 426 QBD.

is one who provides finance by buying motor vehicles and letting them out under hire purchase or conditional sale agreements. Any other purchaser is a private purchaser. The following points can be important:

(i) "Private purchaser" is much wider than "private person"; thus many large public companies will enjoy the "private purchaser" protection of the Act.

(ii) Although the purchaser is a trade or finance purchaser, he may still have Pt III protection if he buys for his private use.[52]

(iii) The term "disposition" can include a fresh hire-purchase agreement. Thus in the third example at the beginning of this chapter the ultimate hirer will be entitled to remain in possession under Pt III even though he finds out about the original agreement before completing his payments.[53]

In *VFS Financial Services Ltd v J F Plant Tyres Ltd*[54]: **2.25**

> V let a truck on hire purchase to D who delivered it to J in settlement of debts owed to J. V sued J for conversion of the truck. Was J protected by the 1964 Act?

The court agreed that J was a "private purchaser", as it did not trade in or finance the acquisition of vehicles. However, there was no "disposition" to J, as the meaning in s.29 was limited to transactions where the vehicle was transferred for money.

Conversely (and controversially) the private purchaser can rescind the agreement and recover all his payments—on the basis of total failure of consideration—if he does so before he has acquired title. In other words, it seems that he can have his Pt III cake and eat it![55]

Two final points can be made. First, there are bound to be serious practical problems in proving that the vehicle was transferred by the hirer or buyer to a private purchaser. The purchaser's job is made somewhat easier by a series of rebuttable presumptions which are to be found in s.28 of the 1964 Act. Secondly, one must always bear in mind that prevention is better than cure. A member of the public who is considering buying a car can always check with HPI.[56] HPI make their information available to the AA, RAC and Citizens Advice Bureaux.

---

[52] See Moore-Bick LJ, obiter, in *GE Capital Bank Ltd v Rushton* [2006] 3 All E.R. 865 CA.
[53] See also *Dodds v Yorkshire Bank Finance Ltd* [1992] C.C.L.R. 92 CA (car held on hire-purchase; hirer sold it as part of a loan agreement; only to take effect if he defaulted (which he did); buyer got Pt III title).
[54] [2013] EWHC 346 (QB).
[55] *Barber v NWS Bank Plc* [1996] C.C.L.R. 30 CA.
[56] See para.2.10 above.

Hire purchase generally

2.26 Suppose X lets out goods to Y on hire-purchase and it then transpires that X is not the owner of the goods. A number of the provisions discussed in this chapter refer to a "disposition" and this is clearly wide enough to cover a hire-purchase agreement. Thus Y could, in appropriate cases, claim the protection of s.2 of the 1889 Act,[57] s.24 or 25(1) of the 1979 Act[58] or Pt III of the 1964 Act. He would also be protected if X had a voidable title, since it will be too late for the original owner to rescind the agreement once third party rights have been acquired.[59]

2. CONSUMER'S RIGHTS AGAINST SUPPLIER

Supplies of goods

2.27 We have dealt at some length with the *nemo dat* rules because it is likely that the real battle in practice will be fought between the original owner and the buyer. We must now consider the position as between consumer and trader. The general principle is clear enough: under a contract to supply goods the transfer of ownership from seller to buyer is a term around which the whole contract revolves.

Section 17(1) provides that "Every contract to supply goods"—sale, hire-purchase, transfer of goods (but not hire):

> is to be treated as including a term—
>> (b) . . . that the trader must have a right to sell or transfer the goods at the time when the ownership of the goods is to be transferred
> (2) Every contract to supply goods, except a contract for the hire of goods or a contract within subsection (4), is to be treated as including a term that—
>> (a) the goods are free from any charge or encumbrance not disclosed or known to the consumer before entering into the contract,
>> (b) the goods will remain free from any such charge or encumbrance until ownership of them is to be transferred, and
>> (c) the consumer will enjoy quiet possession of the goods except so far as it may be disturbed by the owner or other person entitled to the benefit of any charge or encumbrance so disclosed or known.

2.28 Similar provisions to s.17(1) and (2) were implied into sales contracts by s.2 of the 1979 Act, but they used the terminology of "condition" and "warranty", not "term".[60] These provisions have been before the courts many times and presumably similar provisions in the CRA 2015 will receive similar judicial treatment:

---

[57] See para.2.11 above.
[58] See paras 2.16–2.19 above.
[59] See para.2.13 above.
[60] The 1979 Act provisions continue to apply to business-to-business pre-CRA contracts and sales by consumers.

(1) If the goods are delivered in such a form that any sale can be stopped by an injunction there is no "right to sell".

(2) If the supplier is in breach of s.17(1), the consumer may reject the goods[61] and recover the price even though he has used them for some time.[62] If he asks for the return of the price his right will crystallise and will not be affected by anything done *after* this to cure the defect.

(3) If the buyer has incurred other losses or expenses, e.g. the cost of necessary repairs, these can also be claimed from the seller.[63]

An unsettled question is the precise relationship between the right to sell and the *nemo dat* exceptions considered earlier in this chapter. If the seller had no title he would technically have no *right* to sell, even though the effect of the sale would be to pass title to the buyer. Nevertheless, it is inconceivable that a court would allow a claim based on "total failure of consideration" if the buyer got exactly what he paid for, i.e. the property in the goods; in a recent case the Court of Appeal has rejected such a claim.[64] If, however, he was put to trouble and expense in proving his title he might well have a claim.

Can sections 17(1) and 17(2) be excluded?

There may be cases where the supplier of goods is uncertain as to whether or not he has a right to sell and he may wish the buyer to bear this risk. Section 17(4) allows the seller to give a more limited undertaking in a case where there appears from the contract or is to be inferred from its circumstances an intention that the seller should transfer only such title as he or a third person may have. In this type of case the basic title obligations referred to above are replaced by the implied terms in s.17 (5), (6) and (7) about disclosure of encumbrances and charges and quiet possession which are similar to s.17(2) above.   **2.29**

Auctioneers

Where goods are delivered to an auctioneer by a person who is not the owner, the question arises as to whether the conduct of the auctioneer can trigger a claim for conversion. The point arose in a recent case[65] in which the auctioneer returned the goods to the person from whom he had received them; that person, who was not the owner, subsequently sold them on. The judge ruled that, depending on the facts, the true owner might have a claim against the auctioneer. He ruled that: **2.30**

(1) liability will normally only arise where there has been a positive act withholding property from the owner;

---

[61] CRA 2015 ss.17(9) and 19(6). See also Chapter Eight for remedies generally.
[62] *Rowland v Divall* [1923] 2 K.B. 500 CA.
[63] *Mason v Burningham* [1949] 2 K.B. 545.
[64] *Freeman v Walker* (2001) EWCA Civ 923.
[65] *Marcq v Christie Manson and Woods Ltd* [2002] EWHC 2148.

(2) nevertheless, a person who has taken possession of the goods of another can be liable if he has not acted in good faith and without notice; and

(3) the onus of proving good faith is on him.

Other supply of goods contracts

2.31 We mentioned briefly in para.2.01 the different types of "contracts to supply goods". We defined only "sales contracts" there, for these mattered most in relation to sales by non-owners. We shall now consider the other three types defined in the CRA 2015: hire (s.6), hire-purchase (s.7) and transfer of goods (s.8).

Hire

2.32 Section 6(1) states:

> A contract is for the hire of goods if under it the trader gives or agrees to give the consumer possession of the goods with the right to use them . . .

It does not involve the transfer of ownership at all. Examples are the hire of a car for a day, a week or three years (often called a "lease") or of DIY or carpet cleaning equipment.

Section 17(1) implies a term:

> (a) . . . that at the beginning of the period of hire the trader must have the right to transfer possession of the goods by way of hire for that period.

Section 17(3) adds a term

> . . . that the consumer will enjoy quiet possession for the period of the hire . . .

This does not affect the right of the trader to repossess the goods where the contract so provides (s.8).[66]

Hire-purchase agreements

2.33 Although a hire-purchase agreement is not a sale, the s.17 terms which apply to a sale apply to them too.[67] They fall halfway between sales and hire contracts, as can be seen from the definition in s.7. They must satisfy two conditions.

Section 7(2) states the first:

> . . . goods are hired by the trader in return for periodical payments by the consumer. . .

---

[66] Consumer hire was previously governed by similar provisions in the Supply of Goods and Services Act 1982 s.7.

[67] Previously governed by similar provisions in the Supply of Goods (Implied Terms) Act 1973.

Section 7(3) states the second:

> ... ownership of the goods will transfer to the consumer if the terms of the contract are complied with ...

Usually this happens when "the consumer exercises an option to buy the goods" (s.7(3)(a)). In short, it is a hire of goods coupled with an option to purchase.

Under s.17(1)(b) the term "right to sell", as we saw earlier, means that the trader will have a right to sell when the ownership is to pass (this usually occurs when the hirer has completed his payments and exercised his option to purchase). It seems, however, that the hirer may be in an even stronger position under a term implied at common law, i.e. that the owner has the right to sell at the time of delivery to the hirer.[68] A breach of the condition gives the hirer the right to recover all his payments with no set-off for user.[69]

Transfer of goods

Here again s.17 applies in exactly the same way as in relation to sales con-   **2.34**
tracts discussed above. The definition of "a contract for the transfer of goods" in s.8, like the definition of a sales contract in s.5, presupposes a "transfer of ownership" by the trader to the consumer. The difference here is that the consumer provides "consideration otherwise than by paying the price" (s.8(a)) or "the contract is, for any other reason, not a sales or hire-purchase agreement" (s.8(b)).

An example of s.8(a) is an exchange of goods where the consumer pays no money. Contracts for work and materials fall within s.8(b) because the transfer of goods (materials) is coupled with the provision of significant services (work); examples are car repairs, decorations or the installation of kitchens, double glazing or central heating. This is a "mixed contract" within s.1(4), as it is a contract to supply goods within Chapter 2 of the Act and to supply services within Chapter 4 of the Act.[70]

3. IMPROVEMENTS AND REPAIRS

S sells goods to B who spends £1,200 on repairs and improvements. It then   **2.35**
transpires that the goods belong to C who claims them, or their value, from B. It has been well established for many years that, in assessing damages for conversion, credit must be given for improvements made by the defendant.[71] In *Greenwood v Bennett*[72] this principle was applied in interpleader

---

[68] *Karflex Ltd v Poole* [1933] 2 K.B. 251 and more recently (and controversially) *Barber v NWS Bank Plc*, para.2.25 above.
[69] *Warman v Southern Counties Finance Corp* [1949] 2 K.B. 576 CA.
[70] For "mixed contracts" see also ss.1 (6) and 3(7). Previously governed by the Supply of Goods and Services Act 1982 s.2.
[71] *Munro v Willmott* [1949] 1 K.B. 295.
[72] [1973] 1 Q.B. 195.

proceedings between the owner and the improver. This seems fair enough but one point is unclear; if the owner seizes the goods from the improver, does the improver have a cause of action to recover the cost of the improvements from the owner? No English authority supports such a claim, although Lord Denning MR suggested (obiter) that such a claim would be allowed on the basis of unjust enrichment.[73]

2.36   The principle of *Greenwood v Bennett* now appears in statutory form in s.6(1) of the Torts (Interference with Goods) Act 1977. It reads:

> If in proceedings for wrongful interference against a person (the 'improver') who has improved the goods, it is shown that the improver acted in the mistaken but honest belief that he had a good title to them, an allowance shall be made for the extent to which, at the time as at which the goods fall to be valued in assessing damages, the value of the goods is attributable to the improvement.

The section goes on to give a similar right to a subsequent buyer who acted in good faith.[74] If the buyer then sues his seller under s.17(1)(b) of the CRA 2015[75] the seller can claim a similar reduction provided that he acted in good faith.[76]

> O owns a car which is stolen by T who sells it to A. It is worth £800 but A increases its value to £2,000. He then sells it to B for £2,000. O claims the car from B.

If we assume that O has been the owner at all material times, the court may well order O to pay B the sum of £1,200 (the improvement figure reflected in the price paid by B to A) as a condition of getting the car back. In the result, B is out of pocket to the tune of £800. If he then sues A for the return of the £2,000 it seems only right that his claim should be limited to £800 and (assuming that A acted in good faith) s.6(3) allows such a reduction.

2.37   Two final points may be made. It will be seen that the section uses the words "if in proceedings . . . against a person". In other words it does not create a new cause of action. If the owner seizes the goods from the improver, there is nothing in the Act to give the improver a claim against the owner.[77] Secondly, the right to claim compensation for improvements will only be relevant where the improver or his successor in title is liable to the owner and it will not be relevant where the improver or his successor in title has himself become the owner under one of the *nemo dat* exceptions discussed at the beginning of this chapter.

---

[73] For further discussion, see (1973) 36 M.L.R. 89.
[74] s.6(2).
[75] See para.2.27 above.
[76] s.6(3).
[77] He may of course have a claim against the seller—see *Mason v Burningham* [1949] 2 K.B. 545.

CHAPTER THREE

"IT'S A GOOD LITTLE BUS"

(1) During negotiations for the sale of a car the dealer says to the consumer **3.01** "it's a good little bus—I'd stake my life on it". The consumer then takes the car on hire-purchase from a finance company. The steering is defective and the consumer is injured.
(2) The vendor of a site of a petrol filling station tells the prospective purchaser that it should have a throughput of 200,000 gallons per year. This is far too high and the purchaser suffers severe financial loss.
(3) A prospective hirer of barges asks the owner how much they could carry and the owner replies "1,600 tonnes". The hirer makes the contract but the statement is wrong and the hirer refuses to pay the hire charges.

The supplier of goods is likely to make extravagant claims about them **3.02** during negotiations. What are the remedies of the consumer if, as in the three cases cited, the statement turns out to be wrong? The position depends on how the statement is classified. There are at least five possibilities:

(1) The statement may be nothing more than "trader's puff". In this case the consumer has no remedy.

(2) The statement may be a misleading action under the Consumer Protection from Unfair Trading Regulations 2008 (the 2008 Regulations), and, for contracts entered into before 1 October 2014, a misrepresentation at common law. In the latter case, a consumer may have (i) a right to rescind the contract unless it is too late to do so; (ii) a right to damages for deceit at common law if the supplier was fraudulent; (iii) a right to damages under s.2(1) of the Misrepresentation Act 1967 unless the supplier can prove that he had reasonable grounds for believing, and did believe, the statement to be true. However, for contracts concluded after 1 October 2014, the right to claim damages under s.2(1) is no longer available, and a consumer has to rely on the new provisions in the 2008 Regulations (which are discussed at para 8.12 below).

(3) It may be a negligent misstatement giving rise to an action for damages in tort. This branch of the law of negligence is based on the House of Lords decision in *Hedley Byrne & Co Ltd v Heller & Partners Ltd.*[1]

---

[1] [1964] A.C. 465.

(4) It may be a contractual term. In this case the consumer can claim damages; whether he can also treat the contract as discharged depends upon the importance of the term and upon the seriousness and the consequences of the breach.

(5) It may be a collateral warranty giving rise to a collateral contract.

(6) It may form part of the description of the goods (this overlaps with (4) above). If this is so, a breach will be a breach of condition and the consumer can choose between (i) treating the contract as repudiated and claiming damages, and (ii) affirming the contract and claiming damages.[2] Until recently the term "description" has been given a very wide meaning but the pendulum may be swinging the other way.[3]

It remains to add that the supplier may be in breach of the 2008 Regulations[4] and a criminal conviction could lead to an award of compensation.[5]

1. Mere Puff

3.03 The praising of goods by a prospective supplier is a universal fact of commercial life and the lifeblood of the advertising industry. The following phrases are typical:

> "the most popular bike in Britain"
> "clean, healthy and alive"
> "super value for money"
> "the bathroom bargain of the year"

This is typical sales patter; it is not intended to give rise to legal liability and it does not do so. The difficulty is to know where to draw the line between (a) mere puff and (b) a representation or a term. In the above examples the statements were vague and not specific. As soon as the supplier makes an inaccurate specific statement, for example, as to measurements or ingredients, the consumer should have little difficulty in proving an actionable misrepresentation or breach of a contractual term.

3.04 In *Andrews v Hopkinson*,[6] the facts of which appear in Example (1),[7] the dealer who described the car as a "good little bus" was liable for breach of a collateral contract (and also in tort under the rule in *Donoghue v Stevenson*).[8] Collateral contracts are discussed more fully in Section 5 of this chapter.

---

[2] Sale of Goods Act 1979 s.11.
[3] See para.3.30 below.
[4] See para.18.37 below.
[5] See para.17.03 below.
[6] [1957] 1 Q.B. 229.
[7] See para.3.01 above.
[8] [1932] A.C. 562. See para.5.46 below.

2. MISREPRESENTATION

Prior to the amendments to the 2008 Regulations which took effect on 1 **3.05**
October 2014 (see 8.12 below), misrepresentation was a useful doctrine for
dealing with circumstances which could broadly be described as a half-way
house between mere puff and a contractual term. The essence of a misrepresentation is that it is a statement made *before* the making of the contract
which *induces* the other party to enter into the contract. There can, of course,
be an overlap between a misrepresentation and a contractual term; a dealer
may represent a car as being a 2015 model and this may later be incorporated
into the contract. Subject to this, a mere pre-contractual inducement is less
potent than a term of the contract itself, because damages are always available for breach of contract where it causes loss.

Until the enactment of the Misrepresentation Act 1967 it was often vital **3.06**
for the injured party to prove that the statement was something more than a
misrepresentation; the reason was that the only remedy for misrepresentation
was the equitable remedy of rescission, with no right to damages unless there
was fraud. If it was too late to rescind the innocent party might find himself
with no remedy at all. This is what happened in *Oscar Chess Ltd v Williams*[9]
where the following facts arose:

> A consumer who was buying a car was asked by the dealer to state the age of the
> car which he was giving in part-exchange. He said that it was a 1948 model, as
> appeared from the registration book. In fact it was a 1939 model and the dealer
> suffered loss in that the part exchange allowance was too high. He sued the buyer
> for damages.

The Court of Appeal held that the statement made by Mr Williams was a
mere representation and not a contractual warranty. Accordingly, as the law
then stood, no damages could be awarded. In the words of Lord Denning
MR:

> "If, however, the seller, when he states a fact, makes it clear that he has no
> knowledge of his own but has got his information elsewhere and is merely
> passing it on it is not so easy to infer a warranty."

On these particular facts the result of this case might be the same today even **3.07**
after the changes made by s.2 of the Misrepresentation Act 1967 (if the consumer could prove reasonable grounds for his belief) and even after *Hedley
Byrne v Heller*.[10]

If the parties are on an equal bargaining footing the courts may again be
reluctant to find a contractual promise. Thus in *Howard Marine and Dredging
Co Ltd v Ogden & Sons (Excavation) Ltd*,[11] the facts of which appear in
Example 3 at the beginning of this chapter,[12] the statement about the barge

---

[9] [1957] 1 W.L.R. 370.
[10] See para.3.12 below.
[11] [1978] Q.B. 574.
[12] See para.3.01 above.

capacity was held to be non-contractual; in this case, however, the hirers recovered damages under s.2(1) of the Misrepresentation Act 1967.[13]

3.08   If, however, we turn to the normal dealer-consumer situation a statement made by the dealer will frequently be classified as a contractual promise because of the dealer's special knowledge. In *Dick Bentley Productions Ltd v Harold Smith Motors Ltd*[14]:

> A dealer told a prospective buyer that the engine of a second-hand car had done 20,000 miles. It was later discovered that the engine had done 100,000 miles. The buyer claimed damages.

The Court of Appeal gave judgment for the buyer. Here was a statement about a matter within the special knowledge of the seller. It was a contractual warranty and the seller was liable for breach of it.

In this type of case, therefore, the plaintiff would have been best advised to allege in the alternative (i) a contractual term, (ii) a misrepresentation, and (iii) a negligent statement.[15] The advantage of (i) is that the consumer will be entitled to damages for *any* breach of the term, even though the maker had reasonable grounds for believing the statement to be true.

3.09   The various remedies available for misrepresentation will be considered later[16] but before leaving misrepresentation three further points can be made:

(a) It may be necessary to distinguish a representation of *fact* from a mere statement of *opinion*—a problem which can cause particular difficulty on a sale of a painting which is attributed to an old master. Note however that even a statement of opinion can be treated as an actionable misrepresentation if it carries the inference that the maker knew of facts justifying the opinion.[17] A misrepresentation of law can also give rise to liability.[18]

(b) Whether a person relies on the statement is a question of fact. The maker of a statement cannot avoid liability simply by saying "the accuracy of this statement is not guaranteed and the buyer should make his own enquiries". If, in such a case, the buyer *does* rely on the statement he will have the usual remedies for misrepresentation if the statement is incorrect.[19] A recent example of reliance is *Spencer Flack v Pattinson*[20] where the buyer was induced to buy an historic car by a fraudulent misrepresentation that it was "Innes Ireland's 2.5 litre Grand Prix car". The mere fact that the claimant has an opportunity

---

[13] See para.8.05 below.
[14] [1965] 1 W.L.R. 623.
[15] See para.3.10 below.
[16] See para.8.05 below.
[17] *Nelson Group Services (Maintenance) Ltd v BG Plc* [2002] EWCA Civ 547.
[18] *Pankhania v Hackney LBC* reported in Lawtel 11 October 2002, Ch D.
[19] *Cremdean Properties Ltd v Nash* (1977) 244 E.G. 547 CA. As to exclusion of remedies see para.9.46 below.
[20] [2002] EWCA Civ 1820.

to check the statement will not absolve the maker from liability.[21]

(c) The action for damages for misrepresentation is available only where the statement was made by the other party to the contract. Thus it would not be available if, for example, a consumer bought from a retailer in reliance on a statement made by the manufacturer. There may, however, be a claim against the manufacturer if a collateral contract can be established[22] or it is liable in negligence under the rules discussed below.

The relevance of misrepresentation in the consumer context is likely to diminish rapidly now in view of the 2014 amendments to 2008 Regulations (see para.8.12 below).

3. LIABILITY IN TORT FOR NEGLIGENCE

The history of the law of tort is one of gradual and cautious development. **3.10** Although the industrial revolution started in the 18th century, it was not until 1932 that the modern law of negligence was born. Until then it was widely accepted that where A negligently performed a contract with B and thereby caused loss to C, A was not liable to C. It was not until *Donoghue v Stevenson*[23] that the House of Lords, by a bare majority, came down in favour of a more realistic approach. In that case the House decided that in certain circumstances the manufacturer of a product owed a duty of care to the ultimate consumer. The case is also a landmark because Lord Atkin laid down his famous "neighbour" test as the basis of liability in negligence. He said:

> "The liability for negligence . . . is no doubt placed upon a general public sentiment of moral wrongdoing for which the offender must pay. But acts or omissions which any moral code would censure cannot in a practical world be treated so as to give a right to every person injured by them to demand relief. In this way rules of law arise which limit the range of complainants and the extent of their remedy. The rule that you are to love your neighbour becomes in law—you must not injure your neighbour; and the lawyer's question, Who is my neighbour? receives a restricted reply. You must take reasonable care to avoid acts or omissions which you can reasonably foresee would be likely to injure your neighbour. Who, then, in law, is my neighbour? The answer seems to be—persons who are so closely and directly affected by my act that I ought reasonably to have them in contemplation as being so affected when I am directing my mind to the acts or omissions which are called in question."

Despite *Donoghue v Stevenson* there were, and still are, important areas of **3.11** non-liability. In particular the courts have been very reluctant to hold that negligence resulting in purely economic loss gives rise to legal liability; the

---

[21] *Morris v Jones* [2002] EWCA Civ 1790 (defendants liable even though the claimant had three survey reports warning him of damp).
[22] *Shanklin Pier v Detel Products* [1951] 2 K.B. 854. See para.3.20 below.
[23] [1932] A.C. 562. See para.5.46 below.

claimant could not succeed merely by proving that he was a "neighbour" of the defendant within Lord Atkin's test.[24] The reason for this refusal to apply *Donoghue v Stevenson* to statements was their potentially wide-ranging effect. A distinguished American judge referred to the "three indeterminates"—a careless statement might make the maker liable "in an indeterminate amount for an indeterminate time to an indeterminate class".[25] The refusal of the law to provide a remedy was not without its critics. In *Candler v Crane Christmas*[26] Lord Denning adopted a statement from an earlier case:

> "A country whose administration of justice did not afford redress in a case of the present description would not be in a state of civilization."

3.12 It was not until 1964 that the House of Lords altered the law. The case of *Hedley Byrne & Co Ltd v Heller and Partners Ltd*[27] shows a cautious approach and it is difficult to extract one really clear-cut principle from the five speeches. In one sense all the pronouncements in the *Hedley Byrne* case were obiter because the actual decision was that the defendants were absolved from liability because of a disclaimer. The facts were as follows:

> The plaintiffs were advertising agents. They placed orders on behalf of E. Ltd with various newspapers and television. They were personally liable to the sellers of the advertising space and they were anxious to make sure that E. Ltd were financially sound. The plaintiffs' bankers got in touch with the defendants who were the bankers of E. Ltd. The defendants gave favourable references "without responsibility". The plaintiffs thereupon made the contracts. The references turned out to be unjustified and the plaintiffs lost £17,000 on the contracts. They sued the defendants on the references. The House of Lords gave judgment for the defendants.

Lord Reid pointed out that a duty of care existed if there was a "special relationship"; he considered that this could be proved

> "where it is plain that the party seeking information or advice was trusting the other to exercise such a degree of care as the circumstances required, where it was reasonable for him to do that, and where the other gave the information or advice when he knew or ought to know that the enquirer was relying on him."

It is clear from a careful reading of the speeches that the key factor was an assumption of responsibility. In the words of Lord Morris:

> "My Lords, it seems to me that if A assumes a responsibility to B to tender him deliberate advice, there could be a liability if the advice is negligently given."

---

[24] *Hamble Fisheries Ltd v L. Gardner & Sons Ltd*, *The Times*, 5 January 1999, CA and see the building cases discussed in para.5.46 below.

[25] Cardozo CJ in *Ultramares Corporation v Touche* (1931) 255 N.Y. Rep. 170, cited in *Candler v Crane Christmas* [1951] K.B. 164.

[26] [1951] K.B. 164 at 176 (a powerful dissenting judgment).

[27] [1964] A.C. 465.

The case was decided in favour of the bank because (a) the disclaimer made it clear that no responsibility was being assumed, and (b) even without such disclaimer it could well be argued that the only duty expected in this type of case was a duty to be honest.

The recent Court of Appeal decision in *Robinson v P.E. Jones (Contractors) Ltd*[28] underlines the reluctance of the courts to use the "assumption of responsibility" argument to extend the application of *Hedley Byrne* to new areas. Jackson LJ, whose analysis of the relationship between contractual and tortious duties is worthy of study, said at para.76:

> "When one moves beyond the realm of professional retainers, it by no means follows that every contracting party assumes responsibilities (in the *Hedley Byrne* sense) to the other parties co-extensive with the contractual obligations. Such an analysis would be nonsensical. Contractual and tortious duties have different origins and different functions. Contractual obligations spring from the consent of the parties and the common law principle that contracts should be enforced. Tortious duties are imposed by law, as a matter of policy, in specific situations. Sometimes a particular set of facts may give rise to identical contractual and tortious duties, but self-evidently that is not always the case."

In all the decided cases since 1964 the defendants supplied information in answer to an inquiry or in the course of professional duties and the most recent cases[29] indicate that a private consumer (especially at the lower end of the market) is more likely to succeed than a businessman or professional investor; the "reliance" factor mentioned above will often be crucial.[30]

An important pair of cases related to mortgage valuations. *Smith v Bush* and *Harris v Wyre Forest DC*[31] were heard together because similar issues arose. The facts were as follows:

> Mrs Smith and Mr and Mrs Harris applied for mortgages for house purchase. In both cases they paid to the lenders a non-returnable fee for a valuation. In one case the valuer was an independent surveyor and in the other he was an in-house surveyor employed by the lender. In both cases they negligently overvalued the property by failing to discover defects and the buyers suffered loss. Mrs Smith was shown a copy of the valuer's report; the Harrises were not.

In both cases the lenders were under a statutory duty to cause a valuation to be made but the House of Lords held that this was irrelevant. They unanimously held that the negligent surveyor was liable to Mrs Smith[32] and that the council who made the advance to the Harrises was liable for the

3.13

3.14

---

[28] [2011] EWCA Civ 9.

[29] Five of them related to auditors. The leading case on non-liability of auditors is *Caparo Industries Plc v Dickman* [1990] 2 A.C. 605 HL.

[30] For a recent (and rather special) case where the plaintiff succeeded *without* reliance, see *White v Jones* [1995] 2 W.L.R. 187 (solicitors' delay in drawing will; testator died before will was ready; solicitor liable in negligence to two daughters who were due to benefit under that will). Similarly a solicitor was liable to a disappointed beneficiary when he failed to advise a testator to sever a joint tenancy: *Carr-Glynn v Frearsons* [1998] All E.R. 225 CA.

[31] [1990] 1 A.C. 831. The "disclaimer" aspect of the case is considered in para.9.56 below.

[32] The lender too can be sued if he "adopts" the negligent valuation: *Beresford v Chesterfield BC and Woolwich Equitable Building Society* (1990) 10 Tr.L.R. 6 CA.

negligence of their surveyor. What emerges from the case is that the "assumption of responsibility" test is not the true one—or rather the question should be "in what circumstances will a negligent party be *deemed* to have assumed responsibility?". The language of the three substantive speeches is cautious. Lord Templeman said (at p.800):

> "In general, I am of the opinion that in the absence of a disclaimer of liability the valuer who values a house for the purposes of a mortgage, knowing that the mortgagee will rely and the mortgagor will probably rely on the valuation, knowing that the purchaser mortgagor has in effect paid for the valuation, is under a duty to exercise reasonable skill and care and that duty is owed to both parties to the mortgage for which the valuation was made."

The speech of Lord Griffiths shows a typical judicial reluctance to extend the scope of liability. He said (at pp.815–816):

> "I therefore return to the question in what circumstances should the law deem those who give advice to have assumed responsibility to the person who acts upon the advice? I would answer—only if it is foreseeable that if the advice is negligent the recipient is likely to suffer damage, that there is a sufficiently proximate relationship between the parties *and that it is just and reasonable to impose the liability*" (italics supplied).

Finally, Lord Jauncey of Tullichettle stressed the reliance factor in the following passage (at p.822):

> "The four critical facts [in the Smith case] are that the appellants knew from the outset:
>
> (1) that the report would be shown to Mrs Smith;
>
> (2) that Mrs Smith would probably rely on the valuation contained therein in deciding whether to buy the house without obtaining an independent valuation;
>
> (3) that if in these circumstances the valuation was, having regard to the actual condition of the house, excessive, Mrs Smith would be likely to suffer loss; and
>
> (4) that she had paid to the building society a sum to defray the appellants' fee."

After stating that these facts gave rise to a duty of care both to the building society and to Mrs Smith he added:

> "It is critical to this conclusion that the appellants knew that Mrs Smith would be likely to rely on the valuation without obtaining independent advice."[33]

3.15   In a later case[34] (involving a company take-over by a person who had relied on statements made by the company's financial advisers) Hoffmann J was

---

[33] For a further case on similar facts see *Merrett v Babb* [2001] EWCA Civ 214 where the surveyor's firm had ceased to trade and the borrower successfully sued the surveyor in his personal capacity.

[34] *Morgan Crucible Co v Hill Samuel Bank Ltd* [1990] 3 All E.R. 330. The Court of Appeal subsequently held that, on the case as pleaded, a duty of care *might* arise—see [1991] 1 All E.R. 148.

asked to apply the principles set out above so as to impose negligence liability on the advisers. He declined to do so and in an illuminating passage he stressed the "consumer" aspect of the *Smith* and *Harris* cases. He distinguished *Smith* from the case before him as follows (at p.335):

> "First, Mr Smith [*sic*] had paid for the survey; although he had no contract with the surveyor, the relationship was, as Lord Templeman said, 'akin to contract.' [The take-over bidder], on the other hand, had not paid for the audit.
>
> Second, the typical plaintiff in a *Smith v Bush* type case is a person of modest means and making the most expensive purchase of his or her life. He was very unlikely to be insured against the manifestation of inherent defects. The surveyor can protect himself relatively easily by insurance. The take-over bidder, on the other hand, is an entrepreneur taking high risks for high rewards and while some accountants may be able to take out sufficient insurance, others may not.
>
> Third, the imposition of liability on surveyors would probably not greatly increase their insurance costs and push up the cost of surveys because the typical buyer who relies on a building survey is buying a relatively modest house. Takeovers on the Stock Exchange involve huge amounts and the effects on accountants' insurance and fees are unpredictable."

The distinction between the above cases, where the purchasers were buying **3.16** modest residential properties for their own occupation, and commercial cases, where properties are purchased for investment, is highlighted in the recent case of *Scullion v Bank of Scotland (t/a Colleys)*.[35] This is another case against valuers and surveyors, but this time it failed.

> The claimant (S) was a small trader who wished to invest his savings in a buy-to-let flat. His prospective mortgagees instructed the defendants (C) to report on its value. The valuation proved to be much too high. The rent obtained was much lower than S had expected. S sued C in tort for negligence relying heavily on *Smith v Bush*.

The Court of Appeal held that C did not owe a duty of care to S and so S's claim failed. The essential distinction between this case and *Smith* was that C knew that the mortgage was to fund "the purchase of a residential unit, not as the purchaser's residence, but for the purpose of an investment" (per Lord Neuberger at para.46). C did not expect S to rely on its report and it was likely that a buy-to-let purchaser would obtain an independent valuation; this would cover not only the capital value—the only concern of the mortgagees—but also its rental value and other related matters such as the length of the tenancy. The transaction was essentially commercial in nature and did not involve an ordinary domestic householder purchasing his home.

This "commercial" distinction is not an absolute one. Thus an auditor who prepares and certifies the accounts of a company does not thereby owe a legal duty of care to individual shareholders[36] and there is no distinction for this purpose between a private and a commercial investor.

What is the relevance of all this to supplies of goods? If the statement is **3.17**

---

[35] [2011] EWCA Civ 693.
[36] *Caparo Industries Plc v Dickman* [1990] 2 A.C. 605 HL.

made by the supplier it may be useful to plead *Hedley Byrne* as an alternative to other forms of liability. It is unlikely, however, to add a great deal to consumers' chances of success, as the facts will usually disclose a *Bentley v Smith* contractual term[37] an actionable misrepresentation under s.2(1) of the Misrepresentation Act 1967,[38] or a misleading action under the 2008 Regulations as well as a *Hedley Byrne* duty situation. Apart from the inherent uncertainty of establishing such a duty, the claimant is on stronger ground under the 2008 Regulations. There is, however, a possibility that a *Hedley Byrne* claim could be pursued where the consumer has relied on a statement made by the manufacturer (for example, in sales literature or in a leaflet giving instructions for use). There is no doubt, however, that this would represent a major extension of the *Hedley Byrne* rule and in the only modern case in which the matter was raised the claim was rejected.[39]

There is one further possibility. If, for example, the supplier (being a limited company) has gone out of business, a consumer might have a *Hedley Byrne* claim against a director of that company if the personal expertise of that director has given rise to an "assumption of responsibility" for statements made by him.[40]

4. CONTRACTUAL TERMS

3.18   We have already seen that a statement made during negotiations may sometimes be classified as a contractual term.[41] When will this occur? The leading case is *Heilbut, Symons & Co v Buckleton*[42] where Lord Moulton said:

> "An affirmation at the time of the sale is a warranty, provided it appears on evidence to be so intended."

The key word here is the word "intended" and the courts apply an objective test; they do not look into the minds of the parties but at their conduct. In the words of Lord Denning MR:

> "If an intelligent bystander would reasonably infer that a warranty was intended, that will suffice."[43]

3.19   To avoid confusion it must be stressed that the word "warranty" has at least two meanings. In the above examples it is used in its normal sense to

---

[37] See para.3.08 above. See *Huyton SA v Distribuidora Internacional de Productos SA* [2003] EWCA Civ 1104—the claimant had a valid claim for breach of contract, so there was no need to consider misrepresentation.

[38] See para.3.06 above and para.8.05 below.

[39] *Lambert v Lewis* [1980] 2 W.L.R. 299 at 328 CA (the claim was actually brought by an intermediate dealer). In the House of Lords the case was decided on a different point (see para.4.22 below). Note also that statements made by the "producer" in relation to the goods will be relevant in deciding whether they are of "satisfactory quality" (see para.4.26 below).

[40] *Ojjeh v Waller* [1999] C.L.Y. 4405 applying the principles laid down by the House of Lords in *Williams v Natural Life Health Foods Ltd* [1988] 1 W.L.R. 830.

[41] See para.3.08 above.

[42] [1913] A.C. 30.

[43] *Dick Bentley v Harold Smith* [1965] 1 W.L.R. 623 at 627.

mean "a term" or "a contractual promise". A second meaning contrasts a warranty with a condition. For example, the Sale of Goods Act 1979, which applied to consumer contracts concluded before 1 October 2015, states in s.61:

> . . . warranty . . . means an agreement with reference to goods which are the subject of a contract of sale, but collateral to the main purpose of such contract, the breach of which gives rise to a claim to damages, but not to a right to reject the goods and treat the contract as repudiated.

In other words it means a minor term.

If an express statement is classified as a contractual term we have seen that the innocent party can claim damages. Can he also treat the contract as repudiated and reject the goods? The answer is that he may be able to do so, provided that he has been substantially deprived of what he bargained for, which is generally the case where a term is classified as a condition. Also, the Court of Appeal has held that this rigid classification is not exhaustive,[44] and that there were also intermediate stipulations (sometimes called "innominate terms") where the right to reject depended on the seriousness and consequences of the breach.

5. COLLATERAL CONTRACTS

We referred to collateral contracts in para.3.03 above where the leading **3.20** consumer case of *Andrews v Hopkinson* was mentioned. The topic was also mentioned at the end of para.3.09 above where the earlier commercial case of *Shanklin Pier v Detel Products* was cited. These cases illustrate the two situations where collateral contracts (or "collateral warranties" as they are often called) are likely to involve consumers—hire-purchase and manufacturers' guarantees. The situations are similar in that usually they are tripartite and the customers acquire their goods through contracts with a supplier, whereas the warranty is given by a third party with whom they have no other contractual relationship.

Hire-purchase

In hire-purchase cases the three parties are the retailer, the finance company **3.21** and the debtor/customer. As in *Andrews v Hopkinson*, although the initial negotiations for the ultimate acquisition of the goods take place between the customer and the retailer—in that case a car dealer—the goods are sold by the retailer to a finance company which then lets them on hire-purchase to the customer. Thus, no contract for the supply of goods is made between the retailer and the customer whom the retailer introduces to the finance company.

Not surprisingly the dealer may sometimes make extravagant statements

---

[44] *Cehave N.V. v Bremer Handelsgesellschaft GmbH* [1976] Q.B. 44.

about the goods before the above two sequential supply contracts are made. Thus, as in Example (1) at para.3.01 above, the dealer may state that the goods are of high quality: "it's a good little bus". When the goods turn out to be defective, the customer can recover damages against the dealer on the basis that the "warranty" given during the negotiations created a separate, "collateral" contract—the third contract in this triangular legal structure. Since consideration is required for this somewhat artificial contract, the customer provides it by entering into the later hire-purchase contract from which the dealer benefits by selling a car to the finance company and receiving commission from it for the introduction.

3.22   Of course, as the statement is usually oral, it will be more difficult to prove what was said than if it were written. This problem is clearly illustrated by *Brewer v Mann*,[45] another hire-purchase case.

> The customer acquired a second-hand 1930 Bentley Speed Six. She alleged that the dealer had said that it had "a Speed Six engine", which apparently is not always the case in this type of car. Her claim, based on breach of a collateral warranty, succeeded at first instance but the Court of Appeal ordered a retrial because of the trial judge's lack of objectivity.

If at the retrial the judge were to accept her evidence, then she would recover damages against the dealer (the question of rejection did not arise, since the car was acquired directly from the third party, i.e. the finance company).

Manufacturers' guarantees

3.23   Here the three parties are the manufacturer, the retailer and the customer. Although usually manufacturers do not negotiate directly with their consumer end users, it is commonplace for them to give "warranties" or "guarantees" with their products. Thus, although there is no contractual relationship between manufacturers and consumers, here again there is a triangular structure with two sales—by the manufacturer to the retailer (often with a chain of importers or other distributors in between) and by the retailer to the consumer. The manufacturer's warranty is the third contract. This type of collateral contract is fully discussed at paras 5.05 to 5.09 below.

6. DESCRIPTION: SALE OF GOODS

3.24   The final possibility is that the statement formed part of the description of the goods. By s.11 of the Consumer Rights Act 2015:

> (1) Every contract to supply goods by description is to be treated as including a term that the goods will match the description.
> (2) If the supply is by sample as well as by description, it is not sufficient that

---

[45] [2012] EWCA Civ 246.

the bulk of the goods matches the sample if the goods do not also match the description.

(3) A supply of goods is not prevented from being a supply by description just because—

    (a) the goods are exposed for supply, and

    (b) they are selected by the consumer.

This section is a re-enactment of s.13 of the Sale of Goods Act 1979, which continues to apply to consumer contracts entered into before 1 October 2015 when the Consumer Rights Act 2015 entered into force.[46] There is no substantive difference between s.11 of the Consumer Rights Act 2015 and s.13 of the Sale of Goods Act 1979, except that s.11 covers all contract for the "supply" of goods, which includes contracts of sale as well as other supply contracts (see s.3 of the Consumer Rights Act 2015). However, it remains to be seen whether case-law on the scope of s.13 will continue to be followed under s.11, not least because some of those cases are concerned with specifically commercial situations. Nevertheless, they may continue to be of value and we have retained our discussion of the key decisions under the old law in this section.

The section itself is largely self-explanatory. Thus, if a handbag is described **3.25** as "leather" there will be a breach of s.11 if it is plastic; if a car is described as a 2016 model there is a breach of s.11 if it is a 2014 model; if the seller agrees to sell a "woollen skirt" he will be in breach if the material is cotton, rayon or linen. In this type of case the section adds nothing to the general law. It is a central obligation of the seller to supply the goods contracted for and he is guilty of non-performance if he fails to do so.

We now have to consider two problems, namely:

(1) What is a sale by description?

(2) What stipulations form part of the contract description?

What is a sale by description?

The courts have given a wide meaning to this term—in the words of the Law **3.26** Commission "It [is] to all intents and purposes comprehensive". The following examples show how wide it is:

(a) Sales of purely generic goods, e.g. "50 rolls of hand-blocked wallpaper".

(b) Sales of specific goods[47] which the buyer has not seen where he is relying on the description, e.g. "my 2015 VW Golf Plus".

(c) Sales of specific goods which the buyer has seen if they are sold as goods answering a description, e.g. "Canadian salmon".

---

[46] It also continues to apply to private sales.
[47] "Specific goods": see para.6.32 below.

(d) Goods selected by the buyer at a self-service store or supermarket. This is the effect of s.11(3). Thus if a packet on a supermarket shelf is labelled "Scotch salmon" and it contains Canadian salmon there will be a breach of s.11—so also if a label wrongly states the ingredients or quantity.

3.27 A recent case concerning the sale of a painting has confirmed that a sale will only be "by description" if both parties intend the description to form part of the contract.[48]

The principle that goods can describe themselves was affirmed by the courts in the remarkable case of *Beale v Taylor*[49] where the following facts occurred:

> The plaintiff saw an advertisement "Herald convertible white 1961". He went to see it and saw a "1200" disc on the rear of the car. He agreed to buy it for £190 in the belief that he was buying a 1961 Triumph Herald model. Unfortunately, he was only half right; the front part consisted of an earlier model which had been welded on to the rear end of a 1961 Herald 1200. He claimed damages from the seller, but the county court judge dismissed the claim. The Court of Appeal allowed his appeal.

3.28 The court held that the combined effect of the advertisement and the disc was that the seller was offering to sell a 1961 Herald. This was, therefore, a sale by description and the seller was in breach of s.13 of the Sale of Goods Act 1979. Damages were agreed at £125 (the price less the scrap value to the buyer).

It is not clear from the judgments whether the buyer would have succeeded on the strength of the disc alone. It is clear, however, that if a seller says to the buyer "I am offering to sell this to you—I am making no representations and you must exercise your own judgment," there would not be a sale by description.

3.29 This principle was applied and extended in *Harlingdon and Leinster Enterprises Ltd v Christopher Hull Fine Art Ltd*[50] where the seller started by telling the buyer that he had come to sell two paintings by one Gabrielle Münter and then went on to say that he was not an expert in these matters and knew nothing about that particular artist. In holding that this was *not* a sale by description, Nourse LJ in the Court of Appeal said (at p.18):

> "Authority apart, those words [i.e. s.13(1)] would suggest that the description must be influential in the sale, not necessarily alone, but so as to become an essential term, i.e. a condition, of the contract. Without such influence a description cannot be said to be one *by* which the contract for the sale of goods is made."

---

[48] *Drake v Thomas Agnew & Sons Ltd* [2002] EWHC 294 (a statement that the painting was "a Van Dyck" was held to be a statement of opinion only and not part of the decription).

[49] [1967] 1 W.L.R. 1193.

[50] [1991] 1 Q.B. 564. The legal effect of attribution may depend on whether the buyer was (as here) a dealer or a private buyer (see above). Note the strong and convincing dissenting judgment by Stuart-Smith LJ. See *Avora Fine Arts Investment Ltd v Christie, Manson & Woods Ltd* [2012] EWHC 2198 (Ch): buyer relied on Misrepresentation Act 1967 s.2(1), not s.13.

Accordingly, the buyer will fail if, viewed objectively, the court is satisfied that he did not rely on the description. We assume that this will continue to be the case under s.11 of the Consumer Rights Act 2015.

What statements form part of the description?

For a long time, the courts gave an extremely wide meaning to the term "description". The term has been held to include such matters as the quantity, the colour,[51] the measurements, the manner of packing and even the date of shipment. The practical result of this can be very serious from the seller's point of view and unduly favourable to the buyer. If the goods do not comply with their description the buyer can reject the goods, even though he has suffered no loss.[52] In the leading case of *Arcos Ltd v Ronaasen*[53]:

3.30

> Sellers sold a quantity of wooden staves to the buyers. The thickness was given as half an inch. When the goods were delivered the arbitrator found that (i) only 5 per cent were half an inch thick; (ii) a large proportion were between half-an-inch and nine-sixteenths of an inch; (iii) some were between nine-sixteenths and five-eighths of an inch; (iv) a very small proportion were more than five-eighths of an inch; (v) the staves were fit for the buyer's purpose and commercially within, and merchantable under, the contract specification. Despite the finding in (v) the buyer claimed that he was entitled to reject them. The High Court, the Court of Appeal and the House of Lords upheld the buyer's claim.

The judgments in the House of Lords are brief but they emphasise the need for strict compliance. In the words of Lord Buckmaster[54]:

> "If the article they have purchased is not in fact the article that has been delivered, they are entitled to reject it, even though it is the commercial equivalent of that which they have bought."

Lord Atkin, in a well-known passage, commented that:

> "If the written contract specifies conditions of weight, measurement and the like, these conditions must be complied with. A ton does not mean about a ton, or a yard about a yard. Still less, when you descend to minute measurements does half an inch mean about half an inch. If the seller wants a margin he must and in my experience does stipulate for it."

He did, however, go on to add that:

> "No doubt there may be microscopic deviations which businessmen, and therefore lawyers will ignore."

---

[51] *Ojjeh v Waller* [1999] C.L.Y. 4405 QBD—purchase of 17 purple Lalique glass car mascots—colour not authentic—seller liable.

[52] The Sale of Goods Act 1979 s.13 was classified as a condition. The Consumer Rights Act 2015 no longer adopts this classification, but instead makes available a comprehensive set of remedies for consumer contracts, which include both a short-term and long-term right of rejection. See paras 8.19–8.47 below.

[53] [1933] A.C. 470.

[54] [1933] A.C. 470 at 474.

3.31   Another well-known illustration of the doctrine of strict compliance is *Re Moore & Co and Landauer & Co*[55] which, like the previous case, reached the courts via an arbitrator.

> Sellers agreed to sell tinned fruit in boxes containing 30 tins. When delivered some contained only 24 tins. The arbitrator found that there was no difference in the market value of the goods whether they were packed 24 tins or 30 tins in a case. The Court of Appeal upheld a claim by the buyer that he was entitled to reject the entire consignment even though a claim for damages would have failed.

It may be, however, that the position is changing. In a passage which can be equally relevant to consumer cases Lord Wilberforce said this:

> "Some of these cases . . . I find to be excessively technical and due for fresh examination in this House. Even if a strict and technical view must be taken as regards the description of unascertained future goods (e.g. commodities) as to which each detail of the description may be assumed to be vital, it may be, and in my opinion is, right to treat other contracts of sale of goods in a similar manner to other contracts generally so as to ask *whether a particular item in a description constituted a substantial ingredient of the 'identity' of the thing sold, and only if it does to treat it as a condition.*" (italics supplied)[56]

Critical comments such as these presaged a change in law in relation to remedies, so that a non-consumer is no longer able to *reject* for slight breaches.

Special meaning

3.32   If words have acquired a special trade meaning there will be no breach of s.11 if they answer that meaning. Thus in the case of *Grenfell v EB Meyrowitz Ltd*[57] it was proved that the words "safety glass" had acquired a special meaning and that this was known to the buyer. It was held that the sellers were not in breach of s.13 of the Sale of Goods Act 1979 when they supplied "safety glass" goggles which corresponded to the special trade meaning.

Horsemeat and beef burgers—a case study

3.33   In February 2013, the scandal of horsemeat in beef burgers (and who knows what else) hit the headlines. Tesco, Aldi, Waitrose and other supermarkets quickly removed various meat products from their shelves. Why? They were in breach of s.13 of the Sale of Goods Act 1979 and strictly liable whether or not they knew of the adulteration (if the food were unsafe, there would also have been a breach of the satisfactory quality condition in s.14(2) of the Sale of Goods Act 1979 (see para.4.08 below)). Buyers could have rejected such goods and demanded a refund, even if the food were safe to eat. The

---

[55] [1921] 2 K.B. 519.
[56] *Reardon Smith v Hansen-Tangen* [1976] 1 W.L.R. 989 at 989 HL. See the Court of Appeal's approach in *Harlingdon* above, para.3.29.
[57] [1936] 2 All E.R. 1313.

sellers in turn could claim against their sellers and so on up the supply chain to the original seller of the horsemeat masquerading as beef; but as some of the meat came from across the Channel, the success or failure of such claims would depend on what the applicable law was in such international contracts, and also on the contract terms and conditions.

What claims would consumers have against producers such as Findus with beef lasagne containing horsemeat? As there would be no contractual nexus between them and the producers, any claim would be based on the law of tort and in particular the Consumer Protection Act 1987; such a claim would fail, unless the food were unsafe and caused personal injury (see para.5.21 below).

Relationship between description and fitness

A final question which can be important for the consumer relates to the distinction between description and fitness for purpose. If goods are unfit for the buyer's particular purpose, can he allege that there is a breach of s.11 or must he rely on the condition of fitness for purpose under s.10 (considered in Chapter Four)? This is yet another problem where the law is uncertain; the practical importance lies in the sphere of private sales (which continue to fall within the Sale of Goods Act 1979). **3.34**

> Suppose that the seller of a house agrees to sell to the buyer his furniture, lawn-mower and television set. Both the lawnmower and the television set break down almost immediately and a sideboard collapses shortly afterwards.

As the law stands at the moment it is very unlikely that the buyer would have any remedy against the seller. Section 14 of the Sale of Goods Act 1979 only applies to a sale "in the course of a business". There is nothing to suggest that any of the goods have been misdescribed.

One point which is clear is that unfitness for one particular use does not amount to a breach of s.11 of the Consumer Rights Act 2015 (nor would it have of s.13 of the Sale of Goods Act 1979). Thus "herring-meal" in animal feed is still "herring-meal" even if it has defects making it lethal when fed to mink.[58] If, however, the goods have only one use (e.g. "touring skis") it might be arguable that fitness for purpose forms an intrinsic part of the description. Perhaps the courts might adopt the words spoken by Birkett LJ in another context that "a car which will not go is not a car at all".[59] On the other hand, a finding that the goods are not of satisfactory quality may make it unnecessary to consider whether the seller is also in breach of s.11.[60]

---

[58] *Ashington Piggeries v Christopher Hill* [1972] A.C. 441. Such goods might, however, fail to satisfy the new (and expanded) test of "satisfactory quality" as to which see para.4.10 below.
[59] *Karsales (Harrow) Ltd v Wallis* [1956] 1 W.L.R. 936 at 942.
[60] *Clegg v Andersson* [2003] EWCA Civ. 320 (sale of yacht with over-weight keel).

7. Relevance of Pre-contractual Information

3.35   We will see in Chapter Six that there is a requirement to furnish a consumer with all sorts of information before the consumer concludes a contract. These rules were recently updated in the Consumer Contracts (Information, Cancellation and Additional Charges) Regulations 2013 (SI 2013/3134) (the 2013 Regulations). The many items of information required include information about the "main characteristics of the goods". Section 11 of the Consumer Rights Act 2015 therefore provides as follows:

> (4) Any information that is provided by the trader about the goods and is information mentioned in paragraph (a) of Schedule 1 or 2 to the Consumer Contracts (Information, Cancellation and Additional Charges) Regulations 2013 (SI 2013/3134) (main characteristics of goods) is to be treated as included as a term of the contract.

> (5) A change to any of that information, made before entering into the contract or later, is not effective unless expressly agreed between the consumer and the trader.

Of course, all the other items of information required by the 2013 Regulations also become a term of the contract, although these are covered by s.12 of the Consumer Rights Act 2015 instead. This cross-referencing between these two measures makes the law as a whole rather more complex that seems necessary.

8. Other Supply of Goods Contracts

3.36   Prior to the coming into force of the Consumer Rights Act 2015, contracts which were not within the scope of the the Sale of Goods Act 1979 were subject to other legislation, but this included similar provisions for other types of contracts for the supply of goods.[61]

Thus where goods are let out on hire-purchase the condition as to description was implied by s.9 of the Supply of Goods (Implied Terms) Act 1973.[62] Almost identical conditions applied in other cases where the property in goods is transferred to the customer (notably contracts of exchange and contracts for work and materials).[63] Here the relevant statute was the Supply of Goods and Services Act 1982, which also extended to contracts of hire.[64]

Fortunately, one of the happy consequences of the enactment of the Consumer Rights Act 2015 is that the need to classify a supply transaction so as to identify the applicable Act of Parliament has become redundant, and

---

[61] See para.1.18 above.
[62] *Brewer v Mann*, see para.3.22 above: "Bentley Speed Six" was an accurate description.
[63] s.3 of the Supply of Goods and Services Act 1982.
[64] s.8.

now s.11 of the Consumer Rights Act 2015 will apply to *all* types of supply transactions.

9. DIGITAL CONTENT

There is one notable development in the Consumer Rights Act 2015: the introduction of rules dealing specifically with digital content (which includes traditional computer software but also smartphone apps, eBooks and movies streamed on-line), provided this is supplied to the consumer in return for payment of a price. Chapter 3 of Part 1 of the Act introduces a number of new rules which reflect the corresponding provisions applicable to goods. For present purposes, s.36 provides as follows: **3.37**

(1) Every contract to supply digital content is to be treated as including a term that the digital content will match any description of it given by the trader to the consumer.
(2) Where the consumer examines a trial version before the contract is made, it is not sufficient that the digital content matches (or is better than) the trial version if the digital content does not also match any description of it given by the trader to the consumer.

Although this provision looks very similar to s.11 discussed above, one difference is that there is no requirement that the digital content has to be supplied by description.

As with s.11, any pre-contractual information about the main characteristics of the digital content (main characteristics, functionality and interoperability) become a term of the contract by virtue of s.36(3) and (4), which mirror the provisions for goods noted under Section 7 above. Other pre-contractual information about digital content supplied for a price becomes a term of the contract under s.37. If digital content is supplied other than in return for a price, the 2013 Regulations make the pre-contractual information a term of that supply contract instead.[65] **3.38**

---

[65] Under regs 9(3), 10(5) and 13(6).

Chapter Four

"IT DOESN'T WORK"

1. The Problem

(1) A buys a dishwasher. It fails to work. The seller calls on numerous occa- **4.01**
sions to try to put it right. It invariably breaks down again after a few days.
(2) B orders central heating which is installed by X. The radiators leak and
damage the carpet.
(3) C takes his suit to the cleaners. It comes back in a ruined condition.
(4) D buys a pair of new patent leather shoes for a ball. The soles come away
from the uppers almost immediately and D is unable to wear them.
(5) E takes his car to a garage for repair. The garage puts on faulty brake
discs and E is injured when the brakes fail.
(6) F buys an application for his smartphone to record music but all the
recordings are inaudible.

By far the most common consumer complaint is that the goods or services **4.02**
were not up to the expected standard. How does the law protect consumers?
For contracts concluded before 1 October 2015, there were four different sets
of provisions which gave consumers rights against the supplier:

(a) Section 14 of the Sale of Goods Act 1979 (the 1979 Act) for a con-
    tract of sale.

(b) Section 10 of the Supply of Goods (Implied Terms) Act 1973 con-
    tained virtually identical provisions relating to hire purchase agree-
    ments.

(c) Sections 4 and 9 of the Supply of Goods and Services Act 1982 con-
    tained virtually identical provisions in relation to other contracts
    for the transfer of goods (exchange, work and materials, etc.) and
    contracts of hire.

(d) At common law, an analogous condition of fitness for purpose could
    be implied in relation to computer software/digital content.

Although the provisions of all these Acts regarding the quality requirements were essentially the same, it was still necessary to classify the supply
transaction to identify the applicable legislation. This is no longer necessary
because Ch.2 of Pt 1 of the Consumer Rights Act 2015 (the CRA 2015) now
imposes a single set of provisions applicable to all contracts involving the

supply of goods (see s.3 of the CRA 2015 for a full definition of the relevant supply contracts). However, the distinction between the various supply transactions is still important for other purposes—including the passing of property and *nemo dat* rules discussed in Chapter Two.

2. SUPPLY OF GOODS

The general position

4.03 If a contract is for the supply of goods, the obligations of the seller in relation to quality and fitness are governed by ss.9 and 10 of the CRA 2015. These sections are re-enactments of the provisions previously found in s.14 of the 1979 Act, although the new provisions are arranged differently. The substance of the section is not altered, however, and we assume that courts will continue to draw on at least some of the case-law which evolved under s.14 after that section was amended to introduce the now-familiar "satisfactory quality" test.

This test replaced the earlier requirement that goods had to be of "merchantable quality" which was more suitable to commercial contracts. Following a Law Commission Report[1] in 1987 which made proposals for certain changes, the Sale and Supply of Goods Act 1994 gave effect to most of these proposed changes by amending the 1979 Act to introduce the term "satisfactory quality".[2] This test itself was enhanced in 2002 to reflect additional requirements introduced by the EU's Consumer Sales Directive (99/44 EC). All of these developments are now consolidated in the provisions of the CRA 2015.

Let the buyer beware

4.04 In the light of what has been said above, the early law developed on the basis that it was for the parties to make their own bargain—it was up to the buyer to decide whether the goods were merchantable and fit for their purpose before he agreed to buy them. The principle ("caveat emptor" or "let the buyer beware") has been severely eroded but is not entirely extinct. By s.14(1) of the 1979 Act:

> Except as provided by this section . . . there is no implied condition or warranty about the quality or fitness for any particular purpose of goods supplied under a contract of sale.

If, the seller is a private seller the principle of caveat emptor may still apply.

> Suppose that A, a private individual, sells a hedgecutter to B. It is in poor condition and breaks down after a few days. In the absence of any express promise or representation B has no claim against A.

---

[1] Law Com. No.24.
[2] The Law Commission recommended "acceptable quality": see Law Com. No.24 at paras 319–322.

However, contracts between a trader and a consumer are now governed by the provisions of the CRA 2015, which prioritises the requirements discussed below. However, s.18 of the Act includes a provisions which mirrors the old s.14(1) of the 1979 Act. There is one hybrid situation: what about a dealer who sells in the course of a business as agent for a private seller? Section 14(5) of the 1979 Act makes it clear that the seller must endeavour to bring this fact to the buyer's notice to avoid liability. It provides that:

> [The conditions of quality and fitness] apply to a sale by a person who in the course of business is acting as agent for another as they apply to a sale by a principal in the course of a business except where that other is not selling in the course of a business and either the buyer knows that fact or reasonable steps are taken to bring it to the notice of the buyer before the contract is made.

A Scottish case illustrates that a buyer can take advantage of s.14(5) if he **4.05** buys from a dealer without knowing that the dealer is acting for a non-business seller.[3] The CRA 2015 does not contain a provision corresponding to s.14(5) of the 1979 Act. We therefore assume that for the very specific situation addressed by s.14(5), the 1979 Act continues to apply—the provisions of the 1979 Act no longer apply where the CRA 2015 applies (see s.14(9) of the 1979 Act), but the latter Act does not seem to apply to this situation.

Section 14(5) is concerned with the case where a private seller appears to be selling in the course of a business. What about the converse case—trade sellers masquerading as private sellers? Such practices are now covered by para.22 of Sch.1 to the Consumer Protection from Unfair Trading Regulations 2008.[4]

Privity of contract—new law

The conditions of quality and fitness are implied *as between trader and con-* **4.06** *sumer.* If, for example, a mother buys a washing machine and gives it to her daughter as a present then (subject to what is said below) the daughter has no claim against the supplier if it breaks down. The mother would have a claim but she might find it difficult to prove damage flowing from the breach (although she might have a claim if she paid for the cost of repairs).[5] The question of "who made the contract?" may also be relevant if, for example, a group of people go to a restaurant for a meal. It seems that the restaurant makes a contract with each of them, so that each of them would be entitled to claim damages if the supplier were in breach of the implied term.[6]

The mother-and-daughter example given above now has to be considered in the light of the changes made by the Contracts (Rights of Third Parties) Act 1999. The Act provides that a non-party can enforce a contractual term

---

[3] *Boyter v Thomson* [1995] 2 A.C. 628 HL.
[4] See para.18.32 below.
[5] See *Jackson v Horizon Holidays* [1975] 1 W.L.R. 1468 where the Court of Appeal allowed a contracting party to recover damages for a third party's loss (the facts are given at para.8.68 below). But see the comments of Lord Wilberforce in *Woodar Investment Development v Wimpey Construction UK* [1980] 1 W.L.R. 277 HL.
[6] *Lockett v AM Charles Ltd* [1938] 4 All E.R. 17.

if (a) the contract so provides or (b) the contract purports to confer a benefit on the third party—but this will not be so if, on a proper construction of the contract, it appears that the parties did not intend the third party to have enforcement rights. Thus the Act can apply if the matter is expressly dealt with when the contract is made. The following further points should be borne in mind:

(1) The supplier will have the same defences against the third party as he would have had against the original buyer.

(2) The third party must be expressly identified by name, class or description.[7] As the Court of Appeal decided in a recent case, "the use of the word 'express' does not allow a process of construction or implication."[8]

(3) The normal rules as to causation, remoteness and mitigation will apply.

Questions of agency must also be borne in mind in this connection. A woman who does the shopping may do so as agent for her husband or cohabitee, so that *he* would have a claim in contract if the goods turn out to be defective. There is no agency case (so far) the other way round. Thus when a man bought typhoid-infected milk which injured his wife, it was held in *Frost v Aylesbury Dairy Co*[9] that only the husband had a claim in contract. In modern social conditions the courts might well hold that the husband was buying for himself and as agent for his wife; a contrary decision would certainly receive critical comment in the media!

Strict liability

4.07 Section 9 of the 2015 Act requires that the goods "are of satisfactory quality". This imposes strict liability. A case decided under s.9's precursor, *Frost v Aylesbury Dairy Co*, above, held that the absence of negligence is no defence; the trader will not be able to avoid liability by proving that he neither knew, nor ought to have known, of the defect. It is irrelevant that the defect is latent and undiscoverable. The trader is liable though blameless.

If, however, the privity rules bar a claim in contract an injured claimant will have to bring proceedings in *tort*. This used to mean having to prove negligence—by no means an easy task. However, because of the Consumer Protection Act 1987 and the imposition of strict liability in tort on producers and some distributors, the claimant's position improved.[10]

---

[7] See *Crowson v HSBC Insurance Brokers Ltd* [2010] Lloyd's Rep. I.R. 441: contract with company conferred benefit on director.

[8] *Avraamides v Colwill, The Times*, 12 December 2006, per Waller LJ.

[9] [1905] 1 K.B. 608

[10] See paras 5.10 and 5.12 below.

Satisfactory quality: section 9 of the Consumer Rights Act 2015

This provision is arguably the most important statutory weapon for consum-   **4.08**
ers. Where consumers have a complaint about defective goods—failure to
work, durability, appearance, safety, etc.—their first line of attack will be
based on the requirement of satisfactory quality imposed by s.9(1).

At the time of preparing this edition, there is no case-law on the Consumer
Rights Act provisions, so the discussion which follows draws on earlier
case-law. Some of this involves cases applying the "satisfactory quality" test
introduced in 1994, although some of the case-law predating its introduction
continues to be of assistance. It must be borne in mind that pre-1994 cases
will be concerned with the Victorian expression "merchantable quality",
which had a different scope from the satisfactory quality test. In the first case
to apply the satisfactory quality test, *Thain v Anniesland Trade Centre*,[11] the
judge thought that pre-1994 case-law would of limited assistance, but earlier
cases continue to be considered by the courts when applying the current test.
More relevant is another observation by the judge that the application of the
satisfactory quality test is very fact-sensitive, which means that even in cases
with similar facts the application of the satisfactory quality test might result
in different outcomes.

The requirement

Section 9(1), is as follows: **4.09**

> Every contract to supply goods is to be treated as including a term that the
> quality of the goods is satisfactory.

This basic requirement is a departure from the wording of s.14(2) of the 1979
Act, which stated that "where the seller sells goods in the course of a business, there is an implied term that the goods supplied under the contract are
of satisfactory quality". As the CRA 2015 only applies to contracts between
a trader and a consumer, the qualification that the sale has to be in the course
of a business is now redundant.

The reference to "goods supplied under the contract" is also missing from
the new definition, Under the older law, the courts had approached this issue
sensibly, and it was clear that the satisfactory quality requirement applied,
e.g., not only to the *contents* of a bottle or tin but also to the *container*, i.e. the
bottle or tin itself, even if it has to be returned—it is still "supplied" under the
contract even if it has not been sold.[12] Similarly, if the goods actually supplied contain a foreign body (for example, a worm, a snail or a piece of glass)
the totality of the goods supplied may be unsatisfactory.[13]

---

[11] [1997] SLT (Sh Ct) 102.
[12] *Geddling v Marsh* [1920] 1 K.B. 668.
[13] See the interesting case of *Wilson v Rickett Cockerell & Co Ltd* [1954] 1 Q.B. 598 where a
detonator was mistakenly included in a bag of coalite.

When are goods of "satisfactory" quality?

4.10 It will be helpful to cite the key requirements of the satisfactory quality test verbatim:

> (2) The quality of goods is satisfactory if they meet the standard that a reasonable person would consider satisfactory, taking account of—
>
> > (a) any description of the goods,
> > (b) the price or other consideration for the goods (if relevant), and
> > (c) all the other relevant circumstances (see subsection (5)).
>
> (3) The quality of goods includes their state and condition; and the following aspects (among others) are in appropriate cases aspects of the quality of goods—
>
> > (a) fitness for all the purposes for which goods of that kind are usually supplied;
> > (b) appearance and finish;
> > (c) freedom from minor defects;
> > (d) safety;
> > (e) durability.

We shall consider these "aspects" and other matters relating to the definition in turn.

4.11 **Price and sale goods.** The reference to price in s.9(2)(b) mirrors what Lord Reid said in *Brown & Son Ltd v Craiks*,[14] namely, that if a particular description covers different qualities of goods, a buyer who pays a price appropriate to a *superior* quality can reasonably expect to receive that quality, and can regard the goods as unsatisfactory if he receives an inferior quality.

What about goods bought at a "sale" at reduced prices? There is no reported case on this point but a buyer should have no difficulty in satisfying a court that the "sale" aspect is irrelevant; it results from a commercial decision to dispose of surplus stock at bargain prices. It cannot in any way be relied on by the seller to justify the supply of inferior goods. The quality should reflect the higher, pre-sale price.

4.12 **Multi-purpose goods: aspect 9(3)(a).** Under the pre-1994 law, goods which had multiple purposes were regarded as being of "merchantable quality" if they were suitable for at least some of these, but since then, a relevant factor in considering whether goods are satisfactory is to consider whether they are fit for *all* their common purposes. Where goods are unfit for at least one common purpose, then this would support the argument that the goods are not satisfactory.

---

[14] [1970] 1 W.L.R. 752, HL. If, however, the buyer relies entirely on his own judgment, the mere fact that he makes a bad bargain will not give rise to a claim: *Harlingdon Enterprises Ltd v Christopher Hull Fine Art Ltd* [1991] 1 Q.B. 564 (see para.3.29 above).

Appearance and finish: aspect 9(3)(b).   Problems may occur which upset   **4.13**
the consumer even though the goods are still usable. A tabletop may be
scratched, a refrigerator dented, the pattern on a shirt or skirt uneven or the
paintwork on a car chipped or matt.

In a report[15] published by the Consumers' Association in 1979 it was
pointed out that the statutory definition was unsatisfactory in two respects.
First, it concentrated excessively on the fitness of the goods for their purpose
and ignored aesthetic considerations and appearance (dents, scratches, etc.).
Secondly, the reference to the standard which a buyer might reasonably
expect could open the door to an argument that a buyer could not complain if
a new car had "teething troubles" since it was widely known that all new cars
had them. The Law Commission Report[16] refers to a number of cases which
lend some support to these fears[17] but in two later cases these fears have been
largely laid to rest. A case still very relevant on the point is *Rogers v Parish
(Scarborough) Ltd* (decided under the pre-1994 law).[18]

> Mr Rogers bought a Range Rover for £16,000 under a conditional sale agree-
> ment. It was sold as new but it had defects in the engine, gearbox and bodywork
> and the oilseals were unsound at vital junctions. In the six months following
> delivery Mr Rogers drove the car some 5,500 miles while unsuccessful efforts
> were made to rectify the defects. At the end of that period he rejected the car and
> claimed the return of his payments and damages on the basis that the car was
> unmerchantable.

Counsel for the sellers argued that since the car was roadworthy, the defects
did not make it "unmerchantable". The judge at first instance accepted this
view but the Court of Appeal rejected it and found in favour of Mr Rogers.
Mustill LJ said (at 359):

> "Starting with the purpose for which 'goods of that kind' are commonly bought,
> one would include in respect of any passenger vehicle not merely the buyer's
> purpose of driving the car from one place to another *but of doing so with the
> appropriate degree of comfort, ease of handling and reliability and, one might add,
> of pride in the vehicle's outward and interior appearance* [italics supplied]. What
> is the appropriate degree and what relative weight is to be attached to one char-
> acteristic of the car rather than another will depend on the market at which the
> car is aimed.
>
> To identify the relevant expectation one must look at the factors listed in the
> subsection. First, the description applied to the goods. In the present case the
> vehicle was sold as new. Deficiencies which might be acceptable in a secondhand
> vehicle were not to be expected in one purchased as new. Next, the description
> 'Range Rover' would conjure up a particular set of expectations, not the same as
> those relating to an ordinary saloon car, as to the balance between performance,
> handling, comfort and resilience. The factor of price was also significant. At

---

[15] *Merchantable Quality—What does it mean?*
[16] [1995] 2 A.C. 628 HL.
[17] *Millars of Falkirk Ltd v Turpie* (1976) S.L.T. (Notes) 66; *Spencer v Claude Rye (Vehicles) Ltd,
The Guardian,* 19 December 1972; *Leaves v Wadham Stringer (Cliftons) Ltd* [1980] R.T.R.
308.
[18] [1987] Q.B. 933. The other case is *Bernstein v Pamson Motors (Golders Green) Ltd* [1987] 2 All
E.R. 220

more than £16,000 this vehicle was, if not at the top end of the scale, well above the level of the ordinary family saloon. The buyer was entitled to value for his money."

Even if the car is in the middle or lower end of the market it will still be unsatisfactory if (1) the defects have a knock-on effect so that the car can never be restored to its previous condition, or (2) the defects (e.g. oil leak) render it dangerous to drive the car.[19]

This approach is now reflected by the fact that "appearance and finish" are an aspect of satisfactory quality in s.9(3)(b).

4.14 **Minor defects: aspect 9(3)(c).** The list of five aspects also includes aspect (c): "freedom from minor defects". In many cases this will overlap (b) since, for example, a dent in the side of a refrigerator will be a minor defect and also relate to its finish. However, there are often minor defects which affect the function of a product while at the same time not preventing its general use, for example, a faulty light in kitchen equipment such as an extractor hood or oven or a faulty radio in a car. Here aspect (c) can be called in aid and will counter the "teething troubles" argument. The facts of *Farnworth Finance Facilities v Attryde*,[20] a hire-purchase case, illustrates this type of problem where a motor cycle had successively unstable panniers, a faulty headlight switch and a broken chain drive. The consumer succeeded in his claim because of a "congeries of defects".

4.15 **Effect of guarantee.** In the *Rogers* case (above) counsel for the sellers raised a further point—namely that a car was not rendered unmerchantable by defects which the buyer was entitled to have rectified free of charge under the manufacturer's guarantee (or warranty). Mustill LJ was unimpressed. He said (at p.360):

> "Can it really be right to say that the reasonable buyer would expect less of his new Range Rover with a warranty than without one? Surely the warranty is an addition to the buyer's rights, not a subtraction from them, and, it may be noted, only a circumscribed addition since it lasts for a limited period and does not compensate the buyer for consequential loss and inconvenience.
>
> If the defendants are right a buyer would be well advised to leave his guarantee behind in the showroom. This cannot be what the manufacturers and dealers intend or what their customers reasonably understand."

This makes it clear that voluntary manufacturers' guarantees have no bearing on the application of the satisfactory quality test, a matter confirmed more recently by a Scottish court.[21]

4.16 **Second-hand goods.** There have been four cases dealing with "merchantability" of second-hand cars (and they would be decided in the same way under

---

[19] See the judgment of Rougier J in *Bernstein* [1987] 2 All E.R. 220.
[20] [1970] 1 W.L.R. 1053.
[21] *Lamarra v Capital Bank Plc* [2006] CSIH 49.

the satisfactory quality test)). The first was *Bartlett v Sidney Marcus*[22] where the following facts arose:

> The plaintiff bought a second-hand Jaguar car for £950. It was pointed out that the clutch was in need of repair, but the defect was believed to be a small one and the price was reduced accordingly. After driving for 300 miles the plaintiff took the car to a garage who found that the defect was more serious than the plaintiff expected. The cost of repairs came to £84 and the plaintiff claimed this amount from the seller.

The county court judge gave judgment for the buyer but the Court of Appeal allowed the seller's appeal. On the question of merchantability Lord Denning MR pointed out that:

> "On the sale of a second-hand car, it is merchantable if it is in usable condition, even if not perfect. . . . A buyer should realise that when he buys a second-hand car defects may appear sooner or later and, in the absence of an express warranty, he has no redress."

In *Crowther v Shannon Motor Co*,[23] which was also concerned with a second-hand Jaguar, the buyer was more successful.   **4.17**

> The car was eight years old; the engine had done 82,165 miles; the buyer paid a price of £390. He drove the car for another 2,300 miles in three weeks. Then the engine expired. The evidence showed that (a) the engine was in a "clapped out" state when the car was sold to the buyer; (b) the buyer of a Jaguar car could reasonably expect the engine to do 100,000 miles. On these facts the Court of Appeal held that the seller was liable.

In the third case the buyer scored a somewhat Pyrrhic victory. The case was *Lee v York Coach and Marine*[24] and the facts were as follows:

> Mrs Lee bought a second-hand Morris 1100 for £355. Almost immediately it developed defects and it was off the road for a considerable time when the sellers sought unsuccessfully to mend the defects. After seven weeks her solicitors wrote to the sellers saying "we must ask you please to remedy all these defects without delay or to refund £355 to Mrs Lee". The sellers then offered to do some further work on the car; a Department of Environment examiner found very serious defects, and two weeks later a further letter was written by the solicitors. "Mrs Lee would have been justified in rescinding the contract on that basis—that is on the basis that the car was unroadworthy—in our opinion she may still be entitled to do so." Four months later the buyer brought an action claiming the return of the price. The evidence showed (inter alia) that the brakes were so poor that they could not have survived an attempt to test them.

The Court of Appeal held that the car, being unsafe to be driven, was clearly unmerchantable. They also held, however, that neither of the solicitor's letters amounted to a rejection of the car. By the time that the buyer finally

[22] [1965] 1 W.L.R. 1013.
[23] [1975] 1 W.L.R. 30.
[24] [1977] R.T.R. 35

sought to reject (the start of the proceedings) it was too late. Accordingly, she was only entitled to damages and the figure of £100 was not disputed. Presumably Mrs Lee would have seen none of the £100 since the court made no order for costs in the Court of Appeal.

4.18   In another case[25] the Court of Appeal applied the *Rogers* ruling (above) that roadworthiness was not the correct test. Each case would turn on the application of the statutory definition to the particular facts and on the extent to which the actual condition of the vehicle matched the buyer's reasonable expectations.

Perhaps it came as no surprise that the very first reported case to apply the new test, *Thain v Anniesland Trade Centre*,[26] involved a second-hand car which was five years old and had travelled around 80,000 miles. Shortly after purchase, the car developed a fault in the gearbox which was uneconomic to repair and therefore made the car useless. Sheriff MacLeod noted that:

> People who buy second-hand cars get them at less than the original price in large part because second-hand cars have attached to them increased risk of expensive repairs. The price of the Renault, GBP 2,995, was considered reasonable because there was the risk of expensive repair attached to the Renault. In choosing to buy the Renault the pursuer accepted the risk of expensive repair inevitably attaching to a car that was between five and six years old which had over 80,000 miles on the clock

4.19   **Acts to be done before use.**   If both parties contemplate that some act will be done to the goods before use, they must be satisfactory *after* this has been done but not necessarily before. Thus in *Heil v Hedges*[27] the buyer of pork chops failed to cook them properly and became ill as the result of the chops becoming infected by worms. Had she cooked them properly the infection would not have occurred. Her claim for damages failed. On the other hand in the underpants case[28] the pants were sold for immediate use. Therefore the fact that the sulphite might have been removed by washing was held to be irrelevant.

4.20   **Safety: aspect 9(3)(d).**   It is self-evident that the average buyer of goods will be dissatisfied, if they prove to be dangerous and cause death, injury or damage to property or make it necessary to spend money to make them safe. We have already mentioned many cases concerning unsafe goods. For example, in the leading case on strict liability *Frost v Aylesbury Dairy Co*[29] milk was infected by typhoid. *Grant v Australian Knitting Mills* underpants impregnated with a noxious chemical caused dermatitis. In *Lambert v Lewis*, a tow bar broke resulting in a serious accident.[30]

---

[25] *Business Application Specialists v Nationwide Credit Corporation* [1988] R.T.R. 332.
[26] [1997] SLT (Sh Ct) 102.
[27] [1951] 1 T.L.R. 512.
[28] *Grant v Australian Knitting Mills* [1936] A.C. 85. The facts appear in para.5.51.
[29] See paras 4.07 and 4.08 above.
[30] For two recent cases where a lack of safety was a key factor in a successful claim see *Clegg v Andersson* [2003] EWCA Civ 320 and *SW Tubes Ltd v Owen Stuart Ltd* [2002] EWCA Civ 854.

These cases clearly show that if goods are unsafe, they are not of satisfactory quality. The recent Court of Appeal case of *Lowe v Machell Joinery Ltd*[31] is a clear example of unsafe goods.

> The appellants (L) ordered from the respondent (M) a staircase for a barn being converted for residential use. They paid for the goods. When the staircase was delivered, they rejected it as not complying with the contractual obligations and issued proceedings to recover the price. The judge decided that M was in breach of contract, as the staircase did not comply with the Building Regulations, but held that rejection was not justified as it could be modified easily to avoid any breach. L appealed, relying on s.14(2) and s.14(3), which had not even been mentioned at the trial by L's (then) counsel.

The Court of Appeal (Rix LJ dissenting) held that L had a right to reject for breach of what were then the conditions implied by s.14(2) and s.14(3) of the 1979 Act. Section 14(2) was broken: the staircase was not of satisfactory quality, in particular in relation to s.14(2B)(a) (fitness for the goods' common purposes) and s.14(2B)(d) (safety), for it did not comply with the Building Regulations and could not be used legally.

Section 14(3) (which is now s.10 of the CRA 2015) was more debatable. Had L made known their particular purpose? Yes, said the court, since L made it clear to M that the staircase was to be installed in the barn as converted to residential use and did rely on M (see para.46).[32] It was not fit for its purpose as it did not comply with the Building Regulations.

Warnings and instructions. Of course, many products are intrinsically dangerous. Some are so obviously so that no warnings or instructions for use are needed—knives, handsaws and other tools. However, in other cases such as cars, domestic electrical equipment, power tools, gardening machinery, pesticides and medicines it may be difficult or impossible to use them, or to use them safely, unless clear and unambiguous instructions are supplied with the goods. If these are not followed and damage occurs, consumers have no one but themselves to blame. The legal position about instructions under s.9 is identical to that under s.10.[33] Comparable problems occur in relation to manufacturers' product liability in tort, which is considered in Chapter Five.[34]   **4.21**

Durability: aspect 9(3)(e). It is clear from commercial cases involving the sale of rabbits and potatoes that if defects appear soon after purchase this may show that the goods were unsatisfactory at the time of the contract.[35] What does that mean in the consumer context? A vacuum cleaner breaks   **4.22**

---

[31] [2011] EWCA Civ 794.
[32] See para.4.30 below.
[33] See *Vacwell Engineering Co Ltd v BDH Chemicals Ltd* [1971] 1 Q.B. 88.
[34] See paras 5.22 and 5.44 below.
[35] See *Beer v Walker* (1877) 46 L.J.Q.B. 677; *Mash & Murrell v Joseph I Emanuel Ltd* [1961] 1 All E.R. 485.

down after one month, a freezer after eight months, a carpet starts to wear away after 14 months and a dishwasher ceases to operate after 18 months. The consumer *may* be able to show that the goods were unsatisfactory right at the beginning but it will not be easy. If the seller wishes to resist a claim, he will point out that all sorts of things could have caused the breakdown such as misuse and that it is up to the buyer to produce evidence[36] linking the breakdown to the condition of the goods when he bought them. The buyer will argue, "I used the goods in the normal way—a freezer should not break down after only eight months." A House of Lords case lends support to the consumer's argument. In *Lambert v Lewis*[37]—a case concerning a tow bar on a Land Rover—Lord Diplock said:

> "The implied warranty [sic] of fitness for a particular purpose . . . is a continuing warranty that the goods will continue to be fit for that purpose for a reasonable time after delivery. . . . What is a reasonable time will depend on the nature of the goods but I would accept that in the case of the coupling the warranty was still continuing up to the date, some three to six months before the accident, when it first became known to the farmer that the handle of the locking mechanism was missing."[38]

Now the considerable uncertainty in this area (especially at the level of consumer complaints) has been dispelled. The Law Commission recommended[39] an express reference to durability in the Act. This has been done by the inclusion of aspect (e) in what is now s.9(3). Arguments will still rage, though, over what is a reasonable time for goods to last.

A helpful provision here is s.19(14)/(15), which introduces a presumption of non-conformity within the six months from the date of delivery. We shall deal with this shift in the onus of proof when we come to consider the buyer's remedies—see para.8.32 below.

4.23   **Spare parts.**   A consumer may find that his goods become useless because, for example, the retailer does not have a supply of spare parts and the manufacturer has discontinued that particular product or has gone out of business altogether. There is no legal obligation on the seller or manufacturer to carry spare parts,[40] although some trade associations have adopted Codes of Practice which require their members to do so.[41]

Exclusion of matters from the satisfactory quality requirement

4.24   Three exceptions, which operate in quite narrow limits, appear in s.9(4) and are as follows:

---

[36] See para.8.32 below, for the reversal of the burden of proof during the first six months: s.19(14).
[37] [1982] A.C. 225. See also para.5.43 below.
[38] At p.276.
[39] *Daniels v White Ltd and Tarbard* [1938] 4 All E.R. 258 at pp.10, 31–33.
[40] See Law Com. No.160, p.34.
[41] See para.11.04 below.

(4) The term mentioned in subsection (1) does not cover anything which makes the quality of the goods unsatisfactory—

    (a) which is specifically drawn to the consumer's attention before the contract is made,

    (b) where the consumer examines the goods before the contract is made, which that examination ought to reveal, or

    (c) in the case of a contract to supply goods by sample, which would have been apparent on a reasonable examination of the sample.

The first exception in s.9(4)(a) applies where defects are *specifically* drawn to the buyer's attention before the contract is made. This could apply if, for example, a defective clutch or a dent or scratch or other defect was pointed out to the buyer—perhaps with a reduction in price. This is quite common where stores sell shop-soiled showroom models at a discount with labels drawing attention to the particular damage. There could, of course, be room for argument—the buyer might say "the seller told me that the clutch was rather worn but I had no idea I would have to spend £450 on it a week after buying the car".

The second exception in s.9(4)(b) relates to examination where the buyer has examined the goods *before* the making of the contract. The condition does not apply as regards defects which *that* examination ought to reveal. Two points can be made with regard to this exception. First, it applies only to a buyer who has *actually* examined the goods—not to a buyer who has declined an opportunity to do so. Secondly, what is the meaning of "defects which that examination ought to reveal"? This wording was first introduced in 1973 and differs slightly from the wording of the original 1893 Act, i.e. "defects which such examination ought to have revealed". In either case the words appear to refer solely to the examination actually made. If, for example, the buyer of a handbag only examines the outside, she will still be able to complain if on arriving home she finds that the inside has numerous defects including a broken zip (but she could not claim for an external defect which she should have seen, e.g. a broken handle).

There is an old Court of Appeal case which appears to confirm this view.[42]   **4.25** However, in a slightly later case, *Thornett & Fehr v Beers & Son*[43] Bray J at first instance appeared to treat the words "such examination" as if they read "a reasonable examination". He held that (a) the buyers had examined the goods; (b) an examination would "in the ordinary way" have revealed the defect; (c) accordingly, the quality condition was not implied.

It is possible that this decision is wrong on the wording of the Act and it appears to be inconsistent with the *Bristol Tramways* case (which was not cited). It can also be argued that if the case was wrong on the original wording of the 1893 Act, it is even more incorrect on the current wording. Thus, the courts may well refuse to follow it, although the Court of Appeal's

---

[42] *Bristol Tramways v Fiat Motors* [1910] 2 K.B. 831.
[43] [1919] 1 K.B. 486. Not followed in Scotland: *MacDonald v Pollock* [2011] CSIH 12.

ruling in *Bramhill v Edwards*[44] might suggest otherwise The claimants had purchased a US-manufactured second-hand motorhome. Some time afterwards, they discovered that the motorhome was slightly wider than permitted by the relevant road vehicle regulations. The claimants had inspected the interior of the motorhome before purchase, but had not measured its external dimensions. They claimed that the motorhome was not of satisfactory quality because it could not be legally driven in the UK, but this was rejected by the court on the somewhat strange grounds that the regulations were rarely, if ever, enforced on that issue. Auld LJ also made obiter observations on what is now s.9(4), noting that the internal inspection of the motorhome should have indicated that it was wider than permitted, and additionally, the seller's information about the internal measurements should have alerted the consumers to the wider external measurements. However, this reasoning seems to be in conflict with the wording of s.9(4) and we would hope that this approach would not be followed in future cases.

Nevertheless, the moral is clear for consumers—examine goods thoroughly before purchase or not at all.

Public Statements, especially advertising

4.26 Following the implementation of the EU's Consumer Sales Directive (99/44 EC), additional provisions were introduced to give effect to the Directive's requirement to take particular account of public statements. These are now found in s.9(5)–(7):

> (5) The relevant circumstances mentioned in subsection (2)(c) include any public statement about the specific characteristics of the goods made by the trader, the producer or any representative of the trader or the producer.
>
> (6) That includes, in particular, any public statement made in advertising or labelling.
>
> (7) But a public statement is not a relevant circumstance for the purposes of subsection (2)(c) if the trader shows that—
>
>> (a) when the contract was made, the trader was not, and could not reasonably have been, aware of the statement,
>> (b) before the contract was made, the statement had been publicly withdrawn or, to the extent that it contained anything which was incorrect or misleading, it had been publicly corrected, or
>> (c) the consumer's decision to contract for the goods could not have been influenced by the statement.

The moral is obvious: any prospective consumer buyer who is attracted by an advertisement or other public statement made by the producer should bring this to the notice of the seller before the contract is made.

---

[44] [2004] EWCA Civ 403.

However, this provision may cause problems for a retailer caught between a consumer buyer and its own supplier (e.g. a producer or wholesaler). If the consumer makes a successful claim against the retailer based on s.9(5), the retailer as a non-consumer cannot pass the buck to its seller—a piggy in the middle! The retailer's solution is to include an express indemnity in its contractual terms.

Fitness for particular purpose: section 10 of the Consumer Rights Act 2015

Section 10 of the CRA 2015 deals with the situation when a consumer has a particular purpose for the goods in mind and makes this known to the trader in advance. The section reads as follows: **4.27**

(1) Subsection (3) applies to a contract to supply goods if before the contract is made the consumer makes known to the trader (expressly or by implication) any particular purpose for which the consumer is contracting for the goods.

(2) Subsection (3) also applies to a contract to supply goods if—

(a) the goods were previously sold by a credit-broker to the trader,

(b) in the case of a sales contract or contract for transfer of goods, the consideration or part of it is a sum payable by instalments, and

(c) before the contract is made, the consumer makes known to the credit-broker (expressly or by implication) any particular purpose for which the consumer is contracting for the goods.

(3) The contract is to be treated as including a term that the goods are reasonably fit for that purpose, whether or not that is a purpose for which goods of that kind are usually supplied.

(4) Subsection (3) does not apply if the circumstances show that the consumer does not rely, or it is unreasonable for the consumer to rely, on the skill or judgment of the trader or credit-broker.

As with s.9, liability is strict; and the trader may be relieved from liability if the consumer fails to do something to the goods before use.

What is the need for s.10? The key is to be found in the words "any *particular* purpose . . . whether or not that is a purpose for which such goods are commonly supplied". The crucial difference between s.9 and s.10 is this. If the goods are suitable for a consumer's normal, usual or common purposes or needs, they will be of satisfactory quality; if the particular buyer's purposes are also common, the goods will *also* be fit for that purpose—there will be a complete overlap between the two provisions. If, however, the consumer's requirements, needs or purposes are abnormal, unusual, special, extraordinary or "particular", then it will be no defence for the trader to prove that the goods are perfect and not faulty or defective, and so are of satisfactory **4.28** quality in compliance with s.9. The consumer will point out that the goods are perfectly useless! They are *not* fit or suitable for his special or *particular* purposes and so are in breach of s.10. In *Jewson Ltd v Boyhan*,[45] the Court of Appeal commented on the dividing line between the two requirements: "satisfactory quality" reflects a general quality standard, whereas "fitness for a particular purpose" focuses on the particular circumstances affecting the specific case. The former considers the intrinsic aspects of the goods, whereas the latter was concerned with their extrinsic features.

Suppose that a law student goes to a bookseller and says "I want to buy some books which are suitable for examinations on the Legal Practice Course." The seller supplies books which are only suitable for the Bar Professional Training course or University examinations. On these facts the seller would clearly be liable under s.10; but there might well be no breach of s.9.

Common examples are tyres, windscreen wipers or wing mirrors for cars, bags for vacuum cleaners or mobile phone chargers, where the spares or accessories are not defective, but are not suitable and do not fit the particular model which the buyer has pointed out to the seller.

Making known the purpose

4.29 The subsection applies where the purpose is made known "expressly or by implication". In the case of single purpose goods such as a bun or a hot water bottle,[46] the buyer does not have to go through the ritual of spelling out his purpose—this will be implied because it is self-evident.

If, however, the purpose is a special one then the seller will be liable only if that purpose was *expressly* made known. In *Griffiths v Peter Conway Ltd*[47]:

> A lady bought a Harris tweed coat. She had abnormally sensitive skin and contracted dermatitis from wearing the coat. The evidence showed that the coat would not have caused problems apart from this one special fact. It was held that as this fact had not been disclosed to the seller, he was not liable.

Reliance

4.30 There will be no breach of this requirement if the *trader can prove* that the consumer did not rely on the trader's skill or judgment. Suppose that John, an amateur jeweller, goes to a general hardware store and asks for glue suitable for jewellery making. The trader might say "I have no idea whether this brand is suitable—you must decide for yourself and not rely on me". In such a case he would escape liability under s.10 (and perhaps also under s.9 since the circumstances surrounding the purchase would be one of the

---

[45] [2003] EWCA Civ 1030.

[46] See *Priest v Last* [1903] 2 K.B. 148—the case of a bursting hot water bottle. The seller would also be liable under s.14(2), above.

[47] [1939] 1 All E.R. 685. See also *Aswan Engineering Establishment Co v Lupdine Ltd* [1987] 1 W.L.R. 1; *Slater v Finning* [1997] A.C. 473; *Lowe v Machell Joinery Ltd* [2011] EWCA Civ 794. See also *Argos Ltd v Leather Trade House Ltd* [2012] EWHC 1348 (QB): toxic chemical in sachets with leather sofas—not fit for purpose

"circumstances" in s.9(2)). The consumer's reliance on the seller's skill or judgment may well be partial. If the goods turn out to be unfit for the buyer's particular purpose, the seller will be liable unless he can prove that the defect fell outside the area of reliance.[48]

A recent non-consumer case provides a good modern illustration. In *Jewson Ltd v Boyhan*[49]:

> A developer claimed that boilers installed in flats had a low rate of energy retention and that this resulted in a number of prospective buyers dropping out. He sued the supplier of the boilers under s.14. The action failed.

The Court of Appeal held that (1) there was nothing intrinsically wrong with the boilers and accordingly they were of "satisfactory quality"; (2) the case therefore turned on their fitness for a particular purpose under s.10; and (3) it was not reasonable for the buyer to rely on the seller's skill or judgment and accordingly the action failed.

Warnings and instructions

If the instructions supplied with the goods are wrong or misleading this can make the goods unfit for their purpose. If, however, there is a clear warning (e.g. "Do not use after 1 July") a buyer who ignores this cannot complain merely because the damage which he suffers is different from that mentioned in the warning.[50] The position will depend on a number of factors including the experience of the buyer and any previous course of dealing.[51] **4.31**

Credit-broker

The term "credit-broker" is taken from the Consumer Credit Act 1974 which is considered in Part IV of this book. The type of case contemplated by s.10 is that of a consumer who goes to a dealer and tells the dealer the purpose for which he wants the goods. The dealer then sells the goods on to a finance house which in turn sells the goods to the consumer on instalment terms. Although the consumer has bought the goods from the finance company, he will enjoy the protection of s.10 if he makes his purpose known to the dealer (credit-broker) unless he did not rely, or it was not reasonable for him to rely, on the credit-broker's skill or judgment. **4.32**

3. WORK AND MATERIALS

Certain contracts may be classified as contracts for "work and materials" rather than "supply of goods" because, in addition to the transfer of goods, **4.33**

---

[48] *Ashington Piggeries Ltd v Christopher Hill Ltd* [1972] A.C. 441. *BSS Group Plc v Makers (UK) Limited (t/a Allied Services)* [2011] EWCA Civ 809.

[49] [2003] EWCA Civ 1030.

[50] *Wormell v RHM Agriculture (East)* [1987] 1 W.L.R. 1091 (herbicide failed to kill farmer's wild oats because it was used too late in the season).

[51] *Medivance Investments Ltd v Gaselane Pipeworks Ltd* [2002] EWCA Civ 500.

significant services are supplied too. Contracts to repair a house or car, or to insulate a loft, are obvious examples. In the words of Stable J in a case where a hairdresser applied a hair dye to the head of a customer:

> "[It] is really half the rendering of services and, in a sense, half the supply of goods."[52]

The law applies different standards to the two halves of the contractual obligation. On the first half (i.e. the provision of work or services) there is an implied duty to take reasonable care[53]; on the second half (i.e. the provision of materials or goods) there is strict liability under s.9 in respect of satisfactory quality and s.10 as regards fitness for a particular purpose.

As noted earlier, the CRA 2015 now provides a single set of rules regarding all goods supplied to a consumer. In addition, Ch.4 of Pt 1 of the CRA 2015 contains a set of rules regarding the provision of services. Both chapters can apply concurrently to one contract (see s.1(3) of the CRA 2015).

However, this still leaves the question whether, on the facts of a particular case, a claim should be made in respect of the goods themselves or the service provided. The extended definition of "contract of sale" in s.5(2) to include "goods to be manufactured or produced" might suggest that the preferred claim would be in respect of the goods.

4. DIGITAL CONTENT

4.34 Before the CRA 2015 became law, there was a debate as to whether software could be goods. In the case of *St Albans DC v ICL* in a double obiter, Sir Ian Glidewell considered that (1) where a disk containing software is supplied by one person to another, the disk is "goods" for the purposes of s.14 of the 1979 Act; and (2) if the software on the disk is defective, the transferee will have the benefit of the implied condition of reasonable fitness. Aitkenhead J expressed a similar view obiter in *Southwark LBC v IBM UK Ltd* at para.96:

> "CDs are physical objects and there is no reason why they should not be considered as goods. The fact that a CD is impressed with electrons to add functions and values to it simply gives a CD a particular attribute. Thus, if a customer buys a music CD . . . it must be "goods" . . . There can be no difference if the CD contains software."

In the *St Albans* case Sir Ian Glidewell considered (obiter) that the insertion of software into a customer's computer was subject to an implied common law condition of reasonable fitness analogous to that set out above.

4.35 Happily, the CRA 2015 settles this issue by treating contracts for the supply of digital content as a new type of supply contract, and introduces requirements regarding the quality and fitness for particular purposes for digital content which mirror those applicable to goods. Crucially, the digital

---

[52] *Watson v Buckley Osborne Garrett & Co* [1940] 1 All E.R. 174 at 180.
[53] s.49(1) of the CRA 2015.

content must be supplied in return for the payment of a price for these provisions to apply.[54]

We already noted the provision on correspondence of digital content with description in the previous chapter. Section 34 of the CRA 2015 requires that digital content must be of satisfactory quality, and s.34 largely mirrors s.9, although the list of aspects in s.34(3) omits "appearance and finish". Section 35 deals with the requirement that goods have to be fit for a particular purpose and this is identical to provision for goods (s.10).

A new provision is s.40, which deals with digital content supplied "subject to the right of the trader or a third party to modify the digital content". This deals with updates to digital content, a familiar and sometimes irritating feature of all digital content. When digital content is modified, the modified version of the content must also comply with the various requirements of quality, fitness for purpose and description. Additional features may be added, but the digital content must still match its description, as well as any pre-contractual information (unless any change to that information has been agreed with the consumer).

Specific remedies for digital content are also made available, and these are discussed at para.8.19 and following.

---

[54] Consequently, the digital content rules do not apply to "free" downloads of, e.g., smartphone apps (although many are only "free" in the sense that the consumer does not pay money, but often the consumer grants access to personal data instead). An EU proposal could mean that the provisions of the CRA 2015 will in due course be extended to cover other digital content supply contracts: COM (2015) 634 final.

CHAPTER FIVE

"IT WILL COST £1,000 TO MAKE THEM SAFE"

Scheme of this chapter

In the previous chapter we examined the consumer's *contractual* rights against **5.01** his immediate supplier where the goods were faulty. In this chapter we move further afield to consider the consumer's rights against other persons in the distribution chain—including in particular the manufacturer. Such rights can be important for at least three reasons:

(1) A buyer may find that his rights under a manufacturer's guarantee are easier to enforce than the statutory rights against his supplier, where he may have considerable difficulty in proving that the goods were of unsatisfactory quality.

(2) A supplier may be unable to meet the claim—perhaps because it has gone out of business.

(3) The injured party may not have a contract at all; thus a badly constructed car may cause death or injury to passengers and pedestrians while a child may suffer pre-natal injuries caused by a drug supplied to the mother.

This chapter will deal first with *poor quality* goods and then with *dangerous* goods. The distinction is crucial.

Example 1

A buys goods from B which were manufactured by C, e.g. a pen or mobile **5.02** phone. They are of very *poor quality*, do not work and are useless to A unless he spends money on repairing them. The goods are *not* dangerous.

Example 2

The goods in the previous example are a car with defective steering or brakes **5.03** which causes death or personal injury or damage to other property. The goods are *dangerous*.

A. POOR QUALITY GOODS

1. INTRODUCTION

5.04 It is clear from the cases that the law of negligence in *tort* will not help the consumer where the goods are not dangerous, but of poor quality, i.e. safe but shoddy (as in Example 1 above). It is equally clear that Pt I of the Consumer Protection Act 1987 (also a claim in tort, see para.5.11 below) will not help either. That leaves just two rights which exist side by side—a claim under the contract of supply[1] and a contractual claim under a manufacturer's guarantee (in Example 1 against B and C respectively).

2. MANUFACTURERS' GUARANTEES[2]

The nature of a guarantee

5.05 A guarantee is familiar to millions of consumers and it has become an integral part of the purchase of durable goods. The manufacturer usually agrees to replace the goods or defective parts for a specified period (for example, 12 months). The attraction of this for the consumer may be cut down by further clauses requiring the consumer to pay the cost of carriage and sometimes even the cost of labour. Subject to this, a guarantee can have very real commercial advantages for both parties. For the manufacturer, it helps to promote its product and the card which the customer must often sign and return may be valuable for the purposes of market research. For the customer, the guarantee may be a valuable way of sidestepping the hazards of litigation, especially as the remedy which he *really* wants—repair or replacement—may not always be available against the retailer.[3]

There have been very few cases on guarantees and until recently their precise legal status was uncertain; there were (at least in theory) doubts as to how a manufacturer's guarantee could satisfy the legal requirements of offer, acceptance and consideration. Attempts to clarify the position, and to strengthen the consumer's rights, were made by Office of Fair Trading (OFT),[4] the Department of Trade and Industry (DTI) and the National Consumer Council and we summarised them in paras 5.06–5.07 of the Fifth Edition of this book. These domestic initiatives were overtaken by developments in Europe[5] which were transposed by the Sale and Supply of Goods to Consumers Regulations 2002. Similar provisions, slightly amended, now

---

[1] See Chapter Four. Or possibly under a collateral contract: consider Example 1 in para 3.01 above and *Andrews v Hopkinson* [1957] 1 Q.B. 229. See para.3.20 above on collateral contracts generally.

[2] In practice guarantees are sometimes also given by retailers and by suppliers of services (e.g. by suppliers of motor vehicles and electrical appliances). They are often called "warranties".

[3] See para.8.30 below. For the inter-relationship between guarantees and the condition of satisfactory quality see para.4.15 above.

[4] See the OFT Discussion Paper *Consumer Guarantees* published in August 1984, pp.21–23.

[5] See EU Directive 1999/44.

appear in s.30 of the Consumer Rights Act 2015 (CRA 2015), which is set out in full below.

Two points are noteworthy. The definition of "guarantee" in s.30(2) is wide **5.06** enough to cover a guarantee given by a retailer (e.g. car dealer or department store) as well as one given by a manufacturer. Section 30(3) finalises the arguments about their legal status by stating that they take effect as a "contractual obligation".

30 Goods under guarantee

(1) This section applies where—

    (a) there is a contract to supply goods, and
    (b) there is a guarantee in relation to the goods.

(2) "Guarantee" here means an undertaking to the consumer given without extra charge by a person acting in the course of the person's business (the "guarantor") that, if the goods do not meet the specifications set out in the guarantee statement or in any associated advertising—

    (a) the consumer will be reimbursed for the price paid for the goods, or
    (b) the goods will be repaired, replaced or handled in any way.

(3) The guarantee takes effect, at the time the goods are delivered, as a contractual obligation owed by the guarantor under the conditions set out in the guarantee statement and in any associated advertising.

(4) The guarantor must ensure that—

    (a) the guarantee sets out in plain and intelligible language the contents of the guarantee and the essential particulars for making claims under the guarantee,
    (b) the guarantee states that the consumer has statutory rights in relation to the goods and that those rights are not affected by the guarantee, and
    (c) where the goods are offered within the territory of the United Kingdom, the guarantee is written in English.

(5) The contents of the guarantee to be set out in it include, in particular—

    (a) the name and address of the guarantor, and
    (b) the duration and territorial scope of the guarantee.

(6) The guarantor and any other person who offers to supply to consumers the goods which are the subject of the guarantee must, on request by the consumer, make the guarantee available to the consumer within a reasonable time, in writing and in a form accessible to the consumer.

(7) What is a reasonable time is a question of fact.

(8) If a person fails to comply with a requirement of this section, the enforcement authority may apply to the court for an injunction or (in Scotland) an order of specific implement against that person requiring that person to comply.

(9) On an application the court may grant an injunction or (in Scotland) an order of specific implement on such terms as it thinks appropriate.

(10) In this section—

- "court" means—

    (a) in relation to England and Wales, the High Court or the county court,
    (b) in relation to Northern Ireland, the High Court or a county court, and
    (c) in relation to Scotland, the Court of Session or the sheriff;

- "enforcement authority" means—

    (a) the Competition and Markets Authority,
    (b) a local weights and measures authority in Great Britain, and
    (c) the Department of Enterprise, Trade and Investment in Northern Ireland.

5.07   The value of the guarantee to the consumer depends on its terms. The most generous ones provide that:

> If owing to a defect in workmanship or material your appliance breaks down within one [or two] years of purchase we will repair or replace it free of charge.

We have seen, however, that consumers may sometimes be required to pay the cost of transporting the goods; occasionally they even have to pay the cost of labour which can render the guarantee virtually useless. There is also the possibility that the manufacturer may say "there is nothing wrong with this appliance—you have mishandled it". (A similar argument is sometimes advanced by a seller when a buyer complains that the goods are unsatisfactory.) In such a case the consumer might have to negotiate an independent examination of the goods, with the manufacturer paying the whole or part of the cost. The provisions of the various codes of practice (e.g. for new cars)[6] are also relevant.

Further provisions relating to guarantees

5.08   There is still widespread misunderstanding about who is legally responsible for defective products. Such widespread ignorance should have decreased, if not disappeared, as the result of an Order made in 1976[7] whereby a supplier committed a criminal offence if a document setting out his obligations (e.g. the guarantee) failed to draw the consumer's attention to his rights against the retailer. This Order was revoked by the Consumer Protection from Unfair Trading Regulations 2008. The sanction now appears in s.30(8).

Conclusion

5.09   It cannot be stressed too strongly that any rights which the consumer may have under a manufacturer's guarantee do *not* cut down his rights against the

---

[6] See para.11.22 below.
[7] See para.5.06 above.

supplier.[8] In virtually all cases retailers seek to create the false impression in the minds of their customers that the legal responsibility is that of the manufacturer and that, if the guarantee has expired, the retailer is no longer liable. The consumer must be on his guard against this and must be prepared to say (in a loud voice if necessary) "it's *your* responsibility under the Consumer Rights Act". The question of remedies (and their enforcement) is considered in greater detail in Chapters Eight, Eleven and Twelve.

B. DANGEROUS GOODS

1. INTRODUCTION

In the Second Edition of this book it was pointed out that proposals to increase manufacturer's liability from negligence to strict liability had been made by no less than four different bodies—the Law Commission, the Pearson Commission, the Council of Europe and the European Commission. At the time of publication (1 March 1985) some seven years had gone by without any progress; negotiations on the EC draft directive were stalled over the so-called "development risks" defence. It was, however, only a matter of months before a workable compromise emerged and on 25 July 1985 the EC Council of Ministers adopted the Product Liability Directive whereby Member States were required to pass the appropriate legislation by 30 July 1988 (but with the option of excluding the development risks defence). The UK responded before the deadline by passing the Consumer Protection Act 1987 (the 1987 Act). Part I is designed to implement the Directive and came into force on 1 March 1988. **5.10**

It is important to appreciate that Pt I exists side by side with the general law of contract and negligence. In a contract case the consumer will have his (largely non-excludable) rights under the CRA 2015, and in this situation the 1987 Act is virtually irrelevant. As regards non-contractual claims the basic rule is that the consumer will be in a stronger position under the Act because strict liability is the new regime and the need to prove negligence has disappeared. The provisions of Pt I will be examined in detail in the next section of this chapter. It will be seen that there are some situations where the Act does not apply and in these cases the non-contractual consumer will have to fall back on the general law of negligence, which will be briefly considered in the final part of this chapter.

2. PART I OF THE CONSUMER PROTECTION ACT 1987 ("THE ACT")

EU Directives generally start off with a large number of recitals and the second recital of this one declares its policy explicitly: **5.11**

---

[8] See Mustill LJ in *Rogers* [1987] Q.B. 933 (see para.4.15 above): "an addition to the buyer's rights".

> Whereas liability without fault on the part of the producer is the sole means of adequately solving the problem, peculiar to our age of increasing technicality, of a fair apportionment of the risks inherent in modern technological production.

We have seen that Pt I is designed to give effect to the EC Product Liability Directive and s.1(1) expressly so provides.

> This Part shall have effect for the purpose of making such provision as is necessary in order to comply with the Product Liability Directive and shall be construed accordingly.

In the light of s.1(1) above the adviser must refer to the Product Liability Directive if the drafting of the Act is in any way ambiguous.

The basic rule

5.12 By s.2(1):

> Subject to the following provisions of this Part, where any damage is caused wholly or partly by a defect in a product, every person to whom subsection (2) applies shall be liable for the damage.

The words "shall be liable" impose strict liability—a vital change.

In advising the consumer a number of questions must be asked:

(1) Has a *product* been *supplied?*

(2) If yes, did it contain a *defect?*

(3) If yes, did the defect cause *damage?*

(4) If yes, is it the *type* of damage to which the Act applies?

(5) If yes, *who* is liable to the consumer?

(6) Are there any *defences* which may cut down the consumer's rights?

(7) Are there any special *time-limits* for bringing a claim?

Burden of proof

5.13 The Act is silent on this but on general principle the burden will fall on the claimant. This is reinforced by art.4 of the Product Liability Directive which states that:

> The injured person shall be required to prove the damage, the defect and the causal relationship between defect and damage.

In practical terms the abolition of the need to prove negligence may often be of limited value because the task of proving causation can be difficult—especially in medical and pharmaceutical cases.[9]

---

[9] See, e.g. *Kay v Ayrshire and Arran Health Board* [1987] 2 All E.R. 417 HL (penicillin given to child; child became deaf; causal link not proved).

A recent decision about a car is a clear example of this problem. It is the   **5.14**
Scottish case of *McGlinchey v General Motors UK Ltd.*[10] (We need hardly
remind readers that the 1987 Act applies to the whole of the UK.)

> The case concerns a handbrake defect in a three-year-old Vauxhall hatchback
> owned by M. She parked the car on a driveway with a slight gradient near the
> entrance to a cul-de-sac with bollards on either side. She applied the handbrake,
> left the gearbox in neutral and went to the back of the car. It rolled backwards
> and squashed her leg against a bollard. B, a consultant engineer and accident
> claims assessor, inspected the handbrake on the vehicle and found that it was
> operating normally with no obvious defect. He then removed the handbrake
> from the vehicle and tested it on his desk. He noted that the plastic grip on the
> outside of the handbrake lever was detached, possibly impeding the operation of
> the handbrake. B gave evidence that the handbrake had failed to engage on two
> or three occasions during the test on his desk and, although it was only a rare
> occurrence, it was the only means by which he was able to explain the circum-
> stances of M's accident.

M claimed that the manufacturers G were liable under the 1987 Act and at
common law.

The Scottish Court of Session held that M's claim failed. The onus was on
her to prove the cause of the accident, and the occasional failures occurred
only when the handbrake was removed from the car; B had said that failure
in real life operation was only "possible". Thus M failed to prove causation.

An even more recent decision, from England, is *Hufford v Samsung*   **5.15**
Electronics (UK) Ltd.[11]

> A fridge/freezer manufactured by S caught fire while H was out. H brought a
> claim against S under the 1987 Act and for negligence on the basis that the fire
> originated inside the appliance. S alleged that the fire started in some combusti-
> ble material in front of it.
> The High Court dismissed the claim. As to the 1987 Act, H had not discharged
> the burden of proof on him to prove that the product was defective because the
> seat of the fire was in the appliance. The court accepted the opinion of S's expert
> that the material outside the appliance ignited first. (Both parties' experts agreed
> that there was such material there.) As to negligence, the facts did not provide a
> basis for such a claim, for they did not establish a breach of a duty of care, even
> if it had existed.

It will be appreciated from the wording of s.2(1) that partial causation is
sufficient.

Example 3

> Goods manufactured by M injure C; this is due partly to the goods being defec-   **5.16**
> tive and partly to C not following M's instructions. C can recover damages from
> M under the Act—but subject to a reduction for contributory negligence under
> s.6(4).[11a]

---

[10] [2011] CSOH 206.
[11] [2014] EWHC 2956 (TCC).
[11a] See *McGlinchey* on this point too; para.5.14 above.

What is a product?

5.17   We must first consider whether it was a "product" which was defective. Section 1(2) defines "product" as follows:

> "product" means any goods or electricity and (subject to subsection (3) below) includes a product which is comprised in another product, whether by virtue of being a component part or raw material or otherwise.

It is clear that components are included.

Example 4

5.18   CM produces a defective component for M who incorporates it into an end product which he then supplies to D. Both CM and M have produced a "product" and, if the component makes M's product defective, both CM and M are liable under the Act.

If the cause of the component's defect were substandard materials, the materials' supplier would be liable too.

Example 5

5.19   M is a car manufacturer. Its wheels are supplied by C which manufactures them from alloy made by S. A car made by M crashes injuring the passengers. The cause is a broken wheel made from substandard alloy. The car, the wheels (a component part) and the alloy (raw material) are all products. M, C and S are all liable for the injuries.

The term "goods" is defined in s.45(1) to include "substances,[12] growing crops and things comprised in land by virtue of being attached to it and any ship, aircraft or vehicle". What about houses and land? The effect of s.46 is that the seller of a house built with defective bricks does not supply "goods", but if the house collapses and causes "damage",[13] the brick manufacturer can be liable to the injured party under the Act.

Agricultural products

5.20   Although the definition of "goods" includes crops (see above), s.2(4) created an important (and politically sensitive) exception from liability. It excluded liability under the Act "in respect of any defect in any game or agricultural produce if the only supply . . . by that person to another was at a time when it had not undergone an industrial process." However, as a result of the 10 year review of the Product Liability Directive this exception was removed, so that agricultural crops are covered.[14]

---

[12] This is not itself defined in the Act.
[13] See para.5.25 below.
[14] Consumer Protection Act 1987 (Product Liability) (Modification) Order 2000. For a discussion of the previous position, see Fifth Edition, para.5.16.

Is the product defective?

Section 3 rephrases art.6 of the Product Liability Directive in the following **5.21**
words:

> (1) Subject to the following provisions of this section, there is a defect in a
> product for the purposes of this Part if the safety of the product is not
> such as persons generally are entitled to expect; and for these purposes
> "safety", in relation to a product, shall include safety in respect to [com-
> ponents] and safety in the context of risks of damage to property, as well
> as in the context of risks of death or personal injury.
>
> (2) In determining . . . what persons generally are entitled to expect . . . all the
> circumstances shall be taken into account, including—
>
>> (a) the manner in which, and purposes for which, the product has been
>> marketed, its get-up, the use of any mark in relation to the product,
>> any instructions for, or warnings with respect to, doing or refrain-
>> ing from doing anything with or in relation to the product;
>>
>> (b) what might reasonably be expected to be done with or in relation to
>> the product; and
>>
>> (c) the time when the product was supplied by its producer to another;
>
> and nothing in this section shall require a defect to be inferred from the
> fact alone that the safety of a product which is supplied after that time is
> greater than the safety of the product in question.

The above definition of "defect" is broadly similar to the definition of "sat-   **5.22**
isfactory quality" in s.9(2) of the CRA 2015.[15] However, one major distinction must be reiterated. Whereas satisfactory quality covers both unsafe and
shoddy, poor quality goods, defective products in the 1987 Act mean only
unsafe or dangerous products; so "defect" is used in an unusually narrow
sense. The following points can be made:

(1) "Persons generally" can be contrasted with "a person" in art.6 of
the Directive; the expectation standard will be an objective one in
the light of the matters mentioned in the section—notably any safety
representations in advertising material. Thus the mere fact that the
producer was unaware of the defect is immaterial.[16]

(2) The standard of safety that the public are entitled to expect is an
objective one and it will be decided by the judge as an informed representative of the public at large.[17]

(3) Instructions for use and warnings, referred to in s.3(2)(a), now
proliferate, e.g. in a car handbook and the engine compartment. A
warning can make a product safe—provided that it is sufficiently
clear; conversely the absence of a warning can make it unsafe. The
massive cigarette litigation in the United States has largely turned
on the warning factor—and in a class action on behalf of 500,000

---

[15] See para.4.10 above.

[16] Burton J (as he then was) in *A v National Blood Authority* [2001] 3 All E.R. 289.

[17] *Abouzaid v Mothercare (UK) Ltd, The Times*, 20 February 2001—defective attachment to
pushchair—producer liable.

Florida smokers a US jury found a large number of leading tobacco companies liable for deception (see *The Times*, 8 July 1999).

(4) Sometimes products, which are safe when properly used, are misused and for that reason prove to be dangerous. Producers have the unenviable task of trying to anticipate how users may mishandle their products by placing warnings against such misuse on the products or in the instructions. It is significant that s.3(2)(b) asks "what might reasonably be expected" to be done. The position of the adverb is crucial: the question is not whether what is done with the goods is reasonable. People have been known to cut their hedges with rotary mowers or to use a metal ladder while undertaking electrical wiring: if the producer reasonably expects this to happen, a warning should be given—and the best place for a warning is on the product itself, as it is the user who may be in danger and the user may be someone to whom the original buyer sold, gave or lent the product without passing on the instruction leaflet. The interrelation between s.3(2)(a) and (b) is a close one.

(5) The question of what safety persons are entitled to expect brings in what is known as the "cost-benefit" analysis. In relation to medicines a DTI explanatory note contains the following passage:

> Establishing the existence of a defect in a medicine administered to a patient is complicated by the fact that not only is the human body a highly complex organism, but at the time of treatment it is already subject to an adverse pathological condition. . . .
> The more active the medicine, and the greater its beneficial potential, the more extensive its effects are likely to be, and therefore the greater the chances of an adverse effect. A medicine used to treat a life-threatening condition is likely to be much more powerful than a medicine used in the treatment of a less serious condition, and the safety that one is reasonably entitled to expect of such a medicine may therefore become correspondingly lower.

If, however, a product is found to be defective, the mere fact that it is of public benefit is irrelevant.[18]

(6) The relevant time for assessing the safety factor specified in s.3(2) (c) is the time when the product was supplied by its *producer*—not by the retailer. This is often called "the state of the art" factor. The principle is that manufacturers should not be discouraged from improving safety in later models.

Example 6

5.23   In April 2011 M sells to D a car manufactured by him. In August 2011 D sells it to R who sells it to C in 2012. While C is carefully driving the car in 2016 it veers out of control and P is injured. In considering the safety aspects two

---

[18] *A v National Blood Authority* [2001] 3 All E.R. 289.

questions arise, namely (1) what degree of safety could reasonably be expected of a five-year-old car?[19] and (2) what were the relevant safety standards in April 2011? The fact that safer models have been introduced since that time is irrelevant.

(7) In deciding whether a product is "defective" expert evidence is crucial. This can be seen from two cases concerning contraceptives. In one of them[20] a class action was brought alleging that a particular type of oral contraceptive had created an increased risk of thrombosis and other serious injuries. The other case[21] concerned a single contraceptive which had burst during intercourse resulting in a pregnancy. In both cases the court, after considering the expert evidence, rejected the claim. In the former case (which lasted for 42 days) the judge described his own role in the following words:

> "The judge cannot transform himself into some form of super-scientist with access to a level of expertise superior to those who have given the evidence. His role. . . and my role here is to evaluate the witnesses and decide. . . which parts of the evidence are sound and reliable and which are not."[22]

The case of the infected blood

A v National Blood Authority (No.1)[23] involved a class action brought by persons who had received blood which was found to be infected with Hepatitis C. The case was heard by Burton J (as he then was) and his judgment in favour of the claimants was based not on the Act but on the underlying Directive. He described the three-fold objective of the Directive, namely: **5.24**

(1) to increase consumer protection;

(2) to introduce an obligation on the producer which was irrespective of fault by way of strict liability (but not absolute liability); and

(3) to render the compensation of an injured party easier by removing the concept of negligence as an element of liability.

A number of points arising from this judgment have already been mentioned and every point raised by the defendant was rejected. Thus, for example, he held that the producer could not rely on the fact that the medical profession who administered the blood were aware of the risk. He doubted whether a warning would be sufficient to exonerate the defendant from liability. He also rejected a claim that the risk of infection was inherent in all blood. Finally, he gave the development risks defence (as to which see below) a very narrow

---

[19] See *McGlinchey* [2011] CSOH 206: three-year-old car.
[20] *X v Schering Health Care Ltd* [2002] EWCH 1420 QBD.
[21] *Richardson v LRC Products Ltd* [2000] P.I.Q.R. P.114 QBD. For criticism see Charles Lewis, "Wrongful Birth; Rubber-dub-dub" (2000) Med. Lit. 2 (Feb) 8.
[22] See *Hufford* [2014] EWHC 2956 (TCC) (at para.5.15 above).
[23] [2001] 3 All E.R. 289.

interpretation. Writing in (2001) 151 N.L.J. 647 Alison McAdams (a member of the legal team representing the defendant) expressed the view that the judge sought to achieve the object of the Directive "by an alarmingly strained reading of the language of Article 6. The finding is extremely close to one of absolute liability." We do not share that alarm. Its purpose is to impose *strict liability* on the business which puts the unsafe product into circulation, however blameless.

What damage is covered?

5.25   Section 5, which is based on art.9, makes it clear that only three types of damage are covered, namely, death, personal injury or damage to any "private" (as opposed to business) property, i.e. property is excluded by s.5(3) if at the time of the loss or damage it is not—

  (a) of a description of property ordinarily intended for private use, occupation or consum ption; and
  (b) intended by the person suffering the loss or damage mainly for his own private use, occupation or consumption.

Example 7

5.26   A defective heater explodes and damages X's office premises. He cannot recover under the Act.

Two other restrictions must be noted. First (and this is an echo of the distinction between shoddy and dangerous goods)[24] the Act does not cover loss of or damage "to the product itself" or to "the whole or any part of any product which has been supplied with the [defective product] comprised in it".[25] The question is whether the product has damaged something else.

Example 8

5.27   C buys a defective car. It crashes and injures C. The car is a write-off. C can recover for his injuries but not for the cost of replacing the car.

Example 9

5.28   Suppose in the above example the accident is caused by a defective tyre. If the tyre formed part of the car as originally supplied, the answer is the same as in Example 8. If, on the other hand, the tyre was fitted at a later date, the car replacement cost will be "damage to any property"—not to the product itself— and recoverable under the Act against the tyre manufacturer.

The second restriction (designed to exclude small claims) is set out in s.5(4); the Act will not apply where the total damages awarded, exclusive of interest, in respect of *property* do not exceed £275. What if the damages are, say,

---

[24] See para.5.01 above.
[25] s.5(2).

£1,000? The wording of the Act is unambiguous—no deduction is made and £1,000 would be awarded. However, art.9(b) talks of "a lower threshold of 500 ECU". It could be argued—and the French version of the Directive and the EU Commission support this view—that a deduction should be made from *every* award in respect of property. It will be interesting to see how the courts interpret this provision.

It is clear from the wording that any reduction for contributory negligence[26] must be made first.

Example 10

C's damages in respect of private property are assessed at £500 but this figure falls to be reduced by 50 per cent for contributory negligence so that the final figure is £250. The Act does not apply.   **5.29**

Whom can the consumer sue?

First we must emphasise that generally retailers and distributors are not caught, but there are exceptions. Section 2(2) imposes liability on: **5.30**

(1) The "producer" (see para.5.32 below).

(2) Any person who, by putting his name on the product or using a trade mark or other distinguishing mark in relation to the product, has held himself out to be the producer of the product.

Example 11

S, a supermarket, puts its own brand name on a bottle of wine which it sells to B. Unknown to S the wine has been mixed with antifreeze. C becomes violently ill when drinking the "wine" at B's house. C can sue S under the Act. But if S makes it clear that a third party is the producer, e.g. with a label stating "produced for S by M", S is not caught—there is no "holding out".   **5.31**

(3) Any person who has imported the product into a member State from a place outside the member States in order, in the course of any business of his, to supply it to another.

Example 12

F, a French company, imports lethal toys from Taiwan which it then exports to England where one is sold by R to C. C's child is injured.   **5.32**

The English importer is *not* liable under the Act because he imported the toys from another Member State (i.e. France). F, however, *is* liable under the Act and can be sued in England.[27]

(4) A person to whom s.2(3) applies—see para.5.33 below.

---

[26] See s.6(4).

[27] Under a revised version of the EC Jurisdiction and Judgments Convention (operative as from 1 March 2002) a defendant domiciled in a Contracting State can be sued in tort in another Contracting State where the damage is suffered (see art.5). A claim under Pt I of the Act is a claim in tort—see s.6(7). The Act gives the injured consumer a wide choice of where to sue

Returning to para.(1) above, s.1(2) defines a "producer" in relation to a product as:

(a) the person who manufactured it;

(b) in the case of a substance which has not been manufactured but has been won or abstracted, the person who won or abstracted it; this covers mining and quarrying and—unintentionally?—blood and body parts "abstracted" from their donors.

(c) in any other case, a person who has applied an industrial or other process affecting the essential characteristics of the product.[28]

The section 2(3) defendant: anonymous goods

5.33   There may well be cases where the injured party will have great difficulty in identifying the "producer" or the person importing the product into a Member State. To deal with this situation s.2(3) allows him to seek information from another supplier in the chain and makes that other supplier liable if the information is not supplied. Such liability will arise if the following conditions are satisfied:

(a) the injured party requests the supplier to identify one or more of the persons listed in s.2(2) (see para.5.30 above)—whether still in existence or not;

(b) the request is made within a reasonable period after the damage and at a time when it is not reasonably practicable for the person making the request to identify all those persons;

(c) the supplier fails, within a reasonable period after receiving the request, either to comply with the request or to identify the person who supplied the product to him.

Example 13

5.34   The facts are as in Example 12 except that the only person known to the injured party is the retail supplier R. The injured party can ask R to identify the manufacturer and/or the EU importer. R can supply this information or alternatively can say "I bought from X Ltd" (whereupon the injured party can approach X Ltd with a similar request). If R does neither of these things within a reasonable time he will be liable under the Act.

Conclusion

5.35   It will be apparent that the injured consumer has a large number of persons to sue—especially bearing in mind the co-extensive liability of a component

---

(this is known as "forum shopping"); this can be important because the development risks defence (see para.5.39 below) applies in some EU countries but not all.

[28] The term "industrial or other process" is not defined.

manufacturer and an end product manufacturer. He can sue them alone or together and their liability is joint and several; each of them is liable to him for the full amount of his "damage" (see s.2(5)).

What defences are available?[29]

Section 4(1) lists six possible defences lettered (a) to (f), namely: **5.36**

(a) That the defect is attributable to compliance with any statutory or EU *requirement.*

(b) That the person proceeded against did not at any time supply the product to another.

Example 14

M manufactures a crane. While it is being tested on M's premises it collapses and   **5.37**
P is killed. P's estate has no claim under the Act.

The term "supply" is widely defined in s.46. In a hire-purchase case involving dealer—hire-purchaser—finance company the section provides that the *dealer* (and not the finance company) is to be treated as supplying the product to the hire-purchaser—which is what happens in practice (although not in the law of contract).

(c) That the only supply was not in the course of the supplier's business *and* that either s.2(2) does not apply to that person or does so only as the result of things done otherwise than with view to profit.

Example 15

Mrs Jones makes jam for a private function. The jam is defective and a guest is   **5.38**
taken ill. There is no liability under the Act.

(d) That the defect did not exist in the product at the relevant time.[30]

Example 16

M manufactures a car and sells it to D. D sells it to C. C has it serviced by S. C   **5.39**
crashes because S left the wheel nuts loose. M is not liable.

(e) That the state of scientific and technical knowledge at the relevant time was not such that a producer of products of the same description as the product in question might be expected to have discovered the defect if it had existed in his products while they were under his control.

---

[29] The defences must be narrowly confined: *Veedfald v Arhus Amtjkommune, The Times,* 4 June 2001—a case on art.7 of the Directive.
[30] "Relevant time" means the time when the "producer" supplied it to another: s.4(2). See *McGlinchey* [2011] CSOH 206: wear and tear not covered (see para.5.14 above).

It will be recalled[31] that the dispute over this *"development risks"* defence was the prime reason why the EC draft Directive took nearly 10 years to become a Directive. There was strong lobbying from UK industries (especially pharmaceuticals) on the basis that without such a defence research and development would be severely hampered. The argument on the other side is equally compelling—such a defence would leave victims of a future Thalidomide-type tragedy without a remedy. In the event the Directive adopted a compromise—the defence was introduced by art.7(e) but individual Member States were left free to exclude it (art.15(1)(b)) and a few of them exercised their right to do so, e.g. Luxembourg.

The drafting of this provision was hotly debated in Parliament and the Government forced through the present wording in the dying days of the 1986–1987 session just before the 1987 General Election. It is widely felt that the wording is less strict than art.7(e) of the Directive which reads

> that the state of scientific and technical knowledge at the time when he put the product into circulation was not such as to enable the existence of the defect to be discovered.

There is an immense gap between what a producer might be *"expected"* to discover in a particular sector of industry and what he *could* ("enable") discover with all the technical resources available. Nevertheless the ECJ has ruled that the two provisions are not inconsistent.[32]

5.40   In one case[33] (involving an attachment to a pushchair) the producer argued that he was unaware of the defect because "scientific and technical knowledge" in the form of accident reports had not existed at the time of the accident. The argument was rejected; the reports did not amount to "scientific and technical knowledge" and this had not changed since the date of the accident. It has also been held (in the infected blood case (see para.5.24 above)) that the defence ceases to apply once the risk is known—even if the risk from a particular product is unavoidable.

(f) That the defect:

(i) constituted a defect in a subsequent product in which the product in question (i.e. a component) was comprised; and

(ii) was wholly attributable to the design of the subsequent product or to compliance with instructions given by the producer of the subsequent product.

This defence protects a component producer where the reason for the end product being defective is the design or instructions of the end producer.

---

[31] See para.5.10 above.
[32] *EC v UK* [1997] All E.R. (EC) 481.
[33] *Abouzaid v Mothercare (UK) Ltd, The Times*, 20 February 2001.

Example 16

> CM supplies a component to M. The component makes the end product faulty **5.41**
> but only because M's design is faulty. CM is not liable.

When must the claim be brought?

There are two rules—a consumer rule and an overriding supplier rule. For **5.42**
the *injured party* the basic limitation period is three years from (1) the date
on which the cause of action accrued, or (2) (if later) the date on which he
first discovered (or should have discovered) the relevant facts.[34] There is no
distinction between injury and property damage—the period is the same in
both cases.

As regards the *supplier* there is a 10-year cut-off period for each supplier.[35]
This "period of repose", as it is called in the United States, relates to the
particular product, not to the product line; so producers must keep precise
records (showing the exact date when each item was sold) to enable them to
rely on this provision. Traceability is crucial.

Example 17

> CM supplies a component to M in April 2004. M sells the end product to R in **5.43**
> April 2005.
> The 10-year period expires in April 2014 as regards CM and in April 2015 as
> regards M. The fact that no injury has occurred by the cut-off date is immaterial.

3. NEGLIGENCE

It will be appreciated that there will be a limited number of cases where the **5.44**
regime introduced by the Act will not apply and in these cases the injured
party must fall back on the general law of negligence. This will be so where,
for example:

(1) the damage sustained by the claimant (e.g. to business property) is
  not covered by the Act;

(2) the damage to property is £275 or less;

(3) the claim is out of time.

In considering negligence we must stress once again what we said at the
beginning of this chapter—namely the crucial distinction between shoddy
goods of poor quality and dangerous goods. The courts have always been
very cautious about extending the boundaries of liability and one argument
which they have used has been "economic loss". They have held that where

---

[34] Sch.1 para.1, amending Limitation Act 1980 s.11.
[35] As above. This is a "period of limitation" and accordingly the court can exercise its power
to substitute a new party under s.35(5) of the Limitation Act 1980 even though the 10-year
period has expired: *Horne-Roberts v Smith Kline Beecham* [2001] EWCA Civ 2006. See also
O'Byrne v Aventis Pasteur MSD Ltd [2008] UKHL 34.

the only damage is to the product itself, this loss is "economic" and not recoverable in the tort of negligence.[36]

5.45   A recent case reiterated that the tortious route will provide no escape if the contractual route is blocked. In *Robinson v P.E. Jones (Contractors) Ltd*[37] the facts were these:

> The claimant purchased a new house from its builder J. The flues for the gas heating proved to be defective. As R's contractual claim was statute-barred, he sued J in tort for negligence for the cost of £35,000 to rebuild the flues. No one was injured and no damage was caused, so the claim for repairs was a claim for economic or financial loss.

The Court of Appeal unanimously rejected R's appeal. Stanley Burnton LJ succinctly summarised the current legal position:

> "In my judgment, it must now be regarded as settled law that the builder/vendor of a building does not by reason of his contract to construct or to complete the building assume any liability in the tort of negligence in relation to defects in the building giving rise to purely economic loss. The same applies to a builder who is not the vendor, and to the seller or manufacturer of a chattel . . . ." (at para.92)

> "The duty of care in tort applies to damage to other property than that supplied, or to personal injury or death, caused by a defect in the property supplied." (at para.94)

This is so even though the financial loss may be the cost of repairing goods to make them safe (see para.5.52 below).

Donoghue v Stevenson: the snail in the ginger beer

5.46   In relation to dangerous goods the starting point must be the so-called "narrow rule" in *Donoghue v Stevenson*.[38] The facts were as follows:

> A lady took a friend for refreshment to a café in Paisley, near Glasgow. She bought a bottle of ginger beer and two ice creams. The bottle was made of dark, opaque glass, so the contents were invisible. They put the ice creams into tumblers, poured some of the ginger beer on top and drank the concoction. They then poured the rest of the ginger beer into a tumbler and out slid the body of a decomposed snail. They both suffered shock and gastroenteritis. The friend could not sue the café under the Sale of Goods Act 1893 because of the privity of contract rule, so she sued the manufacturers in tort ("delict" in Scotland). They argued that their only duty was a contractual duty to their buyers, e.g. the café and other distributors. The House of Lords disagreed.

---

[36] The first of three House of Lords cases on this point (all concerned with defective construction of buildings) is *D. & F. Estates Ltd v Church Commissioners* [1989] A.C. 177. Note the similar exclusion under the Act: s.5, at para.5.26 above. A similar result was reached in the other two cases that are cited in fn.61 to para.5.52 below.

[37] [2011] EWCA Civ 9. See also para.3.13 above.

[38] [1932] A.C. 562.

The principle of law was stated by Lord Atkin in the following well-known passage:

> "A manufacturer of products, which he sells in such a form as to show that he intends them to reach the ultimate consumer in the form in which they left him with no reasonable possibility of intermediate examination, and with the knowledge that the absence of reasonable care in the preparation or putting up of the products will result in an injury to the consumer's life or property, owes a duty to the consumer to take that reasonable care."

Lord Atkin added that this was a self-evident proposition which no one who was not a lawyer would for one moment doubt.

The duty outlined above is merely one particular type of "duty situation" in the context of the general law of negligence. The cases decided since 1932 show a gradual extension of liability. Thus:

(1) There is no limit to the type of goods covered by the rule. Examples include hair dye, underpants, cars, lifts and even a tombstone.

(2) Liability has been extended beyond manufacturers to cover, for example, repairers, assemblers and distributors. In one case even a car dealer was held liable.[39]

(3) The word "consumer" is not confined to the ultimate buyer; it means anyone likely to be injured by the lack of reasonable care. Perhaps the best illustration is provided by *Stennett v Hancock and Peters*[40] where part of the wheel of a lorry came off and struck a pedestrian on the pavement. She recovered damages from the second defendant who had negligently repaired the wheel shortly before the accident.

(4) The "possibility of intermediate examination" will only defeat the claim if there was a real likelihood of a type of examination which would (or should) reveal the defect. Thus in *Evans v Triplex Safety Glass Co*[41] the buyer of a Vauxhall car was injured when the windscreen shattered. His action against the manufacturers of the windscreen failed for various reasons; one reason was the likelihood of an intermediate examination by Vauxhall before it was fitted into the car; another reason was a failure to prove that the windscreen was defective when it left the manufacturer.

This case can be contrasted with the sale of goods case of *Wren v Holt*[42] where beer containing arsenic was sold by a publican to a customer. The case was fought on the term of satisfactory quality[43] and the publican was liable (and strictly so) even though the customer

---

[39] *Andrews v Hopkinson* [1957] 1 Q.B. 229. See also *Watson v Buckley Osborne Garrett & Co Ltd [1940] 1 All E.R. 174* (see para.4.33 above).
[40] [1939] 2 All E.R. 578.
[41] [1936] 1 All E.R. 283.
[42] [1903] 1 K.B. 610.
[43] See para.4.09 above.

had examined the beer before drinking it; the defect was not discoverable by any normal examination. If the buyer had sued the brewer it would not have been liable unless negligence could have been proved.

Proof of negligence and causation

5.47 As the law stands at present the task facing the injured consumer is not an easy one. He must prove (a) that the product was defective when it left the manufacturer, (b) that this was due to negligence, and (c) that this was the cause of his injury. If the article is completely destroyed in the accident, the claimant's task may well be insuperable, unless the court is prepared to make use of circumstantial evidence.

Was the product defective?

5.48 In many cases this should present no problem; a bun containing a stone, a loaf of bread containing a piece of glass or a car with faulty brakes—these are obvious examples. There may, however, be other cases which are less obvious. Thus in *Evans v Triplex Safety Glass Co*, the facts of which have already been given,[44] the plaintiff failed to prove that the windscreen was dangerous when it left the manufacturer.

In the examples previously given (for example, arsenic in the beer)[45] the product was out of line with the general run of goods produced by the manufacturers. Alternatively, it may be possible to argue that there is a fault in manufacture or design affecting all goods of a particular type. The cost of such a finding could be potentially astronomic for the manufacturer and for intermediate suppliers; they could be faced with a very large number of claims when the problem became known, and they might have to recall all the defective goods for repair.[46] In view of this the courts (both here and in the United States) have been cautious to base a negligence finding on this ground. There have, however, been cases in which the injured party has been successful. Thus in *Lambert v Lewis*[47] the manufacturer of a defective towing hitch which broke and caused a serious accident was held liable to the victims because its design was negligent.

Has the manufacturer been negligent?

5.49 This question and the previous one are closely linked. Thus in *Vacwell Engineering Co Ltd v B.D.H. Chemicals Ltd*[48] the defendants, who manufactured a chemical, were liable in negligence for failing to undertake adequate research to discover, and to warn prospective users, that contact with water

---

[44] See para.5.46 above.
[45] As above.
[46] e.g. the Toyota problems in 2013.
[47] [1982] A.C. 225. See paras 3.17 and 4.22 above.
[48] [1971] 1 Q.B. 88. On warnings, see also *Coal Pension Properties Ltd v Nu-Way Ltd* [2009] EWHC 824 (TCC).

could lead to an explosion. Similarly, in *Wright v Dunlop Rubber Co Ltd and ICI*[49] the Court of Appeal held that ICI were liable in negligence for continuing to market a product with knowledge that it constituted a serious health hazard. Finally in *Fisher v Harrods Ltd*[50] Mrs Fisher recovered damages from Harrods when they sold an untested bottle of cleaning fluid to her husband. She suffered personal injury when it came into contact with her eyes.

The duty owed by the manufacturer at common law does not involve it in strict liability—it is merely a duty to take reasonable care. This is particularly relevant where a manufacturer of (say) a car buys components such as brake linings or wheel bearings[51] which prove to be defective and cause injury to the ultimate consumer. If the manufacturer sources its components from a reliable supplier, has an adequate inspection system and an adequate system for checking faults, this may well be sufficient to show compliance with its duty.

A case from another branch of the law of negligence (employer's liability) is highly relevant here. In *Davie v New Merton Board Mills Ltd*[52] an employer supplied its employee with a tool which the employer had bought from a reputable supplier. The tool had a latent defect which the employer had no means of discovering. The employee was injured when the tool broke and sued the employer for damages for negligence. The House of Lords dismissed the claim on the ground that the employer had not been negligent. In the employment field the principle underlying this case has been reversed by statute[53] but in the product liability field the principle still stands. **5.50**

As already stated, the onus of proving negligence is on the injured party and this can be immensely difficult, especially in the case of a highly complex piece of equipment or a chemical or drug. Evidence of previous accidents caused by the same product is highly relevant and should be sought. Sometimes the facts themselves point to negligence; if a consumer loses a tooth through eating a cake containing a stone, this suggests that the manufacturer had been negligent and, under the doctrine of res ipsa loquitur, the manufacturer will have to adduce evidence from which the inference of negligence can be rebutted.[54] He may say "the defect was in a component and I myself took all reasonable care" or even "I have no idea how the acid got into the lemonade bottle but I had a foolproof system of inspection" (this latter argument was successfully raised in *Daniels v White Ltd and Tarbard*[55] but the decision has been criticised and is unlikely to be followed).[56]

When studying all the vast number of reported cases on negligence (perhaps far too many are reported) one point must never be forgotten;

---

[49] (1972) 13 K.I.R. 255.
[50] [1966] Lloyds L.R. 500.
[51] But in *Walton v British Leyland* (unreported) the defendants were liable in negligence for failure to recall cars when they discovered unexpected defects in wheel bearings.
[52] [1959] A.C. 604.
[53] Employers' Liability (Defective Equipment) Act 1969.
[54] *Moore v R. Fox & Son* [1956] 1 Q.B. 596.
[55] [1938] 4 All E.R. 258.
[56] For a case where the court refused to follow the *Daniels* decision see *Hill v James Crowe (Cases) Ltd* [1978] 1 All E.R. 812.

whether a defendant has performed his duty of care is a pure question of fact and a decision on this point is not a binding precedent for any future case.[57]

Did the defendant's negligence cause the claimant's injury?

5.51   The injured claimant must be able to prove a causal link between the defect, the negligence and his injury. This again can be a difficult matter in practice and the result of the case may turn on the inferences which the court is willing to draw from the facts. In the leading case of *Grant v Australian Knitting Mills*[58] where the claimant, a doctor, contracted dermatitis, the Privy Council accepted his argument that it was caused by an excess of sulphite in underpants manufactured by the defendants. The court reached this decision even though the evidence showed that more than four million of these pants had been sold without complaint. On the other hand, the claimant will fail if the injury would have occurred in any event. Thus, to borrow again from employment law, an employer is generally not liable for failing to provide safety equipment if he can show that the employee would not have worn it.[59] Similarly, a manufacturer of a car will not be liable for faulty brakes if the claimant was driving so fast that the accident would have occurred even if the brakes had been in perfect working order. A "class action" brought by smokers against Gallaghers was dismissed as causation could not be proved.[60]

For what damage can the plaintiff recover?

5.52   Reverting once again to the poor quality/dangerous dichotomy, the final question relates to *potentially* dangerous goods. On which side of the line do they fall? Can the buyer of a car claim in negligence for the cost of repairing brakes in order to avert a serious accident? In the Second Edition of this book we expressed the view that such a claim should be allowed but in two later cases, concerning potentially dangerous buildings, the House of Lords have classified such repair costs as irrecoverable economic loss.[61] Recently the Court of Appeal reiterated the general principle.[62]

---

[57] *Qualcast (Wolverhampton) Ltd v Haynes* [1959] A.C. 743.

[58] See para.4.19 above.

[59] *Qualcast (Wolverhampton) Ltd v Haynes* [1959] A.C. 743; *McWilliams v Arrol* [1962] 1 W.L.R. 295 HL.

[60] *Hodgson v Imperial Tobacco Ltd* (1999) N.L.D. 8 March QBD. For another non-liability case see *Hamble Fisheries Ltd v L Gardner & Sons Ltd, The Times*, 5 January 1999 CA.

[61] *Murphy v Brentwood DC* [1990] 3 W.L.R. 414; *Department of the Environment v Thomas Bates & Son Ltd* [1990] 3 W.L.R. 457. Followed in *Broster v Galliard Docklands Ltd* [2011] EWHC 1722 (TCC).

[62] See para.5.45 above: *Robinson* [2011] EWCA Civ 9.

Chapter Six

"DO I HAVE TO PAY?"

If the supplier of goods or services is guilty of a misrepresentation or a serious **6.01** breach of contract the consumer may be able to rescind the contract or treat it as repudiated. In either case this will relieve him of his obligation to pay the price. Some examples of this were examined in Chapters Two to Four and the matter will be considered again in Chapter Eight. This chapter is concerned with a group of seven unrelated but important topics on which the consumer may seek legal advice. The topics are:

(1) Delivery of unordered goods.

(2) Contracts concluded "at a distance" including internet shopping.

(3) Cancellation of doorstep and distance selling contracts.

(4) Loss of or damage to goods after contract but before delivery.

(5) Unsatisfactory performance of services.

(6) Late performance.

(7) A dispute about the price.

1. I Never Ordered these Goods

An aggressive salesman may try to boost his sales by delivering goods which **6.02** the customer has never ordered, followed by an invoice demanding payment.[1] He clearly hopes that the consumer will be induced, by a combination of ignorance, lethargy and fear, to pay the price. Many years ago there was a considerable outcry at these and similar practices, and there was a growing demand for legislation to curtail them. Eventually this demand was met by the Unsolicited Goods and Services Act 1971 (the 1971 Act). The rights of the consumer are now to be found in reg.27M of the Consumer Protection from Unfair Trading Regulations 2008 (SI 2008/1277) (the 2008 Regulations), as amended.

Before considering these provisions it may be useful to dispose of one problem which has arisen under the general law: is the consumer legally liable if the goods are lost or damaged while they are in his possession?

---

[1] For an example where a company allegedly guilty of this was wound up in the public interest see *Re Forcesun Ltd* [2002] EWHC 443 Ch.

Under the tort of negligence the claimant must prove that the defendant owed him a legal duty of care.[2] A person receiving unordered goods is known as an "involuntary bailee" and does not owe a duty of care. Therefore he will generally not be liable for accidental loss or damage.[3] On the other hand he may be liable for the tort of conversion if he deliberately destroys the goods or converts them to his own use. Where is the line to be drawn? If a tradesman delivers an unordered 10-volume encyclopedia the consumer might well be liable if he puts them outside his house and allows them to disintegrate. However, as we will see below, statutory intervention effectively means that the consumer is unlikely to face any liability in tort.

The current law: the Consumer Protection from Unfair Trading Regulations

6.03   Historically, unsolicited goods and services were dealt with in the 1971 Act, which imposed both civil and criminal sanctions but most of its provisions have been replaced by the reg.27M and para.29 of Sch.1 to the 2008 Regulations. Under the heading "Inertia Selling" reg.27M applies where the trader has engaged in the prohibited practice in para.29 of Sch.1, which prohibits "demanding immediate or deferred payment for or the return or safekeeping of products supplied by the trader, but not solicited by the consumer". This Regulation therefore applies where (a) an unsolicited product is supplied to a consumer by a trader; (b) which the consumer did not solicit; and (c) the trader demands payment, safekeeping or return of the goods. Where this regulation applies, the effect is that the consumer gets a free gift, as per reg.27M:

> (2) The consumer is exempted from any obligation to provide consideration for the products supplied by the trader.
> (3) The absence of a response from the consumer following the supply does not constitute consent to the provision of consideration for, or the return or safekeeping of, the products.
> (4) In the case of an unsolicited supply of goods, the consumer may, as between the consumer and the trader, use, deal with or dispose of the goods as if they were an unconditional gift to the consumer.

Note that (unlike the Act) the regulation has immediate effect; thus if the goods are sent by mistake it will be too late for the sender to recover them. The recipient is not completely safe, however, because the regulation only applies as between himself and the sender; if therefore the goods belong to a third party (for example, a finance company) the rights of that party are unaffected.

6.04   As regards the criminal sanctions these are to be found in reg.12 of the 2008 Regulations and in s.2 of the 1971 Act. Regulation 12 of the 2008 Regulations makes it a criminal offence to infringe the prohibition in para.29 of Sch.1, set out above.

---

[2] *Bourhill v Young* [1943] A.C. 92.
[3] See *Howard v Harris* (1884) Cab. & E. 253.

Although the 2008 Regulations will now be the primary means of combating unsolicited goods and services, the sanction in s.2 of the 1971 Act remains in force. Under this section, an offence is committed where a trader (a) makes a demand for payment for what he knows are unsolicited goods/services which are sent/supplied to another person with a view to his acquiring them otherwise than for the purposes of a business, and (b) he has no reasonable cause to believe that there is a right to payment. An offence is also committed where a person in such a case (1) asserts a right to payment, (2) threatens to bring legal proceedings, (3) places, or threatens to place, the name of any person on a defaulters' list, or (4) invokes, or threatens to invoke, any other collection procedure.

2. I ORDERED THEM ON-LINE

Introduction

In the previous section we were concerned with the obsolescent (or obsolete?)   **6.05**
marketing practice of supplying goods or services, or other products, unasked to consumers with the result that the consumers receive an unexpected present.

Much more frequent nowadays—indeed, so frequent that it is a constant source of irritation to many—is the importunate marketing of goods, services and digital content by various physical and electronic means. It is still common for mail order catalogues and leaflets to constantly drop through letter-boxes; magazines and newspapers are littered with advertisements for everything from the latest health supplement to cruises to luxurious destinations (or both); continual interruptions are caused by telephone calls from call centres pushing telecommunications, utilities, double glazing or fitted kitchens; and commercial breaks on television stridently market their wares. However, more than any other source, the internet with e-mails, social networking sites, smartphone apps and websites generally has become a fertile marketing ground.

Distance Contracts

In none of the examples above are the trader and customer face-to-face. This   **6.06**
is where the Consumer Contracts (Information, Cancellation and Additional Charges) Regulations 2013 (CCR) begin to bite. The CCR implement the EU's Consumer Rights Directive (2011/83/EU) (the Consumer Rights Directive), which primarily merges and enhances earlier directives on doorstep and distance selling.

Our present focus is on "distance contracts", defined by reg.5(1) as "a contract concluded between a trader and a consumer under an organised distance sales or service-provision scheme without the simultaneous physical presence of the trader and the consumer, with the exclusive use of one or more means of distance communication up to and including the time at which the contract is concluded."

All the practices given as examples in the previous paragraph are caught by the CCR, as they fall within the definition of "distance contract" in reg.3(1).

6.07   In order to unpack this definition, it is helpful to refer back to the recitals to the Consumer Rights Directive. In particular, Recital 20 tells us that:

> The definition of distance contract should cover all cases where a contract is concluded between the trader and the consumer under an organised distance sales or service provision scheme, with the exclusive use of one or more means of distance communication (such as mail order, Internet, telephone or fax) up to and including the time at which the contract is concluded.
>
> That definition should also cover situations where the consumer visits the business premises merely for the purpose of gathering information about the goods or services and subsequently negotiates and concludes the contract at a distance.
>
> By contrast, a contract which is negotiated at the business premises of the trader and finally concluded by means of distance communication should not be considered a distance contract. Neither should a contract initiated by means of distance communication, but finally concluded at the business premises of the trader be considered a distance contract.
>
> Similarly, the concept of distance contract should not include reservations made by a consumer through a means of distance communications to request the provision of a service from a professional, such as in the case of a consumer phoning to request an appointment with a hairdresser.
>
> The notion of an organised distance sales or service-provision scheme should include those schemes offered by a third party other than the trader but used by the trader, such as an online platform. It should not, however, cover cases where websites merely offer information on the trader, his goods and/or services and his contact details.

This recital does not clarify everything about the definition, but offers some useful guidance. For example, it clarifies that an "organised distance scheme" includes online platforms (e.g., eBay, Amazon Marketplace or Uber), although such a platform has to be more than an on-line directory. So presumably, an organised distance scheme has to provide a facility for placing an order.

6.08   Of more interest are the "mixed" situations involving both on-line and in-store/face-to-face interactions. Where trader and consumer interact both in-store and at a distance, the contract should not be treated as a distance contract. However, a consumer who is merely a passive browser in the trader's store and then orders goods from that trader on-line can benefit from the rules applicable to distance contracts. Some consumers only visit stores to browse goods and then look for these on-line to get them at a lower price, which on the one hand might seem savvy, but this behaviour is starting to affect the viability of city centre stores.

Earlier regulations (the Distance Selling Regulations 2000 (the 2000 Regulations)) contained a schedule with an indicative list of "means of distance communication". In light of rapid technological advancement (the 2000 Regulations did not even mention the internet as such a means), this list has been dropped.

Regulations' requirements

The 2013 Regulations contain detailed requirements about providing infor-   **6.09**
mation to consumers and various other matters.

Pre-contract information

Regulation 13 requires that the consumer is given specified information   **6.10**
"before a consumer is bound by a distance contract". The list of items of
information to be provided is now incredibly long, and is set out in Sch.2 to
the CCR (which lists 24 separate categories of information!). It must be provided "in a clear and comprehensible manner" and in a "way appropriate to
the means of distance communication used".

Regulation 14 contains special requirements for contracts concluded by
electronic means. In particular, reg.14(3) states that a trader must ensure that
a consumer explicitly acknowledges at the time of placing an order that doing
so entails an obligation to pay (where applicable). In essence, this means that
a consumer is required to click on a button which is labelled "order with
obligation to pay" (reg.14(4)). If a trader does not comply with these requirements, the consumer is not bound by the contract or order (reg.14(5)).

As already discussed (see Chapter Four), by virtue of ss.11(4) and 12
(for goods), 36(3) and 37 (for digital content) and 50(3) (for services) of
the Consumer Rights Act 2015 (CRA 2015), this information is treated as
included as a term of the contract.

Written confirmation

Regulation 16 states that the trader must confirm the contract on a durable   **6.11**
medium, and the contract must include all the information required by Sch.2
(unless this has already been provided on a durable medium). The confirmation has to be provided within "a reasonable time after the conclusion of the
contract" (and no later than delivery of the goods and/or before performance
of a service commences).

Performance

Unless otherwise agreed, the supplier must perform within 30 days[4] begin-   **6.12**
ning with the day after the day on which the contract was entered into or
reimburse any sums paid (see s.28(8)–(12) of CRA 2015.).

Enforcement

Regulation 44 requires the Competition and Markets Authority, or any   **6.13**
other enforcement authority, to consider complaints (unless frivolous or
vexatious). If they find that there has been a breach they are likely to seek
an undertaking from the supplier. If a satisfactory undertaking cannot be
obtained, or if it is broken, reg.45 enables them to apply to the court for an

[4] s.28 of the CRA 2015.

injunction and the court may grant it on such terms as it thinks fit to secure compliance with the 2013 Regulations.

Exceptions

6.14 A few contracts are excepted from the 2013 Regulations by reg.6(2), e.g. contracts via vending machines, use of public phones, or single connections to communications networks. Other contracts are partially exempt by reg.6(1), i.e., only to the extent that the contract falls within one of the types listed in that provision (e.g. the supply of food by regular roundsmen (milk, etc.), rental accommodation, or services of a banking, credit, insurance, personal pension, investment or payment nature).

Making distance contracts

6.15 The 2013 Regulations frequently refer to a contract being "concluded" and sometimes the phrase "consumer is bound" is used instead: they appear to mean the same—the moment when the contract is formed. Not surprisingly they do not set out the contractual principles governing the formation of contracts and it may be helpful briefly to analyse the common law rules. This involves a discussion of offer and acceptance. Two questions have to be answered: (a) who makes the offer?, and (b) when does acceptance occur?

(a) Who makes the offer?

6.16 It is important to decide whether the supplier or consumer is the offeror. If the supplier were the offeror, then as soon as the consumer accepted the offer (e.g. by posting an order form) a contract would be made. This could pose difficult, if not insuperable, problems for the supplier. A seller of goods would usually have limited stocks and be unable to meet an unexpected demand. Conversely, if it is the consumer who makes the offer when placing an order, the supplier will be in a position to choose whether to accept or reject it.

We take the view that the latter solution is correct and the presumption should be that the consumer is the offeror and the supplier the offeree. Case-law on the distinction between an invitation to treat and an offer supports this view.[5] Thus a supplier is merely giving an invitation to treat when including goods or services in a mail order catalogue, newspaper advertisement, door-to-door flyer or letter. The same is true of advertisements on radio or television or the use of fax.

How do e-mail and the internet fit into the rules? The virtue of the common law is its flexibility—there is no need for legislation when a new medium of communication is brought into use. Where suppliers contact consumers electronically, the medium is a modern version of the mail order catalogue and so merely an invitation to treat, so that the consumer's offer to buy may be

---

[5] Goods in shop window—*Fisher* v *Bell*[1961] 1 Q.B. 394; on supermarket shelf—*Pharmaceutical Society of GB* v *Boots Cash Chemists (Southern)* [1952] 2 Q.B. 795.

rejected if the supplier so decides. Thus if, as happened with a well-known retailer, a colour television is advertised at the price of £29.90 with a misplaced decimal point, the supplier is entitled to refuse to accept orders (in that case the other defence was unilateral mistake, as the error was self-evident).

(b) When does acceptance occur?

There are a number of reasons why it is vital to identify the precise moment **6.17** when the contract is made. At that time, both parties become bound (subject to the consumer's cancellation rights: see para.6.23), so that neither the supplier nor the consumer can change their minds with impunity. Further, any later attempt by the supplier to introduce protective terms of business will be ineffectual (see para.9.07 and following). (Thus supplies of goods such as software delivered shrink-wrapped, so that the buyer cannot read the conditions of sale until after the contract is made, are not subject to such hidden terms.)

The general common law principle of acceptance is that it must be communicated to the offeror, i.e. no agreement is made until the offeror is, or could be, aware of the acceptance. The posting rule is exceptional whereby the acceptance is effective as soon as the letter is put in the pillar box.[6] This principle applies whenever the method of communication is fast so that there is no significant interval between the sending and receipt of the acceptance.

(i) Mail order. The postal rule applies where the supplier accepts the order **6.18** by posting an acknowledgment of order; otherwise the delivery of the goods or commencement of the services will be an act of acceptance.

(ii) Telephone. There can be no hard-and-fast rule, as during the negotiation **6.19** either party may make an offer or counter-offer. However, if the line goes dead or the signal fails, so that the offeror does not hear the acceptance, no contract results. Of course, evidential problems are enormous.

(iii) On-line/e-mail. Although there is no authority on this point, we con- **6.20** sider that the offer is made by the consumer, e.g. by clicking on "submit" or "order", and the acceptance occurs if—and only if—the supplier accepts by a further communication to the consumer, e.g. by sending an e-mail acknowledgment or confirmation with a reference for the order or booking. We take this view because, as we stated earlier, this type of transaction is just an up-to-date version of paper mail order. Whether the offeror/consumer has accessed the computer server and actually read the e-mail acceptance is irrelevant, provided it is accessible.[7] It is important to appreciate that on-line ordering is a largely automated process, with little or no human intervention on the trader's side. Many on-line retailers operate fully or partly automated warehousing systems relying on RFID technology to find items ordered by

---

[6] *Adams v Lindsell* (1818) 1 B. & Ald. 681.
[7] See para.6.17 above.

a consumer in the warehouse and to compile the order. A final check and packaging may still be undertaken by human employees.

Terms and conditions

6.21   The principles explained above are, of course, subject to any terms and conditions incorporated into the contract by the supplier. It is almost inevitable that internet purchasing via the web will involve such express terms. For example, one well-known retailer states that they "will confirm receipt of your order by sending an e-mail, . . . however this will not bring into existence a legal binding agreement between us . . . . No contract will exist . . . until your credit/debit card has been charged." Amazon, perhaps the best-known internet retailer, has the following clause lurking amongst its many pages of terms of business:

> Your order is an offer to Amazon to buy the product(s) in your order. When you place an order to purchase a product from Amazon, we will send you a message confirming receipt of your order and containing the details of your order (the "Order Confirmation"). If you are using certain Amazon Services (e.g. Amazon mobile applications) the Order Confirmation may be posted on a Message Centre on the website. The Order Confirmation is acknowledgement that we have received your order, and does not confirm acceptance of your offer to buy the product(s) or the services ordered. We only accept your offer, and conclude the contract of sale for a product ordered by you, when we dispatch the product to you and send e-mail or post a message on the Message Centre of the website confirming to you that we've dispatched the product to you (the "Dispatch Confirmation").

6.22   These and other web suppliers seem to agree with our view that the consumer makes the offer, which is accepted when the supplier does something further, e.g. charging the price to a credit card, e-mailing confirmation that the goods have been sent or, in one reputable High Street chain's terms, the actual sending of the goods.

The legal effect is that neither party is bound during the interval between sending the order and its acceptance, so that meanwhile the consumer may change his mind and revoke his offer—there will be no need to resort to the statutory cancellation rights at that stage.

It is by no means clear that such terms of business will always be successfully incorporated by the supplier. It often takes a time consuming search to find the terms and conditions among the list of other information on the website and then a more detailed search through many pages of terms to discover the relevant provision. The courts may well take the view that the supplier has not taken sufficient or reasonable steps to bring the clause to the consumer's attention[8]; if so, the principle stated in para.6.17 will apply.

---

[8] See paras 9.08 to 9.11 below and in particular *Interfoto*.

3. I Have Changed My Mind

We have just considered problems encountered by consumers when making **6.23** "distance contracts" and the measures in the CCR to protect them. In addition to "distance contracts", the CCR also deal with a separate area of concern: door-to-door sales. Consumers may be caught unawares at home (or at work) and pressurised by unscrupulous traders into making immediate contracts for goods or services, which they may not need or are not good value, by dubious sales techniques, e.g. bargain prices only if contracts are concluded there and then. Utilities and home improvements are sectors where such malpractices are rife—gas, electricity, replacement windows, loft and wall insulation, solar panels.

Legislation giving consumers a chance to reflect privately on the merits of the deal and to change their minds and cancel such contracts was first introduced in 1987: it implemented EC Council Directive 85/577. The Directive, and the implementing legislation (The Consumer Protection (Cancellation of Contracts Concluded away from Business Premises) Regulations 1987[9]) initially applied only to "unsolicited" visits, but the Cancellation of Contracts made in a Consumer's Home or Place of Work etc. Regulations 2008 (the 2008 Doorstep Selling Regulations),[10] which came into force on 1 October 2008, extended to all contracts concluded away from business premises.

Following the adoption of the Consumer Rights Directive and its imple- **6.24** mentation in the CCR, there is now a single set of rules applicable to both distance contracts and "off-premises" contracts which allow a consumer to change his mind in respect of these types of contract.

Regulation 5 of the CCR defines an "off-premises contract" thus:

means a contract between a trader and a consumer which is any of these—

(a) a contract concluded in the simultaneous physical presence of the trader and the consumer, in a place which is not the business premises of the trader;

(b) a contract for which an offer was made by the consumer in the simultaneous physical presence of the trader and the consumer, in a place which is not the business premises of the trader;

(c) a contract concluded on the business premises of the trader or through any means of distance communication immediately after the consumer was personally and individually addressed in a place which is not the business premises of the trader in the simultaneous physical presence of the trader and the consumer;

(d) a contract concluded during an excursion organised by the trader with the aim or effect of promoting and selling goods or services to the consumer;

[9] SI 1987/2117 (as amended).
[10] SI 2008/1816.

The CCR impose detailed obligations on a trader to furnish a consumer with information before concluding a contract—see reg.10 and Sch.2. More limited information is required for repair or maintenance contracts to be performed immediately for a charge not exceeding £170 (reg.11 of the CCR). A consumer also has to be provided with a copy of the signed contract or confirmation of the contract on paper or another durable medium, and this must include all the information required by Sch.2 (reg.12 of the CCR).

The Right to Cancel

6.25   The CCR introduced a single set of rules on the right to cancel applicable to both off-premises contracts (unless the payment to be made by the consumer is not more than £42)[11] and distance contracts. It is perhaps appropriate to stress at this point that there is no legal right to cancel a contract concluded in-store ("on premises") merely because a consumer has changed their mind. That said, many stores offer their own "returns policies", but these are voluntary offers rather than specific legal obligations.

In addition to the contracts excluded from the scope of the CCR altogether, there is an additional list of contracts in respect of which the right to cancel is not available[12]:

(a) for the supply of a medicinal product by administration by a prescriber, or under a prescription or directions given by a prescriber;

(b) for the supply of a product by a health care professional or a person included in a relevant list, under arrangements for the supply of services as part of the health service, where the product is one that, at least in some circumstances is available under such arrangements free or on prescription;

(c) for passenger transport services.

6.26   For other contracts, specific situations are excluded from the right to cancel, including contracts involving[13]:

• the supply of goods for which the price is dependent on fluctuations in the financial market which cannot be controlled by the trader and which may occur within the cancellation period;

• the supply of goods that are made to the consumer's specifications or are clearly personalised;

• the supply of goods which are liable to deteriorate or expire rapidly;

• the supply of alcoholic beverages, where:

---

[11] reg.27(3) of the CCR.

[12] reg.27(2) of the CCR.

[13] See reg.28(1) of the CCR for the full list.

    (i)   their price has been agreed at the time of the conclusion of the sales contract,

    (ii) delivery of them can only take place after 30 days, and

    (iii) their value is dependent on fluctuations in the market which cannot be controlled by the trader;

- concluded at a public auction.

In addition, even where a right to cancel is available, this is lost where:

"(a) in the case of a contract for the supply of sealed goods which are not suitable for return due to health protection or hygiene reasons, if they become unsealed after delivery;

 (b) in the case of a contract for the supply of sealed audio or sealed video recordings or sealed computer software, if the goods become unsealed after delivery;

 (c) in the case of any sales contract, if the goods become mixed inseparably (according to their nature) with other items after delivery."[14]

The cancellation period

6.27 Regulation 29(1) provides the general right to cancel a distance or off-premises contract, which can be exercised at any time during the cancellation period. A consumer seeking to cancel is not required to give any reason—a consumer is free to change their mind.

The CCR have increased the duration of the cancellation period, which now lasts for 14 days.[15] The point at which this period starts varies depending on the type of contract. In the case of a contract for the sale of goods, it starts after the day on which the goods were delivered.[16] There are special provisions in respect of orders comprising multiple goods (the period starts on the date on which the last item was delivered),[17] orders consisting of multiple lots or pieces delivered on different days (it also starts on the date on which the last item was delivered),[18] and orders where goods are delivered regularly on a recurring basis (where the period starts on the date on which the *first* item was delivered[19]). If the contract is a service contract or for the supply of digital content, the period ends 14 days after the day on which the contract was entered into.[20]

---

[14] reg.28(3) of the CCR.
[15] Although under reg.31 of the CCR, this period is extended where the trader has failed to provide the consumer with the relevant information about the existence of the right of cancellation.
[16] reg.30(3) of the CCR.
[17] reg.30(4) of the CCR.
[18] reg.30(5) of the CCR.
[19] reg.30(6) of the CCR.
[20] reg.30(2) of the CCR.

Information about the right to cancel

6.28   Among the many items to be given to a consumer in accordance with Sch.2 is information about the right to cancel the contract (para.(l)). A trader can adopt the model instructions on cancellation provided in Sch.3.

If a trader fails to provide this information at the required time, then the cancellation period does not start until the trader *has* provided the consumer with that information. This should happen within 12 months from the date at which the cancellation period would otherwise have commenced (see above). In any event, the cancellation period will end after 12 months from that date.[21]

Moreover, if, in the context of an off-premises contract, a trader fails to inform the consumer about the existence of the right of withdrawal and possible associated costs (as required by paras (l)–(n) of Sch.2, he will also be guilty of an offence under reg.19 of the CCR.

Cancelling a contract

6.29   To cancel a contract, the consumer has to notify the trader,[22] either by completing a model cancellation form or through any other clear statement to the same effect. A trader can provide an on-line cancellation form on the trader's website for use by the consumer, although a consumer cannot be required to use this.[23]

Once the contract has been cancelled, the obligations of the parties to perform the contract ends.[24]

The trader must reimburse all payments made by the consumer within 14 days.[25] Although this should include delivery charges paid by the consumer, the trader only has to reimburse the equivalent of the least expensive method offered by the trader.[26] If a consumer had selected a more expensive method for quicker delivery, the difference between the cheapest available method and the method chosen cannot be recovered.

There is also a word of warning to consumers who might intend to use their right to "borrow" goods such as expensive clothes for a special event: if the goods have been handled "beyond what is necessary to establish the nature, characteristics and functioning of the goods",[27] which has diminished the

---

[21] reg.31 of the CCR. The CCR are less severe than the 2008 Doorstep Selling Regulations (SI 2008/1816), where a failure to give written information about the right to cancel at the time the contract was made had the immediate effect of preventing the trader from ever enforcing the agreement against the consumer, even where that information was provided by e-mail soon after concluding the contract: *AllPropertyClaims Ltd v Tang* [2015] EWHC 2198 (QB). See also *Cox v Woodlands Manor Care Home Ltd* [2015] EWCA Civ 415 and *Salat v Barutis* [2013] EWCA Civ 1499. Failure to provide this information did not deprive the consumer of the right to cancel: *Robertson v Swift* [2014] UKSC 50.

[22] reg.32(2) of the CCR.
[23] reg.32(4) of the CCR.
[24] reg.33(1) of the CCR.
[25] See regs 34(1) and (4)–(6) of the CCR.
[26] reg.34(2) of the CCR.
[27] reg.34(9) of the CCR.

value of the goods, then the trader is entitled to make a deduction from the sum due to be refunded to reflect this.

If the contract involves the supply of goods, then the trader has to collect **6.30** them where he has offered to do so, or where, under an off-premises contract, goods were delivered to the consumer's home but they cannot be returned by post due to the nature of the goods (e.g. bulky or heavy items).[28] Where this is not the case, the consumer may be required to send the goods back, or hand them over to the trader (or a person authorised by the trader). As far as the goods of returning the goods is concerned, the consumer will have to bear those unless the trader has agreed to do this or failed to inform the consumer that the consumer will be required to pay for those costs.

Special rules apply for contracts involving the supply of digital content: reg.37 of the CCR states that the trader should not supply digital content until the end of the cancellation period. However, the consumer can consent expressly to supply before the end of the period, but must acknowledge that right to cancel will be lost as a consequence.

4. THE SELLER'S STOCK HAS BEEN DESTROYED

We have already seen that where goods are supplied in the course of a **6.31** business, they must be of satisfactory quality.[29] What happens if they were clearly satisfactory at the time of the contract but are accidentally damaged or destroyed at a later date? We must distinguish between total destruction and damage, and the precise form of the contract is also highly relevant.

What has the consumer agreed to buy?

The law draws a distinction between three types of goods: **6.32**

1. **Specific goods.** These are defined as "goods identified and agreed on at the time a contract of sale is made" (s.61 of the Sale of Goods Act 1979 (the 1979 Act)).[30] If therefore a consumer goes into a store and selects and buys a specific DVD player from the shelf, this would be a contract for specific goods.

2. **Purely generic goods.** An example would be where a buyer places an order for a television model like the one in the shop.

3. **Generic goods from an identified source.** An example would be "ten cases of Languedoc wine from the stock in your warehouse".

In 2 and 3 above the goods are "unascertained" goods.

---

[28] reg.35 of the CCR.
[29] See para.4.08 above.
[30] The 1979 Act continues to apply to the points discussed in this section, but only if the contract is a *sale* of goods within the meaning of s.2 of the 1979 Act.

Total destruction

6.33 In case 1 above if the goods are destroyed, they are said to "perish" and s.7 of the 1979 Act provides that:

> Where there is an agreement to sell specific goods and subsequently the goods, without any fault on the part of the seller or buyer, perish before the risk passes to the buyer, the contract is avoided.

So in advising the consumer we must consider (a) fault, (b) risk, and (c) the legal position if s.7 applies.

(a) Fault—if, for example, the seller has been negligent in failing to provide adequate fire precautions, s.7 would not apply and the buyer could sue the seller for damages for negligence and/or non-delivery.

(b) Risk—the 1979 Act contained a special provision on the passing of risk in consumer contracts,[31] but this was replaced by s.29 of the CRA 2015 to implement art.20 of the Consumer Rights Directive (2011/83/EU). Section 29 only applies to sales contracts. Goods remain at the trader's risk until they come into the physical possession of the consumer (or a person nominated by the consumer to take possession of the goods).[32] However, this does not apply where the consumer has commissioned a carrier to deliver the goods and that carrier is not among the options given to the consumer by the trader. In that case, delivery of the goods to the carrier will mean that risk passes to the consumer at that point.[33]

Whilst the old s.20(4) of the 1979 Act was a statuory rule, s.29 gives effect to the provisions on risk by treating a sales contract as including a term to that effect, which seems unnecessary.

(c) Effect of s.7—The contract is frustrated but the Law Reform (Frustrated Contracts) Act 1943 (the 1943 Act) does not apply in a case where specific goods perish; the legal rights of the parties will be governed by the common law rules. Under these rules (a) the buyer does not have to pay the price, (b) if he has paid it, or any part of it, he can recover it on the basis that there has been a "total failure of consideration", (c) he cannot claim damages for non-delivery, and (d) the unfortunate seller cannot claim anything for work done to the goods nor for storage charges.

The position is different in cases 2 and 3 above. Where the goods are purely generic (case 2 above) the fact that the seller's premises have been destroyed by fire will not cut down his liability to the buyer. Unless he has protected

---

[31] s.20(4) of the 1979 Act, inserted by the Sale and Supply of Goods to Consumers Regulations 2002 and revoked by the CRA 2015.
[32] s.29(2) of the CRA 2015.
[33] s.29(3) and (4) of the CRA 2015.

himself by an effective exemption clause (unlikely) he must find goods from elsewhere or pay damages for non-delivery. If, however, the source of the goods is identified in the contract (case 3 above) the destruction of that source before the risk has passed to the buyer will operate to frustrate the contract and in this situation the 1943 Act will apply. The rules are similar to those discussed above except that adjustments can be made for expenses incurred by the seller and benefits received by the buyer before the frustrating event.

Damage

What happens if goods are accidentally damaged while they are still at the seller's risk? This problem could arise if, for example, the television ordered by the buyer is damaged when the delivery van is involved in a road accident for which the seller is not responsible. Presumably the buyer can refuse to accept the damaged goods and then bring an action for non-delivery.

6.34

5. THE PLUMBER WAS A COWBOY

Contracts for services

The contract of "work and materials" (installation of central heating, double-glazing, etc.) was briefly examined in Chapter Four. It will be recalled that such a contract can be divided into two parts—the "goods" part[34] and the "work" part and the legal rules for the two parts are different.

6.35

The "work" part of such a contract is treated like a contract for services. The list of such contracts includes repair, decoration, servicing, maintenance, cleaning, building, storage, carriage of goods and passengers, insurance, the provision of accommodation, entertainment and the whole range of professional services—legal, banking, accountancy, medical, dental, surveying, valuing and so on.

Consumer Rights Act 2015: care and skill

Prior to the enactment of the Supply of Goods and Services Act 1982 (the 1982 Act), there was no statutory obligation on the supplier of a service to carry out his work with reasonable care and skill. Such a duty was first introduced in s.13 of the 1982 Act,[35] which has now been replaced by s.49 of the CRA 2015. Sub-section (1) provides that:

6.36

> Every contract to supply a service is treated as including a term that the trader must perform the service with reasonable care and skill.

Section 49 imposes merely a duty of care and skill on a business supplier of services, rather than imposing strict liability on a service provider to achieve

---

[34] See para.4.33 above where the "goods" aspect is discussed.
[35] For the background to, and commentary on, the 1982 Act see Woodroffe, *Goods and Services—The New Law* (1982). It was a Private Member's Bill and Geoffrey Woodroffe was the draftsman of Pt II (the work or services sections).

a particular outcome. Sections 54–56 introduce new remedies where a trader has fallen short of this requirement (see Chapter Eight).

Two cases under the old s.13

6.37 Although s.13 of the 1982 Act has now been replaced by s.49(1) of the CRA 2015, there has been no change to the legal standard required, and we may consider cases decided under s.13 as illustrations of this test.

One such case on s.13 is *Harrison v Shepherd Homes Ltd.*[36]

> The claimant bought a house from the defendants SH. It stood on cast in-situ concrete ground beams above piled foundations. Cracking in the walls occurred leading to other cosmetic defects.

Ramsey J held that the defects in the properties were caused by defects in the piles of the foundations which had not been constructed in a workmanlike manner. As to their design, he said, "I consider that the usual terms as to the design being carried out with reasonable skill and care and as to fitness for habitation, would be implied under section 13" (at para.50). The award of damages included the cost of remedial work, the diminution in value of the house and the cost of future remedial works. He also awarded "modest" sums for "distress, inconvenience and loss of amenity": £150 per person for each past year and £2,500 in total for the future.

6.38 An unusual case, of special interest to law students taking the Solicitors' Legal Practice Course, is *Abramova v Oxford Institute of Legal Practice.*[37]

> The claimant, a Russian graduate of Oxford University, failed the Legal Practice Course for prospective solicitors on the basis of her third failure of a compulsory subject. She argued that the defendants were negligent because students had to mark their own mock examinations; the teaching in exam techniques was inadequate; and she received inadequate feedback from her tutors.

The High Court held that the claim failed. The approach to a contractual claim based on s.13 of the 1982 Act (and consequently s.49(1) of the CRA 2015) was the same as one brought in negligence—the claimant had to prove a breach of the duty of care satisfying the test in *Bolam v Friern Hospital Management Committee* [1957] 1 W.L.R. 582. She had failed to prove negligence in relation to any of the three matters: the practice of self-marking was not unreasonable; the success of the overwhelming majority of students demonstrated the quality of the teaching; the tutorial advice, assistance and feedback given to her were adequate. It was reasonable to expect adult graduates to take responsibility for their own studies in the light of clear guidance given in the course documents and by the course director at the start of the year.

---

[36] [2011] EWHC 1811 (TCC).
[37] [2011] EWHC 613 (QB).

Express terms

The term included in a contract by s.49(1) of the CRA 2015 requires the **6.39** supplier of services to be careful only. However, more may be said about the service by the trader, and s.50 also treats as a term included in a contract involving the supply of a service anything "said or written to the consumer. . .about. . .the service if

(a) it is taken into account by the consumer when deciding to enter into the contract, or

(b) it is taken into account by the consumer when making any decision about the service after entering into the contract. "

This could cover assurances made by a trader that a service will provide a particular outcome ("your drains will be as new").

In addition, there may be *express* terms in the contract which may go further and impose liability even though the supplier has not been negligent.

In *Platform Funding Ltd v Bank of Scotland Plc (formerly Halifax Plc)*[38]   **6.40**

> the defendants carried on business as valuers and surveyors (trading as "Colleys"). The claimants instructed them to inspect and report on the condition and value of a new house, 1 Bakers Yard. The borrower misled them into inspecting another house nearby. The claimants made an advance and, when the borrower defaulted, repossessed the house and sold it. They sought to recover a shortfall of over £30,000 from the defendants.

The defendants argued that, as their mistake was caused by the borrower's fraud, they were not liable in the absence of negligence. The claimants contended that the obligation to inspect the specified property was unqualified. The Court of Appeal (Sir Anthony Clarke MR dissenting) held that the obligation was unqualified. "By accepting instructions to inspect and value 1 Bakers Yard they undertook an unqualified obligation to inspect the property and were in breach of contract in failing to do so", said Moore-Blick LJ.

Of course, usually such an error will result from negligence, but strict liability applies to the identification of the correct property. It is likely that the courts will limit this higher standard to very special facts. The case does not erode substantially the general principle in s.49(1).

Exclusions

The section was intended to confirm and codify the existing common law. It **6.41** was not intended to enlarge existing areas of liability. Accordingly, s.48(5) gives the Secretary of State power to make orders excluding a service of a description specified in the Order. At the time of writing, no orders had been made under this provision.[39]

---

[38] [2008] EWCA Civ 930.
[39] Orders made under the 1982 Act remain in force but these do not extend to contracts within the scope of the CRA 2015.

Must the consumer pay?

6.42   We revert now to the basic question—does the consumer have to pay the full price if the work of the plumber, electrician, etc., is unsatisfactory? In the vast majority of cases the answer will be "no"; the plumber, etc., will be in breach of the duty of care and skill treated as included in the contract by s.49(1), and the consumer may well be able to treat himself as discharged from the contract altogether. In addition, the CRA 2015 introduced new remedies to require repeat performance or to reduce the price. These remedies are examined more fully in Chapter Eight (see para.8.19 below).

6. They Turned Up Late

6.43   Late performance, whether by sellers, electricians, builders, plumbers, carriers or tour operators, is a frequent source of complaint by consumers. The legal principles governing this topic can be summarised as follows:

(1)   If the contract specifies a date for performance, a supplier of goods or services who fails to perform by that date will be liable in damages for breach of contract (unless this liability has been effectively excluded or unless the contract is frustrated). This claim for damages can be pleaded by way of set-off or counter-claim in an action by the supplier for the price.[40]

(2)   If the contract does not specify a date for performance the supplier must perform within a "reasonable" time. This statutory obligation is imposed on traders supplying a service by s.52 of the CRA 2015. The question of reasonableness is a question of fact[41]; even a long delay will not necessarily amount to a breach of contract if it was due to circumstances beyond the supplier's control.

In a case decided before the 1982 Act, *Charnock v Liverpool Corp*, a car owner took his car to a garage for repair following an accident. A competent repairer would have taken five weeks; the garage gave priority to other work and took eight weeks. It was held by the Court of Appeal that they had failed to carry out the work within a reasonable time and were therefore liable in damages.[42]

(3)   Can the consumer go further and claim to be discharged from the contract altogether? This depends on whether time is "of the essence", i.e. a vital term or, in sale of goods language, a condition. The following statement in *Halsbury's Laws of England* has received judicial approval:

---

[40]   For the assessment of damages, see paras 8.54–8.72 below.
[41]   s.52(3).
[42]   [1968] 1 W.L.R. 1498.

Time will not be considered to be of the essence unless (1) the parties expressly stipulate that conditions as to time must be strictly complied with, or (2) the nature of the subject-matter of the contract or the surrounding circumstances show that time should be considered to be of the essence.[43]

It is probably true to say that under a contract to supply goods or services to a consumer a failure to observe the agreed performance date is not of itself a repudiation of the contract (although see the provisions on delivery of goods in s.28 of the CRA 2015, discussed above). There can, of course, be difficult cases; what about a tour operator who agrees to provide his client with a 15-day holiday in Majorca starting on 1 August but is prevented from carrying out that obligation by reason of industrial action for which he is not responsible? It could be argued that if he is unable to transport his clients on 1 August, he will have broken an essential term of the contract which enables the clients to treat the contract as discharged; alternatively, it might be argued that the contract has been frustrated.[44]

(4) If a reasonable time has elapsed, or if the breach of an essential time clause has been waived, the consumer can serve a notice fixing a time for performance. The time limit in this notice must itself be a reasonable one, but subject to this the consumer can treat the contract as discharged if the supplier fails to perform by the date specified in the notice.[45]

(5) Thus the consumer should always make it clear, in appropriate cases, that the date for performance is vital, e.g. by stating expressly that "time is of the essence".

7. THE PRICE SEEMS RATHER HIGH

Goods

In the case of sale of goods it is fairly rare to find an agreement without a price; indeed the absence of a price may indicate that the parties are still negotiating and that consequently there is no contract at all.[46] Section 8 of the 1979 Act, which is more appropriate to a commercial contract but continues to apply to consumer contracts, provides that the price can be fixed by the contract itself, in manner thereby agreed or by usage. It then goes on to provide that if the price is not fixed in this way, the buyer must pay a reasonable price for the goods.

6.44

---

[43] *Halsbury's Laws of England* (4th edn), Vol.9, para.481, approved by Lord Simon in *United Scientific Holdings Ltd v Burnley Council* [1978] A.C. 904 HL. See also *Bunge Corp v Tradax S.A.* [1981] 1 W.L.R. 711 HL.
[44] In practice the contract will usually deal with the matter in accordance with the ABTA Code of Practice.
[45] *Charles Rickards Ltd v Oppenheim* [1950] 1 K.B. 616 CA.
[46] *May and Butcher v R.* [1934] 2 K.B. 17.

Services

6.45   In the case of services, it is rather more common to call in a repairer or to take a car for a service without agreeing a charge in advance. In such a case the supplier is entitled to claim a reasonable charge by virtue of s.51 of the CRA 2015[47]:

> (1) This section applies to a contract to supply a service if—
>
> > (a) the consumer has not paid a price or other consideration for the service,
> > (b) the contract does not expressly fix a price or other consideration, and does not say how it is to be fixed, and
> > (c) anything that is to be treated under section 50 as included in the contract does not fix a price or other consideration either.
>
> (2) In that case the contract is to be treated as including a term that the consumer must pay a reasonable price for the service, and no more.
>
> (3) What is a reasonable price is a question of fact.

This, of course, is much easier said than done. If a consumer feels that the charge is too high the onus will be on him to find expert evidence to substantiate his claim. He will also be put to great practical inconvenience if the supplier has goods belonging to a consumer in his possession (e.g. a car or a watch being repaired) and refuses to release them until he has been paid. The consumer should also be very careful to limit his potential liability. Instead of saying "the car is starting badly—put it right" he should say "tell me if the work is going to cost more than £100".

Estimates

6.46   Incidentally, what about an "estimate"? If an estimate amounts to an offer which is accepted, the estimate will become the contract price.[48] This, however, is rather unusual and the general rule is that the estimate is not legally binding but merely an indication of the likely charge. If the supplier's bill is much higher than the estimates the court might take the estimate into account in fixing a "reasonable charge". In contrast, a "quotation" is more likely to be an offer to do the job for the quoted charge.[49]

Fixed price contracts

6.47   A very helpful case on the significance of the word "estimate" and whether or not a contract is for a fixed charge (or "fixed price" to use the more usual expression) is the recent Court of Appeal decision in *Sykes v Packham*

---

[47] Provided that there is a "contract" for the service it does not have to be in the course of a business—although it usually is.

[48] *Croshaw v Pritchard* (1899) 16 T.L.R. 45.

[49] See, e.g. VBRA Code, at para.11.23 below.

(t/a Bathroom Specialists).[50] The appellants (S) appealed to the Court of Appeal against the decision on a domestic building contract awarding the respondents (P) a reasonable price for the work done and materials supplied. S claimed that there was a fixed price contract for the sum given in P's "estimate". P cross-appealed on the grounds that it was a cost-plus contract.

The court decided that they were both wrong! There was an implied agreement that a reasonable price would be paid. It was not a cost-plus contract, for as the trial judge had pointed out, there was "no evidence as to what the 'plus' would be". Nor was it a fixed price contract. The document was called an "estimate", but Gross LJ stated at para.23, "I do not think there is any 'magic' in the label 'estimate' . . . I do not regard that label as a term of art." However, the context and the language of the estimate are important. Here the estimate contained round figures and wording such as "approximate materials and equipment" and "approximate labour and expenses costs". (Neither Gross LJ nor counsel mentioned the 1982 Act or s.15. The authors are disappointed that the judiciary appeared to be unaware of the Act even after 30 years—but are hopeful that the new provision in s.51 of the CRA 2015 may gain greater recognition.)

What if the consumer claims that the fixed price is excessive? For example, when the weather is freezing and there are burst pipes everywhere, some plumbers charge very high call-out charges which are agreed in advance on the telephone by householders in an anxious state and not in a mood to bargain. Does the court have power to intervene and reduce the charge to a reasonable one? The answer is "no".

Overcharging a crime?

A different attack on rogue traders may occasionally be launched under **6.48** the criminal law. It is a common scam for itinerant contractors to persuade elderly or vulnerable people that their roofs need repairing or front drives resurfacing and to charge and take cash for exorbitant sums for very little work, which is often unnecessary. In *R. v Baker (Mark)*[51] the Court of Appeal took a severe view of such conduct (though reducing the trial judge's sentences) and imposed sentences of six years' imprisonment for obtaining property by deception on two members of a gang of rogue builders who defrauded 43 householders of £800,000 over four and a half years. Usually they pretended that a roof needed urgent repair. One victim with learning difficulties handed over £75,000.

Extra work

Can a supplier of services claim an additional amount if additional work **6.49** is required? This again depends on what the parties have agreed. If, for example, a builder is employed to convert a loft at a fixed price, the onus will be on him to ensure that the work will comply with the local bye-laws and

---

[50] [2011] EWCA Civ 608.
[51] [2011] EWCA Crim 150.

CHAPTER SEVEN

"THE HOLIDAY WAS A NIGHTMARE"

Legal relationship between the parties

The Law Commission Second Report on Exemption Clauses[1] touches on **7.01** an interesting and difficult question—the precise legal relationship between the customer and the other organisations involved in providing a package holiday (the travel agent, the tour operator, the hotel and the airline).

It is suggested that generally the position is as follows. The customer makes only one contract with one legal entity—the tour operator.[2] This is effected via the travel agent who acts on behalf of the tour operator, not the customer.[3] As the agent is normally known to be acting for a named principal, it will incur no personal responsibility to the customer on the contract.

The contracts for accommodation and transportation are made by the tour **7.02** operator on his own account: only he is responsible to the hotel and airline for these costs, even though the services will be supplied by them to the tour operator's customer. Clearly the tour operator is under an implied obligation to the customer to pay the necessary sums to the carrier and hotel to enable the customer to travel and to stay at the chosen resort without additional payment; if he fails to do so, so that the carrier or hotel refuse to provide their services to the customer unless the customer pays for them direct, the tour operator will have broken the contract with the customer and be liable in damages for such additional charges. Of course, if he does not provide the promised accommodation and facilities, he will be liable for breach of contract too.[4] Damages for mental distress are important here.[5]

Although the travel agent is not a party to the main holiday contract, he may incur liability to the customer in other ways. If he makes untrue statements to the customer about the subject-matter of the contract, for example, hotel amenities, he may be liable (1) in tort for deceit or negligence, or (2) for breach of an implied warranty of authority if the statement is outside his actual authority. Further, he may be in breach of a collateral contract between himself and the customer—a contract collateral to the main contract between the tour operator and the customer. Such rights against the travel agent are unlikely to be needed unless the tour operator is unable to meet

[1] Law Com. No. 69 (1975), para.126.
[2] See Lord Scarman in *Wings Ltd v Ellis* [1984] 3 All E.R. 577 at 586.
[3] For a discussion of this tripartite relationship, paricularly in relation to payment by credit card, see *Connected Lender Liability* (OFT, March 1994), pp.28–30.
[4] See the cases cited in para.8.68 below.
[5] See para.8.63 below.

his responsibilities under the main contract, e.g. because he is bankrupt or in liquidation.

Package Travel Regulations

7.03 The consumer's position has been considerably strengthened by legislation passed to comply with the EC Directive on Package Travel, Package Holidays and Package Tours (90/314).

The Directive was implemented in the UK by the Package Travel, Package Holidays and Package Tours Regulations 1992 (the 1992 Regulations).[6] They keep closely to the wording of the Directive. Clearly the Government was anxious not to be taken to the European Court of Justice, as happened in the field of employment law and sex discrimination, for failure properly to translate European law into national law; the safest route then is to use the same phrases as the Directive (so-called "copy out").

We shall comment on the main provisions, particularly where they improve the consumer's position.

Package

7.04 The 1992 Regulations do not apply to travel or accommodation booked separately, for example, a flight or hotel. Regulation 2(1) defines "package" as follows:

> "package" means the pre-arranged combination of at least two of the following components when sold or offered for sale at an inclusive price and when the service covers a period of more than twenty-four hours or includes overnight accommodation:
>
> (a) transport;
> (b) accommodation;
> (c) other tourist services not ancillary to transport or accommodation and accounting for a significant proportion of the package.

It can be seen that there must be at least two of the three elements. Generally, of course, the package will comprise travel by aircraft, coach, ship or train coupled with accommodation[7] in a hotel, apartment or even on the ship itself in the case of a cruise. However, it is not vital for transport to be included as the package may consist of items (b) and (c). An example given in the Consultation Document *Implementation of EC Directive on Package Travel, Package Holidays and Package Tours (arts 1–6)* (February 1992) by the Department of Trade and Industry suggests that a weekend at a hotel where the price included access to fishing rights or to a golf course, where guests do not generally have these benefits, would be "other tourist services" thus making the arrangement a "package".

---

[6] SI 1992/3288.

[7] In *Administrative Proceedings Concerning AFS Intercultural Programs Finland RY*, *The Times*, 4 March 1999, the ECJ decided that the Directive did not apply to a student exchange, where the student was treated as a member of the host family free of charge.

Organiser and retailer

These terms are used in reg.2(1) to describe the tour operator and travel **7.05**
agent.

Information

There are a number of regulations about information to be given to the **7.06**
consumer. Regulation 5 coupled with Sch.1 prescribes the information to be
included in brochures, e.g. type of accommodation, inclusion of meals, itinerary, price and deposit.

Regulation 7 deals with information to be provided "before a contract
is concluded". This covers such matters as passport and visa requirements,
health formalities and importantly "the arrangements for security for the
money paid over and (where applicable) for the repatriation of the consumer
in the event of insolvency".

This is supplemented by reg.8 which deals with information to be provided "in good time before the start of the journey", for example, the times
and places of intermediate stops and transport connections, and the name,
address and telephone number of any local representative or agent.

We now come to the contents and form of the contract itself which is
governed by reg.9. A written copy of the terms of the contract must be
supplied to the consumer. Depending on the nature of the package, the
contract must contain at least the elements specified in Sch.2. This is set out
verbatim below in view of the importance of these details to the consumer
or adviser.

Elements to be included in the contract if relevant to the particular package
(1) The travel destination(s) and, where periods of stay are involved, the rel- **7.07**
    evant periods, with dates.
(2) The means, characteristics and categories of transport to be used and the
    dates, times and points of departure and return.
(3) Where the package includes accommodation, its location, its tourist cat-
    egory or degree of comfort, its main features and, where the accommoda-
    tion is to be provided in a member State, its compliance with the rules of
    that member State.
(4) The meals which are included in the package.
(5) Whether a minimum number of persons is required for the package to
    take place and, if so, the deadline for informing the consumer in the event
    of cancellation.
(6) The itinerary.
(7) Visits, excursions or other services which are included in the total price
    agreed for the package.
(8) The name and address of the organiser, the retailer and, where appropri-
    ate, the insurer.
(9) The price of the package, if the price may be revised in accordance with
    the term which may be included in the contract under regulation 11, an
    indication of the possibility of such price revisions, and an indication of
    any dues, taxes or fees chargeable for certain services (landing, embarka-
    tion or disembarkation fees at ports and airports and tourist taxes) where
    such costs are not included in the package.
(10) The payment schedule and method of payment.

(11) Special requirements which the consumer has communicated to the organiser or retailer when making the booking and which both have accepted.

(12) The periods within which the consumer must make any complaint about the failure to perform or the inadequate performance of the contract.

Regulation 9(3) states that it is "an implied condition" that the other party complies with the provisions of the regulation, so the consumer will be able to rescind the contract in the event of non-compliance—a serious sanction which should encourage organisers to keep to the rules.

Prices

7.08 Regulation 11 deals with price revisions. Prices are fixed unless the contract "states precisely how the revised price is to be calculated". Even then price revisions are permitted only for variations in transport costs, taxes or exchange rates. No increase can be made during the 30 days before departure or if less than two per cent.

Cancellation and alteration

7.09 There are provisions in regs 12 and 13 entitling the consumer to cancel or to accept an alternative package, with compensation if appropriate, e.g. if the organiser "is constrained to alter significantly an essential term". Force majeure excuses the organiser.

Implied warranties

7.10 Regulation 6 provides that "the particulars in the brochure . . . shall constitute implied warranties . . . for the purposes of any contract to which the particulars relate". The effect is that a consumer will be able to recover damages for breach of warranty, where the services provided by the organiser do not precisely match their description. There will be no need for the consumer to resort to s.13 of the Supply of Goods and Services Act 1982, by proving that the organiser had not exercised reasonable care and skill in the provision of the services, for the warranty implied by reg.6 imposes strict liability. There is one catch, however, for the consumer: there is no implied warranty where the brochure contains an express statement that changes may be made in the particulars contained in it and such changes are "clearly communicated to the consumer before a contract is concluded".

Liability

7.11 Regulation 15 provides that the organiser "is liable to the consumer for the proper performance of the obligations under the contract, irrespective of whether such obligations are to be performed by that other party or by other suppliers of services". This covers liability for sub-contractors too which, as explained in para.7.01 above, is already the legal position in the UK, but it does no harm for the regulation to spell this out.

"Proper performance" does not impose strict liability on the organiser or retailer: it is fault-based.[8]

Unfortunately it goes on to permit limitation clauses which are "not unreasonable". This is the same as the UK position under s.3 of the Unfair Contract Terms Act 1977.

One point for the consumer to watch is that complaints must be speedy— "at the earliest opportunity" to the organiser and to the supplier of the services.

Assignment

One valuable new right is that the consumer may transfer his booking to a third party. However, reg.10 confines this possibility to a case where "the consumer is prevented from proceeding with the package". Will this cover only force majeure circumstances, e.g. illness? It would appear so. A change of mind would not be enough.

7.12

Insolvency

Article 7 of the Directive requires the organiser to prove that there is "security" for refunds and repatriation in the event of insolvency. Regulation 16 obliges the other party to the contract to "be able to provide sufficient evidence of security" for these matters. The organiser is given the option of pursuing a number of different routes: regs 17 to 20 permit bonds, insurance[9] or trust funds to be used. Further, none of these requirements applies where the package is covered by the Civil Aviation (Air Travel Organisers' Licensing) Regulations 1972.[10]

Consumers should protect themselves by paying the tour operator (or hotel, airline, etc., if it is not a "package") by credit card to gain the benefit of s.75 of the Consumer Credit Act 1974.[11] This is vital in these difficult economic times with unexpected insolvencies such as Globespan.

7.13

Enforcement and penalties

Apart from giving the consumer certain contractual rights for breach of the implied terms the 1992 Regulations may result in criminal sanctions against the organiser or retailer. Various criminal offences are scattered throughout the 1992 Regulations. As usual with consumer protection legislation they are enforced by trading standards officers. The penalty for contravention is a fine; a prison sentence cannot be imposed even where the defendant is convicted on indictment.

7.14

---

[8] *Hone v Going Places Leisure Travel Ltd* [2001] 1 All E.R. (D) 102 CA. See also *Codd v Thomson Tour Operators Ltd, The Times*, 20 October 2000 (local, not British, safety standards applied where boy injured in Spanish hotel lift).
[9] See Package Tours (Amendment) Regulations 1995 (SI 1995/1648).
[10] SI 1972/223.
[11] See para.24.08 below. See also, Rutherford, *"Travel agents and the use of credit cards in the travel trade"* (1994) 144 N.L.J. 668.

Distress

7.15   If the tour operator, hotel, airline or other supplier breaks the contract with
the customer, then the customer may recover damages for breach of contract. We discuss remedies in Chapter Eight including the important head of
damages in this context—mental distress, upset, disappointment and injured
feelings (the cases in paras 8.63 and 8.68 below are particularly relevant).

Airline cancellations and delays: EC Regulation 261/2004[12]

7.16   Passengers are frequently delayed at airports in two situations. (1) Sometimes
the delay is caused by overbooking. The airlines assume that some passengers
will prove to be "no shows" and, if more passengers turn up than antici-
pated, the surplus passengers are "denied boarding" and "bumped" onto
later flights. (2) More often delays in take-off or cancellations are caused by
aircraft arriving late or having technical faults or volcanic ash, hurricanes or
snow.

EC Regulation 261/2004 was adopted to protect airline passengers in the
above situations. (The EC Regulation is "directly applicable" and so has not
been transposed into UK law; any claim is based on the Regulation itself.)

It covers three classes of travel disruption—*denied boarding, cancellation*[13]
and delay. The rules are complicated and, although we indicate below sign-
posts through the forest of detail, readers are advised to consult concurrently
the Directive itself set out in Appendix Two.

Not surprisingly it does not cover travel on all airlines throughout the
world. Article 3 applies only to passengers departing (a) from an EU airport
(to any destination on any airline); (b) from outside the EU to an EU airport
on an EU airline. For example, an internal flight in the USA or Australia is not
covered, nor is a flight from India to London on an Arabian or Asian airline.

Two main types of protection are given:

(1) "Compensation". This is quantified by art.7.

(2) "Assistance". This is of two kinds. Article 8 gives a "right to reimbursement or re-routing". Article 9 gives a "right to care".

These protective provisions will now be set out in tabular form for ease of
reference.

Compensation: art.7

7.17   The amount of compensation depends on the length of the flight:

- €250—flights up to 1,500 km;

- €400—flights within EU over 1,500 km, and

---

[12] Set out in Appendix Two.
[13] "Denied boarding" and "cancellation" are defined in art.2.

other flights between 1,500 and 3,500 km; or

- €600—all other flights.

Article 7(2) permits a 50 per cent reduction in some cases where re-routing is offered.

Compensation may be available in three situations:

- denied boarding (art.4);
- cancellation (art.5) (but see para.7.24 below); and
- delay of three hours or more (see below).

Reimbursement or re-routing: art.8

Passengers entitled to this kind of assistance must be offered a choice **7.18** between:

(1) reimbursement of the cost of the ticket and a return flight to their point of departure; or

(2) re-routing to their destination at the earliest opportunity; or

(3) re-routing at a later date

in the following circumstances:

- denied boarding (art.4);
- cancellation (art.5(1)(a));
- delay of at least five hours (but not re-routing in this case) (art.6(1) (c)).

Care: art.9

This kind of assistance comprises the trio of items specified in art.9(1): **7.19**

(a) meals and refreshments;

(b) hotel where a stay of a night or more becomes necessary;

(c) transport to the hotel;

and a fourth in art.9(2):

(d) two phone calls, telex or fax messages or emails.

Passengers have a right to all or some of these when:

- denied boarding—all four (art.4);
- cancellation—(a) and (d) plus, where re-routing, (b) and (c) (art.5(1));

• delay—up to all four depending on the length of the delay and of the flight (art.6).

Information for passengers: art.14

7.20 How can passengers be expected to know and remember these complex protective measures, when met with long delays, cancellation or other problems at an airport? The answer is that there should be no need to do so, as art.14 caters for this in two ways. Article 14(1) provides that at check-in a "clearly legible notice" must be displayed with this text:

> "If you are denied boarding or if your flight is cancelled or delayed for at least two hours, ask at the check-in counter or boarding gate for the text stating your rights, particularly with regard to compensation and assistance."

This is backed up by art.14(2). In the same circumstances the airline must provide each passenger with "a written notice setting out the rules for compensation and assistance".

Not all airlines comply with these rules. This caused severe criticism of British Airways when Heathrow Terminal 5 had just opened and long delays were caused by faults in the baggage handling equipment.

Compensation for "long delay"

7.21 It seems clear from the wording of art.6 that delay, however long, gives no right to compensation; for it does not refer to art.7 and mentions specifically "assistance"—and only "assistance"—four times. Such clarity has been clouded by the European Court of Justice (Grand Chamber) which decided in two Joined Cases on 23 October 2012 that where the delay is for three hours or more compensation under art.7 is available: *Emeka Nelson v Deutsche Lufthansa AG* (C-581/10) and *TUI Travel Plc and Others v Civil Aviation Authority* (C-629/10). The reasoning is impeccable:

(1) Preamble (1) to the Regulations states: "Action by the Community in the field of air transport should aim . . . at ensuring a high level of protection for passengers".

(2) Preamble (2) points out "Denied boarding and cancellation or long delay of flights cause serious trouble and inconvenience to passengers".

(3) "Passengers whose flights are delayed and those whose flights are cancelled must be considered as being in comparable situations, for the purposes of compensation" (ECJ judgment, para.34) and "the principle of equal treatment requires that comparable situations must not be treated differently" (para.33).

(4) So "to alleviate such unequal treatment" passengers whose flights are subject to long delay or cancelled should receive the same compensation (para.38). "The inconvenience suffered by those two groups is the same" (para.36).

(5) But "long delay" is defined as "equal to or in excess of three hours" (para.54).

The ruling of the court was:

"Articles 5 to 7 of Regulation (EC) No 261/2004 . . . must be interpreted as meaning that passengers whose flights are delayed are entitled to compensation under that regulation where they suffer, on account of such flights, a loss of time equal to or in excess of three hours, that is, where they reach their final destination three hours or more after the arrival time originally scheduled by the carrier."

While we consider it likely that an English court would not have given arts 6 and 7 such an interpretation (for there is no ambiguity in art.6 and in contrast arts 4 and 5 both mention "compensation"—presumably an intentional distinction), it was a beneficial result for consumers.

Montreal Convention

A related point also came up for decision in the *Nelson* case. Was there a **7.22** conflict or overlap between the Regulation and the Montreal Convention in relation to the delay? Article 19 of the Convention provides that an air "carrier is liable for damage occasioned by delay". The ECJ held that "damage" means that the damage is "individual to the passengers depending on the various losses sustained by them" (para.50). It does not include a loss of time which is an inconvenience and "is suffered identically by all passengers whose flights are delayed" and whose loss can be redressed "by a standardised measure" (para.52). That loss falls within the Regulation, whereas other damage or loss[14] caused by delay falls within the Montreal Convention (para.58).

In *Dawson v Thomson Airways Ltd*[15] the Court of Appeal had to consider another conflict between the two regimes. Was the period of limitation for claims for compensation under art.7 governed by European law and therefore by the national law of the relevant country (six years in England) or by the Convention (two years: art.35)?

Mr Dawson began proceedings for delay just before the six year period expired and was awarded compensation. The airline argued that he was too late, because the Convention applied, and appealed. The Court of Appeal dismissed the appeal: it was bound to follow decisions of the ECJ such as *Nelson* and *More*[16] that art.7 claims fall outside the scope of the Convention.

A Supreme Court case about the Montreal Convention, again with a possible **7.23** conflict with European law, is *Hook v British Airways Plc, Stott v Thomas Cook Tour Operators Ltd*.[17]

---

[14] *Cowden v British Airways Plc* [2009] 2 Lloyd's Rep. 653: loss does not include distress or loss of enjoyment.
[15] [2014] EWCA Civ 845.
[16] *Cuadrench More v KoninklijkeLuchtvaart Maatschappij N.V.* (C-139/11) (case brought in Spain—Spanish limitation period of 10 years applied). See also *Sturgeon v Condor Flugdienst G.m.b.H* (C-402/07 and C-432/07).
[17] [2014] UKSC 15.

Mr Stott was disabled and a permanent wheel-chair user. He claimed damages for distress, humiliation and injury to feelings (but not personal injury) caused by the tour operator's failure to arrange proper provision for him on a flight from Greece contrary to UK and European disability regulations.

Thomas Cook argued that art.29 of the Convention applied.

As Lord Toulson stated, it is "intended to deal comprehensively with the carrier's liability for whatever may physically happen to passengers between embarkation and disembarkation" (para.61). As he explained, the question whether the claim is outside the substantive or temporal scope of the Convention "depends entirely on the proper interpretation of the scope of that Convention". The case "does not in truth involve a question of European law" (para.59).

Thus as no physical injury occurred during the flight and the Convention applied, the claim failed.

Both Lord Toulson and Lady Hale suggested that it was time for the Convention to be amended to take account of equality rights.

Extraordinary circumstances

7.24   The airline need not pay compensation if it can prove that the cancellation was caused by "extraordinary circumstances which could not have been avoided even if all reasonable measures had been taken".[18] Examples are aircraft grounded by volcanic ash from Iceland or a strike by air traffic controllers.

There are particular problems where a technical fault is the cause. Are these "extraordinary circumstances"? Happily for passengers the answer to the last question is "no". In *Wallentin-Hermann v Alitalia-Linee Aeree Italiane SpA* (C–549/07)[19] the European Court of Justice decided that "technical problems which came to light during maintenance of aircraft, or on account of failure to carry out such maintenance, could not constitute, in themselves, 'extraordinary circumstances'".

In *Jet2.Com Ltd v Huzar*[20] the Court of Appeal reached a similar conclusion in dismissing an appeal by the airline against an award of compensation for delay under art.7(1)(b).

H was delayed for 27 hours because the aircraft had a wiring defect, which was unforeseen and unforeseeable in that it could not have been prevented by prior maintenance or visual inspection. The airline argued that this was an "extraordinary circumstance".

The court agreed with the decision in *Wallentin-Hermann* and stressed the following points.

The focus should be on the source of the problem not its resolution. The concept of "extraordinary circumstances" required that they were out of the ordinary. Difficult technical problems arose in the ordinary operation of a carrier's activity. They were part of the wear and tear. Some were foreseeable and some were not. The fact that a technical problem was unforeseeable did not mean it was unexpected. In this case there were no extraordinary circumstances and the airline must pay compensation.

[18] art.5(3).
[19] *The Times*, 16 February 2009.
[20] [2014] EWCA Civ 791.

Returning to volcanic ash, this was the cause of a cancellation and a long **7.25** delay in Portugal for an Irish passenger in February 2010. Was the cause "extraordinary circumstances"? The case of *Denise McDonagh v Ryanair Ltd* (C-12/11) came before the European Court of Justice (Third Chamber) whose judgment was delivered on 31 January 2013. The facts were these.

> McD was stranded in Portugal for a week when her Ryanair flight was cancelled because of the ash. She incurred hotel expenses of about €1,000. Ryanair refused to pay them. She claimed them under arts 5(1)(b) and 9(1)(b) and (c). She did not seek compensation, accepting that the closure of air space because of the ash was "extraordinary circumstances". Ryanair's strange argument was that the circumstances were super extraordinary! This argument about the meaning of art.5(3) was otiose, since there is no such defence when "assistance" is the basis of the claim.

The ECJ upheld McD's claim for hotel expenses. The court ruled that the closure of European airspace as a result of the eruption of the volcano constituted extraordinary circumstances, but it did "not release air carriers from their obligations in arts 5(1)(b) and 9 to provide care".

CHAPTER EIGHT

"WHAT ARE MY REMEDIES?"

In the previous seven chapters we have considered some of the supplier's **8.01** basic obligations. We now come to the subject of remedies which, as stated in the Preface to the First Edition, is what this book is all about; it is also the area in which the consumer is most likely to seek legal advice. In practice three questions most frequently arise, namely (a) what are the consumer's remedies, (b) can they be excluded, and (c) how can they be enforced? These topics are considered in this chapter and the four following ones.

One preliminary point can be made. This chapter and the next two are concerned with questions of strict law. In Chapter Eleven we shall see that in many cases consumers may be able to sidestep the worry, uncertainty and expense of litigation as a result of voluntary codes of practice drawn up by a number of trade and professional associations with the encouragement of the Trading Standards Institute. We shall also see that a complaint to a trading standards department can lead to a prosecution in certain cases and that this, in turn, can lead to a compensation order.[1]

This chapter is divided into four main parts, namely: **8.02**

1. Remedies for misrepresentation.

2. Remedies for unfair practices under the Consumer Protection (Amendment) Regulations 2014

3. Remedies for breach of contract.

4. Remedies in tort.

By way of final introduction, it should be noted that there have been significant developments in recent years, and especially in the past year, in relation to remedies for defective goods, digital content and services, and in relation to remedies for unfair practices. So, for instance, the Consumer Protection (Amendment) Regulations 2014 introduced new statutory remedies for unfair practices. In addition, the EU-inspired Sale and Supply of Goods to Consumers Regulations 2002 had amended the Sale of Goods Act 1979 (the 1979 Act) and the Supply of Goods and Services Act 1982 (the SGSA), by introducing new remedies (e.g. repair and replacement) for consumers. However, the Consumer Rights Act 2015 now covers these and other remedies for defective goods; extends these remedies to other supply of goods transactions; extends most of

---

[1] See para.16.02 below.

these remedies to digital content transactions; changes the law on the "short term right to reject" goods; and introduces new remedies for defective services. All of these topics will be analysed and explained in this chapter.

1. REMEDIES FOR MISREPRESENTATION

8.03 The remedies for misrepresentation can be summarised as follows:

(1) Fraudulent misrepresentation:

    (a) damages in tort for deceit;
    (b) rescission.

(2) Negligent misrepresentation:

    (a) damages under s.2(1) of the Misrepresentation Act 1967 (the 1967 Act);
    (b) rescission (or damages in lieu under s.2(2) of the 1967 Act).

(3) "Innocent" misrepresentation (i.e. neither fraudulent nor negligent):

    rescission (or damages in lieu under s.2(2) of the 1967 Act).

These matters will now be considered.

Fraudulent misrepresentation

8.04 A person commits the tort of deceit (or fraud) if he makes a false statement of fact knowingly, without belief in its truth, or recklessly (i.e. careless whether true or false) with the intention that it should be acted upon by the claimant who does act on it and thereby suffers damage.[2] In practice, fraud is notoriously hard to prove. If, however, the consumer can prove that, for example, the dealer deliberately misrepresented the age or mileage of a car then, as we have seen, he may have the remedies of damages and/or rescission.[3] If he rescinds the contract he can claim to be put back into his pre-contractual position so that, for example, he can recover any part of the price which he has paid. The action for damages can be considered (a) if the innocent party does not wish to rescind, (b) if one of the bars to rescission applies,[4] or (c) if he has suffered damage over and above the price.

What is the measure of damages for fraudulent misrepresentation? The rules are designed to prove compensation for all loss flowing directly from the fraud, whether reasonably foreseeable or not. Thus, in a sale of goods or land the starting point is the difference (if any) between the price paid by the consumer and the true value of the goods or land.[5] Money spent on repair

---

[2] See the leading case of *Derry v Peek* (1889) 14 App.Cas. 337 HL.
[3] See para.3.06 above.
[4] See paras 8.07–8.08 below.
[5] *Doyle v Olby (Ironmongers) Ltd* [1969] 2 Q.B. 158—a case of the sale of a business.

and improvement before discovering the fraud can also be recovered[6] but not damages for loss of bargain.[7] Damages for personal injury or damage to property can also be recovered.[8] The onus is on the consumer to prove loss and his action will fail if he cannot do so.[9]

Negligent misrepresentation

Until the passing of the 1967 Act the court had no general power to award damages for a non-fraudulent misrepresentation—hence the importance then of proving that there had been a breach of a contractual term.[10] A Law Reform Committee recommended a change in the law and accordingly s.2(1) of the 1967 Act was passed to give a statutory right to damages in certain cases. It reads: **8.05**

> Where a person has entered into a contract after a misrepresentation has been made to him by another party thereto and as a result thereof he has suffered loss then if the person making the representation would be liable in damages in respect thereof had the representation been made fraudulently, that person shall be so liable notwithstanding that the misrepresentation was not made fraudulently, unless he proves that he had reasonable grounds to believe and did believe up to the time that the contract was made that the facts represented were true.

It is clear from the case of *Howard Marine & Dredging Co Ltd v A Ogden & Son (Excavation) Ltd*[11] that a s.2(1) claim is a claim in tort, and the approach in relation to a claim for damages is the same as for fraud.[12] Accordingly, when a claim is brought under s.2(1), the courts may be less likely to find that there has been a misrepresentation in the first place.[13] However, once it has been established that there is a misrepresentation, the effect of s.2(1) is that the misrepresentor must "prove that he had reasonable grounds" otherwise he will be liable under s.2(1). **8.06**

We have seen that the object of damages in tort is to put the innocent party in the same position *as if the contract had never been made*. This can be contrasted with a different rule in contract where the damages are designed

---

[6] As above.

[7] *East v Maurer* [1991] 1 W.L.R. 461 (another business sale; damages awarded for the profits which the plaintiff would have earned if the false statement had not been made).

[8] *Langridge v Levy* (1838) 4 M. & W. 337—exploding gun.

[9] *Latkter v General Guarantee Finance Ltd* [2001] EWCA Civ 875—a case involving the purchase of a Triumph Thunderbird motorbike and a (disputed) representation that it was a 1997 model.

[10] See para.3.06 above.

[11] [1978] Q.B. 574. See also *Naughton v O'Callaghan* [1990] 3 All E.R. 191 (misdescription of race-horse).

[12] *Naughton v O'Callaghan* [1990] 3 All E.R. 191 at 197. See also *Royscot Trust Ltd v Rogerson* [1991] 2 Q.B. 297 CA.

[13] e.g. in applying the inducement requirement, the courts may not consider it to be sufficient that a false statement has been observed or considered by the misrepresentee, or even played supporting role in his decision to enter the contract; rather they may insist that the statement has been a factor that was sufficiently important to be called a real and substantial part of what induced him to enter the contract. See *Avon Plc v Swire Fraser (a firm)* [2000] 1 All ER (Comm) 573 at 633, and *Raiffeisen Zentralbank Osterreich v Royal Bank of Scotland Plc* [2010] EWHC 1392 (Comm); [2011] 1 Lloyds Rep. 123 (85).

to put the innocent party in the same position *as if the contract had been per-formed*. Thus damages for loss of bargain are appropriate to contract but not to tort (the case of *Watts v Spence*,[14] where damages for loss of bargain were awarded under s.2(1) of the 1967 Act, must be regarded as wrongly decided and the judge in a later case refused to follow it).[15]

Rescission

8.07 We can now turn to the equitable remedy of rescission. This has already been mentioned[16] and it only remains to consider the cases where it is not available. There are four well-established bars to rescission and these can be summarised as follows:

(a) where the parties can no longer be restored to their previous position. Thus the right to rescission would disappear if goods were destroyed before the buyer had elected to rescind;

(b) where third party rights have been acquired. Perhaps the clearest example is where B, by misrepresentation, persuades S to sell the goods to B and then resells the goods to C[17];

(c) where the innocent party has affirmed the contract with knowledge of the misrepresentation[18];

(d) where the innocent party has been guilty of unreasonable delay. In the well-known case of *Leaf v International Galleries*,[19] the buyer of a painting, which was described as by J. Constable, sought to rescind for misrepresentation five years after making the contract on discovering that it was the work of another artist. The Court of Appeal held that it was far too late to rescind. In the words of Jenkins LJ:

> "If he is allowed to wait five, ten or twenty years and then re-open the bargain, there can be no finality at all."

If the buyer had claimed damages for breach of the term as to description[20] the claim would presumably have been unanswerable, as it would have been within the six year limitation period for a breach of contract claim.

---

[14] [1976] Ch. 165.
[15] *Cemp Properties (UK) v Dentsply Research and Development Corp (No.2)* [1989] 37 E.G. 126. See also here, *Royscot Trust Ltd v Rogerson* [1991] 2 Q.B. 297 CA, confirming that the correct measure of damages under s.2(1) is the reliance measure.
[16] Above, when discussing fraudulent misrepresentation.
[17] See s.23 of the 1979 Act, see also para.2.09 above.
[18] *Long v Lloyd* [1958] 2 All E.R. 402.
[19] [1950] 2 K.B. 86.
[20] See paras 3.24–3.34 above. But see *Harlingdon and Leinster Enterprises v Christopher Hull Fine Art* [1991] Q.B. 564 (see also para.3.29 above).

Statutory restriction on rescission

If none of these four bars applies, the general rule is that the innocent party   **8.08**
can rescind the contract. The exercise of this remedy can have far-reaching
results.

> Suppose that P buys a house from V for £200,000. V makes a non-fraudulent
> misrepresentation relating to the drains; the defect will cost £800 to put right. V
> has spent the whole of the £200,000 in buying another house.

If P were to rescind, V would have to find £200,000 (and might well be rendered homeless) because of a statement which caused damage of only £800.
It was clearly with this kind of case in mind that s.2(2) of the 1967 Act was
enacted. It provides that

> where a person has entered into a contract after a misrepresentation has been
> made to him otherwise than fraudulently, and he would be entitled, by reason
> of the misrepresentation, to rescind the contract, then, if it is claimed in any
> proceedings arising out of the contract, that the contract ought to be or has been
> rescinded, the court or arbitrator may declare the contract subsisting and award
> damages in lieu of rescission, if of opinion that it would be equitable to do so,
> having regard to the nature of the misrepresentation and the loss that would be
> caused by it if the contract was upheld, as well as to the loss that rescission would
> cause to the other party.

Thus, in the above example, the court would probably refuse rescission and
award P damages of £800.

This power to award discretionary damages only applies where a person
"would be entitled . . . to rescind the contract". In earlier editions of this book
we suggested that this means that damages could be awarded under s.2(2)
only if the innocent party had a subsisting right to rescind at the date of the
hearing, but there are conflicting decisions as to whether this is so.[21]

"Innocent" misrepresentation

If the misrepresentation is neither fraudulent nor negligent, the only possi-   **8.09**
ble remedy is rescission. This is subject to the usual equitable bars[22] and the
court's discretionary power under s.2(2) to award damages in lieu of rescission.

Exclusion clauses

A clause excluding liability for misrepresentation or cutting down the con-   **8.10**
sumer's remedies for misrepresentation is only valid if it satisfies the test of
"fairness".[23]

---

[21] *Thomas Witter Ltd v TPB Industries Ltd* [1996] 2 All E.R. 573 and contrast *Zanzibar v British
Aerospace (Lancaster House) Ltd* [2002] 1 W.L.R. 2333.
[22] See para.8.07 above.
[23] See para.10.25 below.

Misrepresentation and breach of contract

8.11   It is clear from s.1 of the 1967 Act that the innocent party will have remedies for misrepresentation even though the representation has become a term of contract. The precise relationship between the two sets of remedies has yet to be worked out but presumably they are complementary.[24] It has been held that a clause stating "this agreement contains the whole contract between the parties" does not oust a claim for misrepresentation.[25]

2. REMEDIES FOR UNFAIR PRACTICES UNDER THE CONSUMER PROTECTION (AMENDMENT) REGULATIONS 2014

Private Redress under the Consumer Protection from Unfair Trading Regulations 2008

8.12   In Chapter Eighteen, we examine the Consumer Protection from Unfair Trading Regulations 2008 (the 2008 Regulations), which implement the EU's Directive on Unfair Commercial Practices (2005/29/EU). The Directive, and therefore the 2008 Regulations, target the way traders deal with consumers but did not envisage that consumers would have a private right of redress if a trader had engaged in an unfair commercial practice. Consumers who had suffered a loss or other detriment could only seek private redress where the trader's behaviour also constituted a breach of some other private law rule, such as misrepresentation (see 3.2) or duress. There were repeated calls for a private right of redress and eventually, the Law Commissions proposed the introduction of a limited private right of redress for consumers.[26] These recommendations were given effect through amendments made to the 2008 Regulations by the Consumer Protection (Amendment) Regulations 2014.[27]

Following these changes, a private right of redress in respect of a trader's violation of the requirements under the 2008 Regulations will be available if three conditions are met[28]:

> (1) There has to be one of the following types of contract:
>
> > (i) a contract with a trader for the sale or supply to the consumer of a product,
> >
> > (ii) a contract with a trader under which the consumer sells goods to the trader; or
> >
> > (iii) where the consumer makes a payment to a trader for the supply of a product; and

---

[24] See *Naughton v O'Callaghan* [1990] 3 All E.R. 191. See paras 3.04–3.09 above.

[25] *McGrath v Shah* (1989) 57 P. & C.R. 452. This is called an "entire agreement" clause.

[26] Law Commission, *Report 332*/Scottish Law Commission, Report No 226 *Consumer Redress for Misleading and Aggressive Practices* (London: TSO, 2012).

[27] SI 2014/870.

[28] See new reg.27A of the 2008 Regulations.

(2) The trader must have engaged in a misleading action (under reg.5 of the 2008 Regulations) or an aggressive practice (under reg.7 of the 2008 Regulations), or a producer has engaged in such action or practice and the trader could reasonably have been expected to be aware of this practice when the consumer entered into the contract.

(3) The misleading action or aggressive practice must have been a significant factor in the consumer's decision to enter into the contract or make the payment.[29]

The private right of redress is therefore only then available where the misleading action or aggressive commercial practice caused the consumer to conclude a contract with the trader. Although the 2008 Regulations prohibition also extend to the performance of the contract, or its termination, but the new private right of redress is not available in those circumstances. Moreover, a consumer can no longer claim damages for misrepresentation under s.2 of the 1967 Act (in England & Wales)[30] or s.10 of the Law Reform (Miscellaneous Provisions) (Scotland) Act 1985 (in Scotland) where the conduct that would be a misrepresentation also is a misleading action for which the new private right of redress is available.

The Right to "unwind" the contract

The 2014 amendments to the 2008 Regulations introduce a somewhat strange **8.13** new notion to describe a remedy which allows a consumer to bring a contract to an end: a consumer has the "right to unwind" the contract. This right is available for 90 days if the contract is one under which the trader sold or supplied a product to a consumer,[31] and without a time restriction where the consumer sold goods to the consumer or made a payment to the trader for the supply of a product.[32] A consumer who has made a payment which the consumer was not required to make (in part or full), then the consumer is entitled to receive a refund of that payment.[33]

In addition, the product in question must still be capable of being rejected which means that goods or digital content have not yet been fully consumed or a service has not yet been fully performed.[34]

The Right to a discount

Instead of exercising the right to unwind the contract the consumer can **8.14** instead claim the right to a discount[35] on any sums paid (or which are

---

[29] See reg.27C and 27D of the 2008 Regulations for restrictions of the private right of redress in respect of immovable property and financial services.
[30] See new s.2(4) of the 1967 Act.
[31] reg.27E of the 2008 Regulations.
[32] reg.27G of the 2008 Regulations.
[33] reg.27H of the 2008 Regulations.
[34] reg.27E(8) and (9) of the 2008 Regulations.
[35] reg.27I of the 2008 Regulations.

payable). The new provisions in the 2008 Regulations set out how this discount should be calculated[36]:

(a) if the prohibited practice is more than minor, it is 25 per cent,

(b) if the prohibited practice is significant, it is 50 per cent,

(c) if the prohibited practice is serious, it is 75 per cent, and

(d) if the prohibited practice is very serious, it is 100 per cent.

This raises the question how the seriousness of a commercial practice is determined. Here, the new provisions require that it is necessary to consider the behaviour of the person engaging in the practice, its impact on the consumer, and how much time has passed since it took place (although note the derogation in reg.27I(6) and (7)).

The Right to claim damages

8.15   A consumer also has a right to claim damages under reg.27J if the consumer:

(a) has incurred financial loss which the consumer would not have incurred if the prohibited practice in question had not taken place, or

(b) has suffered alarm, distress or physical inconvenience or discomfort which the consumer would not have suffered if the prohibited practice in question had not taken place.

Damages are to cover that loss, or the alarm, distress or physical inconvenience or discomfort in question. Such loss must have been reasonably foreseeable, and seems to depend on the trader being at fault in some way.[37]

Although the introduction of a private right to redress is a welcome development, their practical usefulness has yet to be tested. The rules introduced by the 2014 amendments seem rather complex and will almost certainly require someone trained in consumer law to assist with their enforcement.

3. REMEDIES FOR BREACH OF CONTRACT

8.16   In Chapter Four above, we saw that, in consumer contracts, the terms on description, quality and fitness for purpose of goods have been moved from their original homes, into the Consumer Rights Act 2015 (CRA 2015), which also now imposes the same (description, quality and fitness) terms in

---

[36] reg.27I(4) of the 2008 Regulations.
[37] See reg.27J(4) and (5). The latter provision refers to a number of instances when the trader will not be liable to pay damages.

consumer contracts for digital content, as well as terms (e.g. on reasonable skill and care) in consumer contracts for services.[38] The CRA 2015 also now houses (and in some cases reforms and extends the application of) the remedies on short term rejection, repair, replacement, price reduction and final rejection. The law on all of this was previously spread around various pieces of legislation (in particular, the 1979 Act and the SGSA), and the common law (the latter dealing, e.g. with the right to reject, and its restriction via the concept of affirmation, in contracts for the supply of goods that were not sales contracts (e.g. hire, hire-purchase). The CRA 2015 also deals with remedies related to delivery of the wrong quantity, instalment deliveries, non-delivery and late delivery.

It is proposed to consider first this new regime under the CRA 2015, and then to consider certain other possible remedies available under the general law (specific performance to deal with a trader who refuse to perform the contract at all, rights to terminate the contract that are not covered by the CRA 2015, and compensation for breach of contract which is largely left outside the CRA 2015 altogether).

A. GUARANTEES AND SOME PRACTICAL CONSIDERATIONS

Guarantees

For completeness we should also mention remedies which the consumer may have under a contract of guarantee. This is distinct from the other remedies because the consumer will not have to prove a breach of contract. The precise scope of the remedies will depend on the terms of the guarantee. We have considered some aspects of guarantees in Chapter Five.

8.17

Practical considerations

(1) The supplier will invariably require proof of purchase and the consumer should always insist on getting a sales receipt. He should then keep it in a safe place. His legal remedies will be difficult to enforce without one, although other evidence such as a witness at the time of purchase or a credit card slip will do instead.

8.18

(2) Faced with a consumer complaint the supplier may offer a credit note. This can be useful to the consumer in some cases but he or she must realise that a credit note cannot be used by the supplier to cut down the remedies dealt with in this chapter. Thus where consumers are entitled to their money back, they can refuse to accept a credit note instead.[39]

---

[38] See paras 1.22–1.23 above for the definitions of "trader" and "consumer".
[39] See below on *Duties of Consumers and Traders in Relation to the Right to Reject*.

(1) The "Short Term" Right to Reject in Contracts for the Supply of Goods

8.19 In all contracts for the supply of goods,[40] it is provided the consumer has a right to reject the goods, terminate the contract and receive a refund, where the goods do not conform to the contract either:

(a) by being in breach of the terms on satisfactory quality, fitness for particular purpose, description, compliance with sample, or compliance with a model seen or examined; or

(b) by containing defective digital content; or

(c) by being in breach of the term as to the right to supply the goods.[41]

As a preliminary point here, it should be noted that the consumer has a *right* to reject. He is not bound to do so—he could choose to do nothing, or to exercise another remedy, whether damages for diminution in value or for the cost of having a third party repair the goods, or he could choose to require the seller to repair or replace the goods.[42]

What Does "Refund" Mean?

8.20 "Refund" means the amount of money paid; or if what the consumer transferred under the contract was something other than money, then the same amount of the thing he transferred (or if the same amount of that thing cannot be returned, then the actual thing that was transferred).[43]

It is worth emphasising the points here that if the consumer has paid money, then this (money) is what must be refunded, while if the consumer has provided something else, then this other thing is what must be refunded. In other words the trader cannot insist on providing vouchers or the like if this is not the "currency" in which the consumer paid in the first place.

When is There No Entitlement to a Refund?

8.21 The consumer is not entitled to any refund if he did not transfer money or any other thing to the trader under the contract in the first place, or if whatever was transferred cannot be given back in its original state.[44]

Particular Rules Applicable to Hire and Hire-Purchase

8.22 In contracts for the hire of goods, the right to a refund only covers what has been paid (or otherwise transferred by the consumer) for a period of hire

---

[40] Including sale, hire, hire-purchase, work and materials, exchange, etc.—see CRA 2015 ss.3–8.

[41] ss.19(3)(a), 19(6) and 20(4); and on these conformity standards listed in paras (a), (b) and (c) in the text, see Chapters Three and Four above

[42] On all these remedies, see below.

[43] s.20(10)–(12).

[44] s.20(18)(a)–(b).

that the consumer does not receive due to the contract being terminated.[45] In other words, the consumer is only entitled to be refunded for a hire period that he has paid for, but not received—he is not entitled to a refund for a period of hire that he actually received prior to termination of the contract.[46] In hire-purchase or conditional sales contracts, where the contract is terminated before the whole price has been paid, the consumer is only entitled to be refunded that part of the price that he has actually already paid.[47]

Duties of Consumers and Traders in Relation to the Right to Reject

To exercise the right to reject and obtain a refund, the consumer must indicate to the trader that he is rejecting the goods and treating the contract as at an end—this indication can be by words or actions, so long as it is clear enough to be understood by the trader.[48]   **8.23**

From the time when the right is exercised, the trader has a duty to give the consumer a refund,[49] and the consumer has a duty to make the goods available for collection by the trader or (if there is an agreement for the consumer to return rejected goods) to return them as agreed.[50] Whether or not the consumer is bound under such an agreement to return the rejected goods, the trader is required to bear any reasonable costs of returning them, but this does not extend to any costs incurred by the consumer in returning the goods in person to where the consumer took physical possession of them.[51] This means, e.g. that where goods have been delivered to the consumer, the trader must pay for them to be returned when the consumer rejects them, but if the consumer has taken possession of goods in a shop, then the consumer will need to pay to take them back to the shop.

The refund must be provided "without undue delay, and in any event within 14 days beginning with the day on which the trader agrees that the consumer is entitled to a refund".[52]

Where the consumer paid money under the contract, the refund must be given using the same means of payment as that used by the consumer, unless the consumer expressly agrees otherwise.[53]

The trader is not allowed to impose a fee on the consumer in respect of the refund, e.g. a "processing" or "administration" fee.[54]

---

[45] s.20(13).
[46] Of course, if the period of hire received was affected by the goods being defective, the consumer may still wish to claim damages for this, and the right to do so is preserved by s.20(19).
[47] s.20(14).
[48] ss.20(5) and 20(6).
[49] Subject to any restrictions on the right to a refund, on which see paras 8.26–8.28 below.
[50] s.20(7).
[51] s.20(8).
[52] s.20(15).
[53] s.20(16), so, e.g., if cash was paid, it must be a cash refund, if a card payment was made, the card must be refunded.
[54] s.20(17).

The Short Term Right to Reject and Severable Contracts

8.24   There is a special provision on rejection in the case of a "severable" contract, i.e. where the contract is intended to be divisible, in that different elements of the consideration can be assigned to different elements of the performance. The example given in the CRA Explanatory Notes involves "an agreement to pay pro-rata for some goods supplied, no matter whether others are supplied". The Act provides that in the case of such contracts, depending on the terms of the contract, and the circumstances, the consumer may be permitted to choose whether simply to reject those goods that do not conform to the contract, or to terminate the whole contract and reject all of the goods.[55]

The Short Term Right to Reject and Partial Rejection

8.25   Section 21(1) provides that where the right to reject applies, and the consumer opts not to reject all of the goods and treat the contract as at an end, the consumer can choose whether to reject some or all of the goods that do not conform to the contract, but he may not reject any goods that do conform to the contract.[56]

Loss of the Right to Reject—Then and Now

8.26   Before the CRA 2015, if the contract was one of sale, consumers were covered by the same rules on when the right to reject was lost as applied to other sales. These were the rules on "acceptance" under which consumers lost the right to reject by intimating acceptance, doing an act inconsistent with the ownership of the seller, or failing to reject after the lapse of a "reasonable time".[57] In supplies of goods other than sale, the common law "affirmation" rules applied. In practice consumers tended to be most affected by the "reasonable time" and "affirmation" rules—losing the right to reject after periods between just less than a month, and a good few months, depending on the circumstances.[58]

These previous rules no longer apply, and in all supplies of goods, the position is now as described below. In brief, the normal rule is a simple 30-day cut off period. This does certainly offer less protection than the reasonable time and affirmation concepts, which as indicated, often gave a few months. At the same time, the 30-day rule provides a greater degree of certainty. In addition, we will see below that consumers have other remedies (repair, replacement,

---

[55] s.20(21).

[56] s.21(2) applies the same rule to instalment contracts (and on when consumers can reject in instalment contracts, see also s.26(3)). NB however, that in cases where the goods form a "commercial unit", the consumer cannot reject some of those goods without also rejecting the rest of them (s.21(3)) (a unit is a "commercial unit" if division of the unit would materially impair the value of the goods or the character of the unit—s.21(4)). For the rules on the duties of consumers and traders in relation to rejection and refunds under this "partial rejection" regime, see s.21(5)–(13).

[57] s.35 of the 1979 Act.

[58] See previous editions.

price reduction, final rejection and damages which are not limited to 30 days). Consumers also benefit from the fact that they can no longer lose the right to reject by intimation of acceptance or inconsistent act.[59]

Time Limit for Consumers to Exercise the Short Term Right to Reject

As indicated immediately above, the consumer must normally exercise the right **8.27** to reject within 30 days of the first day after *all* of the following have occurred: ownership has been transferred[60]; the goods have been delivered; and, in cases where the trader is required under the contract to install the goods or take some other action to enable the consumer to use the goods, the trader has notified the consumer that the installation or other action has been taken.[61]

The 30-day period can be extended if the parties have agreed this[62]; although any agreement that fixes a shorter period is not binding on the consumer.[63]

If any of the goods are of a type that can reasonably be expected to perish **8.28** in a period that is shorter than 30 days,[64] then in relation to those goods, the time limit for the consumer to exercise the short-term right to reject, is the end of this shorter period; while the normal 30-day period will continue to apply to any other goods that are part of the transaction and which are not to be expected to perish in less than 30 days.[65]

As highlighted above, the consumer has the *right* to exercise the short term right to reject, and claim a refund, but is not bound to do take this course. So, e.g., the consumer could opt to ask for one of either the repair or replacement remedies discussed below. If such a remedy has not worked out, then, as we shall see below, the consumer is entitled (subject to certain conditions) to request either price reduction or the so called "final" right to reject. However, quite apart from this, if the consumer asks for repair or replacement during the period when he could have asked for the short term right to reject,[66] it is provided that the 30-day period (or any shorter period applicable, e.g. to perishable goods), stops running during a so called "waiting period".[67] The "waiting period" is the period running from when the consumer asks for repair or replacement, to when the trader returns the repaired goods or provides the replacement as the case may be.[68] In such cases if the repaired or replaced goods do not conform to the contract, then the consumer is given

---

[59] But see above on how there is no right to reject where whatever was transferred cannot be given back in its original state.

[60] Or, in the case of hire or hire-purchase, possession has been transferred

[61] s.22(3).

[62] s.22(1), and it is not said that this agreement must be in the original contract, so it appears that it may be in the original contract, or at any later point, e.g. when the dispute arises.

[63] s.22(2).

[64] e.g. food.

[65] s.22(4).

[66] i.e. within the 30-day period, or any shorter period in the case of, e.g. perishable goods, as discussed above in the text. But note also that the repair, replacement and other remedies discussed below are not themselves affected by the time limits applicable to the short term right to reject.

[67] s.20(6).

[68] s.20(8).

the remainder of the 30-day period, or 7 days (whichever of these periods is longer) to exercise the short term right to reject the goods.[69]

(2) Refunds and Recovery of Costs in Digital Contents Contracts

8.29 The above short term right to reject regime does not apply to digital contents (DC) contracts, and there is no short term right to reject DC for breach of the terms as to quality, fitness and description. However, the consumer *is* entitled to a refund in a DC contract, if the trader is in breach of the term requiring that he has the right to supply the DC.[70]

In addition, if the trader is in breach of a term that s.37 requires to be treated as included in the contract, the consumer can recover from the trader any costs incurred as a result of the breach, up to the amount of the price paid for the digital content.[71]

(3) Repair, Replacement, Price Reduction and Final Rejection in Goods and Digital Contents Contracts

Introduction

8.30 Since 2003, in sales contracts, and some other supply of goods contracts (e.g. work and materials contracts, but not hire or hire-purchase contracts), consumers have been entitled to ask for free repair or for a free replacement of non-conforming goods, subject to certain conditions as to possibility and proportionality.[72] Also since 2003, in these same contracts (sale, work and materials, but not hire or hire-purchase), when repair or replacement do not work out, consumers have been entitled to move to a second tier of remedies involving price reduction or rescission.[73] These rights are now placed in the CRA 2015 (rescission now being referred to as the "final right to reject"), and they apply now to all supply of goods contracts (including hire and hire-purchase), and also[74] to DC contracts.[75]

---

[69] s.20(7). NB that, even although consumers are entitled to exercise the "final" right to reject after a failed repair or replacement (see below), it could still be very important in practice to have the alternative right to exercise the short term right to reject, as in the case of the final right to reject, the courts can reduce the refund to take account of use the consumer has had of the goods. While this rule normally only applies after the first six months post sale, with cars, it applies from any time post sale. In the case of the short term right to reject, no such reduction in the refund can be made.

[70] s.42(5); see s.45 on the how, as with goods contracts, the refund must be given without delay, within 14 days, and with the same means of payment as the consumer used to pay for the DC).

[71] s.42(4), and para.3.38 above, on s.37, which includes as a term of the contract, certain information to be provided under the Consumer Contracts (Information, Cancellation and Additional Charges) Regulations 2013 (SI 2013/3134)

[72] This was in order to implement the Sale of Consumer Goods Directive (SCGD), art.3 of Directive 99/44/EEC; the rules, prior to the CRA 2015, being contained in s.48A–B of the 1979 Act and s.11N of the SGSA.

[73] Also following art 3 of SCGD, art 3, and see until the CRA 2015, s.48A–F of the 1979 Act, s.11M–S of the SGSA.

[74] But see below on how in DC contracts, there is only formally a price reduction remedy at the second tier, but that this can sometimes be such as to amount to a full refund.

[75] ss.19(3)(b)–(c), 19(4)(a)–(b), 23(1), 42(2).

In goods contracts these remedies apply where the goods do not conform to the contract either:

(a) by being in breach of the terms on satisfactory quality, fitness for particular purpose, description, compliance with sample, or compliance with a model seen or examined; or

(b) by containing defective digital content; or

(c) by having been installed incorrectly; or

(d) by being in breach of requirements "stated in the contract" (i.e. in breach of an express term).[76]

In DC contracts, these remedies apply where the DC does not conform to the contract by being in breach of the terms on satisfactory quality, fitness for particular purpose, and description.[77]   **8.31**

Note should also be made of s.46, requiring the trader to repair (or provide compensation) where DC that he supplies under a contract, causes damage to a device or DC owned by the consumer, the damage being of a type that would not have occurred if the trader had exercised reasonable care. NB, however, that in many cases where DC causes such damage it will be because it is of unsatisfactory quality, and the consumer will then be able to ask for repair (or replacement) or claim damages for breach of this strict liability provision, which will be easier than entering into debates as to whether there has been a lack of reasonable care.

The burden of proof: six months rule

If the goods or DC break down or develop faults at some point after delivery, a potentially difficult legal task for consumers and their advisers is to prove that the goods were defective when they were first supplied.   **8.32**

To access the short term right to reject and damages remedies, normal rules of evidence apply, i.e. it is for the consumer to show that a defect which has now shown up (e.g. a few months after purchase), existed at the time of the supply. Often, courts take this as easily proven, just by the nature of the defect, e.g. in the case of technical problems with computer, TV, car, etc., if there is no positive evidence of mistreatment by the consumer, courts assume the defect existed at the time of sale. But, with tears, scratches, breaks, etc., traders may allege that there was no defect at the time of the goods or DC being supplied, but rather that the defects that now exist must have been caused by mistreatment of the goods or DC by the consumer. It may be hard for the consumer to disprove this in practice especially to an awkward trader, who knows that the consumer will probably give up, as the low value of the claim may mean that it is not worth going to court.

For the purposes of the repair, replacement, price reduction and final

---

[76] ss.19(3) and (4).
[77] s.42(1).

rejection remedies, consumers are now assisted by a reversal of the burden of proof during a six-month period following delivery of the goods or DC. So, in relation to goods,[78] s.19(14) provides that:

> ... goods which do not conform to the contract at any time within the period of six months beginning with the day on which the goods were delivered to the consumer must be taken not to have conformed to it on that day.

8.33 This is qualified by s.19(15), which provides that s.19(14) does not apply where:

> (a) it is established that the goods did conform to the contract on that day;
>
> (b) its application is incompatible with the nature of the goods or with how they fail to conform to the contract.

This rule originated in art.5(3) of the SCGD and was originally implemented in s.48A–B of the 1979 Act, although the CRA 2015 now makes the rule applicable to other transactions such as hire, hire-purchase and DC, which are outside the scope of the SCGD. In relation to those contracts covered by the art.5(3) of the SCGD, the CJEU has recently held that consumers need only show that the problem has shown itself within six months (no need to show what it's cause was, or that it originates from the trader), it then being presumed that the problem existed in embryonic form at the time of sale. It is then for the trader to prove that this was not the case, i.e. that the problem was caused by something that took place after delivery. The case was *Froukje Faber v Autobedrijf Hazet Ochten BV* (ECLI:EU:C:2015:357, C-497/13). So, on the facts, it was found to be enough for the consumer to show that the car caught fire, it then being for the trader to show this was not because of some defect existing at the time of sale (the car had been scrapped by the time of the case, this in itself making it impossible for the trader to prove there was no defect at the time of the sale).

An obvious example of what is set out in para.(b) of s.19(15) would be goods which have a very short life and which break down or deteriorate after that time, e.g. perishable goods. Take, e.g. food, which deteriorates after the use by date, which date is two weeks after the purchase. So, although this deterioration takes place well within the six-month period, it is incompatible with the goods and the nature of the defect, to presume that the defect existed when the food was supplied.

Repair or replacement

8.34 So, as indicated above, consumers are entitled to ask either for repair or for replacement in relation to non-conformities in goods and DC contracts.[79]

---

[78] For the identical provisions in DC contracts, see s.42(9)–(10).

[79] ss.19(3)(b)–(c), 19(4)(a)–(b), 23(1), 42(2)(a).

"Repair" means bringing the goods or DC into conformity with the contract (ss.23(8) and 43(8)), i.e. fixing whatever makes the goods or DC of unsatisfactory quality, unfit for purpose, etc.; "replacement" is not defined, but involves replacement of the overall thing bought—new TV, car, download, game, app, etc.

This provision brings the law into line with reality by giving the consumer, in many cases, the remedy that he really wants—namely to have the goods repaired or replaced. Previously the question of repair or replacement was a matter of business practice rather than law—and it was very rare for some items (especially cars) to be replaced. In the case of goods,[80] the seller's duty is amplified by ss.23(2) and (5) which provide that:

(2) If the consumer requires the trader to repair or replace the goods, the trader must—

    (a) do so within a reasonable time and without significant inconvenience to the consumer;

    (b) bear any necessary costs incurred in doing so (including in particular the cost of any labour, materials or postage).

(5) Any question as to what is a reasonable time or significant inconvenience is to be determined by taking account of—

    (a) the nature of the goods, and

    (b) the purpose for which the goods were acquired.

The "reasonable time" requirement in s.23(2)(a) will depend on the facts **8.35** of the particular case. In some cases (a wedding dress being an obvious example) the number of days involved in repair/replacement will be critical and, perhaps, decisive. As to "significant inconvenience" (see s.23(2)(a)) this might apply where the repair or replacement disrupts everyday living, e.g. a trader insists on removing/turning off toilet or washing facilities during repairs or replacements.

Section 23(2)(b) is clear that the trader must bear the costs of the repair or replacement. But, what if the replacement involves the removal and reinstallation of defective goods, such as a washing machine or tiles, as happened in *Gebr Weber GmbH v Wittmer and Putz v Medianess Electronics*?[80a] Who bears the cost, the seller or the consumer? The seller, said the European Court of Justice interpreting the SCGD. The seller must either remove and reinstall the goods or pay for that to be carried out, whether or not the seller was obliged to install the goods initially under the contract of sale.

In fact, in the actual case, the consumer had already paid the removal costs, and was claiming the cost of this back from the seller. In such circumstances, the court did say that courts can reduce the amount that the consumer recovers from the trader, to an amount proportionate to the value of the goods.

---

[80] ss.43(2) and (5) contain the equivalent provisions for DC.
[80a] (C-65/09) [2011] 3 C.M.L.R. 27; [2012] C.E.C. 151 and [2001] OJ C226/2 respectively.

What the court did not make clear is whether such a contribution can be required from the consumer where the consumer is asking the trader himself (i.e. the one who is in breach) to do the work. It would seem very strange indeed if the court was saying that the trader can ask for a contribution in such cases. After all, the provision in the SCGD (reflected by s.23(2)(b) above), is very clear to the effect that the trader must bear the costs of carrying out his obligation to repair or replace. In addition, we shall see shortly below that the court also said in this very case that the disproportionality test (below) only involves a comparison between the repair and replacement remedies, and that such a comparison cannot even be made where one of these two remedies is impossible. So, it is hard to see how it is logical to make the argument that replacement is disproportionately expensive relative to (not repair, which was impossible anyway, but) the value of the goods and to use this as a reason to require the consumer to contribute to the cost of the supplier replacing goods. Indeed, it may well be that the only reason the court felt the consumer should contribute in this case is because it was not the original trader who was doing the replacement. At least such a trader can do the work at "cost" price. But if, as happened in the case, someone else has done the work, they will have charged more, in order to make a profit, perhaps making it unfair to expect the original trader to pay the full amount, and therefore more reasonable to expect the consumer to contribute.[81]

8.36   The right to insist on repair or replacement is subject to certain restrictions. For goods contracts (and the same applies to DC),[82] s.23 provides that the consumer cannot require the trader to repair or replace the goods if that remedy (the repair or the replacement) is:

> (3) (a) impossible, or
>   (b) disproportionate compared to the other of those remedies.

> (4) Either of those remedies is disproportionate compared to the other if it imposes costs on the trader which, compared to those imposed by the other, are unreasonable, taking into account—

>> (a) the value which the goods would have if they conformed to the contract,
>> (b) the significance of the lack of conformity, and
>> (c) whether the other remedy could be effected without significant inconvenience to the consumer.

So, e.g., repair might be impossible if goods or DC have been destroyed, or are otherwise beyond repair; while replacement is impossible in the case of unique items, e.g. works of art.

In relation to disproportionality, note that s.23(3)(b) refers to whether repair or replacement is disproportionate in relation to the other of these

---

[81] Whatever is the correct way to read this decision, it is of course not binding on UK courts in relation to hire, hire-purchase and DC contracts, which are outside the scope of the SCGD.

[82] See ss.43(3) and (4) for the same conditions in DC contracts.

remedies. So, the issue is whether repair is disproportionate compared to replacement, or vice versa. The trader cannot refuse either of these remedies on the grounds that it is disproportionately expensive compared to price reduction, refund or some other remedy.[83]

Also, the logic of comparing the two cure remedies in this way, is that if one is disproportionately more expensive than the other, then the consumer is expected to settle for the other, with it still at least being ensured that the consumer can get some form of "cure" remedy. But the consumer cannot do this, if this other one is impossible, so it must be that if one of them is impossible, the disproportionality test cannot be applied to the other, no matter how expensive it is. This was confirmed to be correct in *Gebr Weber GmbH v Wittmer* and *Putz v Medianess Electronics* cases,[84] involving items (floor tiles, in one case, a washing machine in the other) that had been bought from the trader, and then installed by the consumer, but which proved to be defective. It was accepted that "repair" was impossible given the condition of the items and the nature of the installation. So, first of all, as we saw above, it was held that in cases like this, "replacement" would typically mean that the trader would have to remove the items, and install new ones. Secondly, and the key point for present purposes, it was held that the disproportionality test cannot be applied here (the court agreeing that if one cure remedy is impossible, then it would be contrary to the wording and protective purpose of the SCGD, to deprive the consumer of his right to the other cure remedy on the basis that the impossible one is cheaper!!).

When the disproportionality test is actually applied we can see that it involves, in broad terms, asking whether the costs to the trader (of repair or replacement as the case may be) are unreasonable (compared to the other of these remedies). However, this is not looked at in isolation—we can see from criteria (a)–(c), that account needs to be taken of the economic and other significance of the defect[85]; as well as at the inconvenience for the consumer in being required to accept the other remedy (e.g. if a replacement would cost £50 but repair would cost £100, then perhaps repair would be disproportionate, but perhaps not, if replacement goods/DC cannot be provided for some time, especially if the goods are everyday necessities. **8.37**

A final point is that if the buyer asks the seller to repair or replace the goods or DC, he cannot change his mind and ask for the other of these remedies until he has given the seller a reasonable time to effect the remedy that he first asked for; and where the consumer has asked for repair or replacement, he may not change his mind and seek to enforce the short term right to

---

[83] This was confirmed to be the correct reading of these remedies, which derive from SCGD, in Joined CJEU cases C-65/09 and C-87/09, *Gebr Weber GmbH v Wittmer* and *Putz v Medianess Electronics* [2011] OJC226/2. NB that the old provision on this (s.48C(1) of the 1979 Act did—wrongly—allow a comparison to be made with other remedies).

[84] See earlier discussion at para.8.35 above.

[85] e.g. high costs for the trader are less likely to be considered disproportionate, the more serious the defects are.

reject, without first giving the trader a reasonable time to carry out the repair or replacement.[86]

What happens if the seller fails to comply with his statutory repair or replacement obligation? This can have two consequences. First, the court can make an order requiring the seller to perform—on which see the *Remedies and the powers of the court* section, below.[87] Secondly, the failure can trigger the price reduction/final rejection rights which we must now consider.

Price reduction and final rejection

8.38   **Goods Contracts.**   In goods contracts, (under s.24(5)), C can demand price reduction *or* a final right to reject if:

> (i) after one attempted repair or one replacement, the goods still do not conform to the contract, or
>
> (ii) both repair and replacement are either impossible or disproportionate, or
>
> (iii) having requested either a repair or a replacement, this requested remedy is not provided within a "reasonable time" or "without causing significant inconvenience" to the consumer.

The first possibility (one failed repair or replacement—(i) above) is fairly self-explanatory, the point being that the trader has repaired the goods, or he has replaced them, but in either case the goods now provided to the consumer still do not conform to the contract. As for (ii) and (iii), see the earlier discussions above as to "impossibility", "disproportionality", "significant inconvenience" and "reasonable time" concepts.

As with the short term right to reject, the final right to reject (FRR) enables the consumer to treat the contract as at an end, and obtain a refund,[88] and to exercise the FRR, the consumer must indicate to the trader that he wishes to do so.[89] Also, as with the short term right, the consumer must make the goods available,[90] and the trader must bear any reasonable costs of their return to him.[91] Finally, in common with the short term right, the trader must provide the refund without undue delay, and, in any event, within 14 days of agreeing it is due,[92] and must not impose any fee in respect of the refund.[93]

8.39   In contrast with the short term right to reject (which generates a full refund), if the consumer exercises the FRR, the refund may be reduced to

---

[86] ss.23(7) and 43(7).
[87] This can be contrasted with the general reluctance of the courts to grant specific performance—see paras 8.49–8.50 below.
[88] s.20(4) and (10).
[89] s.20(5).
[90] s.20(7)(b).
[91] s.20(8).
[92] s.20(15).
[93] s.20(17).

take account of the use the consumer has had of the goods in the period since they were delivered.[94] This rule normally only applies after six months, i.e. if the FRR is exercised in the first six months after transfer of ownership and delivery, there can be no deduction in the refund to take account of the consumer's use of the goods. However, there is an exception in the case of cars, where such a deduction can be made whenever the FRR is exercised, i.e. whether this is more or less than six months after transfer of ownership and delivery.[95]

The right to a price reduction is the right to require the trader to reduce by an appropriate amount the price the consumer is required to pay under the contract, or to receive a refund from the trader of anything already paid above the reduced amount.[96] The amount of the reduction may, where appropriate, be the full amount of the price or whatever the consumer is required to transfer.[97] In the end what is an "appropriate" price reduction should depend on the extent of the non-conformity—to what extent does it reduce the value of the goods? What would it cost to have them repaired by a third party?

Unlike with the FRR, there is no express provision requiring the trader to provide a price reduction without delay, or within 14 days; and neither is there any express provision saying that no charge can be imposed by the trader.

Digital Content Contracts.   There is no FRR as such in DC contracts (but see below). The consumer can demand price reduction if (i) both repair and replacement are either impossible or disproportionate or, (ii) having requested either a repair or a replacement, this requested remedy is not provided within a "reasonable time" or "without causing significant inconvenience" to the consumer.[98]   **8.40**

So, unlike in the case of goods contracts, there is no "one shot" rule, i.e. no right to demand price reduction just based on there having been one failed repair or replacement.

As in goods contracts, price reduction is the right to require the trader to reduce by an appropriate amount the price the consumer is required to pay under the contract, or to receive a refund from the trader of anything already paid above the reduced amount.[99] Where "appropriate", this may amount to a full refund,[100] but it is not made clear whether DC must be returned in such a case.

As with goods, what is an "appropriate" price reduction must surely turn on the extent of the non-conformity—how much does it reduce the value of the DC, and how much will it cost to have the DC repaired by a third party.   **8.41**

As with goods, a "refund" (which presumably includes also cases where the price reduction is not a full refund, but this is unclear) is to be given without

---

[94] s.24(8).
[95] s.24(10)(a).
[96] s.24(1).
[97] s.24(2).
[98] s.44(3).
[99] s.44(1).
[100] s.44(2).

undue delay, and in any event within 14 days of it being agreed that it is required.[101] Also as with goods, the trader can impose no charge in respect of a refund.[102]

(4) The Right to Reject for Delivery of the Wrong Quantity, Non-delivery and Late Delivery of Goods

Delivery of the wrong quantity

8.42   We have seen that under a non-severable contract the buyer can now accept part and reject part.[103]

It is also necessary to refer to s.25. For consumer contracts, it replaces s.30 of the 1979 Act, and reads as follows:

> (1) Where the trader delivers to the consumer a quantity of goods less than the trader contracted to supply, the consumer may reject them, but if the consumer accepts them the consumer must pay for them at the contract rate.
>
> (2) Where the trader delivers to the consumer a quantity of goods larger than the trader contracted to supply, the consumer may accept the goods included in the contract and reject the rest, or may reject all of the goods.
>
> (3) Where the trader delivers to the consumer a quantity of goods larger than the trader contracted to supply and the consumer accepts all of the goods delivered, the consumer must pay for them at the contract rate.
>
> (4) Where the consumer is entitled to reject goods under this section, any entitlement for the consumer to treat the contract as at an end depends on the terms of the contract and the circumstances of the case.
>
> (5) The consumer rejects goods under this section by indicating to the trader that the consumer is rejecting the goods.
>
> (6) The indication may be something the consumer says or does, but it must be clear enough to be understood by the trader.

Late and non-delivery of goods

8.43   Section 28 deals with late and non-delivery of goods (in sales contracts only), and the right to reject in such circumstances.

Unless there is an agreed time or period for delivery, the contract is taken to include a term that the trader must deliver the goods without undue delay, and in any event, not more than 30 days after the day on which the contract

---

[101] s.44(4).
[102] s.44(6).
[103] See para.8.24 above.

is entered into.[104] If the trader does not deliver within these rules (i.e. the rules on agreed time or period, lack of undue delay or 30 days), then the consumer may treat the contract as at an end if:

(a) the trader has refused to deliver the goods,

(b) delivery of the goods at the agreed time or within the agreed period is essential taking into account all the relevant circumstances at the time the contract was entered into, or

(c) the consumer told the trader before the contract was entered into that delivery in accordance with the above rules was essential.[105]

In any other circumstances, the consumer can require the trader to deliver within a specified period, and if the goods are not delivered within that period, the consumer may treat the contract as at an end.[106]

If the consumer is entitled to treat the contract as at an end on any of the above, but chooses not to, this does not prevent the consumer from cancelling the order for any of the goods or rejecting goods that have been delivered.[107]

(5) Repeat Performance and Price Reduction Remedies in Services Contracts

In services contracts, the CRA 2015 provides for new remedies of repeat performance and price reduction, where the service does not conform to the contract.   **8.44**

In cases where the service does not conform in the sense that the trader breaches a term that s.50 requires to be treated as part of the contract (based on pre-contractual information), but this does not relate to the service, or where the trader breaches the term as to performance of the service within a reasonable time,[108] the only available statutory remedy is price reduction.[109]

Where the service does not conform in the sense that the trader is in breach of the term to carry out the service with reasonable care and skill (s.49), or if the trader breaches a term that s.50 requires to be treated as part of the contract, which relates to the service, then the following scheme applies. The consumer is entitled to repeat performance unless this is impossible.[110] "Repeat performance" is defined as "a right to require the trader to perform the service again, to the extent necessary to complete its performance in conformity with the contract".[111] Repeat performance must be carried out within a reasonable time and without significant inconvenience to the consumer.[112] If repeat performance is impossible, or if it has not been carried out within a

---

[104] s.28(3).
[105] s.28(5)–(6).
[106] s.28(7)–(8).
[107] s.28(10)(a).
[108] see paras 6.39 and 6.43 above on these provisions.
[109] s.54(3) and (5).
[110] s.55(3).
[111] s.55(1).
[112] s.55(2)(a).

reasonable time and without significant inconvenience to the consumer, then the consumer is entitled to price reduction.[113]

8.45   The rules on price reduction are very similar to those applicable to this remedy in goods and services contracts. So, the key provisions in s.56 read as follows:

> (1) The right to a price reduction is the right to require the trader to reduce the price to the consumer by an appropriate amount (including the right to receive a refund for anything already paid above the reduced amount).
>
> (2) The amount of the reduction may, where appropriate, be the full amount of the price.
>
>   . . .
>
> (4) A refund under this section must be given without undue delay, and in any event within 14 days beginning with the day on which the trader agrees that the consumer is entitled to a refund.
>
> (5) The trader must give the refund using the same means of payment as the consumer used to pay for the service, unless the consumer expressly agrees otherwise.
>
> (6) The trader must not impose any fee on the consumer in respect of the refund.

(6) Remedies and the powers of the court

8.46   Section 58 provides for the powers of the court in relation to the award of remedies, and reads as follows:

> (1) In any proceedings in which a remedy is sought by virtue of section 19(3) or (4), 42(2) or 54(3),[114] the court, in addition to any other power it has, may act under this section.
>
> (2) On the application of the consumer the court may make an order requiring specific performance or, in Scotland, specific implement by the trader of any obligation imposed on the trader by virtue of section 23, 43 or 55.[115]
>
> (3) Subsection (4) applies if—
>
>> (a) the consumer claims to exercise a right under the relevant remedies provisions, but

---

[113] s.56(3).

[114] i.e. the short term right to reject goods, the repair, replacement, price reduction and final rights to reject goods; the rights to repair, replacement and price reduction in DC contracts; and the rights to repeat performance and price reduction in services contracts.

[115] i.e. the rights to repair, replacement and repeat performance.

    (b) the court decides that those provisions have the effect that exercise of another right is appropriate.

(4) The court may proceed as if the consumer had exercised that other right.

(5) If the consumer has claimed to exercise the final right to reject, the court may order that any reimbursement to the consumer is reduced by a deduction for use, to take account of the use the consumer has had of the goods in the period since they were delivered.

(6) Any deduction for use is limited as set out in section 24(9) and (10).

(7) The court may make an order under this section unconditionally or on such terms and conditions as to damages, payment of the price and otherwise as it thinks just.

Some reflection is required on subss.(3) and (4). The effect is that if the **8.47** consumer has asked for a remedy such as repair, replacement or repeat performance, but the "relevant remedies provisions" bar such a remedy, the court should proceed on the basis that the consumer had asked for the remedy that these "relevant remedies provisions" make appropriate in the circumstances. According to s.58(8) the "relevant remedies provisions" are the above discussed provisions on repair, replacement and repeat performance, and the related conditions as to impossibility, disproportionality, etc. In other words, subss.(3) & (4) only provide for a requested remedy to be refused, and another one granted, on the basis of these provisions as to impossibility, disproportionality, etc. Subsections (3) and (4) do not provide a general discretion to the court to award a remedy other than that asked for.

    Having said all of this, s.58(2) does arguably contain a more general discretion to refuse specific performance, providing, as it does, that the court "may" (not must or will) award specific performance. Now given, as we have just seen, that s.58(3) separately provides for the court to substitute one remedy for the one requested by the consumer, where this is appropriate based on the "relevant remedies provisions", and that the word "may" in s.58(2) is not qualified by a reference to such provisions, it arguably conveys a more general discretion. This could be important. We should recall that in goods and DC contracts, if repair or replacement is impossible, the effect of the "relevant remedies provisions" is that the other must be granted—the disproportionality test does not apply in such cases. Equally, the disproportionality test does not apply under the "relevant remedies provisions" in relation to the repeat performance remedy in services contracts—the only "defence" under these provisions is the impossibility defence. In short, the "relevant remedies provisions" do not actually allow for refusal of any of the cure remedies on the basis that these cure remedies are disproportionately expensive compared with remedies such as price reduction or damages. This is where the discretion in s.58(2) could be significant, e.g. in allowing the court to refuse specific performance where repair, replacement or repeat performance are disproportionately expensive compared to price reduction, or because they would involve extreme costs, long term commitment, supervision problems, etc.

C. REMEDIES AVAILABLE UNDER THE GENERAL LAW

8.48 The remedies which we have just described exist alongside the remedies available to the consumer under the general law pre-dating the CRA 2015; and generally the CRA 2015 expressly preserves the rights of consumers to demand such remedies (e.g. specific performance, termination of the contract, refund and damages) instead of or in addition to a remedies under the CRA 2015 (so long as this does not involve the consumer recovering twice for the same loss).[116] So, it remains important consider remedies outside the CRA 2015. This will be done by attempting to answer three questions on which a consumer may seek advice, namely:

(1) Can I make them perform the contract?

(2) Can I get my money back?

(3) Can I get compensation?

(1) Can I make them perform the contract?

8.49 We have already dealt above with the right to ask for specific performance under s.58 of the CRA 2015 where goods, DC or services contain non-conformities. However, what about more fundamental non-performance. So, let us suppose that a consumer has ordered goods or DC from a supplier, or work from a builder, and the supplier or builder has failed to carry it out. We have already seen that the consumer may be able to serve a notice making time of the essence; if the supplier or builder then fails to perform by the stipulated date the consumer may be able to treat the contract as discharged.

Let us suppose, however, that the consumer does not want to do this—what he wants is to compel the supplier or builder to perform the contract. In practical terms this may be more trouble than it is worth—the consumer may be better advised to obtain the goods or work elsewhere and claim compensation from the defaulting party.[117] If, however, the consumer insists on performance, can the law help him? Historically the courts of common law granted only the remedy of damages, but the courts of equity supplemented this by granting decrees of specific performance in cases where damages would not be an adequate remedy.

In the case of sale of goods the power to award specific performance is enacted in s.52 of the 1979 Act as follows:

> In any action for breach of contract to deliver specific or ascertained goods the court may, if it thinks fit, on the plaintiff's application . . . direct that the con-

---

[116] e.g see ss.19(9)–(11), 42(6)–(7) and 54(6)–(7).
[117] See para.8.54 below.

tract shall be performed specifically, without giving the defendant the option of retaining the goods on payment of damages. . . .

Now s.52 no longer applies to consumer contracts (CRA 2015 s.100(5)). **8.50**
However, it may still provide a useful guide as to the approach that would be taken by the courts. So, there is the idea of the goods being specific or ascertained. We have already seen that goods are specific if they are identified and agreed upon at the time of the contract.[118] Although the term "ascertained" is not defined in the Act it probably refers to goods which are identified *after* the making of the contract.[119] Thus if a consumer merely orders "a Bosch dishwasher" or "a heated trolley" and the seller, who is out of stock, fails to obtain one, the remedy of specific performance would probably not be available.[120]

Further, the remedy of specific performance is, and has always been, a discretionary remedy and a court will not grant it if damages would be an adequate remedy. In the vast majority of consumer contracts the buyer can get similar goods elsewhere and any loss can be compensated by an award of damages, e.g. for the extra cost. Accordingly, specific performance would not be granted. It follows that the scope of the remedy, in practical terms, is extremely limited. In the case of a contract for services (e.g. building, cleaning or repairing) the remedy is often even less appropriate.[121,122]

There are only two situations in which specific performance is likely to be granted. The first is where the article is unique (perhaps a painting, sculpture or manuscript). The second is where the property in specific or ascertained goods has passed to the buyer and the seller becomes bankrupt or goes into liquidation. Under general principles of insolvency law a creditor can enforce his rights against the estate of an insolvent debtor if those rights are proprietary rather than personal. The consumer should immediately get in touch with the liquidator or trustee in bankruptcy to demand delivery of the goods.

(2) Can I get my money back?

When a consumer makes a contract for the purchase of goods or services he **8.51**
is under a basic obligation to pay the contract price. Thus, if he has booked a holiday at a seaside hotel, he cannot simply cancel his booking. If he does so then, as a matter of strict law, the hotel can keep any deposit; they can even

---

[118] See para.6.32 above.
[119] See Atkin LJ in *Re Wait* [1927] 1 Ch. 606.
[120] As above.
[121] There used to be a rule that specific performance (or a mandatory injunction) would not be granted if this required constant supervision of the defendant's work (*Ryan v Mutual Tontine Westminster Chambers Association* [1893] 1 Ch. 116). The rationale of this rule has always been questionable and it is clear that it no longer exists: *Shiloh Spinners Ltd v Harding (No.1)* [1973] A.C. 721 at 691 HL.
[122] cf. the above discussed cases under the CRA 2015 where the goods, services or DC are defective. Here it may not always be so straightforward, certainly to obtain repair or repeat performance elsewhere—the risk in such cases, especially with complex goods, DC or services, is that the third party charges more and/or makes matters worse, there then being complex debates as to mitigation and causation.

sue him for damages, if they have suffered additional loss by reason of his cancellation and have been unable to mitigate the loss by reletting the room.

There may, however, be cases where the consumer is relieved of his basic duty to pay the price; in these cases he can recover the price (or a deposit) if he has already paid it. This will be so in at least four cases:

(a) where the contract is rescinded for misrepresentation[123];

(b) where specific goods perish before the risk has passed to the buyer[124];

(c) where a contract for the sale of goods is discharged as a result of the supplier's breach; and

(d) where the consumer exercises a contractual or statutory right of cancellation.[125]

Discharge by breach

8.52 We have already dealt above with the statutory right to reject and obtain a refund in goods contracts; and the more limited circumstances, in DC contracts, when a price reduction can amount to a full refund. Here, we are concerned with when there is a common law right to terminate. Given the above statutory rights, any such common law right would be of most significance in DC and services contracts, where there are no statutory rights to terminate the contract.

Under the general law, a contract is discharged by a breach if the innocent party has been deprived of substantially the whole benefit which it was intended that he should obtain from the contract.[126] In other words the question is not "how was this term classified when the contract was made?" but—much more sensibly—"how serious was the breach and what effect did the breach have on the innocent party?" Even if the breach was a repudiatory breach, the innocent party may well have received *some* benefit under the contract and therefore have no right to recover money paid by him— although he will have a claim for damages which could well be equal to, or greater than, the amount of payments made.

Supplies of services

8.53 Finally in contracts for services the statutory obligations as to care and skill, time for performance and price are referred to by the neutral word "term".[127] It is clear therefore that the flexible *Hong Kong* test will apply to them: they are intermediate stipulations.[128] The severity and consequences of the breach are crucial.

---

[123] See para.8.07 above.
[124] See para.6.33 above.
[125] For examples see para.6.23 above.
[126] per Diplock LJ in *Hong Kong Fir Shipping Co Ltd v Kawasaki* [1962] 2 Q.B. 26 at 66.
[127] Supply of Goods and Services Act 1982 ss.13–15.
[128] *Hong Kong Fir Shipping Co Ltd v Kawasaki* [1962] 2 Q.B. 26 at 66.

(3) Can I get compensation?

Rights to claim compensation are reserved by ss.19, 42 & 56. The consumer   **8.54**
is entitled to damages if the other party has broken a term of the contract,
express or implied, and the consumer has suffered loss. It is irrelevant whether
the term is a condition, warranty or intermediate stipulation, or unclassified
as are the most important terms now in the CRA 2015. When we turn to the
difficult question of quantifying the claim we must consider two closely related
problems, namely (a) for what items of loss is the defendant liable, and (b) on
what principles should the compensation be assessed?

For what loss is the defendant liable? Remoteness

The general rules governing remoteness of damage were laid down more than   **8.55**
150 years ago in *Hadley v Baxendale*[129] and more recently by the House of
Lords in *Koufos v Czarnikow Ltd (The Heron II)*.[130] The defendant is clearly
liable for damage arising naturally from the breach (normal loss—first rule).
He is also liable for other damage which can fairly and reasonably have been
within the contemplation of both parties, at the time they made the contract, as
the probable result of the breach of it (unusual loss—second rule). It has been
held that where the general *type* or kind of damage was within the contemplation of the parties, the defendant is liable even though the precise *extent* of the
damage, or the precise form of the damage, was outside his contemplation.[131]

Mitigation

Another basic rule is that of mitigation—the injured party must take reason-   **8.56**
able steps to mitigate his loss. Thus, to take an obvious example, a buyer of
a defective product could not sue the seller for the cost of having it repaired
by a third party if the seller had previously offered to repair it free of charge
or perhaps if a free repair (parts *and* labour) was available under a manufacturer's guarantee.

General principles of compensation

If the damage is not too remote under the rules set out above, the general   **8.57**
principle is that damages should, so far as possible, place the injured party
in the same position as if the contract had been performed properly. Thus,
where a negligent survey causes a buyer to pay too much for a house the
damages will be the difference between the price paid and the lower (defective) value; in *Watts v Morrow*[132] a claim based on the cost of repair when the
defects were discovered was rejected.

---

[129] (1854) 9 Ex. 341 at 354.
[130] [1969] 1 A.C. 350.
[131] *Parsons (Livestock) Ltd v Uttley Ingham & Co* [1978] 1 Q.B. 791 (sale and construction of
     hopper for feeding nuts to pigs; ventilator left unopened; nuts became mouldy; pigs died;
     supplier of hopper liable). See also *Vacwell v B.D.H. Chemicals* [1971] 1 Q.B. 88.
[132] [1991] 1 W.L.R. 1421 CA. See also *Ruxley Electronics v Forsyth* [1996] A.C. 344.

Non-delivery s.51, s.54 and general principles

8.58   In the case of a sale or supply of goods the buyer may have an action for damages against the seller (a) if the seller fails to deliver, or (b) if the seller breaks a condition or warranty. The general principles laid down in *Hadley v Baxendale*[133] appear in statutory form. Thus s.51(2) which deals with non-delivery provides that:

> The measure of damages is the estimated loss directly and naturally resulting, in the ordinary course of events, from the seller's breach of contract.

As an example of this, s.51(3) provided the "available market" rule:

> Where there is an available market for the goods in question the measure of damages is prima facie . . . the difference between the contract price and the market or current price of the goods at the time or times when they ought to have been delivered, or (if no time was fixed) at the time of refusal to deliver.

Sections 51(2) and (3) no longer apply in consumer contracts, but, as indicated, they only ever reflected the general principles from common law in any case, and these principles still apply.

8.59   Let us suppose that John agrees to buy a new Ford Focus car from a dealer for £16,000. The contract provides that the car must be delivered by 1 May but the dealer fails to deliver. By that date the price has increased by £500. If John has to pay an extra £500 to buy one from another dealer, this sum will prima facie be his damages (previously under s.51(3), and now simply under general principles). If, however, he can obtain an identical model elsewhere for the same or a lower price, his loss is nil.

The second rule of *Hadley v Baxendale*, damage within the reasonable contemplation of the parties, is reflected in s.54 of the 1979 Act which reads:

> Nothing in this Act affects the right of the buyer or the seller to recover interest or special damages in any case where by law interest or special damages may be recoverable. . . .

Again, this no longer applies in consumer contracts, but the general principle it reflects does apply. Thus if, as a result of the non-delivery of the car, John loses a valuable business contract, that would be "special damages" and the defaulting dealer will be liable for it only if it was brought to his attention before the agreement was made.

Non-acceptance—s.50 of the 1979 Act

8.60   Consumers should be aware of their duty to take delivery and their liability in damages for non-acceptance. Sometimes they believe (incorrectly) that, having placed an order for goods—a car, carpet, furniture—they can

---

[133] See para.8.55 above.

change their minds and "cancel" the order with impunity. Such cancellation rights are available only where the Consumer Protection (Information and Cancellation) Regulations 2013 apply (see Chapter Six).

If in the example in para.8.59 above John refuses to take delivery, he will be in breach of contract and liable in damages to the dealer. Section 50 of the 1979 Act (which still applies to consumer contracts) provides:

(1) Where the buyer wrongfully neglects or refuses to accept and pay for the goods, the seller may maintain an action against him for damages for non-acceptance.

(2) The measure of damages is the estimated loss directly and naturally resulting, in the ordinary course of events, from the buyer's breach of contract.

(3) Where there is an available market for the goods in question the measure of damages is prima facie to be ascertained by the difference between the contract price and the market or current price at the time or times when the goods ought to have been accepted or (if no time was fixed for acceptance) at the time of the refusal to accept.

8.61 Section 50(2), like s.51(2) above, puts into statutory form rule one of *Hadley v Baxendale*. Section 50(3), like s.51(3) above, gives an example. "Available market"[134] means that demand exceeds supply. Thus if the dealer mitigates his loss and resells the same car to another buyer at the same price, his loss is nil and so are his damages assuming he had only one car to sell and has done so. However, if supply exceeds demand, as is usually the case, s.50(3) is inapplicable and under s.50(2) the dealer will recover his loss of profit on the sale to John, for he could supply all comers and has lost a sale.[135]

Section 50 applies where the seller is left with the goods on his hands by the buyer's refusal to take delivery. If, however, the buyer takes delivery and the property passes to him, the seller will recover the full price under s.49 (the usual debt collection for "goods sold and delivered").

Damages for defective goods—s.53 and general principles

8.62 In this situation damages arising naturally are covered by s.53(2) while abnormal damages are covered by s.54.[136] Like s.54, s.53 no longer applies to consumer contracts, but again, it simply reflects general principles, and these continue to apply. So, where goods are in breach of the terms, e.g., as to quality, fitness, etc., the damages are prima facie the difference between the actual value of the defective goods and their value if they had not been

---

[134] See *Aerocap Partners Ltd v Avia Asset Management AB* [2010] EWHC 2431 (Comm): sale of two Boeing 757s.

[135] *Charter v Sullivan* [1957] 2 Q.B.117; cf. *Thompson v Robinson (Gunmakers)* [1955] 2 W.L.R. 185.

[136] See para.8.59 above.

in breach. This will usually be the cost of repairing the defect.[137] It is clear, however, that damages are not necessarily confined to that amount. Thus, for example, damages for personal injury or death can be recovered on a sale of a defective toy.[138] Then, if a defective car is "off the road" for repair, the buyer will be able to recover from the seller not only the cost of repair but also the cost of hiring a substitute car[139] during this period. The magazine *Which?* has cited a case where a buyer of a leaking caravan spent large sums of money on petrol on numerous journeys to have it repaired. He also planned to have a caravan holiday but was compelled to move into a guest house when the defects reappeared. He successfully recovered both the cost of petrol and the guest house expenses in county court proceedings.

If the seller is in breach of the term on the "right to sell",[140] the damages recoverable by the buyer can include not merely the price paid but also the cost of necessary repairs.[141]

Mental distress

8.63 A head of damages which no legal adviser should forget in a consumer dispute is mental distress, upset, disappointment and injured feelings. The seminal case on this topic was *Jarvis v Swans Tours*, a heart-rending case.[142]

> A solicitor on a fortnight's holiday in the Swiss Alps spent an entire week surrounded by people who could not speak English! As a further insult instead of Swiss cakes he was served crisps and desiccated nut rolls. (As their Lordships pointed out during the hearing, "You don't have to go to Switzerland to get those": Stephenson LJ "You can get them at Crewe": Edmund Davies LJ—*The Times*, 19 October 1972.) Damages of £125 were awarded, double the cost of the holiday, by the Court of Appeal. The description of facilities (including the promise of a fun house party) in the tour operator's brochure was an express term of the contract.

Holiday contracts continue to be a fruitful area for this type of loss.[143]

Damages have also been awarded in proceedings for negligence against a solicitor who failed to obtain a non-molestation injunction for a client.[144]

---

[137] s.53(3) and see *Lee v York (Coach and Marine) Ltd* [1977] R.T.R. 35.

[138] *Godley v Perry* [1960] 1 W.L.R. 9.

[139] *Bernstein v Pamson Motors* [1987] 2 All E.R. 220. Some car hire companies provide cars free of charge on condition that the consumers co-operate with them in bringing proceedings and pay the hire-charges out of damages awarded. The deferment of the hirer's payment obligation amounts to "credit" and the hire agreement will usually be regulated under the Consumer Credit Act 1974 (see para.20.08 below). If the agreement is "improperly executed" (see para.22.02 below) the hirer cannot recover the hire charges from the other driver: *Dimond v Lovell* [2002] 1 A.C. 384. Some 40,000 cases were stayed until the House of Lords had given its ruling in this case.

[140] See para.2.27 above.

[141] *Mason v Burningham* [1949] 2 K.B. 545.

[142] [1973] 1 Q.B. 233.

[143] For further examples, see para.8.68 below.

[144] *Heywood v Wellers* [1976] Q.B. 446. See also *Channon v Lindley Johnstone* [2002] EWCA Civ 353.

The first supply of goods case was *Jackson v Chrysler Acceptances*.[145] This **8.64**
has been followed by two other car cases where the damages were by no
means nominal.[146]

Even so, the courts approach this area cautiously, as can be gleaned from
the remarks of Staughton LJ in *Hayes v Dodd*[147] where the Court of Appeal
disallowed this head of damage in a business dispute:

> "Damages for mental distress in contract are, as a matter of policy, limited to
> certain classes of case. I would broadly follow the classification provided by
> Dillon L.J. in *Bliss v South East Thames Regional Health Authority* [1987] I.C.R.
> 700 at 718:
>
> > '. . . where the contract which has been broken was itself a contract to provide
> > peace of mind or freedom from distress . . . .'
>
> It may be that the class is somewhat wider than that. But it should not, in my
> judgment, include any case where the object of the contract was not comfort
> or pleasure, or the relief of discomfort, but simply carrying on a commercial-
> activity with a view to profit."

In *Watts v Morrow*[148] the Court of Appeal rejected the argument that a **8.65**
contract for the survey of a house was a contract to buy peace of mind. In
this type of case damages for distress should be limited to a modest sum for
physical discomfort and disruption; the court reduced the award from £4,000
to £750.

It is clear from the cases that damages for distress will be kept within
narrow limits. Thus it has been held[149] that customers suing a bank could not
claim damages for distress resulting from alleged unauthorised withdrawals
from service-till machines. Similarly, the undoubted pleasure of a car owner
in driving a Rolls Royce did not give rise to a successful distress claim when
the car was badly repaired.[150]

However, in *Farley v Skinner*[151] the House of Lords extended the param-
eters for distress.

> The claimant wanted to buy a gracious country residence for retirement—"a
> property offering peace and tranquillity was the raison d'être of the proposed
> purchase" (Lord Steyn). He became interested in Riverside House, in the
> country near the Sussex village of Blackboys. It had a tennis court, croquet lawn,

---

[145] [1978] R.T.R. 474. A consumer told a dealer that he wanted a car for a holiday. The car was defective. The county court judge awarded (inter alia) £75 for a spoilt holiday. Increased on appeal to £750 (including other damages).

[146] *Bernstein v Pamson Motors* [1987] 2 All E.R. 220: £150 for spoilt day. *UCB Leasing v Holtom* [1987] R.T.R. 362 CA: £500 for distress where the hire car had three complete electrical failures in four months.

[147] [1990] 2 All E.R. 815 at 824. *Channon v Lindley Johnstone* [2002] EWCA Civ 353.

[148] [1991] 1 W.L.R. 1421. See *Harrison v Shepherd Homes Ltd* [2011] EWHC 1811 (TCC): defective foundations—£150 p.a. for distress and inconvenience.

[149] *McConville v Barclays Bank*, The Times, 30 June 1993. The court formerly known as the Official Referee Court has now been renamed the Technology and Construction Court.

[150] *Alexander v Rolls Royce Motor Co Ltd* [1996] R.T.R. 95.

[151] [2002] 2 A.C. 732. See also *Yearworth v North Bristol NHS Trust*, The Times, 10 February 2009, CA: bailment of sperm lost by hospital.

swimming pool and extensive grounds. As it was only 15 miles from Gatwick Airport, when instructing the defendant surveyor he asked whether it would be affected by aircraft noise. The surveyor reported "We think it unlikely that the property will suffer greatly from such noise". He then bought it in 1991 for £420,000 and spent £125,000 on modernisation. After moving in he quickly discovered that the property was affected by aircraft noise as it was not far away from the Mayfield Stack, a navigation beacon where aircraft circled waiting to land. The trial judge found that the surveyor had been negligent and awarded £10,000 for discomfort. The Court of Appeal, by a majority, allowed the defendant's appeal.

8.66   The claimant's appeal to the House of Lords was allowed unanimously. They rejected the argument that the object of the *entire contract* must be to give pleasure, relaxation and peace of mind as being a narrow reading of the dicta of Bingham LJ in *Watts v Morrow*. Lord Steyn stated (at p.750) that, it is sufficient if it is "a major or important object of the contract". The award of the £10,000 was "at the very top end of what could possibly be regarded as appropriate damages . . . I consider awards in this area should be restrained and modest". However, the court would not interfere with the judge's evaluation.

It is unlikely that earlier cases would be decided differently now, as it is still essential for pleasure or peace of mind to be an important ingredient of the contract. However, in future consumers may succeed if they emphasise at the outset that such a factor is important to them, even though the contract may not be, on the whole, a pleasurable one.

Hire-purchase

8.67   The principles set out above are equally relevant to hire-purchase transactions. Thus in *Yeoman Credit Ltd v Apps*[152] the hirer of a car which took one-and-a-half hours to do three or four miles successfully sued for damages. The damages were assessed at the difference between what the car should have been worth and what it was actually worth; on that basis the hirer recovered all his payments, less a very small allowance for use.

Holiday contracts

8.68   If the customer finds, on arrival at his resort, that his room has been double-booked, or that the hotel does not exist, he can claim the extra cost of having to stay at an equivalent hotel plus (as already stated) damages for mental distress. If the hotel exists but does not have the promised facilities, the remedy will again be damages. In appropriate cases damages can include losses suffered by members of the claimant's family.[153]

---

[152] [1962] 2 Q.B. 508. See also *Jackson v Chrysler Acceptances* [1978] R.T.R. 474, see para.8.64 above.

[153] *Jackson v Horizon Holidays* [1975] 1 W.L.R. 1468 CA. A four-week family holiday in Sri Lanka proved to be a disaster, with very distasteful food apparently cooked in coconut oil, and a shower and no bath. The holiday price was £1,200. Damages of £1,100 were awarded for breach of contract to cover the distress of the husband, wife and child.

An interesting case is *Spencer v Cosmos Air Holidays*[154]:

> The plaintiff booked two weeks' holiday in Spain with the defendants for £266. After about a week the hotelier wrongfully ejected her and her two female companions. They spent two nights sleeping on the beach before the defendants found them alternative, inferior accommodation at a less pleasing resort.

The Court of Appeal awarded her £1,000 for her distress, misery and humiliation, reducing by half the award made by the trial judge.

Of greater importance, though, is the recent Court of Appeal decision in **8.69** *Milner v Carnival Plc (t/a Cunard)*,[155] which contains the most extensive and wide-ranging guidance so far on the assessment of damages in holiday cases. The case is not typical of the holidays enjoyed by most consumers—it concerns a world cruise costing nearly £60,000! The facts were these:

> Mr and Mrs Milner (H and W) booked their preferred cabin with Cunard (C) 18 months before the maiden voyage of the cruise ship Queen Victoria at a discounted price of £59,052 for 106 days. C's brochure lavishly presented the glamour of the world cruise, e.g. "star treatment", "a taste of the high life", and "Queen Victoria embraces the most advanced technology and a host of luxurious innovations".
>
> A storm on the first night damaged their cabin causing loud banging as the floor plates flexed. After two sleepless nights they moved each night to an inside cabin until the ship reached New York four days later. They then moved temporarily to an upgraded cabin for the 17 days to Los Angeles. They refused an alternative cabin as it lacked a bath and hanging space for W's clothes including 21 ball gowns. They then went back to their original cabin to Hawaii, where by agreement they abandoned the cruise after 28 days as the cabin was still too noisy. C refunded £48,270.
>
> They sued C and were awarded £22,000: £2,500 each for diminution in value of their cruise, £7,500 each for their distress and disappointment and £2,000 to W for her wasted expenditure on her ball gowns (about half their cost). C appealed.

The Court of Appeal allowed the appeal and gave the following valuable **8.70** guidance.

(1) Compensation was potentially available for:

- diminution in value;
- consequential pecuniary loss for out of pocket expenses;
- physical inconvenience and discomfort; and
- mental distress.

(2) Diminution in value was the difference between what the supplier contracted to provide and what was actually provided. Here the general disruption, inconvenience and uncertainty as well as the sleepless nights were relevant factors to be balanced against the

---

[154] *The Times*, 6 December 1989.
[155] [2010] EWCA Civ 389.

upgraded cabin. On balance the value of the cruise was diminished by one-third of the price actually paid for 28 days. H and W were awarded £3,500 in all for this.

(3) When assessing damages for physical discomfort, inconvenience and distress the court had to compare expectations with reality. Here the expectations were sky high in view of the advertising. Instead of "star treatment" H and W had a terrible and stressful experience, but not horrendous enough to justify exceptional awards. As the cruise had been cancelled by agreement in Hawaii, they were not entitled to damages for the loss of the pleasures of the rest of the cruise, nor for W's loss of the opportunity to wear her ball gowns. The Court of Appeal then considered comparable awards for psychiatric damage in personal injury cases and for injury to feelings in sex and race discrimination and bereavement cases. They reduced the awards of £7,500 each to £4,000 for H and £4,500 for W.

(4) Warning that judges should ensure that there was no duplication, where two heads of damages were assessed, the court considered £12,000 to be fair and just compensation for C's failure to meet the guests' legitimate expectations.

Cleaners

8.71   If a cleaner negligently ruins or loses a carpet or a suit, the damages will be based on the cost of acquiring a replacement, but this will be subject to a discount for age and use.

Builders

8.72   If a builder, decorator or plumber does a job badly, the damages will normally include not only the money paid to another firm to have it put right but also damages for the resulting inconvenience.[156] If the work is done extremely badly, the consumer may be entitled to refuse to pay anything at all.[157] If, however, the cost of repair or reconstruction is out of all proportion to the resulting benefit, the court will award damages based on "diminution of value" of the property (if any) plus a modest sum for loss of amenity.[158]

4. REMEDIES IN TORT

8.73   Perhaps the most likely case of a tort claim would be where the consumer has a claim against the manufacturer for negligence or under the Consumer Protection Act 1987. In personal injury cases the damages would include loss

---

[156] See, e.g. *Batty v Metropolitan Realisations* [1978] Q.B. 554.
[157] See, e.g. *Bolton v Mahadeva* [1972] 1 W.L.R. 1009.
[158] See the swimming pool case of *Ruxley Electronics v Forsyth* [1995] 3 All E.R. 268 HL.

of actual and future earnings, medical expenses, pain and suffering and loss of amenities. For further details readers are referred to the standard textbooks on tort and to *McGregor on Damages*.

In a case where the same facts give rise to liability in both contract and tort the rules as to damages are being brought very close together.[159]

---

[159] *Parsons (Livestock) Ltd v Uttley Ingham & Co* [1978] 1 Q.B. 791 (see also para.8.52 above).

CHAPTER NINE

"THEY SAY THAT I HAVE SIGNED AWAY MY RIGHTS"

Exemption clauses have been widely used in standard form contracts in the past 60 years or so and have come in for severe criticism from the courts and other bodies. The courts have developed certain techniques to control the legal effect of these clauses. Unfortunately the control exercised by the courts has been unsatisfactory because, with the exception of Lord Denning MR, they have felt themselves unable to break out of the straitjacket of freedom of contract. **9.01**

Accordingly, the use of exemption clauses has been increasingly regulated by statute and the overwhelming majority of these clauses were for a long time controlled by the Unfair Contract Terms Act 1977 (the 1977 Act), in both business to business and business to consumer contracts. These controls were supplemented by the Unfair Terms in Consumer Contracts Regulations 1999, which implemented Directive 93/13/EEC on Unfair Terms in Consumer Contracts and dealt with both exclusion clauses and other types of unfair term, i.e. those imposing unfair obligations or liabilities on consumers. The problem for legal advisers and consumers was the complexity resulting from two concurrent statutory regimes which partly overlap. Now for business to consumer contracts, these two regimes have been merged into a single regime under the Consumer Rights Act 2015 (CRA 2015); while the 1977 Act continues to apply, but only to exclusion clauses in business to business contracts.

Scheme of this and the following chapter

It is proposed to start by examining the attitude of the courts to exemption clauses. These common law rules apply in both business to business and business to consumer contracts. Consideration will then be given to the statutory controls imposed by the 1977 Act. Although these only now apply in business to business contracts, many advisers may deal with smallish business customers who may be affected by exclusion clauses, but will not be protected by the consumer regime under the CRA 2015. The broad scope of the 1977 Act has made the former topic far less important and accordingly it will be examined fairly briefly. A short reference to other legislation will be made at the end of this chapter. **9.02**

Then in Chapter Ten, the new consumer regime under the CRA 2015 will be examined.

Examples

9.03   The first three examples are taken from Law Commission Working Paper No.39, pp.74–88.

> (1) The shipowner shall be exempt from all liability in respect of any detention, delay, overcarriage, loss, expenses, damage, sickness or injury of whatever kind, whenever and wherever occurring, and however and by whomsoever caused of or to any passenger, or of or to any person or child travelling with him or her or in his or her care, or of or to any baggage, property, goods, effects, articles, matters or things belonging or carried by, with or for any passenger or any such person or child.
>
> (2) [The ferry company] shall not be liable for the death or any injury, damage, loss, delay or accident . . . wheresoever, whensoever and howsoever caused and whether by negligence of their servants or agents or by unseaworthiness of the vessel.
>
> (3) The contractors shall not under any circumstances be liable for any loss or damage caused by or resulting from or in connection with fire, howsoever caused.
>
> (4) All cars parked at owner's risk.
>
> (5) In the case of loss or damage the liability of the company is limited to the value of the garment.
>
> (6) All claims within seven days.

Justification

9.04   In deciding on the price of their products suppliers will consider the question of loss apportionment. They can also cut down very substantially on administration overheads by having standard form contracts (thus avoiding the need to negotiate each contract separately) and by avoiding litigation. A survey carried out by Yates in *Exclusion Clauses in Contracts* contains the following passage (2nd edn, p.25).

> The desire to avoid court proceedings in the event of a dispute was also a reason advanced for using exemption clauses which, it was often felt, gave each party a clearer indication of where they stood. . . . Distrust of lawyers' and more especially judges' ability to understand the businessman's problems was very marked.

Criticism

9.05   When due allowance has been made for the points set out above there is no doubt that exemption clauses are open to abuse. The following passage is taken from the Law Commission's Second Report on Exemption Clauses No. 69, para.11, on which the 1977 Act was based:

We are in no doubt that in many cases they operate against the public interest and that the prevailing judicial attitude of suspicion, or indeed of hostility, to such clauses is well founded. All too often they are introduced in ways which result in the party affected by them remaining ignorant of their presence or import until it is too late. That party, even if he knows of the exemption clause, will often be unable to appreciate what he may lose by accepting it. In any case he may not have sufficient bargaining strength to refuse to accept it. The result is that the risk of carelessness or of failure to achieve satisfactory standards of performance is thrown on to the party who is not responsible for it or who is unable to guard against it. Moreover, by excluding liability for such carelessness or failure the economic pressures to maintain high standards of performance are reduced.

1. JUDICIAL CONTROL OF EXEMPTION CLAUSES

9.06 The reasons for judicial hostility to exemption clauses have already been mentioned: ignorance, non-negotiation and inequality of bargaining power. Perhaps the first of these points is the strongest. After all, the law of contract is, or should be, about agreement. If consumers were asked "do you know that you have signed away your right to complain if the cleaners lose the carpet?" or "do you know that you will receive no compensation at all if the carriers damage your furniture?" it is unlikely that their reply could be printed in this book; at all events it is likely to include the word "no". When they made the contract they would reasonably have expected that the work would be done with reasonable care, and that they would receive compensation if this was not so. Their expectations may have been increased by a glowing advertisement in a newspaper or magazine or on television or the internet. Accordingly exemption clauses, which are often inconsistent with their reasonable expectations, are closely scrutinised by the courts.

The courts have to decide two basic problems, namely:

(1) was the clause duly incorporated into the contract? and

(2) does it, on its true construction, cover the event which has occurred?

(1) Incorporation[1]

9.07 The general contractual principles relating to incorporation have been well established for a considerable time.

(a) Signed document

9.08 If the contractual document is signed, this operates as an incorporation of all the terms which appear in that document or which are referred to in it.[2] The signatory will not be bound, however, if by mistake he signed the document

---

[1] For a summary of the rules see the judgment of Boreham J in *John Snow & Son Ltd v Woodcroft Ltd* [1985] B.C.L.C. 48.
[2] The leading case is *L'Estrange v Graucob* [1934] 2 K.B. 394.

without negligence and it turns out to be a document of a fundamentally different kind from the document which he thought that he was signing.[3]

(b) Unsigned document or notice

9.09   If the consumer has not signed a contractual document, a clause will only be incorporated if reasonable steps were taken *before* contract to bring it to his notice. The following cases illustrate how this principle has been applied.

9.10   (i) In the case of *Thompson v L.M.S. Railway*[4] a lady bought a railway excursion ticket containing the words "For conditions see back". The back of the ticket referred to conditions in the railway timetables which were available for purchase. Had Mrs Thompson obtained and read them (by which time she would certainly have missed her train) she would have seen an exclusion clause excluding liability for negligence. The Court of Appeal held that the exemption clause had been incorporated into the contract.

9.11   (ii) The case of *Chapelton v Barry UDC*[5] concerned an exclusion clause on a deckchair receipt. It was held that there was no incorporation; this was not the type of document on which the consumer could reasonably expect to find conditions and therefore the local authority had not taken sufficient steps to bring the clause to the consumer's attention. The court reached a similar "no incorporation" result in two more recent cases where words appeared on the inside of a cheque book[6] and on time sheets.[7]

9.12   (iii) In *Olley v Marlborough Court Hotel*[8] a consumer booked a hotel room. After he had done so he saw an exemption notice in the bedroom. It was held that there was no incorporation since the clause had been introduced too late. The position might have been different if the notice was prominently displayed at the reception desk or if the customer had stayed at the hotel on previous occasions. In the latter case the notice might have been incorporated on the basis of a previous course of dealing. Nevertheless, this principle, which can be more readily implied in commercial contracts,[9] is very rarely applied in consumer contracts.[10]

9.13   (iv) *Thornton v Shoe Lane Parking Co Ltd*[11] is perhaps the best modern example of how the basic rules of "contract" are being adapted, in a realistic way, to standard form consumer transactions.

---

[3] *Saunders v Anglia Building Society* [1971] A.C. 1039, in which the House of Lords emphasised that this so-called *"non est factum"* defence must be confined within narrow limits.

[4] [1930] 1 K.B. 41.

[5] [1940] 1 K.B. 532. In any case it was post-contractual and so ineffective.

[6] *Burnett v Westminster Bank* [1965] 3 All E.R. 81.

[7] *Grogan v Robin Meredith Plant Hire* [1996] C.L.C. 1127 CA.

[8] [1949] 1 K.B. 532.

[9] *Spurling v Bradshaw* [1956] 1 W.L.R. 461.

[10] See, e.g. *McCutcheon v David MacBrayne Ltd* [1964] 1 W.L.R. 125 HL, a notable case, if only because of the appearance in it of a Mr McSporran!

[11] [1971] 2 Q.B. 163. The case was considered in the context of wheel-clamping. The car owner cannot recover damages where there was a clear and prominent sign indicating the risk and the penalty: *Vine v Waltham Forest LBC* [2000] 1 W.L.R. 2383.

Mr Thornton went to park his car at a new multistorey car park—he had not been there before. When he arrived opposite the ticket machine a ticket popped out, the light turned from red to green and he went through and parked his car. The ticket referred to conditions displayed on the premises. These conditions (inter alia) excluded liability for personal injuries caused by negligence. There was an accident caused partly by the defendants' negligence and Mr Thornton was injured.

The Court of Appeal held that the defendants had not taken reasonable steps to bring this particular clause to the notice of Mr Thornton. In the words of Lord Denning MR at p.170:

"It is so wide and destructive of rights that the court should not hold any man bound by it unless it is drawn to his attention in the most explicit way. . . . In order to give sufficient notice, it would need to be printed in red ink with a red hand pointing to it—or something equally startling."

Megaw LJ gave an equally vivid example when he said at p.173:

"It does not take much imagination to picture the indignation of the defendants if their potential customers . . . were one after the other to get out of their cars leaving the cars blocking the entrance to the garages in order to search for, find and peruse the notices! Yet unless the defendants genuinely intended that potential customers should do just that it would be fiction, if not farce, to treat those customers as persons who have been given a fair opportunity, before the contracts are made, of discovering the conditions by which they are to be bound."

Lord Denning MR went so far as to hold that the contract was made when the customer dropped his money into the machine, thereby accepting their offer to park with the result that the conditions on the ticket were introduced too late.[12] The trouble with this approach is that in many cases the customer does *not* put money into the slot—he merely collects a ticket and pays later. Nevertheless both Lord Denning MR and Sir Gordon Willmer were influenced by the finality of a contract made with a machine. To quote again from Lord Denning:

9.14

"The customer pays his money and gets a ticket. He cannot refuse it. He cannot get his money back. He may protest to the machine, even swear at it. But it will remain unmoved. He is committed beyond recall."

These interesting problems may never be decided because it may be unnecessary to do so. If the facts of *Thornton* were to recur, a clause excluding liability for death or personal injury resulting from negligence would in any event be void[13] and accordingly the question of incorporation would have no practical importance. The point might, however, remain relevant if the customer suffered damage to his property. In that case the exemption clause

---

[12] cf. *Olley v Marlborough Court Hotel* [1949] 1 K.B. 532 (see para.9.12 above).
[13] s.2(1) of the 1977 Act: see para.9.34 below.

would be valid if reasonable[14] and accordingly the customer might well raise the argument of "no incorporation" as his first line of attack.

9.15   (v) In *Interfoto Picture Library Ltd v Stiletto Visual Programmes Ltd*[15] (a non-consumer case) the Court of Appeal had to consider the situation where one clause in a set of conditions was particularly onerous.

> SVP, an advertising agency, telephoned IPL, a photographic library, requesting photographs of the 1950s for a presentation for a client. IPL sent by hand 47 transparencies in a bag with a delivery note stating that they must be returned within 14 days.
> Across the bottom of the note were printed nine conditions in four columns, under the fairly prominent heading "CONDITIONS". Condition 2 stated that all transparencies must be returned within 14 days and that "A holding fee of £5.00 plus VAT per day will be charged for each transparency which is retained by you longer than the said period of 14 days. . . ."
> SVP accepted delivery, but did not use them and by an oversight kept them for 28 days. When IPL sent an invoice for £3,783.50, SVP refused to pay, for most libraries charged less than 50p per day.

Hitherto the general approach in the "ticket cases" had been to ask whether the supplier has taken reasonable steps to bring the conditions *as a whole* to the notice of the consumer. However, Lord Denning MR had signposted a different route with his "red ink—red hand" approach in *Thornton v Shoe Lane Parking Ltd.*[16] Following that route the Court of Appeal held in the *Interfoto* case that condition 2, imposing an exorbitant holding fee, was not part of the contract. Dillon LJ stated the principle thus[17]:

> "It is in my judgment a logical development of the common law into modern conditions that it should be held, as it was in *Thornton v Shoe Lane Parking Ltd*, that, if one condition in a set of printed conditions is particularly onerous or unusual, the party seeking to enforce it must show that that particular condition was fairly brought to the attention of the other party."

9.16   Bingham LJ, agreeing that "the plaintiffs did not do what was necessary to draw this unreasonable and extortionate clause fairly to their attention", seemed to be of the view that a more general principle of fairness was being applied[18]:

> "The tendency of the English authorities has, I think, been to look at the nature of the transaction in question and the character of the parties to it; to consider what notice the party alleged to be bound was given of the particular condition said to bind him; and to resolve whether in all the circumstances it is fair to hold

---

[14] s.2(2) of the 1977 Act.
[15] [1988] 1 All E.R. 348. For a recent (unsuccessful) attempt to apply this case to the terms of a scratch-card competition see *O'Brien v M.G.N. Ltd* [2001] EWCA Civ 1279. The court held that there was nothing unusual about the term.
[16] See para.9.13 above. See also his dictum to similar effect in *J. Spurling Ltd v Bradshaw* [1956] 1 W.L.R. 461 at 466, and the comments of Bramwell and Mellish LJJ in *Parker v South Eastern Rly. Co* (1877) 2 C.P.D. 416.
[17] At p.620.
[18] As above. The concept of "good faith" in the context of the Unfair Terms in Consumer Contracts Regulations 1999 is considered at para.10.25 below.

him bound by the condition in question. This may yield a result not very different from the civil law principle of good faith, at any rate so far as the formation of the contract is concerned."

The actual decision (treating the clause as unduly onerous merely because other libraries charged less) is certainly debatable but, subject to this, three final points can be made. First, the clause was not an exemption clause[19] and it will be interesting to see how far the courts will use this "non-incorporation" tool to protect business customers in areas where Parliament has chosen not to do so (business customers are not given statutory protection against clauses such as that in the *Interfoto* case). Secondly, we have already seen how non-incorporation can outflank an argument based on the "reasonableness" test under the 1977 Act. Finally, it remains to be seen how far the principle discussed in *Interfoto* (and particularly the fairness point raised by Bingham LJ) can be called in aid by someone who has *signed* a contract—even though up to now the principle of bringing the conditions to the notice of the consumer has not been relevant in this situation. In other words, *L'Estrange v Graucob*[20] may not be an impassable barrier.

(2) Does the clause cover the event which has occurred?

Even if the clause has been incorporated into the contract it is not automatically effective. The courts have evolved a number of techniques to counter their effect. These techniques may still be relevant in some cases but it must be strongly emphasised that times have changed and, with the arrival of the 1977 Act, the courts will be less concerned with these matters (see para.9.24 below).   **9.17**

(a) Privity

After earlier doubts, the House of Lords decided that an exemption clause between A and B could not protect C—even though C was an employee or contractor engaged by B to perform the contract.[21] This was outflanked by a drafting technique whereby B contracted as agent for his employees/contractors, so that they could enjoy the benefit of the exemption clause.[22] As a matter of strict legal analysis this creates a separate contract between the employees/contractors and the other party, and the performance of the contract would provide the consideration. Presumably such convoluted drafting will now be a thing of the past; the parties will now be able to use the Contracts (Rights of Third Parties) Act 1999 (see para.4.06 above) under which an exemption clause may benefit a third party (s.1(6)).   **9.18**

---

[19] The 1977 Act could not be used to control the clause for that very reason.
[20] See para.9.08 above.
[21] *Scruttons v Midland Silicones Ltd* [1962] A.C. 446.
[22] *New Zealand Shipping Co Ltd v Satterthwaite & Co Ltd* [1975] A.C. 154 PC. See also *Southern Water Authority v Carey* [1985] 2 All E.R. 1077 where the same result was reached by a different route.

(b) Strict construction and the contra proferentem rule

9.19 A party seeking the protection of an exemption clause must show that the wording is clear enough to cover the alleged breach. This is well illustrated by three cases involving sale of goods.

In *Wallis, Son and Wells v Pratt and Haynes*[23] a commercial contract for the sale of seed excluded "all warranties". The seller supplied seed of a different description and the buyer claimed damages. The House of Lords held that the seller had broken a *condition* and that a clause referring only to *warranties* did not protect him. The mere fact that the buyer, in ignorance of the breach, had "accepted" the goods, and was therefore compelled to treat the breach as a breach of warranty,[24] was immaterial.

In *Andrews Bros (Bournemouth) Ltd v Singer & Co. Ltd*[25] the seller sold a "new Singer car" with a clause excluding "implied conditions and warranties". The seller supplied a car which was not new. The Court of Appeal held that he had broken an *express* condition and accordingly a clause which merely referred to *implied* conditions did not protect him.

9.20 In *Nichol v Godts*[26] the sellers agreed to supply rapeseed oil "warranted only equal to sample". They supplied a mixture of rapeseed oil and hemp oil which matched the sample. It was held that the exclusion clause did not protect them from their overriding duty to supply rapeseed oil in accordance with the description.

The rule of strict construction leads on naturally to the so-called "*contra proferentem*"[27] rule which provides that an ambiguity must be construed against the party who introduced the clause. Thus if a claimant has two distinct claims against the defendant (one in contract and one in tort for negligence) an exemption clause may well be construed so as to cover only the former and not the latter.[28] Even words like "the company will not be liable for damage caused by fire" may merely operate as a warning that the company will only be liable if negligent.[29] It follows that clear words are required to cover liability for negligence, for example, "howsoever caused" or "whether or not due to negligence".

(c) Inconsistent oral promise

9.21 An exemption clause will be overridden by an oral promise which is inconsistent with it. Thus in *Mendelssohn v Normand*[30] a suitcase was stolen from a

---

[23] [1911] A.C. 394. Followed in *KG Bominflot BunkerGesellschaft für Mineraloele mbH & Co v Petroplus Marketing AG (the Mercini Lady)* [2010] EWCA Civ 1145. cf. *Air Transworld Ltd v Bombardier Inc* [2012] EWHC 243 (Comm): sale of aircaft—clause effective.

[24] See para.3.19 above.

[25] [1934] 1 K.B. 17.

[26] (1854) 10 Exch. 191.

[27] Literally "against the person proposing it".

[28] See, e.g. *White v John Warwick* [1953] 1 W.L.R. 1285. See also *Casson v Ostley P.J. Ltd* [2001] EWCA Civ1013 (a building case) where a similar result was reached.

[29] *Hollier v Rambler Motors (AMC) Ltd* [1972] 2 Q.B. 71. For a more recent example of the "*contra proferentem*" rule see *Stent Foundation Ltd v MJ Gleeson Group Plc* [2001] B.L.R. 134.

[30] [1970] 1 Q.B. 177. See also *J Evans & Son (Portsmouth) Ltd v Andrea Merzario Ltd* [1976] 1 W.L.R. 1078 CA.

car which the plaintiff had parked at the defendants' car park. An employee of the defendants promised the plaintiff that he would lock the car, but he failed to do so. The Court of Appeal held that a clause excluding "loss or damage howsoever caused" was ineffective.

(d) Misrepresentation

9.22 The courts will not allow a party to rely on an exemption clause if he has misrepresented its effect to the consumer.[31] On the other hand, the consumer may find himself faced with a clause which says that "no employee of the company has any authority to add to or vary these terms". Such a clause is legally binding.[32]

(e) Fundamental breach

9.23 In a number of cases decided before the 1977 Act the courts sought to relieve the consumer from the harsh effects of an exemption clause by holding that it did not cover the breach of a fundamental term[33] or a fundamental breach.[34] The legal reasoning for this doctrine was highly dubious. The House of Lords has twice rejected it[35] and reaffirmed the basic rule that the scope of an exemption clause is always a question of construction and that there is no rule of law preventing the exclusion of a fundamental breach. In a later case the House of Lords warned against the danger of reintroducing the doctrine under another name.[36]

(f) The new approach

9.24 The most recent cases herald a new approach to the construction of exemption clauses; in future the courts will be less willing to adopt a policy of judicial control of exemption clauses because the need for it has gone. Thus in a case decided on the previous law (but with knowledge that the 1977 Act had been passed) Lord Diplock said as follows:

> "My Lords the reports are full of cases in which what would appear to be very strained constructions have been placed upon exclusion clauses, mainly in what today would be called consumer contracts or contracts of adhesion. As Lord Wilberforce has pointed out, any need for this kind of distortion of the English language has been banished by Parliament, having made these kinds of contract subject to the Unfair Contract Terms Act."[37]

---

[31] *Curtis v Chemical Cleaning and Dyeing Co* [1951] 1 K.B. 805 CA.

[32] *Overbrooke Estates Ltd v Glencombe Properties Ltd* [1974] 1 W.L.R. 1335 (a case on auction particulars). In practice, however, the exemption clause can sometimes be overridden by the employee's apparent authority.

[33] "Something narrower than a condition—something which underlies the whole contract:" per Devlin J (as he then was) in *Smeaton Hanscomb & Co Ltd v Setty (Sassoon) Sons & Co (No.1)* [1953] 1 W.L.R. 1468 at 1470.

[34] See, e.g. *Karsales (Harrow) Ltd v Wallis* [1956] 1 W.L.R. 936.

[35] *Suisse Atlantique v N.V. Rotterdamsche Kolen Centrale* [1967] 1 A.C. 361; *Photo Production v Securicor Transport* [1980] A.C. 827.

[36] *George Mitchell (Chesterhall) Ltd v Finney Lock Seeds Ltd* [1983] 3 W.L.R. 163.

[37] *Photo Production Ltd v Securicor Transport* [1980] A.C. 827 at 851.

Quite apart from this, it seems that a clause limiting damages to a fixed amount (a "limitation clause") will not be construed as strictly as a full exclusion clause.[38] It must be said, however, that the reasoning is not convincing although to accept some liability rather than none may be more reasonable.[39]

2. UNFAIR CONTRACT TERMS ACT 1977

Scope of the Act

9.25 The Act operates in five overlapping areas, namely:

(a) negligence;

(b) contractual obligations;

(c) terms implied in contracts for the sale of goods, hire-purchase and certain analogous contracts for the supply of goods;

(d) guarantees and indemnities; and

(e) misrepresentation.

Before considering these areas it is necessary to mention some preliminary points.

Preliminary matters

9.26 (1) The Act does not create new duties—it merely controls clauses which cut down a duty which would otherwise exist or which exclude or modify the remedies available on breach of that duty.

> Let us suppose that Richard runs a small business, is attending a business meeting and parks his business vehicle in a car park and keeps the key. There is a large notice at the entrance: "The company is not liable for any loss or damage to vehicle or contents, whether or not due to negligence of the company or its servants or agents." When Richard comes back to collect his car it cannot be found.

The notice set out above would be controlled by s.2 of the Act[40] and would be subject to the reasonableness test. This, however, is likely to be completely irrelevant; the company can avoid liability on the more basic ground that the transaction was a mere licence and not a bailment and therefore they owed Richard no duty of care. That was the position before the Act[41] and, as already stated, the Act does not create new duties.

9.27 (2) The name of the Act is misleading—it is both too narrow and too wide.

---

[38] *Ailsa Craig Fishing Co Ltd v Malvern Fishing Co and Securicor (Scotland)* [1983] 1 W.L.R. 964—a House of Lords decision on appeal from Scotland.

[39] *Ailsa Craig Fishing Co Ltd v Malvern Fishing Co and Securicor (Scotland)* [1983] 1 W.L.R. 964 at 966 (Lord Wilberforce) and at 970 (Lord Fraser).

[40] See para.9.27 below.

[41] *Ashby v Tolhurst* [1937] 2 K.B. 242.

It is too narrow because it refers only to "contract"; the Act also applies to tortious negligence both at common law and under the Occupiers' Liability Act 1957. It is too wide because it does not control all "unfair terms"; it merely controls exemption clauses and notices.

(3) With very minor exceptions the key provisions of the Act (ss.2–7) apply only to "business liability". By s.1(3) this means:

9.28

liability for breach of obligations or duties arising—

(a) from things done or to be done by a person in the course of a business (whether his own business or another's); or
(b) from the occupation of premises used for business purposes of the occupier.

When we turn to s.14 we find that the term "business" includes a profession and the activities of any government department or local or public authority.

The term "business" crops up at various points in this book. Thus we have already come across it in connection with (a) supply of goods—implied conditions of quality and fitness,[42] and (b) unsolicited goods and services.[43] We shall meet it again later in this chapter when considering the phrase "deals as consumer".[44] It is also critical for certain provisions of the Consumer Credit Act 1974, for example, non-commercial agreements[45] and the licensing provisions.[46]

There are bound to be borderline cases. Is a landlord carrying on a "business" when he lets a block of flats? Is a charity fête a business? The tax cases show that the key factors include the frequency of the transaction, the manner of operation and the profit motive. It is felt that, on these criteria, a charity fête would not be a business, whereas a landlord might well be carrying on a business—especially if he provided services for the tenants.

Reverting now to s.1(3) the question arises as to whether the Act would apply to the premises of a professional person who worked from home. The answer is "yes", because the Act does not require the premises to be used *exclusively* for business purposes. The point is rather academic since the home is unlikely to be plastered with exclusion notices.

(4) Sections 2 to 4 do not apply to certain contracts listed in Sch.1.[47] For the consumer the two most important are (a) contracts of insurance, and (b) any contract so far as it relates to the creation, transfer or termination of an interest in land.[48] The words "so far as" are important. If, for example, a landlord of a block of flats remains the occupier of the common staircase, a notice stating that "visitors enter these premises at their own risk" would be controlled: thus if the landlord negligently allows the staircase to fall into

9.29

---

[42] See Chapter Four above.
[43] See para.6.03 above.
[44] See para.9.36 below.
[45] See para.20.10 below.
[46] See para.21.03 below.
[47] Nor does the Act apply to international supply contracts: s.26.
[48] See *Electricity Supply Nominees v IAF Group* [1993] 3 All E.R. 372—clause in lease excluding tenant's right of set-off not controlled by the Act.

disrepair, he would be liable in damages to an injured visitor under s.2(2) of the Occupier's Liability Act 1957, and the exemption notice would be void by s.2(1) of the 1977 Act (see para.9.34 below).

In relation to insurance the industry successfully lobbied the Government to exclude insurance policies from the Act and in return they issued their Statements of Practice covering life and non-life insurance respectively. There is no corresponding exemption from the CRA 2015.

9.30   (5) The Act repeatedly refers to a clause which "excludes or restricts liability". This clearly covers a clause that "no liability is accepted for any loss or damage howsoever caused", "liability is limited to the contract price" or "liability shall be limited to the cost of replacing the appliance and all liability for consequential loss is excluded".

Then when we turn to s.13(1) we find that:

> To the extent that this Part of this Act prevents the exclusion or restriction of any liability it also prevents:
>
> (a) making the liability or its enforcement subject to restrictive or onerous conditions;
>
> (b) excluding or restricting any right or remedy in respect of the liability, or subjecting a person to any prejudice in consequence of his pursuing any such right or remedy;
>
> (c) excluding or restricting rules of evidence or procedure.

Thus the following would be caught:

(a) "all claims within seven days";

"before starting proceedings the customer must pay £1,000 into a joint bank account";

(b) "no rejection";

"no money back on sale goods: credit note only";

(c) "the report by our engineer shall be conclusive".

9.31   Section 13(1) then concludes with these words:

> . . . and (to that extent) sections 2 and 5 to 7 also prevent excluding or restricting liability by reference to terms and notices which exclude or restrict the relevant obligation or duty.

What does this mean? How can the Act control a clause which prevents a duty from arising? What is "the relevant obligation or duty"? In the earlier editions of this book we suggested that the answer is to adopt the approach of Lord Denning MR in *Karsales (Harrow) Ltd v Wallis*[49] and look at the contract or activity apart from the clause. If, for example, it is a contract giving rise to a condition of reasonable fitness or a duty of reasonable care, the Act would control a clause or notice providing that "no condition of

---

[49] [1956] 1 W.L.R. 936.

fitness is implied herein"[50] or "the occupier shall be under no duty of care". The House of Lords has recently confirmed in *Smith v Eric S Bush*[51] that this is the correct interpretation. Affirming the decision of the Court of Appeal[52] that the disclaimers did not prevent the surveyors having a duty of care Lord Jauncey commented on the concluding words in s.13(1) as follows[53]:

> "These words are unambiguous and are entirely appropriate to cover a disclaimer which prevents a duty coming into existence."

Lord Griffiths adopted a "but for" test[54]:

> "They indicate that the existence of the common law duty to take reasonable care . . . is to be judged by considering whether it would exist 'but for' the notice excluding liability."

Three final points can be made on this topic. First, an agreement in writing to submit present or future disputes to arbitration is *not* a clause "excluding or restricting liability".[55] Secondly, it is thought that the Act does not apply to a genuine "liquidated damages" clause where there is an intention to forecast loss rather than to exclude or restrict liability. Thirdly, the courts have held[56] that the Act does not control a genuine settlement out of court ("I accept this sum [or credit note] in full and final settlement of all claims").

(6) The common law rules as to incorporation, privity and construction mentioned earlier in this chapter remain unaffected, although, as already stated,[57] they will become of far less practical importance. There may, of course, be cases where the common law rules will still be relevant. Thus if the exemption clause is controlled by the reasonableness test[58] this gives the court a wide discretion; so if the party affected by the clause can prove non-incorporation, this will of itself defeat the exemption clause and the question of discretion will not arise. **9.32**

(7) As indicated above the Act no longer applies to business to consumer contracts. To see if a contract counts as a consumer contract, and is therefore not covered the Act, but rather by the CRA 2015, see Chapter Ten below. **9.33**

The areas affected by the Act

(a) Negligence: s.2

Section 1(1) defines negligence as the breach: **9.34**

---

[50] i.e. seeking to displace the primary obligation or duty that would otherwise arise.
[51] [1989] 2 All E.R. 514. The facts are given at para.3.14 above. A similar construction was adopted by Slade LJ in *Phillips Products Ltd v Hyland* [1987] 1 W.L.R. 659 CA.
[52] [1987] 3 All E.R. 179.
[53] At 543.
[54] At 530.
[55] s.13(2).
[56] *Tudor Grange v Citibank* [1991] 4 All E.R. 1.
[57] See para.9.24 above.
[58] See para.9.47 below.

(a) of any obligation, arising from the express or implied terms of a contract, to take reasonable care or exercise reasonable skill in the performance of the contract;

(b) of any common law duty to take reasonable care or exercise reasonable skill (but not any stricter duty);

(c) of the common duty of care imposed by the Occupiers' Liability Act 1957. . . .

This provision encompasses both a contractual and tortious duty of care. In practice the most important example of (a) is to be found in s.13 of the Supply of Goods and Services Act 1982 (see para.6.36 above).

We can now consider s.2—one of the most important sections of the Act. It reads as follows:

(1) A person cannot by reference to any contract term or to a notice given to persons generally or to particular persons exclude or restrict his liability for death or personal injury resulting from negligence.

(2) In the case of other loss or damage, a person cannot so exclude or restrict his liability except in so far as the term or notice satisfies the requirement of reasonableness.

(3) Where a contract term or notice purports to exclude or restrict liability for negligence a person's agreement to or awareness of it is not of itself to be taken as indicating his voluntary acceptance of any risk.

The scope of s.2 is wide. Examples include architects, surveyors, builders, carriers, dry cleaners, cinemas, garages, decorators and holiday tour operators. In all these cases—and there are many more—an exemption clause or notice will be totally void in cases of *death or personal injury*.

If the negligence results in damage to *property* or economic loss, the clause or notice will be effective only if it satisfies the reasonableness test.[59]

9.35   In *Robinson v Jones (Contractors) Ltd*,[60] the Court of Appeal decided that, even if the builder J had owed the householder R a duty of care, the contractual terms limiting its liability to the protection conferred by the National House-Building Council Agreement satisfied the reasonable test in s.2(2). Jackson LJ stated (obiter at para.63) that if R had suffered gas poisoning because of the defective flues, J's liability for that could not be excluded (s.2(1)).

The words "contract term" and "term" cover contractual cases and "notice" covers tortious cases.

(b) Contractual obligations: s.3

9.36   The other really far-reaching provision in the Act—and one bristling with problems—is s.3. It reads as follows:

---

[59] s.11, see para.9.47 below.
[60] See para.3.13 above for the facts.

(1) This section applies as between contracting parties where one of them deals on the other's written standard terms[61] of business.

(2) As against that party, the other cannot by reference to any contract term—

(a) when himself in breach of contract, exclude or restrict any liability of his in respect of the breach; or

(b) claim to be entitled—

(i) to render a contractual performance substantially different from that which was reasonably expected of him, or

(ii) in respect of the whole or any part of his contractual obligations, to render no performance at all,

except in so far as (in the cases mentioned above in this subsection) the contract term satisfies the requirement of reasonableness.[62]

This section is based on the recommendation of the Law Commission in their Second Report on Exemption Clauses[63] and is discussed on pp.52 to 62 of that Report. It applies to a contract between two businesses where it is made on the written standard terms of business of one of them.

So, s.3 applies the reasonableness test in three cases. The first case is where the trader is in breach of contract and the clause excludes or restricts his liability (for example, liability limited to £100). Section 3 is particularly useful where suppliers of goods or services attempt to excuse themselves from liability for late delivery or performance. The second case is where the trader relies on a clause giving him the right to render a contractual performance substantially different from that which was reasonably expected of him. This would apply to a condition on a theatre ticket whereby "the management reserve the right to alter the performance of any member of the cast". In the case of holidays the section would apply to a clause like the one in *Anglo-Continental Holidays Ltd v Typaldos Lines (London) Ltd*,[64] "Steamers, Sailing Dates, Rates and Itineraries are subject to change without notice".

The final case covered by s.3 is where a contractual term gives the trader **9.37** the right to offer no performance at all. It would seem that this provision may be wide enough to cover the so-called "force majeure" clause which is very common in practice. It may provide that "the seller shall not be liable for non-delivery if delay is caused by strikes, lockouts or other acts beyond the seller's reasonable control". Even a clause giving the right of cancellation or termination might be caught by this provision.[65]

One final comment may be made: if a trader tenders a performance substantially different from that "reasonably expected of him", can the clause which allows him to do so ever be reasonable? The question of reasonableness is considered later[66] but it might be reasonable if it formed part of

---

[61] *South West Water Services v ICL* (1999) B.L.R. 420 where a contract was held to have been made on the defendant's written standard terms of business despite extensive negotiation which left the conditions effectively untouched.

[62] See cases cited below.

[63] Law Com. No.69.

[64] [1967] 2 Lloyd's Rep. 61

[65] See Law Com. No.69, para.146.

[66] See para.9.47 below.

an arm's-length business contract between two traders where the trader attacking the clause had exactly the same provision in his own standard terms.

(c) Implied terms: ss.6, 7

9.38   **Sale of goods.**   In business to business sales, the implied terms on title, description, quality and fitness for purpose are still contained in ss.12 to 14 of the Sale of Goods Act 1979. Until 1973 the parties had complete freedom to exclude these obligations, because s.55, as it appeared in the original Sale of Goods Act 1893, provided that "where any right, duty or liability would arise under a contract of sale by operation of law it can be modified or varied by express agreement or by the course of dealing between the parties or by usage if the usage be such as to bind both parties to the contract". This provision was radically altered by the Supply of Goods (Implied Terms) Act 1973 and the controls introduced by that Act were substantially re-enacted by s.6 of the 1977 Act. Section 6 reads as follows:

9.39   **Sale and hire-purchase**

(1) Liability for breach of the obligations arising from—
   (a) section 12 of the Sale of Goods Act 1979 (seller's implied undertakings as to title, etc.);
   (b) section 8 of the Supply of Goods (Implied Terms) Act 1973 (the corresponding thing in relation to hire-purchase), cannot be excluded or restricted by reference to any contract term.

(1A) Liability for breach of the obligations arising from—
   (a) section 13, 14 or 15 of the 1979 Act (seller's implied undertakings as to conformity of goods with description or sample, or as to their quality or fitness for a particular purpose);
   (b) section 9, 10 or 11 of the 1973 Act (the corresponding things in relation to hire-purchase),
   cannot be excluded or restricted by reference to a contract term except in so far as the term satisfies the requirement of reasonableness."

(4) The liabilities referred to in this section are not only the business liabilities defined by section 1(3), but include those arising under any contract of sale of goods or hire-purchase agreement.

There are two basic rules:

(i) The conditions and warranties in s.12 (right to sell) can *never* be excluded.

(ii) A clause excluding or restricting the obligations as to description, sample, quality and fitness, will only be valid if it satisfies the test of reasonableness.

9.40   Despite s.6 a limited amount of "contracting out" is permitted by the sections themselves. Thus it will be recalled that under s.12 of the Sale of Goods Act 1979, the seller can agree to transfer only such title as he himself has,[67] while s.14(2) of the Sale of Goods Act 1979 allows the seller to avoid liability for satisfactory quality in relation to particular defects by drawing the buyer's attention to those defects before the contract is made.[68]

As an exception to the general rule s.6 of the 1977 Act also applies where the seller is *not* acting in the course of a business.[69] This is unlikely to be of great practical importance because private sales are unlikely to contain exemption clauses and because, in relation to quality and fitness, there will be nothing to exclude.[70] Thus the significance of this provision is limited to attempts to exclude liability under ss.13 and 15.

Hire-purchase. The terms implied into a hire-purchase agreement are virtu-   **9.41**
ally identical to those set out above[71] and s.6 of the 1977 Act controls them in exactly the same way as it does in sales of goods.

Other supply of goods contracts. We saw in para.9.39 that the attack   **9.42**
launched by the 1973 Act on exemption clauses in sale and hire-purchase contracts was re-enacted by s.6. This attack was extended to other supplies of goods by s.7: hire, work and materials and exchange.

Miscellaneous contracts under which goods pass. These are dealt with by s.7,   **9.43**
the key provisions being:

> (1A) Liability in respect of the goods' correspondence with description or sample, or their quality or fitness for any particular purpose, cannot be excluded or restricted by reference to such a term except in so far as the term satisfies the requirement of reasonableness.
> (3A) Liability for breach of the obligations arising under section 2 of the Supply of Goods and Services Act 1982 (implied terms about title etc. in certain contracts for the transfer of the property in goods) cannot be excluded or restricted by reference to any such term.
> (4) Liability in respect of—
>
>> (a) the right to transfer ownership of the goods, or give possession; or
>> (b) the assurance of quiet possession to a person taking goods in pursuance of the contract,
>
> cannot (in a case to which subsection (3A) above does not apply), be excluded or restricted by reference to any such term except in so far as the term satisfies the requirement of reasonableness.

(1) Title. It will be recalled that under a contract of hire the owner does   **9.44**
not give an undertaking that he has a "right to sell".[72] An exemption clause controlling this more limited form of title undertaking in hire cases is

---

[67] See para.2.27 above.
[68] See para.4.24 above.
[69] See s.6(4).
[70] See para.4.04 above.
[71] See paras 2.23, 3.20 and 4.37 above.
[72] See para.2.27 above.

controlled by the reasonableness test and is not subject to an outright ban.[73] Subject to this, the controls are virtually identical to those for sale and hire-purchase.[74]

9.45   *(2) Description, quality, fitness.*   It will also be recalled that the implied terms are virtually identical to those implied in sale and hire-purchase cases.[75] Similarly, the controls on exemption clauses contained in s.7 of the 1977 Act are virtually identical to those in s.6—the exemption clause is controlled by the reasonableness test.

If a buyer has a complaint relating to a "work and materials" contract (e.g. repairs to a car) it will be necessary to find out what was wrong. If the *materials* themselves were defective, there is strict liability and an exemption clause would be subject to the "reasonableness" test under s.7. If, however, the complaint relates to the *work* itself, the supplier will only be liable if negligent and a clause excluding this liability will be subject to the "reasonableness" test under s.2(2) (or totally void if the negligence causes personal injury or death).

(d) Misrepresentation

9.46   Exemption clauses relating to misrepresentation have been controlled since the passing of s.3 of the Misrepresentation Act 1967. Section 3 was redrafted by s.8 of the 1977 Act (and then very slightly amended by the CRA 2015), so that it now reads as follows:

> (1) If a contract contains a term which would exclude or restrict—
>
> > (a) any liability to which a party to a contract may be subject by reason of any misrepresentation made by him before the contract was made; or
> > (b) any remedy available to another party to the contract by reason of such a misrepresentation,
>
> the term shall be of no effect except in so far as it satisfies the requirement of reasonableness as stated in section 11(1) of the Unfair Contract Terms Act 1977; and it is for those claiming that the term satisfies that requirement to show that it does.

The first point to notice here is that the law is to be found in s.3 of the Misrepresentation Act 1967 (as amended) and not in the 1977 Act. It follows that the section applies to all contracts (including those excluded from the 1977 Act[76]) and it is not confined to "business liability".

What type of clauses are caught by s.3? Some cases are obvious: "The purchaser shall have no right to rescind this agreement"[77] or "All liability

---

[73] s.7(4).
[74] s.7(3A).
[75] See Supply of Goods and Services Act 1982 at paras 3.20 and 4.38–4.40 above.
[76] Unless it is an international supply contract within s.26: *Trident Turboprop (Dublin) Ltd v First Flight Couriers Ltd* [2009] EWCA Civ 290.
[77] See *Cleaver v Schyde Investments Ltd* [2011] EWCA Civ 929: sale of land—Law Society Standard Condition of Sale 7.1.3 restricted rescission for innocent misrepresentation—Court of Appeal upheld trial judge's decision that sellers had not shown restriction to be fair and reasonable in particular circumstances.

for misrepresentation is excluded". On the other hand a clause stating that "no employee of the company has any authority to make representations on the company's behalf" might be effective.[78] Finally, the contract might state that "although every care has been taken the vendors do not warrant the accuracy of these particulars and the purchaser shall not rely on them". If such a clause were outside s.3 it would severely limit the scope of the section. It seems that if the other party does rely on the incorrect particulars there will be a misrepresentation and the clause will be treated as an exemption clause to which s.3 applies.[79] A clause which is wide enough to exclude liability for fraudulent misrepresentation will not pass the "reasonableness" test.[80]

The reasonableness test

Sections 2, 3, 6, 7 and 8 all refer to the reasonableness test. The concept is not a new one; it has applied to misrepresentation since 1967 and it has applied to the implied terms of sale of goods and hire-purchase contracts since 1973. Section 11 draws a distinction between contractual clauses and non-contractual notices. In the case of a contract the person claiming that the term is reasonable must prove that: **9.47**

> the term shall have been a fair and reasonable one to be included having regard to the circumstances which were, or ought reasonably to have been, known to or in the contemplation of the parties when the contract was made.[81]

Thus the critical date is the date of the contract. For example, a limitation of damages clause which was reasonable at the date of the contract will be upheld even though by the time of the hearing it has become hopelessly inadequate by reason of inflation or by reason of the claimant's loss being far greater than expected.

Three more preliminary points are significant. First, the question is whether the clause is reasonable in relation to *this particular contract*[82]; so what may be reasonable between a supplier and one customer may be unreasonable as against another, e.g. because there may be equality of bargaining power in the one case and not in the other. This poses considerable problems for the draftsman of standard form contracts in that there is no such thing as a clause which is fair and reasonable in itself.

Secondly, the burden of proving reasonableness lies on the supplier; if the factors are evenly balanced, the customer wins the day.[83] **9.48**

This point equally applies to non-contractual notices and disclaimers where the party relying on the notice (e.g. a building society surveyor with

---

[78] See *Overbrooke Estates Ltd v Glencombe Properties Ltd* [1974] 1 W.L.R. 1335.
[79] *Cremdean Properties Ltd v Nash* (1977) 244 E.G. 547 CA.
[80] *Thomas Witter Ltd v T.B.P. Industries Ltd* [1996] 2 All E.R. 573.
[81] s.11(1).
[82] See Slade LJ in *Phillips Products Ltd v Hyland* [1987] 2 All E.R. 620 at 628.
[83] As above. See s.11(5).

a potential liability to a house buyer in the tort of negligence) must show that:

> it should be fair and reasonable to allow reliance on it, having regard to all the circumstances obtaining when the liability arose or (but for the notice) would have arisen.[84]

9.49 Finally, the term must be looked at *as a whole*. Thus in *Stewart Gill v Myer*[85] the plaintiff sought to rely on a clause excluding various remedies including a right of set-off. The Court of Appeal held that the clause read as a whole was unreasonable. However, the court may sever one clause leaving a separate (reasonable) one intact.[86]

The role of the courts

9.50 The concept of reasonableness appears in many areas of the law, including unfair dismissal, matrimonial finance, negligence claims and housing. In relation to the 1977 Act Lord Bridge has emphasised that more than one view is possible. His Lordship dealt with the matter as follows:

> "The court must entertain a whole range of considerations, put them in the scales on one side or the other and decide at the end of the day on which side the balance comes down. There will sometimes be room for a legitimate difference of judicial opinion as to what the answer should be and where it will be impossible to say that one view is demonstrably wrong and the other demonstrably right. It must follow in my view that when asked to review such a decision the appeal court should treat the decision with the utmost respect and refuse to interfere unless it is satisfied that it proceeded upon some erroneous principle or was plainly and obviously wrong."[87]

Guidelines

9.51 In any case involving the reasonableness test the court has a wide discretion and must consider all the relevant circumstances; presumably if the matter comes to court the defendant should be advised to plead the facts on which he relies to support his claim of reasonableness. Schedule 2 contains a non-exhaustive list of guidelines. They apply only to contracts controlled by ss.6 and 7, i.e. to supplies of *goods* where the claimant's claim relies on the *statutory implied* terms.[88] They are as follows:

---

[84] s.11(3).
[85] [1992] 2 All E.R. 257. Followed in *Axa Sun Life Services Plc v Campbell Martin Ltd* [2011] EWCA Civ 133.
[86] *Regus (UK) Ltd v Epcot Solutions Ltd* [2008] EWCA Civ 361.
[87] *George Mitchell (Chesterhall) Ltd v Finney Lock Seeds Ltd* [1983] 3 A.C. 803 at 816. The case was actually decided on an earlier Act but this does not reduce its importance in the present context. See also *Cleaver v Schyde Investments Ltd* [2011] EWCA Civ 929.
[88] s.11(2).

3. "Guidelines" for Application of Reasonableness Test

The matters to which regard is to be had in particular for the purposes of ss.6(3), 7(3) and (4), 20 and 21 are any of the following which appear to be relevant: **9.52**

(a) the strength of the bargaining positions of the parties relative to each other, taking into account (among other things) alternative means by which the customer's requirements could have been met;

(b) whether the customer received an inducement to agree to the term, or in accepting it had an opportunity of entering into a similar contract with other persons, but without having to accept a similar term;

(c) whether the customer knew or ought reasonably to have known of the existence and extent of the term (having regard, among other things, to any custom of the trade and any previous course of dealing between the parties);

(d) where the term excludes or restricts any relevant liability if some condition is not complied with, whether it was reasonable at the time of the contract to expect that compliance with that condition would be practicable;

(e) whether the goods were manufactured, processed or adapted to the special order of the customer.

The first three are of greatest importance. Their broad effect is that if a business buyer, large enough to have bargaining power and with a choice of potential suppliers with whom to negotiate terms, enters into a disadvantageous contract with his eyes open, the court is unlikely to rush to his assistance. The buyer has made a bad bargain and is stuck with it. In contrast if the buyer is a small business, perhaps dealing with a monopoly or with a supplier who belongs to a trade association whose members all adopt standard terms, and does not notice or cannot understand the exemption clause, then the court will probably strike down the clause. He had no real choice—it was a "take it or leave it situation".[89]

No specific guidelines are laid down by the Act in other cases, e.g. contracts for *services*, breach of *express* terms. However, by analogy the courts are applying similar guidelines with particular emphasis on the first three criteria—bargaining power, choice and knowledge. Lord Wilberforce stressed the significance of the first factor in the pre-Act case of *Photo Production Ltd v Securicor Transport*[90]: **9.53**

"After this Act, in commercial matters generally, when the parties are not of unequal bargaining power, and when risks are normally borne by insurance, not only is the case for judicial intervention undemonstrated, but there is everything to be said, and this seems to have been Parliament's intention, for leaving the parties free to apportion the risks as they think fit and for respecting their decisions."

---

[89] See Slade LJ in *Phillips Products Ltd v Hyland* [1987] 1 W.L.R. 659 CA at 629 (clause was one of 43 clauses of plant hire company's terms; used by all members of trade association; not fair and reasonable).

[90] [1980] A.C. 827. The respondents' employee purposely set fire to a factory which he was supposed to be guarding! See also *Regus (UK) Ltd v Epcot Solutions Ltd* [2008] EWCA Civ 361.

The size of print would also be relevant,[91] and a clause is unlikely to be upheld if it is out of line with a Code of Practice adopted by the trader's trade association.[92] It may be that a clause that "the seller can cancel this agreement in the event of strikes, etc." should now be redrafted so as to give a mutual right to terminate. It is also helpful for the contract to specify the factors on which the trader relies in support of his claim of reasonableness. Perhaps we shall see the emergence of a dual price contract, £X with full responsibility or £Y without it. We already see "split clauses"—different clauses dealing with property damage, financial loss, limitation of liability for late delivery and time-limits for claims.

Limitation of damages clauses

9.54 A number of small traders (including travel agents) felt very uneasy about the possibility of having to meet very large, unlimited claims and accordingly during the passage of the Bill Lord Hailsham introduced a new clause which is now s.11(4). Unlike the Sch.2 guidelines, these factors apply to all limitation clauses but not to exclusion clauses. It reads:

> Where by reference to a contract term or notice a person seeks to restrict liability to a specified sum of money, and the question arises (under this or any other Act) whether the term or notice satisfies the requirement of reasonableness, regard shall be had in particular . . . to—
>
>   (a) the resources which he could expect to be available to him for the purpose of meeting the liability should it arise; and
>   (b) how far it was open to him to cover himself by insurance.

This provision is bound to cause problems. Do the "resources" of a sole trader or partner include his private assets? How far afield does he have to search to find insurance? What happens if the premium would destroy or seriously reduce the commercial viability of the transaction? In spite of such difficulties it seems likely that the courts will view more sympathetically a limitation clause, whereby the supplier accepts some liability, than an exclusion clause where the supplier in cavalier fashion refuses to contribute at all to the consumer's loss.[93]

Illustrative cases

9.55 The Act was passed to give added protection to consumers who are nearly always in a weak bargaining position. The problem of widely drawn exemption clauses has not gone away.[94] The following cases show the attitude of the courts.

---

[91] In *The Zinnia* [1984] 2 LL.L.R. 211, Staughton J was minded to strike down the clause on the grounds of (a) size of print, and (b) complexity of language. Unfortunately counsel for the party attacking the clause did not raise this point!

[92] See paras 11.05 and 11.14 below.

[93] See *Ailsa Craig Fishing Co Ltd v Malvern Fishing Co and Securicor (Scotland)* [1983] 1 W.L.R. 964. See also *St Albans DC v ICL* [1996] 4 All E.R. 481 where a limitation clause was held to be unreasonable: the resources of the company and its insurance were relevant factors.

[94] See Chapter Ten below.

The first one is the most important in that the House of Lords has given valuable guidance on the operation of the reasonableness test in a consumer context. Although the Act no longer applies to consumer contracts, it is still useful to consider the case, because it highlights general criteria that could well also be considered in business to business cases; while also hinting at the different ways that these criteria might be applied in business to business cases.

Smith v Bush.[95]   We have already discussed the first point in this case,   **9.56**
namely, whether the surveyors owed a duty of care in tort to the house buyers. To this question the House of Lords unanimously answered "yes".

We now turn to the second point—were the surveyors able to prove that their exemption clauses satisfied the reasonableness test? Again the House of Lords answered the question in favour of the consumers: "no". The judgments of Lords Griffiths and Templeman deserve careful examination. Although Lord Griffiths admitted that it is impossible to draw up an exhaustive list of relevant factors for the court to take into account when applying the reasonableness test, the following extract is crucial for the legal adviser, since he states that these matters should "always be considered"[96]:

"(1) Were the parties of equal bargaining power? If the court is dealing with a one-off situation between parties of equal bargaining power the requirement of reasonableness would be more easily discharged than in a case such as the present where the disclaimer is imposed on the purchaser who has no effective power to object.
(2) In the case of advice, would it have been reasonably practicable to obtain the advice from an alternative source taking into account considerations of costs and time? . . .
(3) How difficult is the task being undertaken for which liability is being excluded? When a very difficult or dangerous undertaking is involved there may be a high risk of failure which would certainly be a pointer towards the reasonableness of excluding liability as a condition of doing the work. A valuation, on the other hand, should present no difficulty if the work is undertaken with reasonable skill and care. . . .
(4) What are the practical consequences of the decision on the question of reasonableness? This must involve the sums of money potentially at stake and the ability of the parties to bear the loss involved, which, in its turn, raises the question of insurance. There was once a time when it was considered improper even to mention the possible existence of insurance cover in a lawsuit. But those days are long past. Everyone knows that all prudent professional men carry insurance, and the availability and cost of insurance must be a relevant factor when considering which of two parties should be required to bear the risk of a loss."

---

[95] [1990] 1 A.C. 831 (see also para.3.14 above).
[96] [1990] 1 A.C. 831 at 858. See also the Scottish case of *Bank of Scotland v Fuller Peiser* (2002) S.L.T. 574 where the court upheld a clause providing that a surveyor was not to be liable to anyone except the borrower.

The effect of this decision is that an exemption clause will not protect a surveyor "in respect of a dwelling house of modest value". The position may well be different where other types of property are valued "such as industrial property, large blocks of flats or very expensive houses",[97] where it may be reasonable for the mortgagee's surveyor to exclude or limit his liability to the buyer/mortgagor.

9.57   **Spencer v Cosmos Air Holidays.**[98]   We discussed this case earlier in relation to damages for distress. The agreement contained a clause whereby the defendants excluded responsibility "for any injury, death, loss or damage which is caused by any negligence of the management or employees of an independent contractor". Without amplifying their reasons the Court of Appeal brushed the clause aside. In the words of Farquharson LJ:

> "It does not bear upon the case at all and does not affect the plaintiff's contractual rights against the defendants—namely, to enjoy 14 days' holiday in the hotel she had chosen."

9.58   **Walker v Boyle.**[99]   During negotiations for the sale of V's house V told P that there was no boundary dispute. This was an innocent misrepresentation which induced P to buy. On discovering the facts P refused to proceed whereupon V claimed specific performance in reliance on Condition 17 of the National Conditions of Sale, which provided that "no misdescription can annul the sale". P claimed that the clause was unreasonable. His claim was upheld. Even though the clause was in the National Conditions of Sale it was not the product of negotiation between the parties or their representatives.[100]

9.59   **South Western General Property Co v Marton.**[101]   Property was described in auction particulars as "long leasehold building land". The particulars failed to disclose major restrictions on development and the buyer would never have bought the property if he had known of this. The particulars provided that the statements were made without responsibility and were statements of opinion only and that it was up to intending purchasers to satisfy themselves as to their accuracy. Croom-Johnson J held that the clause failed to pass the reasonableness test. His Lordship laid great stress on the vital importance of the matter for the buyer. He also pointed out that many prospective buyers attended auctions at short notice and would obviously have no opportunity to check out the particulars.

9.60   **Waldron-Kelly v British Railways Board.**[102]   The defendants agreed to carry the plaintiff's suitcase on "owner's risk" terms. It disappeared. The Board

---

[97] [1990] 1 A.C. 831 at 859 per Lord Griffiths.
[98] *The Times*, 6 December 1989 CA, above, para.8.63.
[99] [1982] 1 W.L.R. 495.
[100] cf. *Cleaver v Schyde Investments Ltd* [2011] EWCA Civ 929.
[101] (1982) 263 E.G. 1090.
[102] [1981] C.L.Y. 303.

sought to limit their liability by a clause which referred only to the weight of the suitcase (equal to £27) and not to its value (£320). The learned county court judge held that the clause failed to pass the reasonableness test.

Woodman v Photo Trade Processing Ltd.[103]   Mr Woodman took photographs of a friend's wedding. The shop to which he brought the film for development displayed a notice limiting liability to the cost of the film. The film came back ruined and Mr Woodman (with the support of the Consumers' Association) claimed that the clause was unreasonable. The county court judge upheld his claim and awarded £75 for disappointment.   **9.61**

St Albans DC v ICL.[104]   ICL were a very substantial company with turnover of £1109 million, profit of £100 million and world-wide liability insurance of £50 million. The contract contained a clause limiting liability to £100,000 (less than their normal standard clause). Scott-Baker J after considering the bargaining strength of the parties, the likely losses of the plaintiffs and other factors, held that the clause failed the reasonableness test: "I do not think it is unreasonable that he who stands to make the profit should carry the risk."[105] The Court of Appeal agreed.   **9.62**

Southwark LBC v IBM UK Ltd.[106]   This is another software case discussed earlier in para.4.34 above. Unlike ICL above, IBM's defence succeeded.   **9.63**

The contract excluded "any implied condition or warranty of merchantability or fitness for purpose". Their exemption clause was held to be fair and reasonable. "Guidelines" (a), (b) and (c) all supported that conclusion. The parties were of broadly equal bargaining strength; S could have contracted with a third party; S knew the terms in view of the protracted negotiation via lawyers.

If any particular trends can be identified form the above cases, perhaps it is that in consumer cases[107] it is taken as obvious that the consumer is in a weaker bargaining position, and this counts against the exclusion clause being upheld; while in business to business cases, each contract is looked at on its merits to see whether the buyer is actually in a weaker bargaining position and this should therefore count against the exemption clause, or whether the parties are of more equal bargaining power, in which case the clause is more likely to be upheld.

---

[103] *Times Business News*, 20 June 1981; *Which?*, July 1981.
[104] [1996] 4 All E.R. 481.
[105] As above, at 711.
[106] [2011] EWHC 549 (TCC).
[107] These are all now dealt with under the unfairness test of the CRA 2015 dealt with in Chapter Ten.

4. OTHER CONTROLS

9.64 Although the 1977 Act is by far the most important example of statutory control of exemption clauses there are many other statutory controls. One of these, s.3 of the Misrepresentation Act 1967, has already been mentioned. There are also a number of other Acts relating to the carriage of passengers by public service vehicle, rail and air. Other examples include the Occupiers' Liability Act 1957, the Defective Premises Act 1972, the Road Traffic Act 1988 and the Consumer Credit Act 1974. For a summary of the statutory controls readers are referred to *Chitty on Contracts*.

CHAPTER TEN

"THESE SMALL PRINT TERMS SEEM VERY UNFAIR"

On 1 July 1995 the Unfair Contract Terms Directive became part of English **10.01** (and UK) law. This was done by Statutory Instrument, namely the Unfair Terms in Consumer Contracts Regulations 1994. They were reproduced with minor drafting amendments, and one change of substance, by the Unfair Terms in Consumer Contracts Regulations 1999 (SI 1999/2083) (the 1999 Regulations).

The Regulations broke new ground by enabling a consumer to challenge not only exemption clauses, but also other terms that "unfair", e.g. terms imposing unfair obligations or liabilities on consumers.[1] They also enabled the Office of Fair Trading (OFT), and certain other bodies, to seek an injunction banning the continued use of such clauses. As indicated in the previous chapter, the Regulations have now been replaced by the new regime on unfair terms contained in the Consumer Rights Act 2015 (CRA 2015), and this regime will be covered in the following pages. This topic should be read together with the powers to seek "enforcement orders" under the Enterprise Act 2002. They are considered in Part III of this book.

Readers should also recall that the Unfair Contract Terms Act 1977 (the **10.02** 1977 Act) (considered in Chapter Nine above) used to apply, but no longer applies, to exemption clauses in consumer contracts. So, for the period since the passing of the 1994 (then the 1999) Regulations, and the passing of the CRA 2015, there were two overlapping statutory regimes applicable to consumer contract terms.

The following points can be made about the previous position, which help to explain the background to the new regime:

(1) In some respects the Regulations went go beyond the 1977 Act because (a) as indicated above, the 1977 Act is (or in relation to consumer contracts, *was*) is largely concerned with *exemption clauses* whereas the Regulations were not so limited in that they covered other types of unfair term and (b) the Regulations controlled a number of contracts (such as insurance, and the leasing of land) to which the 1977 Act does not apply at all. We shall see below that the CRA 2015 follows the approach of the Regulations in both these regards.

(2) In three respects the 1977 Act is (or in relation to consumer contracts,

---

[1] reg.5(1).

was) wider than the Regulations. Thus (a) the 1977 Act is/was not limited to contracts—it also covers non-contractual disclaimers (the CRA 2015 covers both); (b) the 1977 Act is/was not limited to non-negotiated terms, the Regulations were limited to such terms, but the CRA 2015 is not—it covers negotiated and non-negotiated terms; and (c) the 1977 Act applies/applied not only to consumer sales but also to business sales—as we have seen the 1977 Act no longer applies to consumer sales, while the CRA 2015 (following the approach of the now repealed Regulations) only applies to consumer contracts.

(3) So, there was a substantial area of overlap between the 1977 Act and the 1999 Regulations. In this regard, it is important to remember that the Regulations represented the UK's implementation of the Unfair Terms Directive, and so copied out the Directive almost verbatim, in order to ensure that the minimum level of protection required by the Directive, was delivered.

However, the Directive does allow for Member States to provide for a higher level of protection. So, art.8 of the Directive provides that: "Member States may adopt or retain the most stringent provisions compatible with the Treaty in the area covered by this Directive, to ensure a maximum degree of protection for the consumer." This meant for example, that, although the Directive did not cover individually negotiated terms (and following this the Regulations did not), it was perfectly acceptable for such terms to be controlled by the 1977 Act and it is perfectly acceptable for the CRA 2015 to control such terms. It also meant that that, although (following the Directive) no clauses were wholly ineffective under the Regulations (a test of unfairness applied), it was nevertheless acceptable to continue with the position which we saw above under the 1977 Act, whereby some terms were indeed wholly ineffective. In such cases, the consumer would have no need to argue as to the unfairness of the term under the 1999 Regulations. Now, as we shall see below, the CRA 2015 makes the same sort of terms wholly ineffective as were previously made wholly ineffective under the 1977 Act (and adds some other terms to this "wholly ineffective" category) so again, where these sorts of terms are concerned, there will be no need to apply the general test of unfairness under the CRA 2015.

(4) The Law Commission in their Final Report Unfair Terms in Contracts (LC No.298, February 2005) criticised these "inconsistent and overlapping provisions". It proposed a single regime for consumer contracts (more or less following the scheme of the 1999 Regulations, but building in some of the ways in which the 1977 Act offered further protection (e.g. on individually negotiated terms and wholly ineffective terms). This approach was further recommended in the Law Commissions Issues Paper (25 July 2012) *Unfair Terms in Consumer Contracts: a new approach?;* and this is basically the

approach taken in the new consumer regime contained in Part 2 of the CRA 2015.

(5) As indicated above, the CRA 2015 is largely based on the Regulations, which were based on the Directive. Indeed, what has not been said explicitly before now, but which is very important, is that the test of unfairness itself contained in the CRA 2015 is one from the Directive, and the same one that was in the Regulations. We shall see below that a good few cases were decided by the courts under the Regulations, on this test of unfairness. So this case law, and also the approach of regulatory bodies to this test under the Regulations, remain of great value.

1. THE EUROPEAN BACKGROUND

The Directive had an (interrupted) gestation period of some 19 years. Work **10.03** on it started as long ago as 1975, but it was then halted when a large number of Member States (including the UK) introduced domestic legislation in this area. When the dust of this legislation had been given a chance to settle, work on the Directive started again; not surprisingly the comments (especially from industry) were not entirely uncritical.

An EU Directive is normally preceded by Preambles setting out the thinking behind the Directive. This one has a very large number and in this book we have numbered them 1 to 40 for ease of reference. We have already found that these Preambles have been referred to by a court faced with a problem of interpretation. Preambles 5 to 9 provide some of the flavour:

(5) Whereas, generally speaking, consumers do not know the rules of law which, in other Member States than their own, govern contracts for the sale of goods or services;

(6) Whereas this lack of awareness may deter them from direct transactions for the purchase of goods or services in another Member State;

(7) Whereas, in order to facilitate the establishment of the internal market and to safeguard the citizen in his role as consumer when acquiring goods and services under contracts which are governed by the laws of Member States other than his own, it is essential to remove unfair terms from those contracts;

(8) Whereas sellers of goods and suppliers of services will thereby be helped in their task of selling goods and supplying services, both at home and through the internal market;

(9) Whereas competition will thus be stimulated, so contributing to increased choice for Community citizens as consumers.

One general observation can be made; the attempt by the Directive to boost cross-border trade is unlikely to succeed, because the Directive has nothing to say on the vital question of enforcement. In most cases[2] a consumer who

---

[2] The position is different in relation to credit transactions—see the statutory instrument referred to in this paragraph.

is dissatisfied with his purchase must sue in the supplier's home state: see the amended Convention on Jurisdiction and the Enforcement of Judgments (which now forms part of English law under the Civil Jurisdiction and Judgments Act 1982 as amended by SI 2001/3929).

Interpretation

10.04   This Directive (like all Directives) is addressed to Member States and requires them to enact the relevant legislation by a specified date. A question may then arise as to what remedies are available to a consumer if a Member State fails to implement the Directive correctly, or in time, or at all. This is a very live issue; in two cases involving the rights of employees on a business transfer and in the case of collective redundancies the EU Commission took the UK Government before the European Court which held that the UK Government had failed to implement Directives correctly in no less than six respects.[3] Where does this leave the consumer under the Directive which we are discussing? The emerging case law has established a number of points:

(1) The English courts must construe domestic law (the CRA 2015) in such a way as to give effect to the *purpose* of the Directive. This principle was laid down by the House of Lords in *Litster v Forth Dry Dock*[4] and by the European Court in *Marleasing*[5] and more recently in *Faccini Dori*.[6] Since one of the objects of the Directive is to approximate the laws of Member States the courts may well give particular words such as "good faith" a European meaning; anyone putting forward an argument in this area should not do so in purely Anglo-Saxon terms (see also (3) below).

(2) If the CRA 2015 cannot be construed as set out in (1) above, the question arises as to what remedy (if any) is available to a consumer if the Directive has not been correctly implemented. As previously stated, the European Court has been extremely creative and as a result the consumer may have two possible remedies:

(a) If the claim is brought against a public body (an "emanation of the State") the claimant can enforce the Directive directly in the English courts; the public body cannot shelter behind the Government's failure to implement it. The leading case[7] concerned a Health Authority and the concept of "public body" has been widely interpreted to cover public utilities both before[8] and after[9] privatisation.

---

[3] *Commission v UK* [1994] I.R.L.R. 392 and 412.
[4] [1990] 1 A.C. 546.
[5] *Marleasing SA v La Commercial* [1992] 1 C.M.L.R. 305.
[6] [1995] All E.R. (EC) 1 ECJ.
[7] *Marshall v Southhampton Area Health Authority (No.1)* [1986] Q.B. 401.
[8] *Foster v British Gas* [1988] C.M.L.R. 697.
[9] *Griffin v South West Water Services* [1995] I.R.L.R. 15.

(b) Quite apart from this, an aggrieved party may sue the Government for failure to implement the Directive correctly, if the relevant provision was enacted for his benefit and if the failure has caused him loss. Key to understanding this principle is the historic *Francovitch* decision on this point[10] and also the *Factortame* case.[11]

(3) The CRA 2015 is just one example of domestic Regulations passed to implement EU Directives. We have already met three others—two in Chapter Six and one in Chapter Eight. In this connection the comments by Newman J in the case of *Khatun v London Borough of Newham and the Office of Fair Trading*[12] are highly instructive. One of the issues in the case was whether the Regulations could be construed as giving effect to the Directive; accordingly what mattered was the effect of the Directive. He then said this:

"In my judgment it is important not to lose sight of the character of the instrument under interpretative scrutiny. It is not to be construed by the Court as it would construe domestic legislation which is the product of a close, legislative process of debate and amendment and approval by a legislative chamber. It is an autonomous instrument drawn up for implementation by domestic legislation in each Member State. In this context the expressed purpose of the Directive is of paramount significance and is not to be narrowed by legislative or semantic interpretation. Where the Directive will be available in the language of each Member State, too close attention to semantics will place too great a weight upon the problems which can arise from translation. The initial text of the Directive is French but it has no status as the authoritative text."

The last part of this quotation highlights an important point for advisers. In construing any EU Directive the English language version is by no means the end of the story; each of the other languages is equally authentic. In arriving at his decision that the Directive did apply to land contracts the judge took into account the following matters:

(a) the text of the Directive in French, Italian, Spanish and Portuguese;

(b) the use of the French word "biens" (which includes immovable property in French law) in the Directive and also in the European Convention on Human Rights;

---

[10] *Francovitch v Italian Republic* [1992] I.R.L.R. 84 ECJ.

[11] In the *Factortame* case [1991] A.C. 603, the UK Government was held to be in breach of EC law because the Merchant Shipping Act 1988 discriminated against non-UK nationals. Spanish fishermen have sued the UK Government under *Francovitch* [1992] I.R.L.R. 84 ECJ and the courts have held that they were entitled to compensation for their economic loss in an action for breach of statutory duty. Subsequently they accepted a very large offer from the Government to settle their claims.

[12] [2003] EWHC Admin 2326.

(c) a conversation between an EU official responsible for the Directive and an OFT official in the period shortly before the 1994 Regulations were amended;

(d) the text of the "doorstep" Directive under which land contracts were expressly excluded;

(e) legislation and case law in other Member States; and

(f) an OFT argument that the exclusion of land contracts would leave a large gap in the consumer protection aims of the Directive, since 30 per cent of households live in rented accommodation.

2. What Contracts and Notices are Caught?

10.05 The CRA 2015 unfair terms regime applies to a contract between a "trader" and a "consumer", known as a "consumer contract".[13] Section 2(2) provides that:

> "'Trader' means a person acting for purposes relating to that person's trade, business, craft or profession, whether acting personally or through another person acting in the trader's name or on the trader's behalf."

Section 2(3) says that:

> "'Consumer' means an individual acting for purposes that are wholly or mainly outside that individual's trade, business, craft or profession."

For the purposes of both of these definitions, s.2(7) provides that:

> "'Business' includes the activities of any government department or local or public authority."

10.06 What seems apparent here is:

(i) while normally the "consumer" will be the party buying the goods or services, and the "trader" will be the party supplying them, this need not be the case—there is no reference to this, so, e.g., an individual who sells a car to a car dealership can still be classed as a consumer, while the dealership can still be a trader;

(ii) that a company can never be a "consumer" under this regime, as it is surely not an "individual"[14];

(iii) that what matters is the *purpose* of the transaction from the point of view either party, i.e. whether it does or does not have a purpose related or outside any business, trade or profession that person has—the issue is not

---

[13] s.61(1) and (3).

[14] See *Barclays Bank v Kufner* [2008] EWHC 2319 (Comm) on the definition under the 1999 Regulations whether a company.

whether the transaction is a normal activity for that person in the course of any such business, trade or profession.[15]

This leaves two unsettled questions. First, what about mixed use? What happens if a solicitor or doctor buys a car for private use but uses it occasionally for business purposes? Secondly, what happens if the private nature of the purchase is unknown to the supplier (as where the order is given on business stationery)? In the light of what has been said (see para.10.04 above) the court can be directed to other European texts where similar terms appear.[16] On that basis, the first question may well be answered by applying a proportionality test, so that if the car was employed overwhelmingly for private use the Directive (and therefore the CRA 2015) would apply. On the second point the obvious inference must be that a buyer who leads the seller to believe that it is a business sale must take the consequences. **10.07**

By virtue of s.61(4), the regime also covers non-contractual notices to the extent that they relate to rights or obligations traders and consumers, or purport to exclude or restrict a trader's liability to a consumer. "Notice" here includes "an announcement, whether or not in writing, and any other communication or purported communication" (s.61(8)).

3. WHAT CONTRACTS ARE EXCLUDED?

The somewhat curious provisions of Preambles 14 and 15 read as follows: **10.08**

> (14) Whereas [uniform rules of law in the matter of unfair terms] should apply to all contracts concluded between sellers or suppliers and consumers.
> (15) Whereas as a result *inter alia* contracts relating to employment, contracts relating to succession rights, contracts relating to rights under family law and contracts relating to the incorporation and organization of companies or partnership agreements must be excluded from this Directive.

It is rather obvious that such contracts are not consumer contracts, but the CRA 2015 does emphasise this in the case of contracts of employment or apprenticeship, which are excluded by s.61(2).

4. WHAT TERMS ARE NOT CAUGHT?

(1) By virtue of s.73(1), the CRA 2015 does not apply to a term or notice, to the extent that it reflects (a) mandatory, statutory or regulatory provisions of the UK, or (b) the provisions or principles of International Conventions to which the UK or the EU is a party. An obvious example of (a) would be **10.09**

---

[15] In relation to points (ii) and (iii), see *UDT v R & B Custom Brokers* [1988] 1 W.L.R. 321, where under the old "course of a business" test under the Unfair Contract Terms Act 1977, to was found to be possible not to be buying in the course of a business (and therefore to be a consumer) despite being a company and buying at least partly for use in the business albeit an item that such a business would not normally actually trade in.

[16] See, e.g. the Official Report (Guilano-Lagarde) on the Rome Choice of Law Convention, where the point is discussed in relation to art.5 of that Convention.

a contractual term inserted to comply with the Consumer Credit Act 1974 (see para.19.01 below). A further example would be a contract incorporating terms laid down by a regulatory authority under the Financial Services and Markets Act 2000. An example of (b) would be a clause giving effect to the Warsaw Convention on carriage by air.

10.10   (2) The CRA 2015 is only designed to test the fairness of ancillary clauses, rather than to assess fairness in relation to the specification of the main subject matter or the appropriateness of the price. This is made clear by s.64, to which we now turn.

5. MAIN SUBJECT MATTER AND PRICE

10.11   Section 64 provides:

(1) A term of a consumer contract may not be assessed for fairness under section 62 [the section containing the unfairness test] to the extent that—

(a) it specifies the main subject matter of the contract, or
(b) the assessment is of the appropriateness of the price payable under the contract by comparison with the goods, digital content or services supplied under it.

(2) Subsection (1) excludes a term from an assessment under section 62 only if it is transparent and prominent.

(3) A term is transparent for the purposes of this Part if it is expressed in plain and intelligible language and (in the case of a written term) is legible.

(4) A term is prominent for the purposes of this section if it is brought to the consumer's attention in such a way that an average consumer would be aware of the term.

(5) In subsection (4) "average consumer" means a consumer who is reasonably well-informed, observant and circumspect.

10.12   Before proceeding further it should be noted that under the 1999 Regulations (following art.4(2) of the Unfair Terms Directive) the position (in the old reg.6(2)) was also that there could not be an assessment of fairness in relation to the specification of the main subject matter or the appropriateness of the price, although there the condition was that such terms must be in "plain and Intelligible language", whereas now, as we can see, such terms must be "transparent" (i.e. be in plain and intelligible language and be legible), and they must also be "prominent". This prominence requirement has resonance of the "special highlighting"/"red hand" type approaches to incorporation discussed in Chapter Nine above. It will be interesting to see exactly what it requires. Does it merely require charges to be set out prominently in the formal contract, or must they sometimes be in other literature, such as advertising or in later communications between the parties? Do the charges sometimes need to be explained verbally whether in phone or face to face encounters? Do more substantively onerous or unusual charges need to be more prominent than other charges?[17]

---

[17] The Law Commissions recommended this (English and Scottish Law Commissions, *Unfair*

Turning to the general idea that there cannot be an assessment of fairness in relation to the specification of the main subject matter or the appropriateness of the price, the basic principle here is clear enough; a consumer cannot allege unfairness merely because he has made a bad bargain. That said, there is bound to be scope for argument as to what exactly is the main subject matter, or the price. If one takes the case of a clause in a motor policy stating that "the car can only be used by a driver over 25 for social, domestic or pleasure purposes and the insured must pay the first £100 of any claim", it would be a main subject matter provision, whereas a clause stating that "all claims must be notified within 48 hours" would not be a main subject matter provision. Even in the former case the exception would not apply unless the core provision were transparent and prominent as required by the first line of s.64 (2).

We can now consider a series of cases dealing with the question as to what counts as the price and/or main subject matter.

OFT[18] and the Banks

10.13 The running battle between the OFT and the banks culminated in one of the earliest decisions of the new Supreme Court, *Office of Fair Trading v Abbey National Plc.*[19] (Further below, we shall explain the powers of the old Office of Fair Trading (since 2014 re-named the Competition and Markets Authority) and other bodies to challenge terms, and ultimately take action to have them removed from contracts.)

The battleground was reg.6(2) of the 1999 Regulations (the predecessor provision to s.64 of the CRA 2015). The issue, in the words of Lord Phillips, was whether certain bank charges (detailed below) constituted "the price or remuneration, as against the services supplied in exchange".

Credit card and bank charges

10.14 First it is necessary to explain the background to the dispute. Almost every consumer has at some time made a complaint about the amount of charges (often £30 or more) levied by banks, building societies and credit card issuers when a customer draws a cheque which bounces or misses a credit card payment.

The credit card problem was solved in April 2006 when the OFT, after discussions with the eight card issuers, produced a statement of principles for them to follow in setting fair default charges. These should not exceed the administrative costs in the reasonable contemplation of the consumer. The OFT will not take legal action where charges do not exceed £12, which has generally proved to be the norm.

Terms in Consumer Contracts: Advice to the Department for Business, Innovation and Skills, ch.2, 4.46), but it is not provided for in the CRA 2015 provision (s.67(4)).

[18] See the excellent analysis of the following three OFT cases in the Law Commissions, Unfair Terms in Consumer Contracts: a new approach? Issues Paper (2012).

[19] [2009] UKSC 6.

This left open the level of bank charges on current accounts. In March 2007 the OFT began a formal investigation. Four charges were relevant (the "relevant charges"):

- an unpaid item, where a cheque is dishonoured;

- a paid item, where the bank honours a cheque though the account is not in funds;

- a guaranteed paid item, where the bank pays because of a cheque guarantee card though no funds are available; and

- an overdraft excess, where the account is overdrawn without prior authority.

About 20 per cent of the 54 million current account customers incur such charges.

The High Court[20]

10.15   In July 2007 the OFT issued proceedings in the Commercial Court seeking a declaration that reg.6(2) did not apply to such charges. They claimed that the "relevant charges" were (1) penalties at common law; and (2) fell within the Regulations. The eight defendant banks took the opposite view and in particular argued that the charges fell within the exception in reg.6(2).

Andrew Smith J held that (1) the relevant charges were not penalties, as the customers were not in breach of contract in relation to the events giving rise to the charges; and (2) such payments were not made in exchange for the whole package of services supplied by the banks when operating current accounts, so reg.6(2) did not apply to them. The OFT could assess their fairness.

Andrew Smith J's judgment runs to 69 pages. It includes a long, detailed analysis of the eight banks' terms and charges to decide whether they were "in plain, intelligible language" (reg.7), which they were except in "relatively minor aspects".

The Court of Appeal[21]

10.16   The banks appealed against the finding on reg.6(2). The Court of Appeal dismissed the appeal unanimously. The "relevant charges" were not part of the core or essential bargain between bank and customer.

The contingent nature of the charges and the fact that the relevant terms were not specifically negotiated were strong pointers to the conclusion that the charges were not "the price or remuneration" within the meaning of art.4(2) of Directive 93/13 and reg.6(2)(b). Accordingly an assessment of the fairness of the relevant charges was not excluded by reg.6(2)(b).

---

[20] [2008] EWHC 875 (Comm).
[21] [2009] EWCA Civ 116.

The purpose of reg.6(2)(b) was to limit the exclusion to the essence of the price. It was to be construed narrowly or restrictively because it was an exception to what would otherwise be the position. It was not intended to cover incidental or auxiliary terms.

The Supreme Court

The banks appealed again. The Supreme Court unanimously upheld the appeal. The OFT having won the first two rounds was knocked out in round three!   **10.17**

The court agreed that all the relevant charges fell within the exception in reg.6(2)(b) as being part of "price or remuneration". Lord Walker considered (at para.47):

> "Charges for unauthorised overdrafts are monetary consideration for the package of banking services supplied to personal current account customers. They are an important part of the banks' charging structure, amounting to over 30 per cent of their revenue stream from all personal current account customers. The facts that the charges are contingent, and that the majority of customers do not incur them, are irrelevant. . . Even if the Court of Appeal's interpretation had been correct, I do not see how it could have come to the conclusion that charges amounting to over 30 per cent of the revenue stream were (para.111) 'not part of the core or essential bargain'."

The court was not persuaded by the view of the Court of Appeal that the package should be divided into the "core or essential bargain" comprising those matters to which the typical consumer would have regard when deciding whether to enter into the agreement with the bank and those provisions which were "incidental or ancillary" such as overdrawing on his current account and so fell outside reg.6(2).[22]

While this decision prevents the Competition and Market Authority (CMA) (the new name for the OFT) from intervening in relation to the adequacy or appropriateness of the price (provided plain, intelligible language has been used[23]) the charges "will still be open to attack by the OFT [CMA] on the ground that they are 'unfair' as defined by reg.5(1), but that attack cannot be founded on an allegation that the Relevant Charges are excessive by comparison with the services which they purchase, for that is forbidden by Regulation 6(2)(b)" (per Lord Phillips at para.57). The implication here is that there might be other ways in which such charges might be said to be unfair, e.g. that it allows for unequal treatment—those inadvertently exceeding overdrafts are treated very harshly in comparison with others perhaps?   **10.18**

The Supreme Court agreed that the charges were not penalties. As Lord Phillips explained at para.83, "It is not a breach of any of the standard form contracts under consideration to overdraw, or attempt to overdraw, on a current account."

---

[22] See Lord Phillips at paras 69 and 80 and Lord Mance at para.98.
[23] Now, of course, the requirements are that the provisions must be transparent and prominent— see above.

Future solutions

10.19 On 27 December 2009, shortly after the Supreme Court judgment, the OFT announced in a press release that it had "concluded that any investigation it were to continue into the fairness of current unarranged overdraft charging terms under the Unfair Terms in Consumer Contracts Regulations would have a very limited scope and low prospects of success". Other options ranged from voluntary action to legislation. It would "discuss these issues intensively with banks, consumer groups and other organisations" and report on progress by the end of March 2010. The banks then agreed to introduce "transparency measures", e.g., annual summaries of account costs, and in late 2011 "additional commitments", e.g., text alerts about low balances.

The Supreme Court itself suggested legislation. Lord Walker, reflecting on the fact that the Government had decided to transpose the EU Directive as it stood rather than to confer the higher degree of consumer protection afforded by the national laws of some other Member States—for example, Netherlands and Spain—wondered whether "Parliament may wish to consider whether to revisit that decision". Lady Hale, though, considered "it may not be easy to find a satisfactory solution".[24]

OFT v Foxtons

10.20 The OFT was more successful in its claim against Foxtons, the well-known estate agents. In *Office of Fair Trading v Foxtons Ltd*[25] F's terms provided for the payment by landlords of commission on the introduction of a tenant and on a renewal by or a subsequent sale to the tenant. The OFT claimed that (1) the renewal and sales commissions were not part of "the main subject matter of the contract" within reg.6(2)(a) so as to escape an assessment of fairness; (2) the terms were not "in plain, intelligible language" as required by reg.7; and (3) the provisions relating to such commissions were unfair.

Mann J decided all these issues in the OFT's favour. (1) The renewal and sales commissions were not part of the core bargain. A typical consumer would approach F to find a tenant for an initial term; a renewal or sale would be a subsidiary matter. (2) The terms had not been drafted in plain and intelligible language. Parts of the renewal terms were too vague and hidden away in the document. (3) All the relevant provisions were unfair.

OFT v Ashbourne

10.21 Another recent success of the OFT occurred after years of negotiation with the defendants. The *Office of Fair Trading v Ashbourne Management Services Ltd*[26] was concerned with two other statutory provisions in addition to the Unfair Terms in Consumer Contracts Regulations. For completeness we

---

[24] Lord Walker at para.52. Lady Hale at para.93.
[25] [2009] EWHC 1681 (Ch).
[26] [2011] EWHC 1237 (Ch).

shall discuss all three aspects here and refer back to this discussion where relevant later in this book. The facts were these.

> The defendants A carried on the business of recruiting members for gym and health and fitness clubs, providing standard form agreements for their use and collecting payments from members under those agreements. A advised gym clubs to adopt agreements with specified minimum membership periods of 12 to 36 months. Members who wished to terminate their agreements were described by X as defaulters and dealt with by registering or threatening to register their defaults with a credit reference agency.

The OFT sought declarations that these were unfair commercial practices and injunctions restraining A from using such agreements and from relying on any unfair terms in existing agreements.

The OFT contended that (1) clause 2 of the gym agreements "YOU MUST PAY THE MONTHLY MEMBERSHIP SUBSCRIPTION FOR THE NEXT . . . MONTHS ('THE MINIMUM MEMBERSHIP PERIOD')" was not a core term within reg.6(2). Anyway A's agreements were regulated consumer credit agreements under s.8 of the Consumer Credit Act 1974 (the 1974 Act), which did not meet the requirements of s.61(1)(a); (2) the terms of A's agreements providing for a minimum membership period were unfair within the meaning of the 1999 Regulations; (3) by reporting information about gym members to credit reference agencies, A had adopted unfair commercial practices contrary to the Consumer Protection from Unfair Trading Regulations 2008 (the 2008 Regulations).

The High Court held: **10.22**

(1) The agreements were not credit agreements within the 1974 Act, but agreements under which the member made payments each month for the continuing provision of gym facilities.

(2) Clause 2 was the main subject of the agreement. It was a core term "because it defines the period during which the member is entitled to use the facilities of the gym club and, in return, must pay a particular monthly subscription" (per Kitchin J at para.152). Even so A's agreements did not address the tendency of the average consumer to overestimate the use they would make of the gym and that they were likely not to attend at all after two or three months. A's advice to clubs to have minimum membership periods was calculated to take advantage of naïve consumers using gyms and the agreements contained a trap for them. The agreements caused a significant imbalance in the parties' rights and obligations to an extent which was contrary to good faith, so they were unfair under the 1999 Regulations.

(3) As the agreements were not regulated consumer credit agreements, the information reported to credit reference agencies was inaccurate. Reporting the fact that an individual owed a debt which was really only unliquidated damages was an unfair commercial practice which

harmed the collective interests of consumers contrary to the 2008 Regulations. The OFT was entitled to the declarations and injunctions.

After that decision the OFT began an investigation in January 2012 into health clubs and gym contracts. In March 2013 it announced that three companies with almost a million gym users had agreed to improved membership conditions, e.g. by reducing cancellation periods. The companies were Bannatyne Fitness, David Lloyd Leisure and Fitness First.

ParkingEye Limited (Respondent) v Beavis (Appellant)

10.23 This case[27] is the most recent to be decided on the core term issue.

ParkingEye Ltd agreed with the owners of the Riverside Retail Park to manage the car park at the site. ParkingEye displayed numerous notices throughout the car park, saying that a failure to comply with a two-hour time limit would "result in a Parking Charge of £85". On 15 April 2013, Mr Beavis parked in the car park, but overstayed the two-hour limit by almost an hour. ParkingEye demanded payment of the £85 charge. Mr Beavis argued that the £85 charge was unenforceable at common law as a penalty, and/or that it was unfair and unenforceable by virtue of the 1999 Regulations. The Court of Appeal upheld the first instance decision rejecting those arguments.

The Supreme Court dismissed Mr Beavis' appeal, concluding that the clause was neither a penalty, nor was it unfair under the 1999 Regulations. We will explain the reasoning as to why the term was not unfair below. However, the key point for present purposes is that the court took the view that the unfairness did at least apply. The view was that the charge did not fall within the price exclusion, because (unlike in a case such as Abbey National) it was not provided in exchange for any services. Rather it was a charge for a default (a breach) by the consumer and was therefore covered by the test of unfairness. It was said that:

> "The £85 is described in the notice as a 'parking charge', but no one suggests that that label is conclusive. In our view it was not, as a matter of contractual analysis, a charge for the right to park, nor was it a charge for the right to overstay the two-hour limit. Not only is the £85 payable upon certain breaches which may occur within the two-hour free parking period, but there is no fixed period of time for which the motorist is permitted to stay after the two hours have expired, for which the £85 could be regarded as consideration. The licence having been terminated under its terms after two hours, the presence of the car would have constituted a trespass from that point on. In the circumstances, the £85 can only be regarded as a charge for contravening the terms of the contractual licence" (Lords Neuberger and Sumption at para 94).

27 [2015] UKSC 67.

6. Individually and Non Individually Negotiated Terms

The Regulations (following the Directive) only applied to terms that had **10.24** not been individually negotiated (typically standard terms), and not to terms which had been individually negotiated.[28] This exclusion has been removed, so individually negotiated terms are now covered by the test of unfairness. Of course, the only terms in consumer contracts that tend to be negotiated are core provisions, e.g. on price or main subject matter and these are, as we have seen, excluded in their own right from the test of unfairness. The main reason for removing the exclusion was probably to remove the scope for traders to put consumers off by claiming that terms had been negotiated (perhaps pointing to some formal declaration the consumer had signed claiming the terms had been negotiated, when this had not happened in reality. Of course, if ancillary terms are genuinely the result of negotiation, then, although they are now subject to the test of unfairness, the existence of the negotiation will be at least a factor in favour of them being held to be fair.

7. When are Terms and notices Unfair?

Broadly reflecting 3.1 and 4.1 of the Directive, s.62 provides as follows: **10.25**

(1) An unfair term of a consumer contract is not binding on the consumer.
(2) An unfair consumer notice is not binding on the consumer.
(3) This does not prevent the consumer from relying on the term or notice if the consumer chooses to do so.
(4) A term is unfair if, contrary to the requirement of good faith, it causes a significant imbalance in the parties' rights and obligations under the contract to the detriment of the consumer.
(5) Whether a term is fair is to be determined—

    (a) taking into account the nature of the subject matter of the contract, and
    (b) by reference to all the circumstances existing when the term was agreed and to all of the other terms of the contract or of any other contract on which it depends.

(6) A notice is unfair if, contrary to the requirement of good faith, it causes a significant imbalance in the parties' rights and obligations to the detriment of the consumer.
(7) Whether a notice is fair is to be determined—

    (a) taking into account the nature of the subject matter of the notice, and
    (b) by reference to all the circumstances existing when the rights or obligations to which it relates arose and to the terms of any contract on which it depends.

It is clear then that the fairness of a term must not be looked at in isolation **10.26** but in the context of the contract as a whole—including the price and the

---

[28] Regulation 5(1), and see the old regs 5(2)–(4) defining negotiation.

consumer's reasonable expectations. The reference to "another contract on which it is dependent" would enable the court to examine, e.g., the terms of a contract between a lender and a debtor when assessing the fairness of a term in a contract of guarantee or indemnity. As with the 1977 Act (see para.9.47 above) it is the time of the contract that is the critical time for assessing fairness.

It is to be noted that s.63(1) refers to Pt 1 of Sch.2 to the Act containing "an indicative and non-exhaustive list of terms" that may be regarded as unfair for the purposes of this part. These are discussed in paras 10.47–10.92 below.

The central unfairness concept is, of course, that contained in subss.(4) and (6)—the idea that the term or notice causes a significant imbalance, contrary to good faith. In *Director General of Fair Trading v First National Bank*,[29] the House of Lords (now of course, the Supreme Court) took the view that for a term to be unfair there would need to be a significant imbalance in rights and obligations to the detriment of the consumer *and* a violation of the requirement of good faith; these being separate, if connected, requirements.

10.27   So, dealing first with significant imbalance/detriment, the House of Lords related this to the substantive features of the term; there being a significant imbalance where the term is "so weighted in favour of the supplier as to tilt the parties' rights and obligations under the contract significantly in his favour" (Lord Bingham at 1307). This would be the case where terms give unduly beneficial rights to the trader or impose undue burdens on the consumer. Lord Bingham said that:

> "The requirement of significant imbalance is met if a term is so weighted in favour of the supplier as to tilt the parties' rights and obligations under the contract significantly in his favour. This may be by the granting to the supplier of a beneficial option or discretion or power, or by the imposing on the consumer of a disadvantageous burden or risk or duty."[30]

The reference to "the granting to the supplier of a beneficial option or discretion or power" will usually cover exemption clauses and terms giving traders the right to vary their performance; while "imposing on the consumer of a disadvantageous burden or risk or duty" refers to terms where traders impose some onerous obligation or liability on the consumer (whether greater than the law would normally impose, or perhaps contrary to what consumers would reasonably expect).[31]

Lord Bingham also said that the indicative list of terms (as indicated above, this is now in Pt 1 of Sch.2 to the CRA 2015), provided guidance as to unfairness in substance.

10.28   Turning to good faith, Lord Bingham equated good faith with "fair

---

[29] [2001] UKHL 52; [2001] 3 W.L.R. 1297.

[30] [2001] 3 W.L.R. 1297 per Lord Bingham at 1307.

[31] See discussion by C. Willett, *Fairness in Consumer Contracts: The Case of Unfair Terms*, (Ashgate, 2007), and C. Willett, "General Clause and the Competing Ethics of European Consumer Law in the UK" C.L.J. 2012, 71(2), 412–440.

and open dealing". He said that "openness" meant that terms should be "expressed fully, clearly and legibly"; not containing "concealed pitfalls or traps"; and being given "appropriate prominence" where they might "operate disadvantageously" to the consumer. He said that said that fair dealing:

> "requires that the supplier should not, whether deliberately or unconsciously, take advantage of the consumer's necessity, indigence, lack of experience, unfamiliarity with the subject matter of the contract [or] weak bargaining position . . ."[32]

Lord Steyn considered that there was "a large area of overlap" between the significant imbalance and good faith limbs of the test. Indeed, he rejected the idea that good faith is primarily concerned with procedural matters, saying that:

> "Any purely procedural or even predominantly procedural interpretation of the requirement of good faith must be rejected."[33]

At the same time it seems clear that he did view procedural matters as being relevant to good faith. He approved Lord Bingham's statement that good faith was about "fair and open dealing".

Taking all of this together it appears that if a term excludes or restricts **10.29** liability, or imposes an onerous obligation or liability on the consumer, it will often cause a significant imbalance to the detriment of the consumer. The question will then be whether there has been a violation of good faith. This appears to involve a combined analysis of the degree of unfairness in substance and various aspects of procedural fairness (in particular the degree of transparency, but also whether (as will usually be the case) the consumer is in a weaker bargaining position and this appears to have been taken advantage of.

It seems arguable that in some cases the degree of significant imbalance and detriment caused in this way will be sufficient in itself to lead to the conclusion that the requirement of good faith has not been complied with. This was not confirmed by the House of Lords, although it was by the Court of Appeal[34]; and the House of Lords did not express any view to the contrary. This seems most likely to be the case where the indicative list of unfair terms is concerned.

---

[32] [2001] 3 W.L.R. 1297 per Lord Bingham at 1308.
[33] [2001] 3 W.L.R. 1297 per Lord Steyn at 1313.
[34] See the view of Beale "Legislative Control of Fairness: The Directive on Unfair Terms in Consumer Contracts" in Beatson and Friedmann, *Good Faith and Fault in Contract Law* (OUP, 1995) pp.232 and 245, cited with approval by the Court of Appeal at [2000] Q.B. 672 at 686; [2000] 2 All E.R. 759 at 769; and see C. Willett, "General Clause and the Competing Ethics of European Consumer Law in the UK" C.L.J. 2012, 71(2), 412–440.

ParkingEye Limited (Respondent) v Beavis (Appellant)[35]

10.30   This provides a good recent example of the approach of the Supreme Court
to application of the test of unfairness (for the facts see above). According
to the Supreme Court, even if the charge of £85 did cause a significant
imbalance, this did not arise "contrary to the requirements of good faith",
as ParkingEye and the owners had a legitimate interest in inducing Mr
Beavis not to overstay in order to efficiently manage the car park for the
benefit of the other users of the nearby shops, the charge was no higher than
was necessary to achieve that objective, and the reasonable motorist would
have, and often did, agree to such a charge (Lord Neuberger at 106–109,
Lord Mance at 188–214, and Lord Hodge at 284–288). Lord Toulson dis-
sented, emphasising the high level of protection intended by the Unfair
Terms Directive,[36] the fact that the burden is on the supplier to show that
the consumer would have agreed to the terms in individual negotiations on
level terms, that it was not reasonable to assume this to be so in this case,
and that ParkingEye had not produced sufficient evidence to this effect
(309–315).[37]

8. TERMS THAT ARE ALWAYS UNFAIR

10.31   Certain terms are always ineffective, i.e. they are always viewed as unfair and
not binding, without the need to apply the test of unfairness. Some of the
most important of these are discussed below.

> • (in goods contracts), terms excluding or restricting: the terms and
> rights set out in Chapter Four, on satisfactory quality; fitness for
> particular purpose; compliance with description, sample or model;
> other pre-contract information included in contract; installation as
> part of conformity of the goods with the contract; goods not con-
> forming to contract if digital content does not conform; trader's to
> have right to supply the goods, etc.; delivery of goods; and passing
> of risk (s.31(1)).

"Excluding or restricting" includes "preventing an obligation or duty arising
or limiting its extent" (s.31(3)), and excluding or restricting a right or remedy
in relation to the above terms or rights (s.31(2)); so it covers both excluding or
restricting the above terms and rights, and also excluding any of the remedies

---

[35] See para.10.23 above.
[36] Generally see the recent CJEU case, *Aziz v Caixa d'Estalvis de Catalunya, Tarragona i
Manresa* (C-415/11) [2013] 3 C.M.L.R. 89, which provides guidance as to how to interpret the unfairness test, and which was relied upon in the Supreme Court's judgement in
ParkingEye.
[37] This case again shows the vastly differing views there can be as to what is "fair", depending
on how much one focusses, on the one hand, on business self-interest, freedom of contract,
etc., or, on the other hand, on consumer protection needs. On this see C. Willett, "General
Clause and the Competing Ethics of European Consumer Law in the UK" C.L.J. 2012, 71(2),
412–440.

flowing from breach of these terms or rights, i.e. repair, replacement, rejection, damages, price reduction, etc. (see Chapter Eight above).

Section 31(2) provides that excluding or restricting also covers:

"(b) [making] such a right or remedy or its enforcement subject to a restrictive or onerous condition,

(c) [allowing] a trader to put a person at a disadvantage as a result of pursuing such a right or remedy, or

(d) [excluding or restricting] rules of evidence or procedure."

However, "an agreement in writing to submit present or future differences to arbitration" does not count as an exclusion or restriction of liability (s.31(4)).   **10.32**

For examples as to how the almost identical provisions in the 1977 Act work, see para.9.30 above.

- (in digital contents contracts) terms excluding or restricting: the terms and rights set out in Chapter Four, on (digital content to be of satisfactory quality; fitness for particular purpose; compliance with description; other pre-contract information included in contract); and the trader's right to supply digital content (s.47(1)).

Note that the same approach is taken in digital contents contracts as in goods contracts, as to what counts as exclusion or restriction of liability (excluding or restricting the terms and rights themselves, the remedies, using the other techniques outlined above) (see s.47(2)–(4)).

- (in services contracts), terms excluding or restricting: the terms set out in Chapter Eight on reasonable care and skill[38]; information about trader or service to be binding; reasonable price and reasonable time. Again, the same approach is taken as in goods and digital contents contracts, as to what counts as exclusion or restriction of liability (excluding or restricting the terms and rights themselves, the remedies, using the other techniques outlined above) (s.57(1), (2), (4)–(6), and it is also specifically provided that a term is ineffective if it would prevent the consumer in an appropriate case from recovering the price paid or the value of any other consideration (s.57(3)).

9. DUTY OF COURT TO CONSIDER FAIRNESS OF TERM

Traditionally, in civil proceedings, it is for the party who stands to benefit   **10.33**
from a particular rule, to raise this rule in argument before the court, e.g.,

---

[38] See also ss.65 and 66 on the ineffectiveness of excluding liability for death or injury caused by negligence (this extending beyond contractual duties to take reasonable care, to cover, e.g. the tort of negligence).

for the consumer to question whether a term satisfies the test of unfairness. However, a series of cases from the CJEU have established the principle that courts should often raise the issue of fairness "ex-officio", i.e. even if issue has not been raised on behalf of the consumer. The idea is to recognise that, otherwise, the point may not be raised, as consumers may sometimes be unrepresented, or represented by a lawyer who may not be a specialist in this field.[39]

Following this jurisprudence from the CJEU, s.71 of the CRA 2015 provides that:

> (2) The court must consider whether the term is fair even if none of the parties to the proceedings has raised that issue or indicated that it intends to raise it.
> (3) But subsection (2) does not apply unless the court considers that it has before it sufficient legal and factual material to enable it to consider the fairness of the term.

10. Effect of Unfairness

10.34 As we can see above, an unfair term or notice is not binding on the consumer, although this does not prevent the consumer choosing to rely on the term or notice (ss.62(1)–(3)). Where a term is not binding on the consumer, it is provided that the contract "continues, so far as practicable, to have effect in every other respect" (s.67).

11. Transparency and Terms with Different meanings

10.35 We have already come across a reference to plain language in relation to the main subject matter and price exclusions. There are two further provisions related to language and meaning. First, there is s.68, which provides that:

> (1) A trader must ensure that a written term of a consumer contract, or a consumer notice in writing, is transparent.
> (2) A consumer notice is transparent for the purposes of subsection (1) if it is expressed in plain and intelligible language and it is legible.

One imagines that a clause which meets the standards of the "Plain English campaign" should pass the reg.7 test. Knowledge that the particular consumer does not speak English, or that English is not his first language, will be taken into account in assessing good faith and fairness.

The requirement of plain language is greatly to be welcomed. If there is a breach of this provision, there is no direct sanction for the individual consumer. However, as we saw above, lack of transparency will mean that price and main subject matter terms become subject to the test of unfair-

---

[39] e.g. *VB Pénzügyi Lizing Zrt v Ferenc Schneider* (C-137/08) [2011] 2 C.M.L.R. 1; [2011] C.E.C. 973.

ness, and as we also saw this lack of transparency will help a term to fail the test of unfairness (see Lord Bingham in the *First National Bank* case). We will also see below that lack of transparency could affect the meaning of a term and this could be significant. Finally, we shall see further below that regulators can act to have terms removed on the basis that they are not transparent.

It is heartening to note that from the very beginning that the OFT (now the CMA) has taken a purposive and positive approach to the issue of plain, intelligible language. Indeed there is a strong emphasis throughout on the principle that before they enter into any contract consumers must be able to read and understand all its written terms.

The following points are also worthy of note: **10.36**

(1) Some firms are tending to use forms which were drafted with business customers in mind and which use language which is inappropriate to consumers.

(2) The terms must be within the understanding of ordinary consumers without legal advice.

(3) Legal jargon must be avoided. There is all the difference in the world between "all conditions and warranties are excluded" and "we are not legally responsible if the machine breaks down". Other terms to avoid include "consequential loss", "vicarious liability", "mitigation" and "this is without prejudice to your statutory rights".

(4) The need for "plain, intelligible language" goes beyond mere vocabulary and covers such matters as using short sentences, avoiding double negatives, minimising cross-references and legibility (size and colour of print coupled with the colour and quality of the paper).

(5) A set of terms should be user-friendly and should use "we" and "you". The OFT Bulletin 3 set out the whole of the British Fuel (Oils) Ltd's contract of domestic gas supply as a model of clear and helpful drafting. Here is one clause in that contract:

> If we cannot supply you with gas for some reason which is beyond our control, for example damage to the pipeline system, then you will not be able to claim that we are in breach of our arrangement with you but we will take all steps that are reasonably practicable to secure the supply of gas to you.

In virtually all cases the central factor is one of knowledge (or lack of it).[40] The number of consumers who know and understand what they are signing is minute. In an address given years ago in 1997 Pat Edwards (who was then Director of Legal Affairs at the OFT) referred to the serious problem of tackling the "impenetrable jargon" in some consumer

---

[40] *Spreadex Ltd v Cochrane* [2012] EWHC 1290 (Comm): 49 pages of complex paragraphs—unfair.

contracts but she then proceeded to sound a note of cautious optimism. She said:

> "One of the most encouraging aspects . . . has been the willingness of suppliers—in the end—to rewrite their contracts totally and in plain intelligible language
>   . . . It seems likely that the use of plain language, and the dropping of substantial unfairness, tend to go hand in hand. Doubtless, once terms are seen in the cold light of ordinary language, unfairnesses which were decently veiled by jargon and complexity stand out as the excrescences they are and the scales fall from the suppliers' eyes" (OFT Bulletin 4, p.26).

10.37   Aside from the transparency, s.69 provides that:

> (1) If a term in a consumer contract, or a consumer notice, could have different meanings, the meaning that is most favourable to the consumer is to prevail.
> (2) Subsection (1) does not apply to the construction of a term or a notice in proceedings on an application for an injunction or interdict under paragraph 3 of Schedule 3.

Section 69(1) is very similar to the idea of *contra proferentem* construction discussed in Chapter Nine. So, if traders do not draft terms transparently, they run the risk that the court finds ambiguity which will be read in favour of the consumer, e.g. an exemption clause will be read not to be as broad in what it excludes as the trader actually intends. The point of s.69(2) is in cases where regulators are acting against terms (see further below) it is actually better if the term is given an interpretation that is *not* favourable to the consumer interest. This after all is the way in which it might be understood by consumers, potentially allowing it to cause maximum prejudice.

Choice of law evasion

10.38   A trader may seek to avoid the unfair terms regime Regulations (or the Directive) by a clause which applies, or purports to apply, the law of a non EEA Member State. Section 74(1) makes it clear that this is not possible if the contract has a close connection with the territory of an EEA Member State.

12. COMPLAINTS AND ENFORCEMENT

10.39   Section 70 refers us to Schs 3 and 5 to the CRA 2015, which sets out the powers of the CMA (formerly the OFT) and various other so called "regulators" to take preventive action to obtain the removal of unfair terms from contracts.

Who are the "regulators" having enforcement powers? (Sch.3, para.1)

10.40   (a) the Competition and Markets Authority (CMA)

(b) the Department of Enterprise, Trade and Investment in Northern Ireland,

(c) a local weights and measures authority in Great Britain,

(d) the Financial Conduct Authority,

(e) the Office of Communications,

(f) the Information Commissioner,

(g) the Gas and Electricity Markets Authority,

(h) the Water Services Regulation Authority,

(i) the Office of Rail Regulation,

(j) the Northern Ireland Authority for Utility Regulation, or

(k) the Consumers' Association.

Duty to consider complaints (Sch.3, para.2)

A person who alleges that a term or notice is unfair can make a complaint to   **10.41**
the CMA and/or to another regulatory body. The CMA may consider such
a complaint. If a regulator other than the CMA intends to consider a complaint, it must notify the CMA of this, and must then consider the complaint.
In either case the CMA or other regulator must give reasons for a decision
not to apply for an injunction.

Injunctions and Undertakings (Sch.3, paras 3–6)

The CMA or other regulator can apply to the High Court[41] or to a county   **10.42**
court for an injunction against any person appearing to the CMA or other
regulator to be using or recommending a term or notice that is either wholly
ineffective, or in breach of the breach of either the unfairness test or the
transparency requirements set out above. This is subject to one qualification; a qualifying body can only apply if it gives to the CMA not less than
14 days' written notice of its intention to do so (or such shorter period as the
CMA may agree). When the matter comes to court it can grant the injunction on such terms as it thinks fit, whether in relation to the term initially
complained about or any term or notice, of a similar kind or with a similar
effect.

A regulator may accept an undertaking from a trader against whom it has
applied, or thinks it is entitled to apply, for an injunction. This is the much
more typical route than actually seeking an injunction. The undertaking
would typically be to the effect that the trader would delete or amend a term
or notice to make it fair, transparent, etc. Where a regulator other than the
CMA accepts an undertaking, it must notify the CMA of who has given the
undertaking and the conditions attached to it.

---

[41] See *Office of Fair Trading v Foxtons Ltd* [2009] EWCA Civ 288.

Publication, information and advice (Sch.3, para.7)

10.43   This is largely self-explanatory and is of considerable practical importance. It reads as follows:

> (1) The CMA must arrange the publication of details of—
>
>> (a) any application it makes for an injunction or interdict under paragraph 3,
>> (b) any injunction or interdict under this Schedule, and
>> (c) any undertaking under this Schedule.
>
> (2) The CMA must respond to a request whether a term or notice, or one of a similar kind or with a similar effect, is or has been the subject of an injunction, interdict or undertaking under this Schedule.
>
> (3) Where the term or notice, or one of a similar kind or with a similar effect, is or has been the subject of an injunction or interdict under this Schedule, the CMA must give the person making the request a copy of the injunction or interdict.
>
> (4) Where the term or notice, or one of a similar kind or with a similar effect, is or has been the subject of an undertaking under this Schedule, the CMA must give the person making the request—
>
>> (a) details of the undertaking, and
>> (b) if the person giving the undertaking has agreed to amend the term or notice, a copy of the amendments.
>
> (5) The CMA may arrange the publication of advice and information about the provisions of this Part.

10.44   Acting under this final provision, the OFT used to publish regular Bulletins setting out (1) some of the current OFT thinking and policy in exercising their enforcement powers and (2) details of action taken by the OFT (and other qualifying bodies) against named firms in relation to potentially unfair terms. This practice has ceased, but other OFT (and now CMA) publications contain a mine of information. For a repository of past work and a guide to the unfair terms regime under the CRA 2015, see *https://www.gov.uk/government/publications/unfair-contract-terms-cma37*.

On the powers to obtain documents from traders see Sch.5 to the CRA 2015.

13. POLICY AND PRACTICE OF THE OFT/CMA

10.45   Very few cases under the Regulations reach the courts but many thousands of clauses have been, and are still being, considered by the OFT (now the CMA). Thus, to take a random example, Bulletins 21 and 22 reveal that in the six months from July to December 2002 no less than 765 clauses were amended or abandoned as the result of enforcement action by the OFT (in

the same period a further 38 clauses were revised in the light of enforcement action by other qualifying bodies—principally weights and measures
authorities).

If they consider that a complaint reveals a potentially unfair term the OFT
would adopt a three-pronged approach, and this is likely to be the ongoing
approach of the CMA:

(1) They would first open a dialogue with the firm, inviting them to
    modify or delete a term which, in their opinion, is unfair.

(2) If this proved unsuccessful and unconstructive, they would seek an
    undertaking.

(3) Finally, as a last resort, they would seek an injunction.

In a press release (33/2000) the OFT pointed out that their success in achiev-   **10.46**
ing alteration to potentially unfair terms without litigation in more than 4,800
cases has saved hundreds of millions of pounds. However, in 1999 the OFT
did launch proceedings against First National Bank in relation to a clause in
a loan agreement which provided that contractual interest would continue to
run even after judgment. The Court of Appeal held that the clause was indeed
unfair but the House of Lords disagreed.[42] The unsuccessful litigation on
bank charges is another example of the CMA's determination to try to curb
unfair practices (see paras 10.13–10.18 above).

14. Clauses Which may be Unfair: Schedule 2

As already stated, there is an indicative and non-exhaustive list of the terms   **10.47**
which may be regarded as unfair (the so-called "grey list"). The words
"indicative and non-exhaustive" should be constantly borne in mind—Pt 18
of the OFT Unfair Contract Terms Guide (2001) gives examples of clauses
which they consider as potentially unfair even though they are not mentioned
in the Schedule.

The list in para.1 of Sch.2 comprises 17 examples lettered (a) to (q). We
set them out below with a comment on each clause and, in some cases, an
example. The list opens with the words "Terms which have the object or
effect of:" and then follow the 17 examples.

(a) excluding or limiting the legal liability of a seller or supplier in the event of   **10.48**
    the death of a consumer or personal injury to the latter resulting from an
    act or omission of that seller or supplier;

Comment.   Thus in one case the OFT achieved the deletion of the following   **10.49**
clause:

---

[42] *Director General of Fair Trading v First National Bank* [2001] UKHL 52; [2001] 3 W.L.R.
1297.

The company does not accept responsibility for the failure of any fire protection equipment in the event of a fire.

In another case, a clause stated that persons using the equipment or facilities at a gymnasium did so at their own risk. It was amended so that it started with the words, "In the absence of any negligence or other breach of duty . . ."

10.50   (b) inappropriately excluding or limiting the legal rights of the consumer *vis-à-vis* the seller or supplier or another party in the event of total or partial non-performance or inadequate performance by the seller or supplier of any of the contractual obligations, including the option of offsetting a debt owed to the seller or supplier against any claim which the consumer may have against him;

10.51   **Comment**.   The following example of a para.(b) term relating to Microsoft software is a good illustration of a change in substance and in the use of plain intelligible language.
Before:

> LIMITED WARRANTY. MICROSOFT warrants that the support provided hereunder shall be substantially as described. THIS WARRANTY IS EXCLUSIVE AND IS IN LIEU OF ALL OTHER WARRANTIES AND MICROSOFT DISCLAIMS ALL OTHER WARRANTIES, EXPRESS OR IMPLIED, INCLUDING, BUT NOT LIMITED TO, WARRANTIES OF MERCHANTABILITY AND FITNESS FOR A PARTICULAR PURPOSE.

After:

> LIMITED WARRANTY. MICROSOFT warrants that it will provide Support with reasonable care, within a reasonable time and substantially as described in this Agreement. MICROSOFT does not make any other promises or warranties about Support service.

This is a clear example of balancing the interests of supplier and consumer; the OFT acknowledged that the supplier also needs to protect his interests— but not to the extent provided by the original term. This group of potentially unfair terms is by far the largest section of the OFT illustrations; Bulletins 21 and 22 contain no fewer than 153 examples identified by the OFT in the six-month period (July to December 2002); they include terms excluding or limiting liability for defective performance, non-performance or delay, time limits, excluding or restricting set-off and using "guarantees" to restrict liability. We must once again stress two essential points which apply to every illustration; they merely represent the opinion of the OFT and not the opinion of a court, and each term under discussion must be considered in the context of the contract as a whole and not in isolation.

10.52   (c) making an agreement binding on the consumer whereas provision of services by the seller or supplier is subject to a condition whose realisation depends on his own will alone;

Comment. This could catch a servicing agreement where the consumer was **10.53** required to pay an annual fee even though the supplier might decide to discontinue carrying spare parts for that particular item (see OFT Bulletin No.5 at p.76).

    (d) permitting the seller or supplier to retain sums paid by the consumer **10.54** where the latter decides not to conclude or perform the contract, without providing for the consumer to receive compensation of an equivalent amount from the seller or supplier where the latter is the party cancelling the contract;

Comment. This highlights one of the key concepts of "unfairness", **10.55** namely the one-sided nature of a particular provision. Essentially the clause covers three distinct situations, namely a term giving the seller or supplier the right to forfeit (1) a pre-contractual deposit, (2) a deposit liable to be forfeited if the consumer "cancels" and (3) a deposit liable to be forfeited if the consumer breaks the agreement. Under the general law (1) a pre-contractual deposit is recoverable by a consumer as of right if the contract does not happen, (2) a "cancellation" deposit is presumably forfeitable as of right as being the price paid by the consumer for a right not available to him or her under the general law, and (3) a deposit payable on breach can be forfeited unless it amounts to a penalty. In all these cases a deposit (being a payment indicating that the consumer "means business") must be distinguished from a part-payment which the consumer can recover (subject to a set-off for damages) if the event giving rise to payment has not yet arrived.

The idea in (d) appears to be that a deposit forfeiture clause may be unfair if it is not matched by a "reverse deposit"—a totally new concept. Here is an OFT illustration (omitting the company's name).

Before:

> No order which has been accepted by (the Company) may be cancelled by (the Customer) except on terms that the Customer shall indemnify (the Company) in full against any losses and costs incurred by (them) as a result of cancellation. A MINIMUM CANCELLATION CHARGE of 25% OF THE CONTRACT PRICE WILL BE PAYABLE BY THE CUSTOMER IN THE EVENT THAT (THE COMPANY) ACCEPTS SUCH CANCELLATION.

After:

> You cannot cancel an order unless you . . . pay any losses and costs we suffer because of the cancellation. If we cancel the contract, we must pay you any losses or costs you suffer because of the cancellation.

Readers will be familiar with cases where a cancellation charge is imposed by a hotel without any attempt by them to re-let the accommodation or to calculate the costs saved by the cancellation. Such terms can now be open to challenge.

    (e) requiring any consumer who fails to fulfil his obligation to pay a dispro- **10.56** portionately high sum in compensation;

10.57   **Comment**. Under a loan agreement the *initial* rate of interest is a "core" provision and therefore falls outside the Regulations if it is expressed in plain, intelligible language (and it may well be that a reference to a "flat" rate without a reference to the "true" rate based on the amount from time to time outstanding could be attacked). Paragraph (e) relates to the rate of *default* interest (which might be attacked under the general law as a penalty). The word "disproportionate" must refer to the size of the transaction, the extent of the default and to the loss that this causes to the other party. The OFT has persuaded traders to reduce the amount of default interest on credit cards and to replace a "termination" clause by a "suspension" clause.

10.58   **(f)** authorizing the seller or supplier to dissolve the contract on a discretionary basis where the same facility is not granted to the consumer, or permitting the seller or supplier to retain the sums paid for services not yet supplied to him where it is the seller or supplier himself who dissolves the contract;

10.59   **Comment**. This lack of mutuality as a key feature of unfairness has already been mentioned in relation to (d). An obvious example would be a clause in a policy of insurance giving the insurer (but not the insured) a discretionary right to cancel the policy during the period of insurance. The OFT Bulletins give a number of illustrations of one-sided termination rights covering a wide variety of activities including blinds, computer systems, leases, football club membership and satellite TV. In a widely publicised success story, the OFT persuaded Sky TV to change its terms of business so that (1) Sky will have no right to terminate during the "minimum period" unless the customer is in breach, and (2) more significantly, the customer will have a termination right if, for example, Sky varies the conditions or withdraws one of the Channels falling within the Option chosen by the customer.

10.60   **(g)** enabling the seller or supplier to terminate a contract of indeterminate duration without reasonable notice except where there are serious grounds for doing so.[43]

10.61   **Comment**. A contract of hire or storage or a contract for the provision of accommodation may give the supplier the right to terminate without notice. Clearly such a clause, which could put the consumer in great difficulty, is potentially unfair unless serious grounds exist for it. Examples of the latter would include the consumer becoming bankrupt or his cheques being dishonoured.

10.62   **(h)** Automatically extending a contract of fixed duration where the consumer does not indicate otherwise, when the deadline fixed for the consumer to express this desire not to extend the contract is unreasonably early;

10.63   **Comment**. A contract of hire or a maintenance contract for one year might provide that "this contract will be automatically extended to three years unless the consumer informs the company in the first three months that he

---

[43] But see para.10.83 below.

does not wish this to occur". In the vast majority of cases the consumer would be blissfully unaware of this provision until it is too late.

> **(i)** irrevocably binding the consumer to terms with which he had no   **10.64**
> real opportunity of becoming acquainted before the conclusion of the
> contract;

Comment.   One obvious example would be a clause in a train ticket stating   **10.65**
that "passengers are carried on our conditions of carriage which can be
inspected at our Head Office" (see *Thompson v LMS Railway*[44]). Then
again, terms not expressed in plain, intelligible language or put in minute
print could be unfair under this provision. This can be regarded as one of
the most important of the Sch.2 terms. In the words of the OFT (Bulletin 4,
p.10):

> We interpret a "real" opportunity as something more than the theoretical right
> to refer to a book held by the operator. While it is not practicable to put much
> information legibly on the back of a normal sized ticket, it is by no means
> impossible to take reasonable steps—for example by displaying posters in ticket
> offices—to alert consumers to, and summarise, significant provisions which they
> might not otherwise realise applied to them, and ignorance of which could cause
> them detriment.

One potential trap for consumers is the possibility that they may place an
order by phone, fax or internet and then find themselves bound by conditions
of sale of which they were unaware. There is a strong argument that, under
general principles of contract law, the conditions will not bind the consumer
because they were introduced too late (see para.9.12 above). Quite apart from
this, the OFT has persuaded a supplier to give the consumer a "money-back"
seven-day cancellation right for unopened and unused goods if he does not
agree to the hidden conditions.

In the context of leases the tenant may be required to observe the terms
of a head lease or the terms of the landlord's insurance. The tenant will be
unaware of those terms and accordingly the OFT has succeeded in obtaining
deletion.

> **(j)** enabling the seller or supplier to alter the terms of the contract unilaterally   **10.66**
> without a valid reason which is specified in the contract[45];

Comment.   Under the general law neither party can vary the terms of a   **10.67**
concluded contract, unless the contract itself gives such a right. The exercise
of such a right (e.g. altering the duration of the contract or the time fixed for
performance) would clearly undermine what the consumer expects and it
may therefore be unfair.

The OFT attitude was that "any term in any kind of contract that effectively gives an unrestricted power to vary significant terms for captive consumers creates a contractual imbalance that is likely to be considered unfair"

---

[44] [1940] 1 K.B. 41 (see para.9.10 above).
[45] See para.10.44 below.

(Bulletin 5, p.10). This was written when criticising the terms of business of Northern Rock Plc which (1) gave Northern Rock the right to restructure their customers' accounts (involving a reduction in the rates of interest) without notice to the customers, and (2) prevented the customers from moving their money to another account without incurring a penalty. The OFT persuaded Northern Rock to change this policy. They also persuaded BSkyB to modify a "right to vary" clause and a health club to delete the following term:

> We reserve the right to alter hours of business if found necessary and change the annual membership system and/or price structure.

10.68   (k) enabling the seller or supplier to alter unilaterally without a valid reason any characteristic of the product or service to be provided;

10.69 **Comment**.   If a building contract specifies the materials to be used, a clause giving the builder the right to substitute different materials may well be unfair.

A kitchen company was persuaded to restrict a substitution clause from "if for any reason the company is unable to supply a particular piece of furniture" to "if for any reason beyond the company's reasonable control . . .". The OFT also examined the following term in the conditions of a ferry company:

> The company accepts no liability for any inaccuracy in the information contained in this publication, which may be altered at any time without prior notice, and also reserves the right to alter, amend, or cancel any of the arrangements shown in this publication.

This was changed to:

> We reserve the right, *before you book*, to vary the services described in our brochures, including prices and departure dates, and to designate a different ferry for a particular journey.

10.70   (l) providing for the price of goods to be determined at the time of delivery or allowing a seller of goods or supplier of services to increase their price without in both cases giving the consumer the corresponding right to cancel the contract if the final price is too high in relation to the price agreed when the contract was concluded[46];

10.71 **Comment**.   It is common to find a price escalation clause as, for example, "the price quoted is the price prevailing at the date of the contract and the seller reserves the right to increase the price if this should prove necessary by reason of increases in the cost of work or materials". Similarly an order for a new car may contain a clause that the price will be the "price in the manufacturer's list at the date of delivery". Such clauses may be unfair, unless they give the consumer the option of pulling out.

---

[46] See para.10.84 below.

The OFT persuaded traders to modify price increase terms by (1) making the increases index linked, (2) giving the customer a termination right if the price is increased, or (3) improving that right. They also came across a term used by a trader with the improbable name of .0.0.0.0.0.0.1.A.A.A. Abbeyflow Ltd stating that "the quoted prices will be adjusted to meet any price variation in labour or materials occurring after the date of quotation". The term was deleted.

> (m) giving the seller or supplier the right to determine whether the goods or services supplied are in conformity with the contract, or giving him the exclusive right to interpret any term of the contract;

10.72

Comment. An example of this is: "the certificate of the company's surveyor shall be conclusive", or a clause in a building contract giving the supplier the right to decide that defects have been rectified.

10.73

> (n) limiting the seller's or supplier's liability to respect commitments undertaken by his agents or making his commitments subject to compliance with a particular formality;

10.74

Comment. A clause might provide "we are not responsible for any statements made by our agents or employees in negotiating this contract unless authorised in writing by a director". Under the general law a clause limiting the authority of an agent is effective[47] but in a consumer transaction the consumer is likely to rely heavily on the salesman and a "small print" clause of this type may well be unfair.

10.75

A common clause, which can operate unfairly, is the so-called "entire agreement" clause which effectively prevents the consumer from relying on any other document, letter or oral statement (especially promises made by an enthusiastic salesman). The matter is discussed in a five-page survey in the OFT Bulletin 2, p.14. An advertising company agreed to delete a clause which bluntly stated that "no verbal agreements will be honoured" and a security company agreed to the following plain-English variation. Before:

> All the terms of the Contract between the Company and the Customer are contained in the Contract and in these conditions and no oral or written arrangements . . . not contained in the Contract shall be in any way binding on the Company.

After:

> The Company intends to rely upon the written terms set out here and on the other side of this document. If you require any changes, please make sure that you ask for these to be put in writing. In this way we can avoid any problems surrounding what the Company and you the Customer is expected to do.

> (o) obliging the consumer to fulfil all his obligations where the seller or supplier does not perform his;

10.76

---

[47] See fn.78 at para.9.46 above.

10.77 **Comment**. The unfairness of such a provision (which overlaps with (c) above) is self-evident. In one case a clause bound ticketholders to the contract even where the supplier defaulted in supplying what was agreed at the time of ticket purchase. It was deleted.

10.78   **(p)** giving the seller or supplier the possibility of transferring his rights and obligations under the contract, where this may serve to reduce the guarantees for the consumer, without the latter's agreement;

10.79 **Comment**. Under the general law the burden of a contract cannot be assigned; the *assignor* remains liable to perform. If the contract does confer a right to assign obligations, the consumer might thereby lose the value of a long-term guarantee. The clause may therefore be unfair.

10.80   **(q)** excluding or hindering the consumer's right to take legal action or exercise any other legal remedy, particularly by requiring the consumer to take disputes exclusively to arbitration not covered by legal provisions, unduly restricting the evidence available to him or imposing on him a burden of proof which, according to the applicable law, should lie with another party to the contract;

10.81 **Comment**. This provision overlaps paragraph (m) above. The ground is already largely covered by the Arbitration Act 1996 (see para.11.45 below).

Modifications

10.82 Paragraph 2 of Sch.2 modifies three of the preceding provisions ((g), (j) and (l)); a clause which satisfies the modifying provisions is less likely to be unfair. However, it must be stressed that

> any standard term will be seen as being unfair, whether or not it appears in (or is excluded from) the list if it fails the unfairness test . . .. The purpose of the Schedule is to *illustrate this test* . . .. Similarly, the restrictions to the scope of the Schedule found particularly in paragraph 2 . . . exemplify situations in which— despite their apparent similarity to what is included in the Schedule—certain kinds of terms may nonetheless not produce "imbalance, detriment or lack of good faith" (OFT Bulletin 5, p.10).

The modifications in para.2 are set out below.

10.83   **(a)** Paragraph 1(g) is without hindrance to terms by which a supplier of financial services reserves the right to terminate unilaterally a contract of indeterminate duration without notice when there is a valid reason, provided that the supplier is required to inform the other contracting party or parties thereof immediately.

10.84 **Comment**. The "valid reason" can be contrasted with "serious grounds" in (g). Presumably the reason is not limited to default or insolvency by the consumer but can include reasons personal to the lender (such as a decision to withdraw from house mortgage loans). Although the proviso is not expressed in plain, intelligible language, the spirit of the Regulations suggests that the reason must be set out as part of the termination terms.

(b) Paragraph 1(j) is without hindrance to terms under which a supplier of **10.85**
financial services reserves the right to alter the rate of interest payable
by the consumer or due to the latter, or the amount of other charges for
financial services without notice where there is a valid reason, provided
that the supplier is required to inform the other contracting party or
parties thereof at the earliest opportunity and that the latter are free to
dissolve the contract immediately.

Comment.   On a strict reading of this proviso (and the placing of the comma) **10.86**
the words "where there is a valid reason" appear to qualify the words "other
charges" but not the words "rate of interest"; in other words a term that "the
lender may by written notice increase the rate of interest payable to the lender
or decrease the rate of interest payable to the borrower" would not be within
(j) provided that it also allowed the consumer to respond to the notice by
terminating the contract. This seems surprising and the French text (which
omits the commas) points to a different conclusion.

Paragraph 1(j) is also without hindrance to terms under which a seller or supplier **10.87**
reserves the right to alter unilaterally the conditions of a contract of indeterminate duration, provided that he is required to inform the consumer with reasonable notice and that the consumer is free to dissolve the contract.

Comment.   It will be recalled that a term may very well be unfair if it gives **10.88**
the supplier the right to alter the terms of the agreement and to hold the consumer to a bargain different from the one he originally made.
    If the supplier finds it necessary to alter a term in a contract of indetermi-
nate duration, this proviso allows him to insert a contractual term to that
effect provided that the consumer is then given the option of walking away
from the contract. This proviso is not limited to contracts for financial services.

(c) Paragraphs 1(g), (j) and (l) do not apply to: **10.89**
—transactions in transferable securities, financial instruments and other
products or services where the price is linked to fluctuations in a stock
exchange quotation or index or a financial market rate that the seller or
supplier does not control;
—contracts for the purchase or sale of foreign currency, traveller's
cheques or international money orders denominated in foreign currency.

Comment.   These two provisos permit sellers or suppliers to insert altera- **10.90**
tion/termination clauses in cases where the seller/supplier's calculations can
go wildly wrong as a result of share or currency fluctuations beyond his
control.

(d) Paragraph (l) is without hindrance to price-indexation clauses, where **10.91**
lawful, provided that the method by which prices vary is explicitly
described.

Comment.   A general price escalation clause may well be unfair under (l) **10.92**
above, but a clause for price adjustment by reference to (for example) the
retail price index might not be caught.

15. CONCLUSION

10.93 There is a Latin maxim *"ubi ius, ibi remedium"*[48] which broadly means that a right is valueless unless there is an effective remedy. A large part of this chapter has dealt with enforcement by regulatory bodies—but this is essentially machinery for protecting *future* consumers. Whether the rights of an individual consumer have any real value must depend on whether those rights can be enforced without too much hassle and expense. We shall consider this in the next two chapters.

---

[48] Literally, "where a right, there a remedy".

Chapter Eleven

"HOW DO I ENFORCE MY RIGHTS WITHOUT GOING TO COURT?"

In the previous chapters we have considered the consumer's rights and rem- **11.01**
edies and attempts to exclude them or to cut them down. We come now to the
all-important question—how can the rights be enforced? The lawyer tends to
think immediately of court proceedings but especially in this branch of the
law the courts should only be used as a last resort—if only because the cost of
proceedings may exceed the amount in dispute.

Scheme of this chapter

A short introduction will be followed by an examination of codes of **11.02**
practice—one of the most important developments in the consumer field.
Our discussion will then focus on the Ombudsman schemes which play an
increasingly significant role in consumer redress. This will be followed by
sections dealing with arbitration, alternative dispute resolution and legal
advice.

1. How to Start

The obvious first step is to contact the supplier. If the client himself does not **11.03**
receive satisfaction he could call in to see his solicitor or a Citizens Advice
Bureau (CAB) or contact the Citizens Advice Consumer Helpline. A letter,
fax or email sent to the head office, or to the chief executive, may produce
results. Alternatively, a member of the staff of the Trading Standards
Department might make a telephone call or visit the shop to see what the
shop has to say. These Departments are anxious to adopt a neutral role—to
play the part of conciliator rather than advocate.

If the suppliers are not co-operative, the next step might be to contact
their trade association. This is especially relevant if they are members of a
trade association with an Approved Code of practice. This is considered at
para.11.10 below.

Mention must also be made of the press, both local and national, radio
and television. Many of these bodies have someone dealing with consumer
matters and if they are satisfied that the consumer has had a raw deal, they
may print or publish a story about it. Needless to say they will take great
care to get their facts right because damages for defamation can be very
high.

2. Codes of Practice

A. INTRODUCTION

11.04   One method of improving standards of business practice across the board is to introduce legislation (with criminal sanctions) on such matters as safety and unfair commercial practices.[1]

Another method is to leave it to the different sectors of commerce to put their own houses in order by the introduction of voluntary codes of practice by the various trade associations. The development of voluntary codes can be regarded as one of the most significant contributions which the Fair Trading Act 1973 (the 1973 Act) made to the protection of individual consumers and accordingly it may be useful to examine this topic in some detail.

The regime introduced by the 1973 Act came to a halt in 2001 and was replaced by the Office of Fair Trading's (OFT) new approach under the Enterprise Act 2002.[2] Support for the existing codes was withdrawn on 31 December 2001. The OFT gave its support to 42 codes. These included cars, electrical appliances, travel, laundries and cleaners, mail order trading and double glazing. A full list of the codes is given in the following table to show the wide range of sectors covered by this regime from 1974 to 2001 (its successor regime from 2002–2013 covered only 12 sectors (see para.11.22 below)).

11.05

Operative from	Code
1974	AMDEA (Association of Manufacturers of Domestic Electrical Appliances): Principles for Domestic Electrical Appliance Servicing.
1975	ABTA (Association of British Travel Agents): Codes of Conduct.
1975	VBRA (Vehicle Builders and Repairers Association): Code of Practice for Vehicle Body Repair (Motor Car and Caravan Sector).
1976	RMI (Retail Motor Industry Federation Ltd): SMTA (Scottish Motor Trade Association): SMMT (Society of Motor Manufacturers & Traders): Code of Practice for the Motor Industry.
1976	NAMSR (National Association of Multiple Shoe Repairers): Society of Master Shoe Repairers: Code of Practice for Shoe Repairs.
1976	TSA (Textile Services Association Ltd): Code of Practice for Domestic Laundry and Cleaning Services.
1976	FDF (Footwear Distributors Federation): Code of Practice for Footwear.
1976	RETRA (Radio, Electrical and Television Retailers' Association (RETRA) Ltd):

---

[1] See paras 16.01 and 18.32 below.
[2] See para.11.10 below.

Code of Practice for the Selling and Servicing of Electrical and Electronic Appliances.

1978   MOTA (Mail Order Traders' Association):
            Catalogue Mail Order Code of Practice.

1979   Photographic Industry Code of Practice.

1980   DSA (Direct Selling Association Ltd):
            Direct Selling Code of Practice.

1981   GGF (Glass and Glazing Federation):
            Code of Ethical Practice.

1984   Motorcycle Code.

1987   FLA (Finance and Leasing Association):
            Code of Practice.

1988   CCTA (Consumer Credit Trade Association):
            Code of Practice.

1988   NCCF (National Consumer Credit Federation):
            Code of Practice.

1988   CCA (Consumer Credit Association of the United Kingdom):
            Code of Practice.

1989   LPFA (London Personal Finance Association Ltd):
            Code of Practice.

1989   British Holiday and Home Parks Association Ltd:
            National Caravan Council: .
            Code of Practice for Letting Holiday Caravans.
            Code of Practice for Selling and Siting Holiday Caravans.

1989   SMMT (Society of Motor Manufacturers and Traders):
            Code of Practice for Mechanical Breakdown Insurance Schemes.

1989   BDMA (British Direct Marketing Association Ltd):
            Direct Marketing Code of Practice.

1991   CSA (Credit Services Association):
            Code of Practice.

1995   BVRLA (British Vehicle Rental and Leasing Association):
            Code of Conduct.

1995   BRC (British Retail Consortium):
            Code of Practice for Extended Warranties on Electrical Goods.

1996   ABIA (Association of British Introduction Agencies):
            Code of Practice for Introduction Agencies.

1997   STAR (Society of Ticket Agents and Retailers):
            Code of Practice.

1998   OEA (Ombudsman for Estate Agents Scheme):
            Code of Practice for Residential Estate Agents.

1998   NTDA (National Tyre Distributors Association):
            Code of Practice for Tyre and Fast Fit Trade.

Advantages?

11.06 Whether voluntary codes and self-regulation are to be preferred to legislation is a matter of debate. The advantage from the point of view of industry is that traders are allowed to police themselves, but this in turn may be disadvantageous to the consumer. It is clear from the results of monitoring exercises undertaken by the OFT that, predictably, not every member of a trade association honours its code. More surprisingly, not every trade association checks to ensure that its members follow the code, which was such a serious failing as to prevent the code being approved under the OFT regime (see para.11.12 below).[3]

Another serious disadvantage of relying on voluntary methods is that, even if all members of an association comply with their obligations, the rogues in the trade may well not be members. This is particularly true of the motor trade.

However, some advantages can be cited. (1) Legislation would necessarily be of a general nature and inappropriate for setting precise standards for a particular industry, for example, pre-delivery inspections of cars or service calls within three days for electrical appliances. (2) Businesses are more likely to comply with their own optional rules than with statutory obligations imposed against their will. (3) Codes can be improved by re-negotiation; for example, the ABTA Code was amended after a year to include surcharges and overbooking, both common causes of complaint. (4) Codes go beyond the existing law, in recommending practices which impose on suppliers obligations or restrictions not otherwise attaching to them, and thus consumers' rights are enhanced.[4] (5) The opportunity for conciliation and arbitration affords a cheap and quick mode of resolving disputes instead of taking action in the courts.

Sanctions for non-compliance

11.07 An increasingly important question is how codes of practice should be enforced. The most obvious way is for the trade association itself to deal with recalcitrant members. Some associations have very wide powers, including fines and expulsion, and are prepared to use them. However, many have no real sanctions and can do little more than apply the "club" threat of social ostracism by their peers.

It has been suggested, optimistically in our view, that an individual consumer may enforce a code against a member of a trade association by claiming that a breach of contract occurs when a trader fails to comply with a practice, on the basis that the contract includes an implied term that the trader will comply with the code. In view of the limitations placed by the courts on implied terms such a plea is unlikely to succeed.[5] Of course, it is possible for a consumer to incorporate a code expressly when making the

---

[3] On monitoring and other aspects of codes see Woodroffe, "Government Monitored Codes of Practice in the United Kingdom" (1984) 7 *Journal of Consumer Policy* 171; Cranston, *Consumers and the Law* (2nd edn), pp.31–42.

[4] For examples, see Woodroffe, "Government Monitored Codes of Practice in the United Kingdom" (1984) 7 *Journal of Consumer Policy* 171.

[5] The narrow "business efficacy" test in *The Moorcock* (1889) 14 P.D. 64.

contract, but it would be unrealistic to expect all but the most enthusiastic and well-informed consumers to remember to refer to the point in their conversation when ordering a carpet or taking a car in for a body repair.

In contrast the criminal law will sometimes provide a more effective route. For example, the Consumer Protection from Unfair Trading Regulations 2008 (the 2008 Regulations)[6] contain a number of provisions about codes of conduct, e.g. Sch.1: "1. Claiming to be a signatory to a code of conduct when the trader is not".[7]

Duty to trade fairly

A far-reaching proposal was to impose on traders a statutory "duty to trade fairly". A suggestion to this effect was put forward by Lord Borrie, the then Director General of Fair Trading, in a lecture[8] discussing the self-regulatory system of advertising control: **11.08**

> "The duty not to publish misleading advertisements could be seen as a precursor to a more general statutory duty to trade fairly in consumer transactions, a duty which would not be enforceable apart from sectoral or general retail codes of practice giving it practical expression. Such codes could be prepared by the DGFT after consultation with relevant trade associations and the codes would need to be given some form of ministerial or parliamentary approval before becoming effective."

The OFT floated the idea in 1986 with a discussion paper, *A General Duty to Trade Fairly*. However, such a bold approach was not welcomed by industry in a period of free market economy. In the end the Director General reluctantly admitted in *Trading Malpractices*[9] that "the original proposals were over-ambitious in aiming in one provision both to raise trading standards generally and to improve the prospects for consumer redress" and came down in favour of a complete overhaul of Pt III of the 1973 Act. More than a decade later that happened when the Enterprise Act 2002 repealed Pt III.[10]

The idea of a duty to trade fairly, though, did not go away. New impetus came from the European Commission which in 2003 proposed a Directive on Unfair Commercial Practices.[11] The Directive was duly adopted on 11 May 2005 and is considered with the 2008 Regulations in Chapter Eighteen.

"Raising Standards"

The early optimism engendered by self-regulation and the proliferation of codes supported by the OFT subsided in the late 1990s. At the end of 1996 the OFT issued a consultation paper *Voluntary Codes of Practice*. This was **11.09**

---

[6] See para.18.37 below.
[7] See also Sch.1 para.3, and reg.5(3).
[8] "Laws and Codes for Consumers" [1980] J.B.L. 315 at 324.
[9] OFT (July 1990), para.1.5. The arguments for and against the general duty appear on p.21.
[10] See para.18.13 below.
[11] Directive concerning unfair business-to-consumer commercial practices in the internal market (COM (2003) 356 final).

followed in 1998 with its report *Raising Standards of Consumer Care— Progressing beyond codes of practice*. The OFT's suggested change in policy was set out on p.5 of the report:

> The main change suggested is to introduce standards to replace codes, with a core standard applicable to all business and sectoral versions where necessary. A key element would be access to effective, low-cost independent redress, without recourse to the courts. The standards would be drawn up under the British Standards Institution.

B. OFT APPROVED CODES OF PRACTICE: 2002–2013

Modern markets: confident consumers

11.10   The Department of Trade and Industry (DTI) (now Business, Innovation & Skills (BIS)) did not take up the proposal to introduce standards instead of codes when it published its important and extensive White Paper, *Modern markets: confident consumers* (Cm.4410) in July 1999. However, in its new approach to codes it accepted that effective redress was vital and that a logo to identify Approved Codes was desirable. Its support for codes was made clear in para.4.3:

> Codes of practice can play an important part in protecting consumers' rights and in offering a higher level of consumer protection and service than the basics set down in law. Consumers with a complaint to make overwhelmingly turn first, as they should, to the seller for a solution. Codes are a way for:
>
> - *business* to assure customers that they will get value and that, if there is a problem, there is an effective way to solve it. And for business to gain a marketing advantage by using a code's logo in their advertising.
> - *consumers* to know that they are dealing with a reliable supplier, and that redress is accessible if something goes wrong.

In due course many of the proposals in the White Paper were implemented by the Enterprise Act 2002. Section 8(2) gave the OFT the power to approve consumer codes and s.8(3) imposed a duty to specify the criteria for approval.

New approach: Consumer Codes Approval Scheme (CCAS)

11.11   The OFT issued a consultation paper and published its response in July 2001: *Consumer codes of practice: the OFT's response to the consultation* (OFT 344). It confirmed its view that "codes of practice should deliver benefits to consumers beyond the law". It set out the core criteria to form the basis of the new regime.

Two stages

11.12   A two-stage approach was adopted:

> *Stage One* Code sponsors, such as trade associations, developed codes which complied with the core criteria. If successful, they were informed that they had "achieved stage one status".
>
> *Stage Two* They were then invited to take part in Stage Two, when they

had to prove that they had fulfilled the promises made at Stage One. If successful the OFT endorsed and promoted the code, which could then be used in the businesses' marketing by displaying the logo "OFT Approved Code".

It proved to be a thorough, but rather slow, process indicating a justified reluctance of the OFT to approve codes which did not meet its strict criteria precisely. Stage Two could not be rushed, since the OFT required evidence to verify that the code sponsors' promises made at Stage One had been performed.

However, this painstaking scrutiny of codes caused disappointment and frustration in some sectors where code sponsors, though initially keen to gain approval, lost their enthusiasm for the new regime. It may have become difficult for the OFT to encourage businesses to devote considerable time and resources to bringing their existing codes up to the standard required by the core criteria, when so few surmounted the hurdles of Stages One and Two. An illustration of the time-consuming process is the Carpet Foundation's code. It was submitted to the OFT for assessment in October 2004, completed Stage One in August 2005 and became an Approved Code in January 2007—27 months for a simple sector of business.

The three main elements causing lengthy negotiations appear to be that the codes had to include (1) rights for consumers which go beyond their existing rights rather than merely state that members comply with the law; (2) real sanctions against members for non-compliance; (3) monitoring procedures to check compliance by members and consumer satisfaction.

Twelve codes achieved full OFT approval by reaching Stage Two, while **11.13** two were en route at Stage One:

Stage One

> SafeBuy
> The Property Ombudsman (Letting)

Stage Two

> Bosch Car Service
> The Carpet Foundation
> The Property Ombudsman Ltd (Sales)
> Direct Selling Association[12]
> Motor Codes Ltd (New Car Code)
> Vehicle Builders and Repairers Association Ltd
> British Association of Removers
> Debt Managers Standards Association
> British Healthcare Trades Association
> Renewable Energy Association
> Institute of Professional Willwriters
> Motor Codes Ltd (Service and Repair)

---

[12] Not transferred to Chartered Trading Standards Institute (below).

Core criteria

11.14 The "core principles" were outlined in the White Paper. These had been translated in detail into the core criteria. In May 2002 the OFT published *Core criteria for consumer codes of practice. Guidance for those drawing up codes of practice* (OFT 390). It was updated in March 2008. We comment now on some of the criteria.

General Principles

11.15 The core criteria are preceded in the OFT *Guidance* by some general principles which "before reading the detail of the core criteria it is important to understand". These principles are set out in paras 1.1 to 1.7 of the *Guidance*.

Content (para.3)

11.16 Various unrelated matters are contained in this section. They include staff training, high-pressure selling, delivery dates, cancellation rights, warranties and protection of prepayments.

Complaints (para.4)

11.17 Procedures must be "speedy, responsive, accessible and user friendly". This rubric applies to both complaints handling and redress schemes. Pre-contractual material must publicise access to the system. Conciliation should be available.

Low cost redress is probably the most important feature of all. Decisions must be binding on the business, but not on the consumer who may still go to court if dissatisfied. (This is similar to ombudsman schemes, but contrasts with normal arbitration where a decision is binding on both parties and blocks off access to the courts.) As the criterion states, it is "to act as an alternative to seeking court action *in the first instance*" (our emphasis).

Monitoring (para.5)

11.18 A vital feature is the development of performance indicators (e.g. mystery shopping) to measure the effectiveness of the code and consumer satisfaction.

The code sponsor must provide the OFT with a written report annually with information on complaints, conciliations and its redress scheme, and also on monitoring and its disciplinary process.

Enforcement (para.6)

11.19 There must be procedures for handling non-compliance by code members, including independent disciplinary procedures, and a range of sanctions for non-compliance, e.g. fines and expulsion.

Conciliation and arbitration

As we have just seen in para.11.17 above, the criteria for an Approved Code **11.20** require conciliation to be available and all the codes discussed below include it. We suggested in para.11.03 that dissatisfied customers should first bring their complaints to the attention of the manager of the business. If the complaint is not resolved, then it may be appropriate to seek the help of a CAB. If the complaint relates to new goods, the customer may agree to the manufacturer being brought in. Where the dispute is still not settled and the trader is a member of a trade association, the customer should ask the association to conciliate. No charge is made for this service.

However, it should be remembered that the association may appear to the consumer, rightly or wrongly, to lack impartiality and to be prejudiced in favour of its own member.[13]

Where a code provides for arbitration the customer is required to pay a small fee, often refundable where the claim is upheld: this is the limit of liability where the arbitration is on the basis of "documents only". The fee does not cover the full cost of arbitration, the balance being borne by the trade association. Normally the arbitration will be "documents only", for the expense of oral arbitrations is prohibitive.

Publicity and information

It is not enough to introduce legislation and codes of practice to bolster the **11.21** consumer in his perpetual confrontation with the business world. Such rights are useless unless he knows of them and can exercise them. To ensure that as far as possible the consumer is made aware of his rights the core criteria require publicity by code sponsors.

It is difficult to know whether the effect of consumer legislation and the codes has been to improve the quality of goods and services. The main culprits have regularly been motor vehicles, furniture and floor coverings, household appliances and electronic equipment, and clothing and footwear, with secondhand cars usually taking the gold or silver medal. One area giving an increasingly major headache to consumers, particularly in view of the large sums of money usually at risk, is that of home improvements (including double glazing).

As we pointed out earlier,[14] the OFT withdrew support from the existing codes at the end of 2001. We now turn our attention to the 12 OFT Approved Codes.

C. TWELVE OFT APPROVED CODES

New cars: Motor Codes Ltd

The Society of Motor Manufacturers and Traders was one of the first trade **11.22** associations to gain the support of the OFT to its code of practice in 1976. Its

---

[13] cf. Ombudsman schemes, where independence and impartiality are prerequisites to membership of the Ombudsman Association (see para.11.47 below).
[14] See para.11.04 above.

New Car Code of Practice was the first to receive OFT approval in September 2004. Motor Codes Ltd, a wholly-owned subsidiary of the Society of Motor Manufacturers and Traders (SMMT), was formed to administer the New Car Code which was relaunched in April 2009 as the Motor Industry Code of Practice for New Cars. It is more limited than the original code in that it covers only the sales of new cars and their warranties and imposes duties on manufacturers only (SMMT members) and not on car dealers.

Body repairs: VBRA

11.23 The Vehicle Builders and Repairers Association's [VBRA] Consumer Code of Practice has its origins in 1975 when the OFT first gave its support to it. It became an OFT Approved Code in October 2004. It is concerned mainly with repairs to car bodies.

Bosch Car Services: BCS

11.24 Robert Bosch Ltd is the first organisation to obtain OFT approval to a code within the car repair and service sector. Members of the code are independent garages.

Direct selling: DSA[15]

11.25 The Direct Selling Association [DSA] Code of Practice for Consumers was drawn up in 1980 by the DSA in consultation with the OFT after an OFT study had identified consumer problems arising out of party plan selling. It became an OFT Approved Code in December 2004.

Removals: BAR

11.26 The British Association of Removers [BAR] secured OFT approval for its code in February 2008.

Among its many provisions one is worthy of note. If the remover cancels within 10 working days or less of the removal date, the customer will obtain a full refund plus 50 per cent.

Estate agents: Property Ombudsman

11.27 The Code of Practice of the Property Ombudsman is unique among the OFT codes in that it was prepared by an Ombudsman Scheme. It became an Approved Code in September 2005. The Ombudsman for Estate Agents (OEA) since 1998 has been open to independent residential estate agents who have chosen to join the OEA.

It changed its name to The Property Ombudsman in May 2009 and the code[16] is now called the Code of Practice for Residential Estate Agents.

The Code applies only to residential buildings sold with vacant possession.

---

[15] Not transferred to the Chartered Trading Standards Institute (see para.11.36 below).
[16] Covers 96% of UK estate agents.

Carpets: Carpet Foundation

In January 2007 the OFT approved the Carpet Foundation Consumer Code **11.28** of Practice for exclusive use by Registered Specialist Retailers. It has two categories of members: manufacturers (owners of the "Quality Mark") and independent retailers known as "Registered Specialists". The code covers the sale and fitting of domestic carpets.

Debt management: DEMSA

The Debt Managers Standards Association (DEMSA) received OFT approval **11.29** for its code in December 2008. It represents companies which, for a fee, act for debtors in negotiating with creditors to repay their debts. (A better route for debtors is to seek free advice from a CAB or money advice centre!)

Healthcare products: BHTA

The British Healthcare Trades Association (BHTA) has had an OFT **11.30** Approved Code since September 2009. Its members supply various equipment and other products, e.g. stair lifts, mobility vehicles, prosthetics. Such sales often involve home visits.

Renewable energy: REAL

The Renewable Energy Assurance Limited (REAL) received OFT approval for **11.31** its "REAL Consumer Code" in November 2011. The code covers the sale, installation and servicing of small-scale energy generating systems such as solar electricity and water heating, wind electricity and ground and air source heat pumps.

Will writers: IPW

The Institute of Professional Will Writers (IPW) Code of Practice embraces **11.32** both the drafting of wills and the administration of estates.

Car service and repair: Motor Codes Ltd

This is the second code administered by Motor Codes Ltd (see para.11.22 **11.33** above for their New Car Code). It is called the Motor Industry Code of Practice for Service and Repair. A Brief Guide appears on their website and is available from member garages.

D. CTSI CONSUMER CODES APPROVAL SCHEME (CCAS)

We mentioned earlier that in April 2013 the Chartered Trading Standards **11.34** Institute (CTSI) took over responsibility from the OFT for Approved Codes.
    The plan for the new CCAS was set out in a CTSI document published on 21 December 2012. We give below a few points from the plan:

(1) The CCAS scheme is self-funding with sponsors paying membership fees.

(2) To separate the running of the scheme from the CTSI a new company was formed for this purpose: the Consumer Code Approval Board Limited with a Board of seven members.

(3) There are also a Consumer Advisory Panel[17] and a Code Sponsors Panel, whose functions speak for themselves.

11.35 The "Proposed core criteria and guidance" for the CCAS were approved by the CCAS Board on 2 February 2013. Like the OFT criteria the procedure has two stages.

The CCAS Annual Report 2015[18] emphasizes the importance of the "Core Criteria". On p.13 it states:

> " At the heart of the scheme is a set of core criteria that covers the following:
>
> - Organisation criteria
> - Preparation
> - Content of Codes
> - Handling complaints
> - Monitoring of codes
> - Enforcement of codes
> - Publicising codes
>
> Each one of these core criteria has a set of much more detailed criteria that sit underneath them."

The avowed overall aim is "to streamline the approval procedure".

That approach is to be applauded, for the OFT scheme, which lasted for 12 years, produced only 12 Approved Codes, as we have seen. A strike rate of one per year was disappointing, to say the least. Some potential sponsors were put off by the time taken even to reach Stage One.

11.36 The new CTSI process has been much swifter with eight Approved Codes achieving Stage Two status in three years:

> Checkmate
> Glass and Glazing Federation
> Home Insulation and Energy Systems
> Motor codes (vehicle warranty products)
> RAC Service and Repair Code
> RAC Used Vehicle Code
> The Property Ombudsman (residential lettings)
> Trust My Garage

Of the 12 OFT Approved Codes described above 11 were transferred to the CTSI Scheme—the DSA chose not to do so; so there are now 19 CCAS Codes. More are in the pipeline with six having achieved Stage One approval:

---

[17] Geoffrey Woodroffe is a member of the panel.

[18] See *http://www.tradingstandards.uk* for this report and other information about CTSI and CCAS.

Advantage Partners in New Build
Building Lifeplans
Consumer Code for Home Builders
Consumer Code for New Homes
The Furniture Ombudsman
International Construction Warranties Ltd

E. EIGHT CTSI APPROVED CODES

Car sales: RAC

This Code and the RAC Service and Repair Code are the latest two CCAS **11.37**
Codes. Its full title, the RAC Used Vehicle Code, indicates its purpose and
ambit.

Car service and repairs: RAC

The RAC Service and Repair Code is the fourth CCAS code covering this **11.38**
sector (the other three are Bosch, Motor Codes Ltd and Trust My Garage).

Car service and repairs: "Trust My Garage": RMI

The Trust My Garage [TMG] Code of Practice is administered by Retail **11.39**
Motor Industry Standards & Certification (RMISC). It sets out the obligations that members of the TMG Code have to their customers when carrying
out car repairs.

All members of the TMG Code are members of the Independent Garage
Association (IGA), which is part of the Retail Motor Industry Federation
(RMI).

Car warranties: Motor Codes Ltd

The Motor Industry Code of Practice for Vehicle Warranty Products is the **11.40**
third Motor Industry Approved Code administered by Motor Codes Ltd. (Its
New Car Code and Service and Repair Code were OFT Approved Codes and
are described in paras 11.18 and 11.29 above.)

It covers the sale of car warranty and insurance products including:

- mechanical breakdown insurance

- roadside assistance

- extended warranties/guarantees

- tyre and key insurance

- GAP guaranteed asset protection

- MOT insurance.

Glass and glazing: GGF

11.41 The Glass and Glazing Federation's [GGF] Consumer Code of Practice is the first code in the glazing sector. It covers a wide range of products. Doors and windows are obvious examples. Conservatories and renewable energy products are included too.

Home insulation and energy: HIES

11.42 The Home Insulation and Energy Systems [HIES] Quality Assured Contractors Scheme is the company which administers The HIES Scheme Rules & Code of Practice. This binds all HIES members, who must pass an Accredited Installers accreditation process.

The Scheme covers a wide range of products, e.g.:

- solar and wind energy products

- air source heat pumps

- wall, roof and pipework insulation

- secondary glazing

- hot water showers and systems.

Unusually complaints may be made to an ombudsman—Ombudsman Services.

Lettings: The Property Ombudsman

11.43 The Letting Code is the second Approved Code administered by The Property Ombudsman (TPO). (The first was the Code of Practice for Residential Estate Agents approved under the OFT CCAS regime and described in para.11.27 above.) The Code of Practice for Residential Letting Agents, as its full title states, covers businesses concerned with letting or management services of residential property. It is followed by an estimated 85 per cent of such agents.

New home warranty: Checkmate

11.44 Its full title is the Checkmate Consumer Code for Builders of Homes for Sale. It is the first code to receive full approval in the new home sales sector. It is administered by Checkmate, a division of Lockton Companies LLP.

Members who join the scheme—builders and developers—provide latent defects insurance for new homes ("new home warranty").

3. PUBLIC UTILITIES—NEW CONSUMER COUNCILS

11.45 In September 1998 the Government published a consultation paper setting out proposals for consumer councils for the energy, water and telecommunications sectors. In the next few years these proposals were implemented. (1) A consumer Council for Water was set up in 2005. (2) The mammoth Communications Act 2003 required the regulator OFCOM to establish a Consumer Panel (membership to be approved by the Secretary of State) while ss.52–54 require public providers to establish independent dispute resolution procedures. (3) The Consumer Council for Gas and Electricity was set up under the Utilities Act 2000.

The Consumers, Estate Agents and Redress Act 2007 made further changes **11.46** by giving to the new National Consumer Council ("Consumer Focus") the functions of Postwatch and Energywatch. With the imminent demise of Consumer Focus in 2013 these functions will be transferred to the new Regulated Industries Unit which in turn will transfer to Citizens Advice in 2014.

These bodies assist consumers in three ways:

(a) They act as independent and influential consumer advocates with a voice at the heart of the regulatory system—advising utility regulators, utility companies and others on consumer issues.

(b) They have the specific task of handling consumer complaints against utility companies where they have not been resolved by the company. They will be expected to mediate a satisfactory settlement wherever possible; if enforcement action is necessary they will pass the complaint to the relevant regulatory authority. They will also be expected to work with the utility companies to reduce the causes of complaints.

(c) They should provide consumers with good quality information and advice on how to get the best deal from the utility markets; influential councils and well-informed consumers can play a key part in driving standards up and prices down.

A former energy Minister John Battle told consumers to put behind them the traditional British reluctance to complain. He urged them to "expect and demand good service, remembering that you can take your business elsewhere. In the United Kingdom, the most open energy market in the world, it's cool to complain." (DTI Press Notice P/99/617.) With ever-increasing energy prices these remarks continue to be topical.

4. OMBUDSMAN SCHEMES

Comparison with codes of practice

We have already suggested that from the consumer's point of view codes **11.47** of practice suffer from the disadvantage that they do not appear to provide a completely impartial method of resolving disputes. However, the CTSI's approach to codes with its stringent core criteria for Approved Codes strengthened the consumer's position in those sectors where codes were ultimately approved.[19] As conciliation is often carried out by employees of the relevant trade association, there may be some justification for the scepticism of consumers in believing that he who pays the piper calls the tune.

Of course, where a code of practice gives a complainant the opportunity of going to arbitration—and we have seen that not all codes do so—then without doubt the arbitrator will act independently and reach a fair and impartial conclusion. However, it should be remembered that although conciliation is free, the consumer must usually pay for arbitration. Then again a decision by an arbitrator is binding on the parties and final—the claimant cannot ignore it and later sue in the courts. None of these disadvantages is present in the ombudsmen schemes discussed below. All of the ombudsmen are independent and impartial. In every case the service is provided free of charge. If the complainant rejects the ombudsman's decision, litigation in the courts is almost always still available.

11.48   If then codes of practice have not provided consumers with suitable redress procedures, are other routes of alternative dispute resolution (usually nowadays blessed with the acronym ADR) to be preferred? *Raising Standards*[20] came down firmly in favour of ombudsmen schemes in 1998:

> Use indicates that ombudsmen schemes are more popular with consumers than is trade-association-sponsored independent arbitration. There are a number of perceived benefits. They include: the fact that they are free to consumers; the ombudsman's ability to investigate cases as well as adjudicate on them; and the general perception (perhaps largely based on the objective stance perceived to have been taken by the better known operators in the financial services sector) that ombudsmen appear to be impartial. In response to the OFT's earlier consultation paper, some consumer bodies felt that arbitration was not suitable for consumer problems. Their view was that the nature of the process, with the element of legal confrontation, was off-putting. They also considered that successful arbitration required some semblance of equity in the knowledge and abilities of the parties, which is seldom present in consumer cases. Ombudsmen schemes also seem preferable from the OFT's perspective. (para.3.43)

This official support for ombudsmen was preceded by judicial support in the shape of Lord Woolf, whose proposed reforms of litigation—case management, practice, procedure, costs—came into force in April 1999. *Access to Justice*, his interim report to the Lord Chancellor in June 1995, recommended:

> 63. The retail sector should be encouraged to develop private ombudsman schemes to cover consumer complaints similar to those which now exist in relation to service industries; the government should facilitate this.
>
> 64. The relationship between ombudsmen and the courts should be broadened, enabling issues to be referred by the ombudsman to the courts and the courts to the ombudsman with the consent of those involved.

---

[19] See para.11.11 above.
[20] See para.11.09 above.

Background

The origins of ombudsman schemes can be found in the Nordic countries. In **11.49** the UK most of the schemes have been set up by statute and many, particularly the earlier schemes, are concerned with complaints about the activities of public bodies, including central and local government. Others, though, are voluntary and were set up at the expense of the businesses concerned to deal with complaints about particular sectors of the service industries. All the schemes have one thing in common, namely they exist to deal with complaints from members of the public about the way in which members of the schemes carry out their business, e.g. delay, carelessness, inefficiency or discourtesy. Ombudsmen must not be confused with regulators such as OFCOM or the Financial Conduct Authority, as the sole function of ombudsmen is to provide redress to individuals, not to control or supervise a business sector.

Ombudsman Association

The use of the term "Ombudsman" can be misleading in that it gives the **11.50** impression that, whenever the word is used, the adjudicator will be impartial. It is a matter of regret that sometimes the term is used to describe someone who is concerned with handling complaints either on behalf of a trade association or even on behalf of a single organisation such as a newspaper or local authority; obviously in neither of these cases is the person independent.

To enable the public to identify genuine, independent ombudsmen the British and Irish Ombudsman Association was set up in 1993. It is now called simply the Ombudsman Association. Only those schemes are admitted to voting membership which satisfy its strict criteria, namely independence, effectiveness, fairness and public accountability. Of these four factors the crucial one is independence and it is this which distinguishes recognised ombudsmen schemes from other complaints procedures. (There are also many more Complaint Handler and Associate Members.)

Association members

The UK voting members cover the following sectors: **11.51**

Energy

Estate agents (Property)

Financial services

Furniture

Glazing

Health services

Higher Education (Independent Adjudicator)

Housing

Independent Football

Legal services

Local government

Parliamentary

Pensions

Police (Northern Ireland)

Removals

Retail

Surveyors

Telecommunications

Waterways

Details of the various schemes can be found at *http://www.ombudsmanassocia tion.org/*.

The largest scheme by far is the Financial Ombudsman Service (FOS) created by the Financial Services and Markets Act 2000. It brought together eight different complaints handling organisations, not all of which were ombudsmen schemes; the best known were probably banking, building societies and insurance. The FOS jurisdiction was extended to cover consumer credit from 6 April 2007.[21] Recently it has been almost overwhelmed by PPI complaints (Payment Protection Insurance).

Most ombudsmen are now creatures of statute with voluntary schemes becoming fewer—the Property Ombudsman for Estate Agents is a continuing example.[22]

Jurisdiction and powers

11.52   The extent of the jurisdiction of a particular ombudsman depends on the particular scheme. For example, the private sector schemes do not usually cover all members of the industry. Thus, the Ombudsman for Estate Agents (now the Property Ombudsman) was initially concerned only with the large chains of estate agents owned by banks, building societies and insurance companies and could not deal with complaints against independent estate agents.[23]

To discover the extent of the jurisdiction, powers and duties of a particular scheme the consumer adviser will normally need to peruse its terms of reference or rules which where appropriate will reflect the memorandum and articles of association of the company operating the scheme.

Usually complaints have to be brought within a specified time-limit and cannot be dealt with if the complainant has already issued court proceedings.

---

[21] s.59 of the Consumer Credit Act 2006.

[22] The Funeral Ombudsman Scheme (Geoffrey Woodroffe was the Ombudsman through its time) was a voluntary scheme which ceased after the trade associations funding it withdrew their support, despite the low financial costs.

[23] See para.11.27 above.

Procedures

Here again the adviser must look at the details of the particular scheme. **11.53**
However, generally ombudsmen cannot consider a complaint until they are
satisfied that the complainant has given the business concerned the opportunity to try to resolve the complaint by its own in-company complaints
procedure. Once the ombudsmen are satisfied that such procedures have been
exhausted, they will then try to resolve the dispute by acting as a conciliator.

If conciliation fails, the ombudsmen will commence their formal investigation and collect all the relevant evidence. Generally there will not be an
oral hearing and the adjudication will be based on written evidence only. In
reaching a decision the ombudsman will take into account such matters as
the terms of the contract, codes of practice, previous decisions and in some
schemes what is "fair and reasonable".

Remedies

One of the main aims of the ombudsman is to try to improve the quality **11.54**
of service in a particular organisation or industry. Thus if the ombudsman
upholds a complaint, he may well make a recommendation that the business
practices or procedures of the respondent organisation should be altered
and improved to prevent a repetition of the problem. Sometimes an apology
by the business will satisfy a complainant—it is strange how frequently an
organisation, though at fault, will be absolutely certain that it has acted properly and efficiently and refuse to budge, while all the complainant desires is a
formal apology that a mistake had been made. Often, though, the complainant will seek financial compensation. The maximum which can be awarded
depends on the scheme; for example, the FOS may award up to £150,000.
Failure by an organisation to carry out its services carefully and efficiently
may cause distress to the complainant and some schemes contain express
power for the ombudsman to award compensation for aggravation and distress. This may have a maximum of £750.

Sanctions

Throughout this chapter we are concerned with the effectiveness of pro- **11.55**
cedures. What can be done if a recommendation or award by an ombudsman is ignored by the respondent organisation? The answer depends on the
particular scheme. In some schemes a monetary award is legally binding on
the organisation. In other schemes the recommendation and award by an
ombudsman are not legally enforceable; but the business organisation with
rare exceptions complies with the ombudsman's decision.

The ultimate sanction for non-compliance is publicity. Every ombudsman publishes an annual report, which will normally give examples of
complaints made in the previous year and statistics on the number and
type of complaints without naming the organisations involved. However,
if an organisation were to fail to comply with a decision, in some schemes
the ombudsman would have the power to name the culprit; it is the fear of

the commercial effect of such adverse publicity which stimulates businesses into compliance.

5. ARBITRATION

Cheap, quick, informal?

11.56 Until 1971 the consumer, faced with a supplier who was not prepared to meet his proper obligations, had no choice but to abandon his complaint unless he was determined enough to launch himself upon the uncertain seas of litigation. The prospect of such action caused the consumer considerable anxiety for three principal reasons. First, it was likely to be expensive because of the level of legal fees. Secondly—and a related point—although he could save legal fees by conducting the case himself, he was put off playing the role of the litigant in person by the formality and complexity of court proceedings. Thirdly, he knew litigation to be a long-winded affair and was unhappy at having the doubtful outcome hanging over him like the sword of Damocles for years on end. Thus, the layman saw access to his legal rights guarded by a Cerberus whose three heads were expense, delay and formality.

11.57 These disadvantages were particularly identified in the 1960s and fully discussed in *Justice out of Reach*, the 1970 report by the Consumer Council. The report proposed a nationwide system of small claims courts, drawing partly upon experience in North America. (It is salutary to recall that the county courts were set up in 1846 to provide the sort of forum being ardently espoused a century and a quarter later.) The county court arbitration scheme was inaugurated in 1973. The small claims track now caters for court-based small claims.[24]

The consumer adviser must remember, however, that most of the codes of practice discussed in this chapter provide for low cost, documents only arbitration arranged by the relevant trade association. It must be stressed, though, that if consumers agree to their disputes being resolved by arbitration, they are normally bound by the arbitrator's decision. They cannot ignore it and then try the courts later in the hope that the district judge adopts a different attitude. This is the crucial distinction between arbitration and the ombudsman schemes.

Consumer arbitration

11.58 The codes of practice approved by the CTSI do not compel consumers to take advantage of an arbitration scheme, if available, and point out that the complainant is free to take the alternative route of suing in the courts. This contrasts with the type of clause common in commercial contracts which makes arbitration a condition precedent to action in the courts (the so-called "*Scott v Avery*"[25] clause).

Such clauses can operate unfairly and legislation to control them has been

---

[24] See para.12.12 below.
[25] (1856) 5 H.L.C. 811.

in force since 1988. Under s.91 of the Arbitration Act 1996 (the 1996 Act) a clause referring present or future disputes to arbitration is to be treated as "unfair" under Pt II of the Consumer Rights Act 2015 (which we discussed in Chapter Ten) where the value in dispute does not exceed a specified amount—currently £5,000 (SI 1996/3211). The 1996 Act is wider than the Regulations because, by s.90, the term "consumer" includes a company or partnership.

6. ALTERNATIVE DISPUTE RESOLUTION

Alternative dispute resolution has been high on the agenda at the EU level. **11.59** Following the Green Paper *on alternative dispute resolution in civil and commercial law*,[26] two significant measures were adopted: a regulation to establish a platform for the online-resolution of consumer disputes (ODR Platform)[27] and a Directive on alternative dispute resolution for consumers.[28] The Directive was given effect in UK Law by the Alternative Dispute Resolution for Consumer Disputes (Competent Authorities and Information) Regulations 2015.[29] The purpose of the Directive is to ensure that there are ADR mechanisms available for every type of consumer dispute, and much of the Regulations are concerned with the process for establishing and certifying ADR schemes. Much of this work is undertaken by the CTSI, alongside the regulators in the regulated sectors. Whilst participation in ADR is not made mandatory for businesses, there is an obligation to inform consumers about the availability of ADR schemes. Many existing Ombudsman schemes will continue to operate, but for sectors which did not previously have such schemes, so-called "residual bodies" have been appointed. One such body is the Retail Ombudsman, which offers ADR between consumers on the one hand, and retailers (in-store and online), supermarkets, garden centres, restaurants and takeaways, hotels and leisure providers, boiler installation and repair providers, and airlines, on the other hand. A list of certified bodies, both in the UK and throughout the EU, can be viewed on the European Commission's website.[30]

In addition, it is possible to utilise the ODR Platform to submit a claim online for ADR, particularly for goods or services acquired online.[31]

This builds on a long-established EU initiative known as the ECC-Net which enables consumers in one EU country to contact ADR organisations in other countries. Its UK European Consumer Centre is run by the CTSI.

---

[26] COM (2002) 196 final. See also Directive 2008/52/EC on certain aspects of mediation in civil and commercial matters which applies only to cross-border disputes.

[27] Regulation 524/2013/EU on online dispute resolution for consumer disputes (2013) OJ L165/1.

[28] Directive 2013/11/EU on alternative dispute resolution for consumer disputes (2013) OJ L165/63.

[29] SI 2015/42, amended by the Alternative Dispute Resolution for Consumer Disputes (Amendment) Regulations 2015 (SI 2015/1392).

[30] *https://webgate.ec.europa.eu/odr/main/?event=main.adr.show*.

[31] This can be accessed at *https://webgate.ec.europa.eu/odr/main/index.cfm?event=main.home. show&lng=EN*.

7. ALTERNATIVE DISPUTE RESOLUTION MEDIATION

11.60 In Chapter Ten of our Fourth Edition we wrote that ADR was "increasingly in the news as the cost of legal aid continues to rise faster than general inflation". Much water has flowed under the bridge in the years since then as clients and the courts have sought to avoid the cost and delay of litigation. The Civil Procedure Rules, which are considered in the next chapter, give the court wide powers to stay a case so that the parties can explore ADR; also, an unreasonable refusal to consider ADR (both before and after the start of proceedings) will be taken into account when the court awards costs. For small claims the cost of litigation is usually out of all proportion to the amount in dispute—hence the value of ADR. There are two main ADR organisations—namely the Centre for Dispute Resolution (CEDR) and ADR Group; the latter is probably more suitable for smaller cases. The Chartered Institute of Arbitrators also provided ADR services for consumers via its subsidiary IDRS Ltd which in 2011 was sold to CEDR.

11.61 The procedure varies from one mediation to another but essentially it involves getting the parties to reach their own agreement—rather than leaving it to a third person (the judge). A typical mediation will proceed as follows:

   (1) Before the mediation starts the parties will be asked to prepare written position statements and to sign the mediation agreement; this confirms that anything said during the mediation is, and will remain, confidential.

   (2) The parties will then come together and meet the mediator; he will ask each of them to make an opening statement.

   (3) The parties then retire to separate rooms and the mediator will shuttle between them—exploring the strength and weakness of each party's case in more detail and finding out what their main concerns are. In these separate discussions he will endeavour to get the parties to narrow their differences until an agreement emerges and this will then be recorded in writing.

CHAPTER TWELVE

"WHAT HAPPENS IF I GO TO COURT?"

1. FUNDING THE ACTION

Conditional fees

As previously explained, a solicitor can enter into a "conditional fee agree- **12.01**
ment" (CFA) (or "contingency fee agreement" see para.12.03 below) with
his client under powers contained in the Courts and Legal Services Act 1990
and Orders made under that Act. The agreement will usually provide that
(1) no costs are payable if the case is lost and (2) the solicitor can charge his
usual hourly rate plus a success fee if the case is won. The amount of the
success fee is a matter for agreement but it can be as high as 100 per cent of
the usual charging rate. The widely used words "no win, no fee" are seriously
misleading for two reasons. First, the agreement will normally be limited to
the solicitor's own fees and will not normally include court fees and other
outgoings such as experts' fees. Secondly, the client must realise that he may
have to pay the other side's costs if he loses (although this is unlikely if the
case is allocated to the small claims track as to which see para.12.12 below)
and insurance is essential to cover this risk.

Under the conditional fee regime, the client's chances of legal representation will depend on the willingness of a solicitor to take the case and finding
an insurer who is prepared to do so.

A solicitor can agree to limit his client's liability for costs to the actual **12.02**
amount of costs recovered from the other side, so the client receives any
compensation without deductions, but this might be difficult to negotiate for
a consumer dispute.

As from April 2013 the success fee paid to a party's lawyer under a conditional fee agreement and the premium for "after the event" (ATE) insurance
will no longer be recoverable from the losing party. Litigants will still be able
to enter into CFAs and take out ATE insurance but will have to pay these
costs themselves. Success fees in personal injury cases will be capped at 25
per cent of the damages, excluding damages for future care and loss. The cap
will apply to net damages after Department for Work and Pensions (DWP)
benefit recovery. A likely outcome of these changes is that litigants will negotiate down success fees and insurers will reduce ATE premiums.

Contingency fees

Contingency fee agreements—"damages based agreements"—will be a **12.03**
funding option in all types of civil litigation. A lawyer's fee is calculated as a

percentage of the damages recovered, with no fee payable if the client loses. Costs recovered from the losing party are used to pay part of the contingency fee. In personal injury claims there will be a 25 per cent cap on the amount of damages, excluding damages for future care and loss, that can be taken as a lawyer's contingency fee. In all non-personal injury claims (excluding employment tribunal cases) there will be a 50 per cent cap on the amount of damages.

2. PROCEDURE

Introduction

12.04 The Civil Procedure Rules (the Rules) have been in force since 26 April 1999. Designed to eradicate the three evils of litigation at that time—delay, uncertainty and cost—they have succeeded on the first two but have been judged to have failed to deal effectively with the third. Costs greatly exceeding the value of matters being fought over are still a common occurrence. The appellate courts are continually counselling practitioners against such excesses and encouraging all the courts to monitor and control the level of costs by the use of costs estimates and cost-capping. In the meantime, court fees have also continued to rise as part of the move towards the civil courts becoming self-financing. At the same time, the reforms have led to a decrease in the number of cases and an increase in the number of cases which settle at an earlier stage.

Although, since the inception of the Rules, there have been over 40 sets of regulations which have amended and updated them (together with a body of case-law) most of them have been of a "tidying-up" nature rather than wholesale reform. The Rules themselves have proved fairly robust and Human Rights compliant. There have been some perceived areas of weakness, particularly with regard to service of proceedings (Pt 6) and they were changed in 2008 to make them less opaque and contradictory.

The following are the key distinguishing features of the Rules, namely:

(1) openness and "cards on the table"—no more last minute ambush;

(2) co-operation with the court and the other side and early disclosure of documents;

(3) proportionality;

(4) on-going attempts to settle—using the courts as a last resort;

(5) case management by the court; and

(6) pre-action protocols.

The overriding objective

The Rules are divided into Parts and many of them are supplemented by
Practice Directions—a number of which are longer and more detailed than
the Rules themselves. Part 1 sets out the overriding objective which must be
constantly borne in mind both before and during the conduct of the case. It
reads as follows:

> 1.1(1) These Rules are a new procedural code with the overriding objective of
> enabling the court to deal with cases justly and at proportionate cost.
>
> (2) Dealing with a case justly and at proportionate cost includes, so far as is
> practicable–
>
> (a) ensuring that the parties are on an equal footing;
> (b) saving expense;
> (c) dealing with the case in ways which are proportionate –
>
> (i) to the amount of money involved;
> (ii) to the importance of the case;
> (iii) to the complexity of the issues; and
> (iv) to the financial position of each party;
>
> (d) ensuring that it is dealt with expeditiously and fairly;
> (e) allotting to it an appropriate share of the court's resources, while
> taking into account the need to allot resources to other cases;
> and
> (f) enforcing compliance with rules, practice directions and orders.
>
> 1.2 The court must seek to give effect to the overriding objective when it –
>
> (a) exercises any power given to it by the Rules; or
> (b) interprets any rule subject to rules 76.2, 79.2 and 80.2.
>
> 1.3 The parties are required to help the court to further the overriding objec-
> tive.
>
> 1.4 (1)   The court must further the overriding objective by actively manag-
> ing cases.
>
> (2)   Active case management includes –
>
> (a) encouraging the parties to co-operate with each other in the
> conduct of the proceedings;
> (b) identifying the issues at an early stage;
> (c) deciding promptly which issues need full investigation and trial and
> accordingly disposing summarily of the others;
> (d) deciding the order in which issues are to be resolved;
> (e) encouraging the parties to use an alternative dispute resolution
> procedure if the court considers that appropriate and facilitating
> the use of such procedure;
> (f) helping the parties to settle the whole or part of the case;
> (g) fixing timetables or otherwise controlling the progress of the case;
> (h) considering whether the likely benefits of taking a particular step
> justify the cost of taking it;
> (i) dealing with as many aspects of the case as it can on the same occa-
> sion;
> (j) dealing with the case without the parties needing to attend at court;
> (k) making use of technology; and
> (l) giving directions to ensure that the trial of a case proceeds quickly
> and efficiently.

Two observations can be made. First, much of the necessary technology to assist the court in managing cases is now in place. Courts now have

the benefit of recording equipment, computers for the judges, an electronic diary and a database system as well as templates for the production of word processed orders. Some courts also have video link facilities. The Rules have been amended to provide for telephone conferences to be the standard pattern for many interim and directions hearings for which suitable conference equipment has been installed in judges' chambers. Secondly, these management powers are supplemented by Pt 3 which contains sanctions for non-compliance with a court order or direction; these include striking out a claim or defence or ordering a defaulting party to pay money into court.

Pre-action Protocols

12.06 There are now at least nine Pre-action Protocols (PAPs), including Construction and Engineering, Defamation, Personal Injury, Clinical Disputes, Professional Negligence, Judicial Review, Disease and Illness, Housing Disrepair and Rent Arrears. They have been structured with one central aim—to encourage the early settlement of cases. If we take the personal injury protocol as an example, we can pick out five points:

(1) The claimant must send two copies of a letter of claim to the defendant as soon as sufficient information is available to substantiate a realistic claim and before questions of quantum are addressed in detail.

(2) The defendant must reply and identify his insurer within 21 days.

(3) The insurer must reply within three months stating whether liability is denied and, if so, giving reasons.

(4) If the defendant denies liability his denial must be accompanied by any documents in his possession which are relevant to the issues.

(5) Part 36 of the Rules enables either party to make an offer to settle and there may be serious costs consequences if the matter comes to court and it is found that a party has unreasonably failed to make or to accept an offer.

New PAP

12.07 There is now a new "catch-all" PAP the aim of which is said to be as follows:

"Aims

1 The aims of this Practice Direction are to –
  (1) enable parties to settle the issue between them without the need to start proceedings (that is, a court claim); and
  (2) support the efficient management by the court and the parties of proceedings that cannot be avoided.

2 These aims are to be achieved by encouraging the parties to –

> (1) exchange information about the issue, and
>
> (2) consider using a form of Alternative Dispute Resolution ('ADR')"

The new provisions make it clear that the court will expect the parties to have complied with this Practice Direction or any relevant PAP. The court may ask the parties to explain what steps were taken to comply prior to the start of the claim. Where there has been a failure of compliance by a party the court may ask that party to provide an explanation.

The court may decide that there has been a failure of compliance by a party because, for example, that party has—

(1) not provided sufficient information to enable the other party to understand the issues;

(2) not acted within a time limit set out in a relevant pre-action protocol, or, where no specific time limit applies, within a reasonable period;

(3) unreasonably refused to consider ADR; or

(4) without good reason, not disclosed documents requested to be disclosed.

If, in the opinion of the court, there has been non-compliance, the sanctions which the court may impose include—

(1) staying (that is suspending) the proceedings until steps which ought to have been taken have been taken;

(2) an order that the party at fault pays the costs, or part of the costs, of the other party or parties (this may include an order under r.27.14(2) (g) in cases allocated to the small claims track);

(3) an order that the party at fault pays those costs on an indemnity basis (r.44.4(3) sets out the definition of the assessment of costs on an indemnity basis);

(4) if the party at fault is the claimant in whose favour an order for the payment of a sum of money is subsequently made, an order that the claimant is deprived of interest on all or part of that sum, and/or that interest is awarded at a lower rate than would otherwise have been awarded;

(5) if the party at fault is a defendant, and an order for the payment of a sum of money is subsequently made in favour of the claimant, an order that the defendant pay interest on all or part of that sum at a higher rate, not exceeding 10 per cent above base rate, than would otherwise have been awarded.

12.08 The principles that should govern the conduct of the parties are that, unless the circumstances make it inappropriate, before starting proceedings the parties should—

> (1) exchange sufficient information about the matter to allow them to understand each other's position and make informed decisions about settlement and how to proceed;
>
> (2) make appropriate attempts to resolve the matter without starting proceedings, and in particular consider the use of an appropriate form of ADR in order to do so.

Further, the parties should act in a reasonable and proportionate manner in all dealings with one another. In particular, the costs incurred in complying should be proportionate to the complexity of the matter and any money at stake. The parties must not use the PAP Practice Direction as a tactical device to secure an unfair advantage for one party or to generate unnecessary costs.

ADR

12.09 The directions contain clear encouragement to the parties to settle rather than litigate. The Practice Note to the Pre-action Protocols suggests some of the ways in which matters might be resolved without litigation, including:

- Discussion and negotiation.
- Early neutral evaluation by an independent third party (for example, a lawyer experienced in that field or an individual experienced in the subject matter of the claim).
- Mediation—a form of facilitated negotiation assisted by an independent neutral party (see para.11.60 above).

Some county courts are already starting to offer such services and litigants are reminded at various stages of the benefits of compromise over uncertain and costly litigation.

It is expressly recognised that no party can or should be forced to mediate or enter into any form of ADR. At the same time, the cases show that a party who unreasonably fails to mediate can incur a costs penalty.

Costs

12.10 Strictly speaking, there are no costs within the pre-action protocols themselves except on a retrospective basis, i.e. if proceedings do not settle and litigation ensues, the court can consider any costs incurred as part of the pre-action process. The rules provide for costs-only proceedings to be issued where all other matters have been resolved. These proceedings may, however, be defeated by a defendant filing an acknowledgement disputing the use of such proceedings. Thereafter the claimant has to issue proceedings for the *whole* of the claim and not just the costs.

What happens next?

If court proceedings become necessary the next stages are as follows: **12.11**

(1) The claimant will file a "claim form" at the appropriate court. He can file in the county court regardless of value. A case can be issued in the High Court if the value of the claim is not less than £25,000 (or £50,000 in personal injury cases) but straightforward cases so issued are likely to be transferred out at some point to a convenient local county court for hearing.

(2) The particulars of claim can form part of the claim form or they can be served separately. They will contain details of such matters as the defects in the goods and the loss or damage sustained by the claimant. Both the claim form and any separate particulars must be verified by a "statement of truth".

(3) The court will issue the claim form (on payment of the appropriate fee) and will serve it on the defendant (unless the claimant wishes to serve it himself).

(4) Within 14 days of service of the particulars the defendant must file:

(a) an admission; or
(b) a defence; or
(c) an acknowledgement of service (giving him a further 14 days to file a defence).

Failure to take steps (b) or (c) can lead to a default judgment.

(5) As soon as a defence is filed, the court will send to the parties a directions questionnaire.

(6) Part 26 of the Rules deals with the vital question of allocation. A court officer will consider the claim form and the defence will then allocate the case into one of the three tracks—small claims, fast or multi. For consumers and their advisers the small claims track will be the most important one; this is the normal track where the amount in dispute is £10,000 or less. The fast track (and fast is the operative word) is for cases where the amount in dispute is between £10,001 and £25,000 and the hearing will not last more than one day. The multi track is for cases (1) over £25,000 or (2) cases in the fast track band which will take more than one day. The claim form must indicate the band into which the claim falls and Pt 26 sets out the matters which must be taken into account. Note that the value of the claim is not the only relevant factor; thus, for example, a "small"

claim may be allocated to a different track if it involves the construction of an exemption clause which will affect many other cases.

Money claims can now be issued and responded to online. See *http://www.*
moneyclaim.gov.uk.

In the remainder of this chapter we will look in some detail at the small
claims track and then briefly at the fast and multi tracks.

Small claims track (Part 27)

12.12   The emphasis is on informality and costs limitation—so that a person with a
small claim can bring it to the court without the need to instruct a solicitor.

To achieve the object set out above, Pt 27 of the Rules contains the following provisions:

(1) A number of the rules which apply elsewhere will not apply in the
small claims track. They include (a) disclosure of documents, (b) the
strict rules of evidence, (c) most of the rules about experts, (d) most
of the rules about hearings and (e) the provisions of Pt 36 relating
to offers to settle and payment into court (these have costs consequences which are not appropriate to small track cases).

(2) At the allocation stage the procedural judge may:

(a) give "standard directions" in the Notice of Allocation and fix
a date for hearing;
(b) give "special directions" in the Notice of Allocation and fix a
date for hearing;
(c) fix a date for a preliminary hearing (if, for example he feels
that the claim or the defence has no reasonable chance of
success); or
(d) give notice that he proposes to decide the case on the papers
without a hearing and invite the parties to notify the court by
a specified date if they agree.

"Standard directions" will include a direction that each party shall,
at least fourteen days before the hearing, file and serve on each other
party copies of all documents (including experts' reports) on which
he intends to rely. The term "special directions" covers such matters
as the inspection of documents, experts, witness statements and
video evidence; it also covers directions appropriate to the type of
case which have been provided for by Practice Directions including
road traffic cases, vehicle repairs, holiday and wedding claims—see
Appendix A to Practice Direction 27, para.2.2 for further detail. The
standard form of directions used by many courts requires the parties
to send copies of documents on which they intend to rely to the other
party at least 14 days before the hearing. The list includes "experts'
reports" but the standard form does not make it clear that such
reports may only be relied upon if permission is given by the court.

(3) The case will normally (but not invariably) be heard by a district judge in his room; the general rule is that hearings should be open to the public but this will not not be so if (a) the hearing is held away from the court or (b) the judge orders a hearing in private—he can do this if the parties agree or on certain other grounds listed in Pt 39.

(4) A party can present his case personally, or by a lawyer or lay representative (if the party is present).

(5) As stated above, the strict rules of evidence do not apply. Thus, for example, evidence need not be on oath and a party can rely on a witness statement even though the witness is not present—although the statement must be verified by a statement of truth. Expert evidence can only be used if the court has granted permission—and this will usually be limited to a written report from a single expert jointly instructed.

(6) The judge can adopt any method of proceeding that he considers fair and can limit cross-examination. Judges have traditionally taken a very pro-active role in small claims cases (especially as many of the claimants will not have a lawyer to present their case) and the rules reflect this (see r.27.8 and Practice Direction 27, para.4.3).

(7) If a party is unable or unwilling to attend the hearing, he can, at least seven days before the hearing, give written notice to the court and the other party that he will not be attending and asking the court to decide the case in his absence. A failure to send this notice is likely to lead to the case being struck out—although the rules allow the absent party to apply within fourteen days to have a judgment set aside if he can show a good reason for non-attendance and a reasonable prospect of success at the hearing.

(8) Appeals from a small claims decision are the same as for any other appeal from a final decision of a court. Permission to appeal is required from the trial judge or the appellate judge. This permission will only be given where the court considers that the appeal stands a real prospect of success or there are some other compelling reasons why the appeal should be heard.

(9) A person with a small claim may be reluctant to use the courts for two reasons—fear of the complexity and fear of having to pay the other side's costs if he loses. The rules seek to overcome both of these fears. We have already dealt with informality; we must now mention that the general power to award costs to the winner is heavily circumscribed in the small claims track. Under r.27.14 the court can order a party to pay to the other party:

   (a) fixed costs on issue of proceedings (see Pt 45);
   (b) any sum paid for legal advice not exceeding £260, but only in injunction or specific performance proceedings;

(c) court fees paid by the other party;

(d) reasonable witness expenses (including that of the litigant) for travelling or other expenses involved in staying away from home to attend a hearing;

(e) loss of earnings for a litigant or witness limited to £95 per person per day;

(f) £750 for court approved expert;

(g) the costs of a transcript for an appeal; and

(h) such further costs as the court may summarily assess to be paid by a party who has behaved unreasonably, e.g. by their misconduct of the action, failing to attend a hearing, unreasonably failing to settle.

12.13   Costs on a successful appeal are limited in exactly the same way as the costs at first instance. In the small claims track they are limited to the fixed costs of issue, court fees, witness expenses, loss of earnings, experts' fees and (rarely used) the fixed costs of obtaining an injunction. The only escape from the rigours of the fixed costs regime would be for the successful party to convince the circuit judge hearing the appeal that the unsuccessful party has behaved unreasonably; if he succeeds on this point the circuit judge can summarily assess the costs without the small claims limitation.

This general inability to recover costs from the other side, and the need to balance the value of the claim against the cost of enforcing it, are key issues for solicitors consulted in small claims cases (the problems are much less acute if the client has legal expenses insurance). The solicitor may feel that he or she should take a "behind the scenes" advisory role, perhaps drafting the letter of claim and/or the claim form. This division of functions is known in the USA as "unbundling" and it will be interesting to see whether it takes off here (see an article by Suzanne Burn in *Busy Solicitors' Digest*, July 1999).

The fast track (Part 28)

12.14   The need to reduce delay is one of the central aims of the Rules and the fast track is a prime example. This is the normal track for cases where:

(1) the value of the amount in dispute is between £10,001 and £25,000;

(2) the trial is likely to last for no longer than one day; and

(3) oral expert evidence at the trial (where allowed) will be limited to

(a) one expert per party in any expert field; and
(b) expert evidence in two expert fields.

Once a case has been allocated to the fast track the district judge will consider whether further details of the claim or defence are necessary, whether the case can be disposed of summarily and whether a preliminary hearing is necessary. Subject to this, he will make an order for directions which is likely to include a strict (and largely immovable) timetable; this will be geared to a fixed trial date not more than 30 weeks from service of the directions.

There are detailed rules as to disclosure of documents, exchange of witness statements, exchange of experts' reports, a "pre-trial checklist" and the preparation of a "trial bundle" limited to those documents which are really required. Also (and this is of great importance) the court will have an on-going power to control the cost of litigation; the rules require the parties to prepare costs estimates (present and future) on every court appearance.

It is also important to appreciate that under Pt 46 an award of costs for the trial advocate is severely limited. Also, if the case is not finished in one day (and a day is normally limited to five hours), there is no scope for increasing the figures set out above. Bearing in mind how difficult it will be to move the trial date, it is vital that the timetable is adhered to as closely as possible in order to avoid difficulties as the trial date approaches.

The multi-track (Part 29)

This is the normal track for (a) claims in excess of £25,000 and (b) claims **12.15** within the fast track band where the case is likely to last for more than one day or where the rules relating to expert evidence (see above) are not satisfied. Although the cases in this track are not subject to the severe time constraints of the fast track the court will nevertheless strive to fix a trial date at as early a stage as possible, such date being as immovable as the trial date for fast track. There may be two occasions on which the judge will meet the parties' lawyers (and in many cases the clients will also be present) to plan the conduct of the case. The first of these meetings is the Case Management Conference at which the judge is likely to give directions—this can involve approving directions which the parties have agreed between themselves. The second meeting is known as the Pre-Trial Review and it may take place after completion of a pre-trial checklist. The trial advocates will meet the trial judge about 8–10 weeks before the hearing date (a) to explore the possibility of settlement before the full trial costs are incurred, and (b) if settlement is not possible, to prepare an agenda for the trial. At both of these meetings (neither of which is compulsory) the judge will be fully prepared and he will expect the same of the lawyers. In moving the case forward at these meetings the r.1 overriding objective must be constantly borne in mind by all concerned. Costs budgeting will be of increased importance in these cases.

Jackson Reforms

See the latter part of Appendix One for a note on these reforms.   **12.16**

3. PRECEDENTS

For a selection of county court precedents in consumer cases see Appendix **12.17** One.

Part II

THE CONSUMER AND THE CRIMINAL LAW

CHAPTER THIRTEEN

INTRODUCTION

In Part I we have examined the position of consumers as far as the civil law is concerned. We saw that it is not enough for them to show that they have a right of action, for example, for breach of contract or negligence. Their main problem is how to enforce that right. The proportion of complainants who are prepared to sue to enforce their rights is small. This encourages traders to assume that they can adopt careless and sloppy practices with impunity. If they can get away with providing shoddy goods and incompetent service, traders will be tempted to lower their standards by the prospect of increased profitability. Not only is this clearly contrary to the interests of consumers; it is equally unfair to the honest trader who endeavours to maintain high standards and at the same time to compete with the rogues operating in the same line of business. **13.01**

In pursuing its two-fold aim—to protect consumers and to ensure that honest traders are able to make a living on equal terms without the need to resort to the malpractices of their dishonest competitors—Parliament has increasingly turned to the sanctions of the criminal law in its search for control. This approach has the significant advantage for the consumer that the expensive and time-consuming process of regulating the rogue is entrusted to public officials who usually have a duty—not merely a power—to enforce its provisions. If the provisions of the criminal law also enable consumers to obtain compensation,[1] it will be unnecessary for them to rely on the rights explained in Part I: they will be superfluous.

The full range of criminal controls is very extensive. The following examples show some of their ambit. **13.02**

(1) The Food Safety Act 1990[2] controls the quality of food. Section 14 prohibits the sale of "any food which is not of the nature or substance or quality demanded by the purchaser", for example, containing maggots, mould or metal.

(2) The Weights and Measures Act 1985 empowers trading standards inspectors to test weighing and measuring equipment, and also makes it an offence to deliver short weight when goods are sold by weight, number or other measurement.

(3) The Consumer Credit Act 1974 creates a large number of criminal

---

[1] See para.17.03 below.
[2] Repealing most of the Food Act 1984.

offences, e.g. carrying on a consumer credit business without a authorisation.[3]

(4) The General Product Safety Regulations 2005 (the 2005 Regulations) impose a general safety requirement prohibiting the supply of unsafe goods.[4]

(5) The Consumer Protection from Unfair Trading Regulations 2008 (the 2008 Regulations) regulate a wide range of commercial activities,[5] many of them previously controlled by the Trade Descriptions Act 1968 and Pt II of the Consumer Protection Act 1987 (the 1987 Act).

13.03 The most important provisions of the Trade Descriptions Act 1968 (the 1968 Act) and all of Pt III of the 1987 Act were repealed by the 2008 Regulations. We shall discuss them briefly in Chapters Fourteen and Fifteen respectively in view of their historical importance—they were in force until 26 May 2008—and the continuation in force of some minor provisions of the 1968 Act. (Readers will find a much more detailed analysis of the 1968 Act in earlier editions of this book.) In Chapter Fifteen we also discuss payment surcharges.

Next in Chapter Sixteen we survey those statutory provisions which protect the consumer against unsafe goods, now to be found in Pt II of the 1987 Act and the 2005 Regulations.

Finally in Chapter Seventeen we consider the important question of compensation for the victims of criminal offences; how can they obtain financial redress for any loss which they may have suffered as a result of the convicted person's failure to comply with the criminal law? Two aspects are examined—orders for compensation under the Powers of Criminal Courts (Sentencing) Act 2000 and the limited right to bring civil proceedings for breach of statutory duty.

---

[3] See para.21.08 below.
[4] See para.16.45 below.
[5] See para.18.37 below.

CHAPTER FOURTEEN

"THE DESCRIPTION MISLED ME"

1. INTRODUCTION

This chapter is concerned almost entirely with the Trade Descriptions **14.01**
Act 1968 (the 1968 Act). Some of its provisions continue in force and are
discussed later, but the two main offences—false descriptions of goods
and services—disappeared on 26 May 2008 with the repeal of ss.1 and 14
by the Consumer Protection from Unfair Trading Regulations 2008 (SI
2008/1277) (the 2008 Regulations). However, we shall briefly outline them
below because of their historical importance—they were in force for 40
years.

Instead the 2008 Regulations will now protect consumers, in particular by
reg.5 on "misleading actions" with its detailed list of matters in reg.5(4) and
(5) and by the black list of prohibited practices in Sch.1.

Why was the whole of the 1968 Act not repealed? Two reasons can be dis- **14.02**
cerned. First, two practices fall outside the EU Unfair Commercial Practices
Directive (discussed in Chapter Eighteen) which the 2008 Regulations implemented. They concern false representations as to royal approval in s.12 and
false trade descriptions on imported goods in s.16 (see paras 14.14 and 14.15
below). Secondly, the provisions as to offences, defences and enforcement in
ss.18–20, 23–31, 33–36 and 38–39 had to be retained because other legislation
refers to them, e.g. s.93 of the Trade Marks Act 1994.

Originally the 1968 Act also contained the provisions relating to misleading prices, but they became separately controlled by Pt III of the Consumer
Protection Act 1987,[1] until its repeal too by the 2008 Regulations.

Historical background

As early as 1423 an Act was passed regulating the marking of silver plate. **14.03**
Others dealt with the marking of gold and other precious metals, cutlery
and linen. The first statute to cover goods in general was the Merchandise
Marks Act 1862 which was replaced in 1887 by an Act of the same name.
This was added to by later statutes culminating in the Merchandise Marks
Act 1953.

Apart from these statutes dealing specifically with marking, there are related
Acts dealing with other aspects of the supply of goods. For example, the
Weights and Measures Act 1985 is particularly concerned with the *quantity* of

---

[1] See Chapter Fifteen.

goods being sold, e.g. coal and petrol, whereas the 1968 Act is also concerned with *quality*. There is one major similarity between the two Acts, namely, that their provisions are enforced by trading standards officers[2] (formerly known as inspectors of weights and measures) employed by local authorities. Whilst the above legislation has the effect of protecting the consumer, most of the legislation, like that relating to patents and trade marks, was passed with the intention of protecting one trader or manufacturer against unfair competition from another.

14.04 The position with regard to trade descriptions generally was looked into by the Committee on Consumer Protection, generally known as the Molony Committee, which published its Final Report in 1962.[3] It paid particular attention to the working of the Merchandise Marks Acts and highlighted a number of defects:

> (a) The Acts were limited in their scope since they were relevant only where a description had been "applied" to goods, i.e. where goods had been physically marked with labels, dies, blocks, etc. Thus oral statements and many advertisements were not covered.

> (b) Whatever the merits of the Acts, they were not generally enforced. The Acts of 1891 and 1894 gave the Board of Trade and Ministry of Agriculture, Fisheries and Food respectively the *power* to enforce the regulations; the Local Government Act 1933 gave a similar power to local authorities. Yet nobody was under a *duty* to enforce them.

14.05 These defects were cured by the passing of the 1968 Act. The preamble to the 1968 Act discloses the two main offences:

> (a) applying a false trade description to *goods* or supplying goods with such a description (section 1);

> (b) making a false statement as to the provision of *services*, accommodation or facilities (section 14).

Before considering these offences, two important general features of the Act need to be grasped. First, the Act operates in the criminal area only: Secondly, it applies only to suppliers in the course of a trade or business, i.e. not to private suppliers.

2. GOODS

14.06 Section 1(1) prohibited false trade descriptions of goods until its repeal in 2008. The offences created by s.1 were offences of strict liability.

---

[2] See para.14.25 below.
[3] Cmnd.1781.

Although charges under these provisions often involved an element of dishonesty, as was pointed out by the Divisional Court in *Alec Norman Garages Ltd v Phillips*,[4] it was not necessary for the prosecution to prove dishonesty.

Applying a trade description:

14.07 The offences under s.1 and s.16 (see para.14.15 below) occur when a person applies a false trade description to goods. A wide meaning is given by s.4 to the word "applies".

It covers:

(i) markings on the goods themselves, e.g. labels;

(ii) markings on anything in which the goods are supplied, e.g. packaging;

(iii) markings on anything in which the goods are placed, e.g. display units, vending machines, point-of-sale material;

(iv) oral statements, specifically mentioned in s.4(2).

Meaning of trade description

14.08 Section 2(1) defines a trade description as "an indication" of any of the matters exhaustively listed in its 10 paragraphs:

(1) A trade description is an indication, direct or indirect, and by whatever means given, of any of the following matters with respect to any goods or parts of goods, that is to say—

(a) quantity, size or gauge;
(b) method of manufacture, production, processing or reconditioning;
(c) composition;
(d) fitness for purpose, strength, performance, behaviour or accuracy;
(e) any physical characteristics not included in the preceding paragraphs;
(f) testing by any person and results thereof;
(g) approval by any person or conformity with a type approved by any person;
(h) place or date of manufacture, production, processing or reconditioning;
(i) person by whom manufactured, produced, processed or reconditioned;
(j) other history, including previous ownership or use.

Is it false?

14.09 Let us assume that there is a trade description within the meaning of s.2.

The next question to consider is whether the trade description is a false trade description. Section 3(1) states simply and clearly that "a false trade description is a trade description which is false to a material degree".

---

[4] [1985] R.T.R. 164.

3. Services

14.10 An area not covered by the Merchandise Marks Act 1953 was services. This novel extension of criminal liability from goods to services doubtless accounted for a more tentative approach in s.14 as compared with s.1. The offence of making false or misleading statements about services, accommodation or facilities was not an offence of strict liability, as can be seen from the wording of s.14(1):

> It shall be an offence for any person in the course of any trade or business—
>
>> (a) to make a statement which he knows to be false; or
>> (b) recklessly to make a statement which is false;

This is the other important offence repealed by the 2008 Regulations.

4. Property

14.11 Section 14 of the 1968 Act included statements about "accommodation", such as holiday hotels, and "services" covered services relating to building, e.g. by an architect or builder. However, although some aspects of building and sale were covered, the 1968 Act did not apply to general statements about properties for sale such as their location or characteristics.

Eventually the Property Misdescriptions Act 1991 was passed: a Private Member's Bill advocated by the Consumers' Association. It remains in force, as the EU Unfair Commercial Practices Directive, though it is a maximum Directive, allows Member States to "impose requirements which are more restrictive or prescriptive" in relation to immovable property (art.4.9).

Section 1(1), provides:

> Where a false or misleading statement about a prescribed matter is made in the course of an estate agency business or a property development business, otherwise than in providing conveyancing services, the person by whom the business is carried on shall be guilty of an offence under this section.

The main impact is upon estate agents. It is intended to dissuade them from indulging in their previous practice of giving extravagant descriptions which often at best were half-truths—"the pretty cottage adjoining farmland" which turns out to be a one-up, one-down terraced house with open country at the front, but a noisy car exhaust and tyre fitting centre overlooking the back garden.

Its ambit also extends to a "property development business". Section 1(5) (f) provides that a statement is caught in this case only if the business is concerned with "the development of land" *and* the statement is made "with a view to disposing of an interest in a building or part of a building, constructed or renovated in the course of a business".

An offence is committed where the statement relates to "a prescribed matter", i.e. prescribed in an order made by the Secretary of State (s.1(5) (d)).

The Property Misdescriptions (Specified Matters) Order 1992[5] contains **14.12** a long list of prescribed matters, e.g. location, view, fixtures and fittings, accommodation, surveys, treatments, history, council tax, easements.

The defences, enforcement and penalties are similar to those relating to the 1968 Act discussed below. Thus the familiar "due diligence" defence is available (s.2). However, on conviction the defendant may be fined, but not imprisoned (s.1(3)).

5. TWO CONTINUING OFFENCES

As we mentioned earlier, although ss.1 and 14 on misdescriptions of goods **14.13** and services have been repealed, two offences are extant.

Royal approval

Section 12 makes it an offence for a trader (1) to give a false indication that **14.14** his goods or services are of a kind supplied to or approved by any member of the Royal Family, or (2) to use an emblem signifying the Queen's Award to Industry without the authority of Her Majesty.

A new s.12(3) is added by the 2008 Regulations[6] excluding anything that is a commercial practice, as defined by the 2008 Regulations, unless it is unfair.

The Department for Business, Innovation & Skills (BIS) (formerly the Department for Trade and Industry (DTI)) consider that displaying such a flag or banner over a business building would be outside the 2008 Regulations and an offence under the 1968 Act.

Imported goods

Section 16 prohibits the import of goods into the UK where a false trade **14.15** description is applied to them outside the UK and it relates to the place of manufacture, production, processing or reconditioning. This would apply, for example, to knives made in Korea or clothes made in China and labelled "Sheffield England" or "Made in Italy" respectively.

6. DEFENCES

As we pointed out in para.14.01, the provisions about defences and offences **14.16** were not repealed by the 2008 Regulations.

---

[5] SI 1992/2834.
[6] Sch.2 Pt 1, para.10.

The general defence

14.17 The defence provided by s.24(1) reads as follows:

> In any proceedings for an offence under this Act it shall, subject to subsection (2) of this section, be a defence for the person charged to prove—
>
> (a) that the commission of the offence was due to a mistake or to reliance on information supplied to him or to the act or default of another person, an accident or some other cause beyond his control; and
> (b) that he took all reasonable precautions and exercised all due diligence to avoid the commission of such an offence by himself or any person under his control.

It may be split into five defences. The defendant must prove that the commission of the offence was due to any one of the following causes:

  (i) a mistake;

 (ii) reliance on information supplied to him;

 (iii) the act or default of another person;

 (iv) an accident;

  (v) some other cause beyond his control.

As Lord Templeman pointed out in *Wings Ltd v Ellis*,[7] where the company failed to invoke s.24, "Good intentions and mistake do not by themselves constitute a defence. The accused must plead and prove the circumstances specified in section 24".

Mistake

14.18 As far as mistake is concerned this is available only where the mistake is of the defendant himself; it cannot be used where someone else's mistake is involved (e.g. an employer pleading the mistake of an employee).[8]

Act or default of another person

14.19 The defence most frequently relied upon is that the offence was due to the "act or default of another person". When an employer is charged, he may rely on the default of an employee. However, when the employer is a company, it is necessary to distinguish between those employees who are the *alter ego* of the company, when their defaults are the company's defaults, and those employees who are not thus identified with the company which can then claim that the defaults are those of "another person". The difficulty was fully discussed by the House of Lords in *Tesco Supermarkets v Nattrass*,[9] a case involving s.11 (now repealed):

---

[7] [1984] 3 All E.R. 577 at 594.
[8] *Birkenhead & District Co-operative Society Ltd v Roberts* [1970] 1 W.L.R. 1497.
[9] [1972] A.C. 153.

Soap powder was advertised in a supermarket "Radiant 1 shilling off giant size 2/11d". This was intended to apply only to "flash packs" which were marked "1 shilling off recommended price". As the supermarket had run out of these packs, ordinary packs were on display. A customer was charged the full price of 3/11d for one of these.

Their Lordships held that where the person charged is a limited company, **14.20** the only persons who can be identified with the controlling mind and will of the company are the board of directors, the managing director and any other superior officer[10] to whom the board has delegated full discretion to act independently from the board. Thus, though a general manager may be the company's *alter ego*, the supermarket manager was not. Accordingly, since the offence was caused by his failure to ensure that sufficient flash-packs were available, Tesco were able to rely on his default.

To establish this defence the defendants must not merely produce the list of staff who might have been at fault; they must at least try to identify the actual person responsible by carefully investigating the circumstances to discover how the offences occurred.[11] Further, to rely on this defence s.24(2) requires the defendants at least seven clear days before the hearing to serve on the prosecutor a written notice giving such information as they have to identify the other person.[12] The reason for this provision is to enable the prosecution to consider whether to proceed directly against the other person either for one of the main offences or under the by-pass provision in s.23.[13]

Due diligence defence

It is not enough for the defendant to prove one of the five defences in s.24(1) **14.21** (a). He must also prove that he falls within what is now popularly known as the "due diligence defence", a defence frequently found in consumer protection legislation, namely "that he took all reasonable precautions and exercised all due diligence to avoid the commission of such an offence by himself or any person under his control".[14] These factors have generally been considered by the courts in relation to the default defence.

Sampling

Suppliers dealing with large quantities of goods and relying on sampling must **14.22** show that they have been taking reasonable precautions and been duly dili- gent. In *Rotherham Metropolitan BC v Raysun (UK) Ltd*[15]:

---

[10] By s.20 such officers may be prosecuted too, where the offence has been committed with their consent or connivance.
[11] *McGuire v Sittingbourne Co-operative Society Ltd* [1976] Crim.L.R. 268.
[12] See *Birkenhead & District Co-operative Society Ltd v Roberts* [1970] 1 W.L.R. 1497.
[13] See para.13.23 above.
[14] s.24(1)(b).
[15] *The Times*, 27 April 1988. See also *Amos v Melcon (Frozen Foods)* (1985) 149 J.P. 712, DC: "rump steak" was really silverside of beef; insufficient evidence of sampling; no defence.

The defendants, large-scale importers of Far East products, imported once a year about 100,000 packets of children's wax crayons from Hong Kong. Their agents there had samples analysed and had to send back only adverse reports: none was received. The defendants tested in England a single packet. They sold the crayons as "poisonless". The black crayons contained excessive amounts of toxic material.

The Divisional Court rejected their defence under s.24(1). They had not checked that the Hong Kong analyses were in fact taking place and their sample in England was "very moderate".

The by-pass provision

14.23 Although the so-called "by-pass provision" in s.23 is not a defence, it is appropriate to deal with it at this point in view of its close interaction with the defence in s.24(1). Section 23 states:

> Where the commission by any person of an offence under this Act is due to the act or default of some other person that other person shall be guilty of the offence, and a person may be charged with and convicted of the offence by virtue of this section whether or not proceedings are taken against the first-mentioned person.

Thus where X commits an offence, but the real culprit is Y, Y may be prosecuted for the offence committed by X. It is irrelevant whether or not proceedings have been taken against X. The corollary is that if no offence is committed by X, Y cannot be prosecuted under s.23.[16]

It can result in an offence being committed by a private person who cannot otherwise be charged, because he is not acting "in the course of a trade or business". Thus even if Y were a private person, he could be charged under s.23.[17]

Advertisements

14.24 Section 25 affords a special defence in the case of advertisements. In any proceedings for an offence relating to the publication of an advertisement the defendant is free from liability if he can prove that (a) the advertisement was received and published in the course of a business involving such publication, and (b) he did not know and had no reason to know that the publication would amount to an offence under the Act. The defence protects not only the publishers themselves, e.g. of newspapers and magazines, but also those who arrange for the publication of advertisements, e.g. advertising agencies.

---

[16] *Cottee v Douglas Seaton (Used Cars) Ltd* [1972] 1 W.L.R. 1408.
[17] *Olgeirsson v Kitching* [1986] 1 W.L.R. 304 DC.

7. ENFORCEMENT

One of the major defects of the Merchandise Marks Acts was the absence of **14.25** anybody with a duty to enforce their provisions. Section 26(1) clearly places the obligation of prosecution on trading standards officers in the following unequivocal terms: "It shall be the duty of every local weights and measures authority to enforce within their area the provisions of this Act."

To assist the inspectors in carrying out their duties s.27 gives them the power to check compliance with the Act by making test purchases.

Section 28 of the Act enables them to enter premises to make spot checks **14.26** and, if reasonable cause for suspicion of an offence exists, to require production[18] of the books and documents of the business.

Before instituting proceedings the local authority must give notice to BIS. Such liaison helps to prevent numerous prosecutions in different areas for the same offence, for example, for goods or services advertised and supplied nationally. However, multiple prosecutions do sometimes occur.

A prosecution must be brought within three years of the commission of an offence or one year from its discovery, whichever is the earlier.[19]

8. PENALTIES

If proceedings are brought summarily, a fine not exceeding £5,000 may be **14.27** levied in respect of each offence. If the defendant is convicted on indictment, not only may the fine be unlimited but imprisonment of up to two years may be imposed—both penalties may be meted out.[20] Occasionally prison sentences are imposed but the Divisional Court stated in *R. v Haesler*[21] that imprisonment is normally reserved for cases involving dishonesty.

---

[18] "Produce" does not mean "hand over and allow to take away": *Barge v British Gas Corp* (1983) 81 L.G.R. 53 DC.
[19] s.19(1). But see also s.19(2) and (4).
[20] s.18.
[21] [1973] Crim.L.R. 586.

CHAPTER FIFTEEN

"THE PRICE WAS WRONG"

1. HISTORICAL BACKGROUND

For the last 40 years various statutory attempts have been made to control **15.01** misleading price claims. Some have adopted a very detailed approach, others a broad-brush approach. As with all very specific regulations businesses and their legal advisers spend (or waste?) long hours seeking and exploiting loopholes in their battle with consumer protection agencies. Hence the Government has resorted to "principles based" regulation exemplified by the Consumer Protection from Unfair Trading Regulations 2008 (the 2008 Regulations) (discussed generally in Chapter Eighteen) which repealed Pt III of the Consumer Protection Act 1987.

The 2008 Regulations have particular provisions about price on which we comment later in this chapter. Before doing so we shall briefly explain the earlier approaches to the problem of misleading prices which may help to put the current statutory solutions into perspective (previous editions of this book examine the earlier legislation in some detail).

Trade Descriptions Act 1968

The Molony Committee in 1961 recommended[1] that the problem should **15.02** be tackled by including in the definition of trade description "the former or usual price of any goods". However, instead the Trade Descriptions Act 1968 endeavoured to deal with the mischief with separate price provisions contained in s.11. It created three offences: (1) false comparisons with a recommended price; (2) false comparisons with the trader's own previous price; (3) an indication that the price is less than that actually being charged.

Recommended prices[2]

The first offence caused little difficulty inasmuch as it was easy to prove **15.03** from manufacturers' lists whether or not an offence had been committed. However, the Act had no deterrent effect on the practice of manufacturers setting unrealistically high recommended prices (so-called "sky prices") to enable retailers to offer an apparent bargain to their customers by discounting.

---

[1] At para.636.
[2] The Resale Prices Act 1976 makes it unlawful to impose minimum resale prices (resale price maintenance or RPM) on distributors.

Previous prices

15.04 The second offence was similar to the first offence except that the false indication related to the price at which the supplier previously offered the goods.

Overcharging

15.05 The third offence was expressed in very wide terms and covered situations where the customer was charged a higher price than he would have expected to pay in view of the indications as to price given to him by the supplier.

Consumer Protection Act 1987 Pt III

15.06 The purpose of Pt III of the Consumer Protection Act 1987 was to adopt a much more flexible approach than the previous legislation in the hope that this would cope with the constantly changing commercial practices and marketing techniques of the modern world. This more general approach could be found in the main offence created by s.20(1) of giving a misleading price indication. The offence covered "any goods, services, accommodation or facilities". This was complemented by s.26 giving power to make regulations to be activated when particular practices required specific provisions.

Bureaux de Change

15.07 The only regulations made under s.26 and preserved by the 2008 Regulations are the Price Indications (Bureaux de Change) (No.2) Regulations 1992.[3] Their purpose is obvious from their title: they are concerned with transparency and information for consumers. Any traveller will have seen the effect of these regulations when obtaining foreign currency. For example, the selling, buying and commission rates must be stated. If the rates for travellers' cheques and notes are different, that must be shown. This information must be given "clearly and prominently" and must be visible to consumers as they either approach or enter the bureau de change.

2. THE 2008 REGULATIONS

15.08 As we have seen, the 2008 Regulations[4] repealed the Pt III of the Consumer Protection Act 1987, leaving as its only trace the Order discussed in para.15.07 above.

The regulation of prices now falls within the 2008 Regulations, of which a number of provisions are aimed specifically at prices.

Regulation 5 is concerned with "misleading actions", which we discuss more generally in para.18.45 below. Here we draw attention only to reg.5(2) (a). With reference to a commercial practice which "contains false informa-

---

[3] SI 1992/737. See CPR Sch.3, para.5.
[4] SI 2008/1277.

tion", it directs attention to reg.5(4). This contains a list lettered (a) to (k) of relevant matters: two are important on pricing:

    (g) the price or the manner in which the price is calculated;
    (h) the existence of a specific price advantage.

The black list of unfair practices in Sch.1 also needs to be considered. Paragraphs 5 and 6 are both concerned with prices and the malpractices of bait advertising and bait and switch respectively. Paragraph 20 deals with "gratis", "free" and "without charge" offers which are not really so.

3. PRICE MARKING

We complete our brief survey of consumer protection measures about prices **15.09** with a comment on the Price Marking Order 2004 (SI 2004/102). It implements EU Directive 98/6/EC on consumer protection in the indication of prices of products offered to consumers.

Article 4 requires a trader who indicates that a product is for sale to indicate its sale price in sterling. There are exceptions, e.g. in art.3: auctions, works of art and antiques. Advertisements for products are also exempt if they are aural, on television, shown at a cinema or inside a small shop (280 square metres or less: art.1(2)).[5]

There are special provisions about sales at reduced prices (art.9) and precious metals (art.10).

Where a trader sells products from bulk and certain pre-packaged goods, he must indicate the unit price (art.5). Schedule 1 contains a long list of the relevant unit of quantity for specified products ranging from coffee to coal and pies to pipe tobacco.

4. PAYMENT SURCHARGES

Background

For many years consumers have been penalised by being required by some **15.10** suppliers, particularly when paying for goods or services by credit, debit or charge cards, to pay a surcharge of X per cent or £Y on top of the cash price.

This practice was rife with low cost airlines until the Office of Fair Trading (OFT) intervened in 2012 after a super complaint by Which? about the travel industry. Which? identified three practices detrimental to consumers:

- advertising incomplete prices where the surcharges are hidden or appear at the very end of an online purchase ("drip pricing");

- providing no practicable alternative; and

---

[5] art.5(3) and Sch.2.

- charging more than the cost of processing the consumer's payment.

15.11 The OFT solved the problem by pointing out that such practices could fall foul of the 2008 Regulations as breaches of reg.5 (misleading actions) and reg.6 (misleading omissions).[6] Voluntary agreements followed with a number of travel companies and in July 2012 12 airlines agreed to scrap debit card surcharges.[7]

The problem, though, was more widespread. In September 2012 the Department for Business, Innovation & Skills (BIS) issued a consultation paper on the *Early implementation of a ban on above cost payment surcharges* (URN 12/1008). It proposed to implement art.19 of the EU Consumer Rights Directive 2011/83/EU earlier than 2014.

2012 Regulations

15.12 The Government acted swiftly and three months later the Consumer Rights (Payment Surcharges) Regulations 2012[8] were made. They came into force on 6 April 2013. The essential ban appears in reg.4 and (except the first five words) is a copy out of art.19. Regulation 4 reads as follows:

A trader must not charge consumers, in respect of the use of a given means of payment, fees that exceed the cost borne by the trader for the use of that means.

The Regulations apply only to contracts made between consumers and traders after they came into force. They cover supplies of goods, services, utilities and digital data. In August 2015 BIS issued guidance on the Regulations, available at *https://www.gov.uk/government/uploads/system/ uploads/attachment_data/file/452405/BIS-15-343-BIS-payment-surcharges- guidance.pdf*.

Exclusions

15.13 (1) Regulation 5(2) lists 11 categories of excluded contracts. They include social and health services, financial services, residential rentals, new buildings and food and drink supplied by regular roundsmen.

(2) Regulation 6 exempts temporarily—until 12 June 2014 at the latest—two types of business: micro-businesses (fewer than 10 employees) and new businesses. Details appear in the Schedule to the Regulations.

---

[6] See paras 18.45 and 18.48 below.
[7] OFT estimated that £300 million was spent on airline surcharges in 2010.
[8] SI 2012/3110. NB minor amendments made by the Consumer Contracts (Information, Cancellation and Additional Charges) Regulations 2013 (SI 2013/3134) Sch.4.

Sanctions

The weakest sanction for the consumer against the trader is that by reg.10 the **15.14** excessive fee is unenforceable: the contract is still valid. We foresee that many traders will continue to apply high fees hoping to be paid by uninformed consumers.

However, persistent rogues may find their local trading standards department applying for an injunction under reg.8.

A third sanction is an enforcement order under Pt 8 of the Enterprise Act 2002.[9] It is noteworthy that a breach of the Regulations will not be a criminal offence.

---

[9] See Enterprise Act 2002 (Part 8 EU Infringements) Order 2013, and para.18.13 below on the Enterprise Act 2002.

CHAPTER SIXTEEN

"THE GOODS AREN'T SAFE"

1. INTRODUCTION

In Chapter Five we considered Pt I of the Consumer Protection Act 1987 **16.01** (the 1987 Act) which imposes *civil* liability on *producers* of unsafe goods. In this chapter we turn to Pt II of the 1987 Act and the General Product Safety Regulations 2005 (the 2005 Regulations)[1] which impose *criminal* sanctions on *producers and suppliers* of unsafe goods (and only *consumer goods* in relation to the general safety requirements). First this legislation will be placed in its historical context by briefly reviewing its legislative predecessors.

We have seen in earlier chapters that often consumer protection legislation is concerned as much with shoddy, poor quality goods as with dangerous goods. However, in many statutes a different approach is adopted where death or personal injury is concerned: provisions are likely to be more stringent or restrictive than in cases where only financial or economic loss results. Thus under s.65(1) of the Consumer Rights Act 2015 (CRA 2015), a clause excluding liability for negligence is void in the case of death or personal injury.[2] In other areas the same emphasis is placed on ensuring that the individual is protected against death or injury. For example, the Health and Safety at Work, etc. Act 1974, s.6, ensures that articles for use at work are safe when properly used.

Concern for safety at home should be as serious as concern for safety **16.02** in the work place. Forty years ago the Foreword to *Consumer Safety: A Consultative Document*[3] provided ample evidence.

> About 7,000 people in Great Britain die each year from accidents in the home, over a tenth of them from fires. This is comparable to the number killed on the roads. In addition over 100,000 receive hospital in-patient treatment for home accident injuries. No central statistics are kept for those not admitted to hospital, but it is estimated that in England and Wales 650,000 receive out-patient care in hospitals and 500,000 attend their general practitioner for treatment.
>
> Apart from the toll of human suffering which these figures represent, there are substantial economic costs, both direct—through damage to property, as in the case of the 50,000 or so fires in the home each year—and indirect—e.g. the cost of medical treatment and hours lost from work.
>
> This Consultative Document is concerned with ways of reducing the cost and

---

[1] SI 2005/1803 implementing the 2001 EC General Product Safety Directive, see para.16.26 below.
[2] See para.10.32 above.
[3] Cmnd.6398, (1976).

suffering caused by home accidents. It considers how information, publicity and education on causes of home accidents and means of avoiding them can be improved; and in particular it discusses how the law can best ensure that goods which reach consumers are as safe to use as the public may reasonably expect.

As the last paragraph states, the Green Paper paid particular attention to the way in which the law could be improved with a view to ensuring that goods used by the consumer are safe. At that time this branch of the law was regulated by the Consumer Protection Acts 1961 and 1971. Several of the proposals contained in the paper for improving the legal protective framework were incorporated in the Consumer Safety Act 1978 (the 1978 Act).

Consumer Safety Act 1978

16.03   Its main purpose was to prevent dangerous goods reaching the market or, if they had done so, to prohibit their further sale. The most important changes effected by the Act were these:

(1) It gave any Secretary of State much more flexible powers to make regulations to ensure that goods are safe and to prohibit the supply of unsafe goods.[4]

(2) It enabled quick action to be taken to ban the supply of dangerous goods by the use of "prohibition orders"[5] and "prohibition notices".

(3) It provided power by the service of a "notice to warn" to require manufacturers and distributors of goods, which were found to be dangerous only after they had been sold, to publish notices warning the public of the danger.[6]

(4) It imposed an enforcement duty on local authorities.[7]

These improvements are retained in the 1987 Act.

Consumer Safety (Amendment) Act 1986

16.04   Less than six years after the 1978 Act came into force the Government published a White Paper, *The Safety of Goods*,[8] setting out the Government's conclusions with regard to the effectiveness of the consumer products safety legislation. It contained proposals for amending the 1978 Act with a view to strengthening its provisions. One example mentioned in the White Paper illustrated the difficulties. In 1981 over a hundred types of electrical hair-curling brushes were imported in large numbers, mostly from Asia. They failed to satisfy the regulations on matters such as insulation, but this hazard

---

[4] s.1.
[5] s.3(1). Prohibition orders are no longer available: see para.16.16 below.
[6] As above.
[7] s.5(1).
[8] Cmnd.9302, (1984).

did not become apparent until they had reached the shops and market stalls, been sold and were in use. It proved to be an expensive, time-consuming exercise to track down the unsafe appliances and have them removed from sale. In the interval, a death or serious injury could easily have occurred.

The purpose of the recommendations was to introduce preventative measures to assist in identifying and halting the supply of unsafe goods before they reached the shops; to enable enforcement officers to suspend the supply of apparently unsafe goods; and to introduce a general safety duty on all suppliers.

The Consumer Safety (Amendment) Act 1986 (the 1986 Act) added the first two of those new weapons to the armoury of the enforcement authorities. They both reappear in the 1987 Act:

(1) Customs officers were given power to detain imported goods for two days and to pass on information to trading standards officers, who would thus be given time to activate their other procedures.

(2) Trading standards officers were empowered to serve suspension notices to prohibit supplies of goods for up to six months, and to apply to the court for an order that goods be forfeited and destroyed.

Related compensation provisions were also enacted.

2. CONSUMER PROTECTION ACT 1987 PT II

The proposal that there should be a general statutory duty on suppliers to supply safe consumer goods was first put forward in the consultative document *Consumer Safety.*[9] The absence of this duty on suppliers of consumer goods contrasted with the duty on suppliers of articles for use at work imposed by the Health and Safety at Work, etc. Act 1974. The Government's policy remained consistent and was reiterated in para.34 of the White Paper[10]: **16.05**

> The Government accepts that there is a case for widening the scope of the Act to place a general obligation on the suppliers of consumer goods to achieve an acceptable standard of safety where it is reasonable to expect them to anticipate and reduce risks arising from those goods. This would induce a greater sense of responsibility on the part of those suppliers who currently regard themselves as unaffected by legislation (and who may not be adequately deterred by the common law duty of care). At the same time it would provide wider scope for swift remedial action by enforcement authorities in the case of newly identified dangerous products.

This "general safety requirement" (GSR) was the novel feature of the 1987 Act but it has been repealed and replaced by the GSR contained in the 2005 Regulations.[11] Otherwise the 1987 Act is in the main a consolidating statute bringing together in Pt II the provisions of the 1978 and 1986 Acts. **16.06**

---

[9] Cmnd.6398, (1976).
[10] Cmnd.9302, (1984).
[11] See para.16.30 below.

The regulatory regime now consists of the following measures which we shall consider below.

(1) Safety regulations impose specific requirements in relation to a particular type of product.

(2) Prohibition notices, notices to warn and suspension notices provide back-up powers to control particular traders dealing in unsafe goods.

(3) The GSR in the 2005 Regulations prohibits producers from placing unsafe consumer products on the market and imposes on distributors a duty of care in this respect. These Regulations are considered in a separate section at the end of this chapter.

As a preliminary it is necessary to look at some key words defined in the 1987 Act.

Key definitions

16.07 The definitions are found in various places. Those definitions relating to the Act as a whole are found in ss.45 and 46 (some of these have already been discussed in Chapter Five in relation to Pt I); those relating only to Pt II appear in s.19; and a few of more limited importance are given in the relevant section itself.

Safe

16.08 This is the core of Pt II—it is essentially concerned with dangerous, unsafe goods, not with shoddy goods of poor quality (this is true of Pt I too). Section 19(1) gives this meaning to the word "safe":

> "safe", in relation to any goods, means such that there is no risk, or no risk apart from one reduced to a minimum, that any of the following will (whether immediately or after a definite or indefinite period) cause the death of, or any personal injury to, any person whatsoever, that is to say—
>
> (a) the goods;
> (b) the keeping, use or consumption of the goods[12];
> (c) the assembly of any of the goods which are, or are to be, supplied unassembled;
> (d) any emission or leakage from the goods or, as a result of the keeping, use or consumption of the goods, from anything else; or
> (e) reliance on the accuracy of any measurement, calculation or other reading made by or by means of the goods,
>
> and "safer" and "unsafe" shall be construed accordingly.

It can be seen that goods do not have to be absolutely safe, but the risk at

---

[12] s.19(2) amplifies this aspect.

worst must be "reduced to a minimum". This is a commonsense approach, since otherwise some products would be outlawed, e.g. motor vehicles, lawn mowers, power saws.

It is enough to refer to some of the regulations made under the 1961 and 1978 Acts[13] to find examples of unsafe goods: explosive oil heaters or lamps; toys with sharp edges or spikes or loose doll's eyes; flammable nightdresses; retreaded motor tyres. **16.09**

Electrical appliances provide frequent examples; here faulty insulation brings with it the hazard of electrocution—electric blankets, hair-curling brushes, vacuum cleaners and electric razors.

The importance of (b) lies in making regulations relating to the effectiveness of safety equipment, e.g. life jackets, buoyancy rafts, fire extinguishers; for the risk arises not from the product itself but from the fact that, when circumstances occur in which the equipment is in "use", it is found at that late, critical stage to be unsuitable and thus to expose the user to risk. The significance of the word "keeping" can be seen in relation to labelling requirements on goods which create a hazard if not safely stored, e.g. garden pesticides.

Examples of the other factors in the list may be helpful:

(c) flat pack furniture, unassembled bicycles;

(d) household cleaning fluids, microwaves, gas cylinders;

(e) tyre pressure gauges, speedometers.

Goods

The definition of "goods" in s.45(1) is very wide and is not confined to consumer goods: **16.10**

> "goods" includes substances, growing crops and things comprised in land by virtue of being attached to it and any ship, aircraft or vehicle.

However, safety regulations may not be made in respect of crops, water, food, feeding stuff, fertilisers, mains gas, drugs and medicines.[14]

Supply

A supply is caught only if made "in the course of carrying on a business (whether or not a business of dealing in the goods in question[15]) and as principal or agent."[16] The business supply is covered; the private supply is not. **16.11**

---

[13] These regulations continue in force until replaced by new regulations.

[14] s.11(7).

[15] s.46(5). These clarifying words did not appear in the equivalent provision of the 1961 Act. But in *Southwark LBC v Charlesworth* [1983] C.L.Y. 3311 the Divisional Court reached the same conclusion: a shoe repairer who sold an unsafe electric fire through his shop breached the Electrical Equipment (Safety) Regulations 1975 (SI 1975/1366).

[16] s.46(1).

What types of transaction are "supplies"? The definition provides a detailed answer:

    (i) Sale.

    (ii) Hire or loan.

    (iii) Hire-purchase.

Section 45(2) provides that in the case of hire, hire-purchase, credit sale or conditional sale agreements, "the supplier" is not the provider of the credit (the "ostensible supplier") but "the effective supplier" who is enabled to provide the goods by virtue of such financial facility.

Example

16.12   D wishes to acquire on credit terms a car owned by a dealer S. S sells the car to a finance house C. C lets the goods on hire-purchase to D. S is "the supplier" under the 1987 Act. (To use Consumer Credit Act jargon, the credit-broker S (not the creditor C) is the supplier.)

    (iv) Work and materials.

    (v) Exchange, e.g. for trading stamps.

    (vi) Provision under a statutory function, e.g. the NHS.

    (vii) Gift, e.g. a prize.

Safety regulations

16.13   Safety regulations are an old feature of this area of consumer protection. Indeed, regulations orginally made under the Acts of 1961 and 1978 continue in force. The current offences for contravention of safety regulations are to be found in s.12, e.g. supplying goods prohibited by regulations. It is s.11 which contains the regulation-making power:

> (1) The Secretary of State may by regulations under this section ("safety regulations") make such provision as he considers appropriate for the purposes of section 10(3) above and for the purpose of securing—
>
>   (a) that goods to which this section applies are safe;
>   (b) that goods to which this section applies which are unsafe, or would be unsafe in the hands of persons of a particular description, are not made available to persons generally or, as the case may be, to persons of that description; and
>   (c) that appropriate information is, and inappropriate information is not, provided in relation to goods to which this section applies.

Thus regulations may cover not only the goods, but also information about them. Further, s.11(1)(b) makes it clear that they may relate to the supply of goods to certain groups only, a doubtful point in earlier legislation, e.g. fireworks not to be sold to children.

The possible contents of regulations are illustrated by a list set out in s.11(2). **16.14**
They include provisions relating to:

(i) composition or contents, design, construction, finish or packing;

(ii) standards to be approved, e.g. British Standards;

(iii) testing or inspection, e.g. manufacturers' quality control procedures to prevent faulty batches of aerosol cans from reaching the market;

(iv) marks, warnings, instructions or other information on goods, e.g. warning symbols, first-aid instructions, lists of ingredients in cosmetics; or prohibiting the giving of "inappropriate information", e.g. misleading marks or insignia.

The regulations may also prohibit the supply of goods or components which are unsafe or do not satisfy the requirements of the regulations. Thus a permanent ban may be imposed on dangerous products which the Secretary of State considers to be inherently unsafe irrespective of design or construction, e.g. oral snuff.

Revocations

With the wide-ranging control originally given by the GSR in the 1987 **16.15**
Act and currently by the GSR in the 2005 Regulations (see para.16.30 below) there is no longer any need for some of the regulations which are concerned only with specific products. Thus from 1 October 2012, 14 regulations were revoked pursuant to the Government's policy of reducing red tape: the Product Safety (Revocation) Regulations 2012 (SI 2012/1815) revoked some regulations made between 1972 and 2009 and relating to—

All Terrain Motor Vehicles

Asbestos Products (in part)

Bunk Beds

Children's Clothing (Hood cords)

Child Resistant Packaging

Cooking Utensils

Fireguards

Gas Appliances

Gas Catalytic Heaters

Gas Cooking Appliances

Imitation Dummies

Magnetic Toys

Stands for Carry-Cots

Wheeled Child Conveyances.

Emergency procedures

16.16   Extensive consultation is required by s.11(5) before the making of regulations. As many months may elapse in this way, the 1978 Act contained power
for the Minister to make prohibition orders to by-pass the normal regulation-
making procedures as a temporary measure in an emergency.[17]

Prohibition orders have now disappeared and been replaced by the
expedited procedure set out in s.11(5). The Secretary of State may make
regulations without consultation for a 12 months maximum where "the
need to protect the public requires that regulations should be made without
delay".[18]

Notices

16.17   The Act contains various powers to stop the distribution, or further distribution, of unsafe goods.

Suspension notice[19]

16.18   If an enforcement authority reasonably suspects that a trader is supplying
goods in contravention of a safety provision, it may serve a "suspension
notice" on him. This will prevent him disposing of his stock for a maximum
of six months. The authority may have to pay compensation, if there was no
contravention after all. A separate, but sometimes related, route is to apply
to the court for forfeiture of the goods, which usually involves their destruction.[20] In neither of these cases is a conviction of the trader a prerequisite;
only a "contravention" is needed.

Prohibition notice[21]

16.19   Like the suspension notice, the "prohibition notice" is aimed at a particular trader. It is served by the Secretary of State and prohibits the supply of
unsafe goods. This is a useful follow-up to the local authority's suspension
notice.

The power is rarely used. No such notice had been issued since 1992,
until the banning in April 2003 of "yo-balls"—toy balls made of a jelly
like material attached by an elastic strap to a finger loop. They could
pose a risk of strangulation to children and so did not meet the requirements of the Toys (Safety) Regulations 1995.[22] The Department of Trade

---

[17] See the Second Edition of this book, pp.238–240, for an explanation of this procedure.
[18] e.g. Fireworks Regulations 2003 (SI 2003/3085).
[19] s.14(1).
[20] s.16.
[21] s.13(1)(a).
[22] SI 1995/204, made under s.11 of the 1987 Act.

and Industry (DTI) served prohibition notices on three English and two Scottish companies.

Notice to warn[23]

Prohibition notices are appropriate where goods are still in the hands of the suppliers. What can be done if the goods have already reached the public and are in daily use? Prior to the Act the most that the DTI could do was to ask manufacturers to publish a warning or itself to issue a press notice. Responsible manufacturers and importers readily do so. The motor industry is a good example; as soon as any apparent defect reveals itself as a danger, e.g. brakes, the producer gives it widespread publicity and advises owners to take in their vehicles to be checked.

    Now it is possible for the Secretary of State to serve a "notice to warn" on any trader requiring him to publish a specified warning about unsafe goods at his own expense.

16.20

Recall

A major defect in the 1987 Act was that no one had the power to order manufacturers to recall dangerous products, although in practice they do recall such goods to avoid being sued under Pt I of the 1987 Act or for negligence.[24]

    However, the 2005 Regulations[25] revoking the General Product Safety Regulations 1994 (the 1994 Regulations),[26] at long last gave enforcement authorities the power to require the recall of dangerous products.[27]

16.21

General safety requirement (GSR)

The wide-ranging GSR imposed on suppliers by s.10 of the 1987 Act was the linch-pin of UK safety legislation until its virtual replacement by the GSR originally imposed by the 1994 Regulations and its ultimate repeal by reg.46 of the 2005 Regulations. Accordingly our discussion of the 1987 Act GSR will be brief.

    No longer was it necessary to bring in regulations piecemeal when particular products proved to be dangerous. This was the difficulty faced by the enforcement authorities before the 1987 Act, when the closing of various specific loopholes by regulations was no help in tackling another type of unsafe product when it appeared on the market.

    Section 10(1) contained the GSR offence:

16.22

    A person shall be guilty of an offence if he—

      (a) supplies any consumer goods which fail to comply with the general safety requirement;

---

[23] s.13(1)(b).
[24] See Chapter Five.
[25] See para.16.26 below.
[26] SI 1994/2328.
[27] See para.16.43 below.

    (b) offers or agrees to supply any such goods; or

    (c) exposes or possesses any such goods for supply.

Unlike the safety regulations made under Pt II and the product liability provisions of Pt I of the 1987 Act, it was confined to *consumer* goods, i.e. "ordinarily intended for private use or consumption".[28]

Defences and penalties

16.23   The familiar defence is available that the accused "took all reasonable steps and exercised all due diligence[29] to avoid committing the offence", with the usual duty to notify the prosecutor of the identity of anyone else who is being blamed.[30]

The penalty for any of the offences is the same—on summary conviction a maximum fine of £5,000 and up to six months' imprisonment.[31]

Enforcement

16.24   Although the 1961 Act merely gave a discretionary power to trading standards inspectors, s.27(1) makes it their duty to enforce the provisions creating the offences explained above. Whether with the limited resources available to them local authorities are managing to cope with their ever-increasing responsibilities—the Consumer Credit Act 1974 is also their problem—is debatable. Nevertheless this duty is one which they must do their best to fulfil, unless the Secretary of State exercises the power given to him by s.27(2) to transfer the duty elsewhere. Sections 28 and 29 give the authorities the usual related powers of purchase, entry and seizure, testing, etc., and s.30 enables a customs officer to detain imported goods for two days.

Civil remedy

16.25   In the following chapter breach of statutory duty is examined.[32] The Acts of 1961 to 1987 are unusual among the criminal statutes concerned with consumer protection in expressly affording the victim a civil remedy. Section 41(1) offers the remedy and s.41(4) prevents it being snatched away by invalidating any exclusion clause. Further, any contractual rights of the victim remain untouched.[33] However, this civil remedy applies only to breach of the safety regulations, not of the GSR. In practice it is rarely, if ever, used.

---

[28] s.10(7).

[29] *Balding v Lew-Ways Ltd* [1995] Crim. L.R. 878: non-compliance with Toys (Safety) Regulations 1989 (SI 1989/1275); not "due diligence" to rely on analyst's report that toy complied with British Standard.

[30] s.39(1) and (2). See *Riley v Webb* [1987] Crim. L.R. 477.

[31] e.g. s.12(5).

[32] See para.17.10 below.

[33] s.41(3).

3. GENERAL PRODUCT SAFETY REGULATIONS 2005

1992 EU General Product Safety[34] Directive

We have just seen that the policy of ensuring that the consumer is protected   **16.26**
from dangerous goods had been implemented in the UK by taking two complementary routes, First, legislation was introduced enabling regulations
to be passed to regulate particular kinds of products which were inherently
hazardous.[35] Such "vertical legislation" copes only with narrow sectoral
problems which are attacked piecemeal, leaving the holes in the dyke to be
plugged as and when they appear. So the second route was taken of introducing "horizontal legislation" with the imposition of a GSR by the 1987 Act.[36]

Of course, such problems exist at the European level too and can be met
with similar solutions. The importance of safety was emphasised in point 72
of the 1985 EU White Paper *Completing the Internal Market* which stated
that the health and safety of workers and consumers were interests which
should be taken into account in the 1992 programme. This very same point
was referred to in July 1985 when the European Commission submitted to
the European Council a Communication concerning a *New Impetus for a
Consumer Protection Policy*. This Communication gave a special priority to
consumer safety.

Then in 1989 the EU Commission submitted its proposal for a Directive on   **16.27**
General Product Safety. Horizontal legislation already existed in such other
influential countries as France and Germany. Indeed, in this area as in others
there was a marked distinction between the approach adopted by the northern Member States and the southern or Mediterranean Member States whose
legislation on product safety was much less stringent. These anomalies are
highlighted in the Preamble to the 1992 Directive:

> Whereas some Member States have adopted horizontal legislation on product
> safety, imposing, in particular, a general obligation on economic operators to
> market only safe products; whereas those legislations differ in the level of protec-
> tion afforded to persons; whereas such disparities and the absence of horizontal
> legislation in other Member States are liable to create barriers to trade and dis-
> tortions of competition within the internal market.

One difficulty was how to dovetail specific EU or national rules relating to
particular products or product sectors into the general safety duty at the core
of the Directive. Should the specific and general duties be mutually exclusive
or should they overlap? The Directive comes down firmly on the former solution—no overlap.

Another hotly debated issue was whether the Directive should cover all products or only consumer products. The original plan was to include only consumer
products. Although as the debate continued the scope of the draft directive was
widened to encompass all products (whether manufactured or agricultural, new

---

[34] 92/59/EEC.
[35] See para.16.13 above.
[36] See para.16.22 above.

or used), the Directive in its final form was watered down again: it applies only to consumer goods and excludes some second-hand goods.

The Directive on General Product Safety was finally adopted on 29 June 1992 and was supposed to come into force within two years. The implementation of the GPS Directive within the UK was delayed until 3 October 1994. This was the date when the 1994 GPS Regulations took effect.[37]

2001 EU General Product Safety Directive[38]

16.28   On 3 December 2001 an amended GPS Directive was adopted and came into force on 15 January 2002. Its purpose, stated in the preamble, is "to complete, reinforce and clarify some of the [1992 Directive's] provisions in the light of experience as well as new and relevant developments on consumer product safety". It mainly re-enacts the provisions of its predecessor, which was repealed from 15 January 2004. Member States should have transposed the Directive into national law by that date, but once again the UK Government was late with an implementation date of 1 October 2005.

There is one major innovation—art.8(f) entitles Member States to order the recall of a dangerous product from consumers.

Relationship to 1987 Act

16.29   We saw in the previous section that the UK already had in place a GSR introduced by the 1987 Act. Its virtual existence was limited to seven years as the main effect of the 1994 GPS Regulations was to make the GSR in s.10 redundant; it has been repealed now by the 2005 Regulations.[39]

2005 GSR

16.30   The essence of the 2005 Regulations appears in reg.5:

> (1) No producer shall place a product on the market unless the product is a safe product.
> (2) No producer shall offer or agree to place a product on the market or expose or possess a product for placing on the market unless the product is a safe product.
> (3) No producer shall offer or agree to supply a product or expose or possess a product for supply unless the product is a safe product.
> (4) No producer shall supply a product unless the product is a safe product.

Unlike the GSR in the 1987 Act this is limited to a producer. However, it is backed up by a complementary provision in reg.8 aimed at distributors:

> (1) A distributor shall act with due care in order to help ensure compliance with the applicable safety requirements and in particular he—

[37] SI 1994/2328.
[38] 2001/95/EC.
[39] reg.46.

(a) shall not expose or possess for supply or offer or agree to supply, or supply, a product to any person which he knows or should have presumed, on the basis of the information in his possession and as a professional, is a dangerous product; and

(b) shall, within the limits of his activities, participate in monitoring the safety of a product placed on the market, in particular by—

    (i) passing on information on the risks posed by the product,

    (ii) keeping the documentation necessary for tracing the origin of the product,

    (iii) producing the documentation necessary for tracing the origin of the product, and cooperating in action taken by a producer or an enforcement authority to avoid the risks.

(2) Within the limits of his activities, a distributor shall take measures enabling him to cooperate efficiently in the action referred to in paragraph (1)(b)(iii).

It can be seen that the producer is more in peril in that reg.5 creates an offence of strict liability, whereas the distributor's offence depends on his actual or presumed knowledge that the products are dangerous. Regulation 8(1)(b)(ii) imposes an additional traceability duty on distributors compared with the 1994 Regulations. Contraventions of regs 5 or 8(1)(a) are the most serious offences (see para.16.45 below). **16.31**

Both offences involve the supply of dangerous products to consumers. To discover the precise meaning of these words we need to look closely at some key definitions in reg.2.

Key definitions: reg.2

Product

"Product" is defined as follows: **16.32**

> "product" means a product which is intended for consumers or likely, under reasonably foreseeable conditions, to be used by consumers even if not intended for them and which is supplied or made available, whether for consideration or not, in the course of a commercial activity and whether it is new, used or reconditioned and includes a product that is supplied or made available to consumers for their own use in the context of providing a service. "product" does not include equipment used by service providers themselves to supply a service to consumers, in particular equipment on which consumers ride or travel which is operated by a service provider;

A few comments need to be made.

(1) Although the wording does not state so expressly, clearly the Regulations apply only to goods and not to services themselves, like the Product Liability Directive.[40]

(2) The supply must be in the course of a "commercial activity". Thus a private sale by a consumer is not caught.

---

[40] See para.5.17 above.

(3) Consumer goods fall within the Regulations.[41] A product will be caught if it is "intended for consumers"; presumably it is the producer's intention which matters here. For example, if a producer makes a chainsaw intending it to be sold to and used only by trained foresters, this would fall outside these words of the definition even if occasionally one of the chainsaws was sold on by a trade customer to a member of the public, perhaps in a garden centre.

16.33   More problematical are the words "likely, under reasonably foreseeable conditions, to be used by consumers". Suppose that in the above case the producer discovered that his chainsaws were frequently being sold on to consumers, perhaps in contravention of his terms of sale to the trade. Arguably once the producer discovers this, it can be said that his products are covered by the Regulations. Such difficulties will clearly arise in the case of building or gardening equipment hired out by the day, e.g. cement mixers, scaffolding, rotavators. The same is true of vans; large numbers of these are hired to consumers on a short-term basis to move house, etc., although the proportion of vans sold by producers to van and car rental companies is small compared to the sales to businesses which use the vans for their own transport purposes.

One further comment needs to be made on the definition by looking at its last sentence. Its purpose is to take outside the Regulations products which are actually being used by a trade or business even though such a product might equally be available for purchase by consumers. For example, if a hair dryer is used by a hairdresser in her salon, the equipment will fall outside the Regulations, whereas if the customer were to buy the same thing from the hairdresser, it would be covered. Taxis and private-hire cars are clearly excluded too.

16.34   (4) It does not matter whether the product has been sold or given away in view of the words "whether for consideration or not".

(5) Unlike the GSR in the 1987 Act, second-hand goods are not excluded. Indeed, the definition expressly states that a product may be "new, used or reconditioned".

However, two related exceptions appear in regs 4 and 30. A supplier of goods to be reconditioned or repaired or of antiques will not be caught provided he informed the consumer of the special facts.

Antiques are not defined. Presumably a judge would take into account whether the price reflected merely its utilitarian value or whether it took account of the age and perhaps rarity of the artefact.

The second exception will apply only where the supplier "informs" the consumer that the second-hand product is to be repaired or reconditioned before use (see reg.4). From the point of view of the supplier it will provide valuable evidence, if the sale note states this specifically.

---

[41] Contrast the 1987 Act; see para.16.10 above.

Producer

The definition is as follows: **16.35**

"producer" means

    (a) the manufacturer of a product, when he is established in a Member State and any other person presenting himself as the manufacturer by affixing to the product his name, trade mark or other distinctive mark, or the person who reconditions the product;

    (b) when the manufacturer is not established in a Member State—

        (i) if he has a representative established in a Member State, the representative,

        (ii) in any other case, the importer of the product from a state that is not a Member State into a Member State;

    (c) other professionals in the supply chain, insofar as their activities may affect the safety properties of a product;

This definition bears a close resemblance to the definition of producer given in the Product Liability Directive.[42] The definition includes businesses which are not "producers" in the ordinary sense of the word.

(1) The manufacturer himself is obviously included, but only if his business operates within the EU.

(2) Even though the producer may not be the actual manufacturer, if he gives the impression that he is the manufacturer ("presenting himself") by the way in which the goods are marked, he is treated as the producer.

(3) A business which reconditions its products is a producer, for example, a retailer taking goods in part-exchange and reselling after putting them in working order.

(4) Where there is no EU manufacturer, his representative carries the responsibility instead—presumably that means his agent. If there is no agent, the importer of the product into the EU is treated as the producer.

(5) Other businesses are also caught, even though they are merely distributors, if their "activities" may affect the product's safety. Examples would include a motor dealer conducting a pre-delivery inspection or a tyre distributor fitting replacement tyres.

Distributor

Distributor means: **16.36**

---

[42] See para.5.30 above.

a professional in the supply chain whose activity does not affect the safety properties of a product.[43]

A "distributor" is someone whose activities do not affect the product's safety;
if they do so, he will fall within the meaning of "producer" (see (5) above).
Such a business may also be a producer because of "own labelling", reconditioning or being the EU importer (see (2), (3) and (4) above).

Dangerous and safe products

16.37   A "dangerous product" is "a product other than a safe product". The latter
is defined in the following way:

> "safe product" means a product which, under normal or reasonably foreseeable
> conditions of use including duration and, where applicable, putting into service,
> installation and maintenance requirements, does not present any risk or only
> the minimum risks compatible with the product's use, considered to be accept
> able and consistent with a high level of protection for the safety and health of
> persons. In determining the foregoing, the following shall be taken into account
> in particular—
>
> (a) the characteristics of the product, including its composition, packaging,
>   instructions for assembly and, where applicable, instructions for installa
>   tion and maintenance,
> (b) the effect of the product on other products, where it is reasonably foresee
>   able that it will be used with other products,
> (c) the presentation of the product, the labelling, any warnings and instruc
>   tions for its use and disposal and any other indication or information
>   regarding the product, and
> (d) the categories of consumers at risk when using the product, in particular
>   children and the elderly.
>
> The feasibility of obtaining higher levels of safety or the availability of other
> products presenting a lesser degree of risk shall not constitute grounds for
> considering a product to be a dangerous product;

Although the wording is not exactly the same, many of the factors appearing in this definition are reminiscent of the factors mentioned in the definition of "defect" in the Product Liability Directive[44] and also in s.3 of the
1987 Act. Again, instructions are important and here they are spelt out to
include assembly, maintenance, use and disposal. One important feature
is (d), highlighting particular categories such as children who might be at
serious risk.

16.38   Another similarity appears in the sentence at the end about other
products being less risky. In s.3 of the 1987 Act the words are aimed at
later products being safer than the product in question, whereas in these
Regulations the comparison is between other products currently available.
The Regulations also acknowledge that "higher levels of safety" may be
obtained.

---

[43] reg.2.
[44] See para.5.21 above.

Clearly the definition is not imposing on producers a duty to place on the market only perfectly safe goods. No product can be absolutely safe, so that the broad test is whether the risk has been reduced to an acceptable level. The beginning of the definition indicates as much by stating that a safe product is one which "does not present any risk or only the minimum risks compatible with the product's use, considered to be acceptable and consistent with a high level of protection for the safety and health of persons". However, although a product may be safe in spite of there being "minimum risks", the emphasis on "a high level" of safety shows that producers should not be chary of spending a few pounds on introducing new safety features which will not price the goods out of the reach of the average consumer.

It should be noted, and we have made this vital point elsewhere, that the Regulations are not concerned at all with products which are shoddy and of poor quality. Their aim is simply to ensure that goods are not dangerous.

Information and monitoring

The GSR imposed on producers by reg.5 and the duty on distributors by **16.39** reg.8 are intended to fulfil that aim, i.e. to prevent dangerous goods being supplied to consumers. However, even manufacturers with high standards and excellent quality control may make mistakes and place a product on the market which has unexpected and dangerous features. As a matter of self-interest manufacturers usually monitor the use of their products and react quickly, if the products turn out to be unsafe; otherwise they might be sued in tort or prosecuted. That self-interest is bolstered by the statutory requirements in regs 7 and 8(2).

Regulation 7 is addressed to producers:

(1) Within the limits of his activities, a producer shall provide consumers with the relevant information to enable them—

    (a) to assess the risks inherent in a product throughout the normal or reasonably foreseeable period of its use, where such risks are not immediately obvious without adequate warnings, and

    (b) to take precautions against those risks.

(2) The presence of warnings does not exempt any person from compliance with the other requirements of these Regulations.

(3) Within the limits of his activities, a producer shall adopt measures commensurate with the characteristics of the products which he supplies to enable him to—

    (a) be informed of the risks which the products might pose, and

    (b) take appropriate action including, where necessary to avoid such risks, withdrawal, adequately and effectively warning consumers as to the risks or, as a last resort, recall.

(4) The measures referred to in paragraph (3) include—

    (a) except where it is not reasonable to do so, an indication by means of the product or its packaging of—

>   (i) the name and address of the producer, and
>   (ii) the product reference or where applicable the batch of products to which it belongs; and
>   (b) where and to the extent that it is reasonable to do so—
>   (i) sample testing of marketed products,
>   (ii) investigating and if necessary keeping a register of complaints concerning the safety of the product, and
>   (iii) keeping distributors informed of the results of such monitoring where a product presents a risk or may present a risk.

16.40 Regulation 8(1)(b) and (2) is addressed to distributors and is set out above in para.16.30.

These Regulations are concerned with ensuring that the consumer is informed of potential risks and dangers and so can take precautions to prevent being harmed. The second aspect of the information provisions is concerned with monitoring the products while in use, so that the producer can withdraw the product from the market, if necessary. These monitoring provisions appear in reg.7(3), backed up by the possible measures listed in reg.7(4) and coupled with the distributor's duties specified in reg.8(1)(b) and (2).

Where, probably as a result of monitoring, a producer or distributor knows that a product on the market is dangerous, reg.9 compels them to notify an enforcement authority in writing.

Compliance with EU rules

16.41 The policy adopted by the Directive and so by the Regulations, where there might be an overlap between the GSR and specific EU or UK rules, is to dis-apply the GSR in such cases. In deciding whether a product is covered by the Regulations or not the following sequence is suggested.

(1) First, consider reg.3. If *all* aspects of safety fall within specific EU rules, the Regulations do not apply at all.

(2) In contrast where such specific EU rules deal with only *some* aspects of safety, the GSR will apply to all other aspects. Regulation 3 deals with this possibility too.

(3) Where there are no EU rules one turns to reg.6(1). It provides that where a "product conforms to the specific rules of the law of part of the United Kingdom . . . the product shall be deemed safe . . .". This is self-explanatory.

(4) In the absence of the above rules the GSR applies. Regulations 6(2) and (3) give a list of factors to be taken into account in assessing whether the product conforms to the GSR, e.g. voluntary UK standards, codes of good practice and the state of the art.

Enforcement

Enforcement, as usual, is placed in the busy hands of local authority trading   **16.42**
standards services.[45] They are given substantial powers to serve various
"safety notices":

(1) "a suspension notice" to prohibit temporarily the placing of a
product on the market while they organise safety checks, etc (reg.11);

(2) "a requirement to mark" dangerous products with warnings (reg.12);

(3) "a requirement to warn" the public of risks (reg.13);

(4) "a withdrawal notice" prohibiting the placing of a product on the
market (reg.14); and

(5) "a recall notice" (reg.15). This is discussed below (para.16.43).

Regulations 16 and 17 contain a number of supplementary provisions
about safety notices and details of appeals procedures. As a final resort
enforcement authorities may apply to the court for a forfeiture order, which
will usually result in the dangerous products being destroyed (reg.18).

Recall

We have commented in early editions on the inability of public authori-   **16.43**
ties to order the recall of unsafe products which have already reached the
public. We consider the most important reform introduced by the 2001
Directive and the 2005 Regulations is the power to serve a recall notice
given by reg.15. Such a procedure is expensive for business, since the cost
of contacting customers who have the unsafe products can be enormous:
advertisements in the press and, where the current ownership is known (cars
are the best example), direct postal contact too. Regulation 15 is inevitably
very detailed to ensure that the interests of business as well as of consumers
are taken into account. Thus, a recall notice may not be served where other
action would suffice (reg.15(4)).

Compulsory recalls are rare, for businesses are keen to act quickly to
protect their own interests by recalling unsafe products voluntarily. If goods
are dangerous, civil claims by injured consumers are likely—against retailers
for breach of contract because the goods are not of satisfactory quality (see
Chapter Four) or in tort against producers under the 1987 Act or for negligence (see Chapter Five).

Frequent examples occur in the motor industry. Toyota have recalled their   **16.44**
cars a number of times since 2010 and in 2016 Volkswagen and Porsche
recalled more than 800,000 cars worldwide "as a preventative measure"
because of problems with foot pedals.

The immense cost of recalls is shown by the £5.3 billion set aside by

---

[45] reg.10.

Volkswagen in 2015 to cover the cost of recalling 11 million cars. The company was caught using illegal software to cheat in diesel emission tests in the United States. In the UK 1.2 million Volkswagens, Audis and Skodas have been affected and recalled.

An example of a compulsory recall is "Bigen" hair dye recalled in 2016. It had dangerous side effects and infringed the Cosmetic Products (Safety) Regulations.

Offences and Penalties

16.45   The offences are listed in reg.20. The most serious are contraventions of the GSR in regs 5 and 8(1)(a).[46]

The penalties, also in reg.20, are most severe for those two contraventions: a maximum of twelve months' imprisonment and a fine of £20,000, if convicted on indictment. For lesser offences the figures are three months and £5,000.

The usual "due diligence" defence is provided by reg.29.

Civil liability

16.46   The question for consumers is whether the Regulations enable a civil action to be brought. The answer is an unambiguous "no", given by reg.42. The consumer's right of action in the civil courts will be based on the contractual or the tortious position mentioned in para.16.43.

RAPEX and monitoring

16.47   In the previous pages we discussed the transposition into the law of the UK of those Articles of the Directive which are concerned with the responsibilities of producers and distributors. The 2005 Regulations are not confined to those matters. The Directive has a broader scope and deals, in the Articles and the Annex, with the duty of public authorities to monitor compliance with its provisions and to ensure that, if dangerous products reach the market, action is taken by the appropriate Member State to have them withdrawn from the market.[47]

The onus lies on the Member States to make appropriate monitoring arrangements and to establish or nominate appropriate authorities to effect compliance by suppliers with the GSR.[48] Regulations 32 to 39 deal with the interrelation between BIS, the European Commission and enforcement authorities and with market surveillance and public information.

16.48   Emergency procedures are specially built into the Directive. Where there is a "serious and immediate risk", the Member State must ensure that there is a "rapid exchange of information" between its own authorities.[49] If the

---

[46] See para.16.31 above.
[47] art.6.
[48] art.6.
[49] Food is excluded from RAPEX.

grave risk is not merely local, it must immediately inform the Commission.[50] RAPEX (the Community System of Rapid Exchange of Information) was originally introduced in 1984 by a Council decision.[51] BIS is the central contact point for RAPEX in the UK.

In limited circumstances the Commission may take the initiative[52]—there was some anxiety in a number of countries that the Brussels bureaucracy, as they saw it, would be too keen to interfere. The Commission will be assisted by a new Committee on Product Safety Emergencies.

Safety of services

Neither the EU Directives nor home grown UK legislation extend beyond the safety of goods to cover services too. Recently, however, there has been some activity in Brussels on this important topic. The European Commission published a consultation paper "*Safety of Services*" in August 2002 suggesting a number of options such as data collection to monitor the safety of service activities. The most significant proposal was a general safety obligation on service providers similar to the GSR in the 2001 GPS Directive. It appears from the EC Commission's report to the Council and Parliament in June 2003 that lack of evidence of specific internal market problems makes it difficult to justify substantive Community action. Even so, six months later the ball was gently played back to the Commission by a Council Resolution[53] asking the Commission to consider how far safety might be improved by adopting European standards on services and to bring forward proposals for action by October 2004. We still await developments with interest, but probably not in the immediate future.

16.49

Proposed reforms

In Brussels the Commission staff have been busy again. On 13 February 2013 they published a *Product Safety and Market Surveillance Package* (COM (2013) 78 final) (*the Package*) containing proposals for new Regulations on Consumer Product Safety and on Market Surveillance. If adopted, they would repeal the 2001 GPS Directive and also transfer the market surveillance provisions and RAPEX to the new Market Surveillance Regulation.

16.50

The *Proposal for an EU Regulation on Consumer Product Safety* and the *Proposal for a Regulation on Market Surveillance* are explained in BIS/13/1045. A *Summary of the Responses to Consultation* is given in BIS/13/1295.

One of the main reasons for the delay in adopting *the Package* has been the UK industry's strong objection to the introduction of origin marking— the indication of country of origin by manufacturers and distributors. Its purpose is apparently to facilitate greater traceability. It is arguable that the strict liability imposed on producers by Pt 1 of the 1987 Act has already

16.51

---

[50] reg.33(5); art.12.
[51] See now Commision Decision of 16 December 2009 laying down guidelines for management of RAPEX (2010/15).
[52] art.13. See reg.35.
[53] [2003] OJ/C299/1.

achieved this objective. Retailers and intermediate distributors, if held liable to their buyers, will want to pass the buck up the supply chain, as will end producers vis-à-vis their component or materials suppliers. So traceability has been crucial for decades.

By the time the Eleventh Edition of this book is published *the Package* may have reached its destination.

CHAPTER SEVENTEEN

CRIME AND COMPENSATION

1. INTRODUCTION

A commonly held view of the consumer protection lobby is that it is a waste **17.01** of effort for Parliament to amend and improve upon the long-standing statutory rights of consumers and to launch assaults across a broad front on attempts to rob the consumer of those rights by unfair terms. Often consumers clearly have a right of action for breach of contract, but of what benefit are their rights unless machinery exists to enable them to be enforced without difficulty? The real need is for reform to be concentrated upon the enforcement of existing rights rather than the creation of new ones and for information and education to ensure that consumers are aware of those rights.

We discussed in Chapter Eleven enforcement under the civil law. We saw that frequently the consumer has no alternative to suing the recalcitrant trader in the county court; for there is often no ombudsman scheme in a particular sector nor even a trade association able or prepared to bring about a settlement of the complaint by conciliation or to discipline the trader for falling below the standards set out in a code of practice. In such circumstances there are clearly considerable advantages to consumers if they can reap some benefit from the fact that the trader has committed a criminal offence in addition to having broken one of its civil obligations. However, it should be borne in mind that criminal offences are not created for the purpose of providing consumers with compensation, as was pointed out in para.281 of the 1976 Review of the Trade Descriptions Act 1968:

> We believe that compensation is primarily a matter for the civil law, and that an award of compensation under the Powers of the Criminal Courts Act should be regarded as a windfall rather than a right which itself justified prosecution under the Act.

It is proposed in this chapter to deal with two aspects of recovery arising out of the criminal law. First, we shall look at the power of the courts on conviction to award compensation under the Powers of Criminal Courts (Sentencing) Act 2000 (the 2000 Act). Secondly, we shall consider the circumstances in which it is possible to sue for breach of statutory duty.[1]

---

[1] See para.17.10 below.

2. Powers of Criminal Courts (Sentencing) Act 2000

17.02 The recommendations of the 1970 Widgery Report with regard to the remedies available under the criminal law for compensating victims of crime were broadly carried into effect by the Criminal Justice Act 1972. The particular provision which now concerns us was replaced by s.130 of the 2000 Act.[2]

In essence it enables the court to order a convicted person to pay compensation for any damage resulting from the offence. The section states:

> A court by or before which a person is convicted of an offence, instead of or in addition to dealing with him in any other way, may, on application or otherwise, make an order (in this Act referred to as "a compensation order") requiring him (a) to pay compensation for any personal injury, loss or damage resulting from that offence or any other offence which is taken into consideration by the court in determining sentence.

This discretionary power is available whenever there has been a conviction in any court, including a magistrates' court. It is especially valuable in cases where the loss may be too small to justify the cost of civil litigation.

Maximum

17.03 The amount of compensation where the conviction is on indictment in the Crown Court is unlimited.

In *R. v Connors (Patrick)*[3] C was convicted on indictment of the offence of aggressive commercial practice.

> He had coerced a man of 81 into agreeing to a series of works at his house, e.g. a block paving drive, a special drain, redecoration and a roof repair. The victim paid £16,400 cash. The works were carried out either badly or not at all. C's appeal to the Court of Appeal against a compensation order of £16,400 was dismissed.

In the magistrates' court it is limited to £5,000.[4] This limit relates to each offence of which the accused is convicted; so if a supplier is convicted of four offences, the order may reach £20,000.

Special care must be taken when the accused asks for other offences to be taken into consideration for which he has not been prosecuted. No additional sums may be awarded in respect of such t.i.c. offences.[5]

Example

17.04 A tour operator publishes a brochure containing false statements in contravention of reg.5 of the Package Travel Regulations 1992.[6] Forty people from different parts of the UK book holidays in reliance on the brochure. The tour

---

[2] Itself replacing the Powers of Criminal Courts Act 1973.
[3] [2012] EWCA Crim 2106.
[4] s.131 of the 2000 Act.
[5] See H. Street, "Compensation Orders and the Trade Descriptions Act" [1974] Crim. L.R. 345.
[6] See para.7.06 above.

operator, when prosecuted in one area, asks for the 39 other offences to be taken into consideration. The magistrates' order for the 40 offences cannot exceed £5,000 in total.

From the point of view of the victims in this example it would be preferable for separate charges to be brought in each area, so that altogether the orders would have a ceiling of £200,000.

Type of loss

The compensation may relate to "any personal injury, loss or damage". **17.05** Thus claims for breach of contract or for the tort of negligence are covered. Further, the Act is wide enough for an order to be made in respect of loss for which no civil remedy is available: in such a case in the absence of a successful prosecution the victim has no remedy.[7]

Assessment

As the assessment of compensation will commonly be made by lay magis- **17.06** trates, it is inappropriate for the power to be exercised in complicated cases, e.g. where the principles of remoteness of damage need to be understood and applied. An order will be made only in straightforward cases. Lawton LJ explained the court's approach in *R. v Thomson Holidays Ltd*[8]:

> "Parliament, we are sure, never intended to introduce into the criminal law the concepts of causation which apply to the assessment of damages under the law of contract or tort. . . . [The court] must do what it can to make a just order on such information as it has. Whenever the making of an order for compensation is appropriate, the court must ask itself whether loss or damage can fairly be said to have resulted to anyone from the offence for which the accused has been convicted."[9]

The defendants were convicted under s.14 of the Trade Descriptions Act 1968 for making a false statement in their brochure that a hotel had a night club and swimming and paddling pools. Compensation of £50 was awarded to the complainant.

A separate point to bear in mind is that the victim must show that the defendant is liable for the amount claimed. In *R v Vivian*[10] the Court of Appeal quashed an order in respect of damage to a car alleged to have been done by a thief in a collision, as there was no proof that he was responsible for all the damage: further, the appellant claimed that the sole estimate given for the repairs was excessive. Talbot J. said[11] that the view of the court was that "no order for compensation should be made unless the sum claimed by

---

[7] See *R. v Chappel* [1984] Crim. L.R. 574.
[8] [1974] Q.B. 592 at 599. See also *Stapylton v R* [2012] EWCA Crim 728.
[9] See also *R. v Daly* [1974] 1 All E.R. 290; *R. v Kneeshaw* [1974] 1 All E.R. 896: the machinery is intended "for clear and simple cases" (per Lord Widgery CJ).
[10] [1979] 1 All E.R. 48.
[11] [1979] 1 All E.R. 48 at 50.

way of compensation is either agreed or has been proved". This appears to leave a large loophole for defendants and certainly makes it necessary in this type of case for victims to be less perfunctory in preparing claims, e.g. by obtaining more than one estimate.

17.07   Situations where it would be appropriate to make an order include misdescribed goods, e.g. clocked or misdescribed cars, where the reduction in value or cost of repair can be easily proved, and holiday cases where part of the cost can be refunded to take account of inconvenience and loss of enjoyment.

In determining whether to make an order and, if so, for what amount, the court must take into account the defendant's means[12] and generally limits the award to a sum which he can manage to pay over two or three years. Thus in *R. v McIntosh*[13] the Court of Appeal revoked a £90 order against a burglar on the grounds that he had no means and would find it hard to obtain employment on his release from prison because of his wooden leg— surprisingly not an impediment to the nefarious activities of this Long John McSilver in a trade where one would expect agility to be a sine qua non! Similarly it is not generally appropriate to make an order where the defendant is sentenced to a significant period of imprisonment, unless he has assets in hand to pay the compensation.[14]

How to apply

17.08   No procedure is laid down for making the application for compensation. Generally it is enough for the victim to forewarn the clerk or prosecutor before the trial commences, so that the application may be brought to the notice of the court after conviction and the victim then heard. Alternatively the court may act of its initiative without an application. Although it is customary for the prosecution to pass on a request for compensation, they are not under a duty to conduct an inquiry into the defendant's means.[15]

An order is enforceable in the same ways as a fine. Thus the court may impose a term of imprisonment in default.

Interrelation with civil claims

17.09   Generally the trial of the criminal charge will be held some time before any civil proceedings reach that stage. In the subsequent civil proceedings two points must be borne in mind. First, the conviction may be used in evidence.[16] Secondly, when awarding damages the court must take into account sums paid under the order.[17]

If exceptionally the civil proceedings have already come to an end, whether

---

[12] s.35(4).
[13] [1973] Crim. L.R. 378. See also *Stapylton v R* [2012] EWCA Crim 728: award of £8,500 at £100 per month quashed.
[14] *R. v McCullough* (1982) 4 Cr. App. R. (S.) 98 CA; *R. v Morgan* (1982) 4 Cr. App. R. (S.) 358 CA.
[15] *R. v Johnstone* (1982) 4 Cr. App. R. (S.) 141.
[16] s.11 of the Civil Evidence Act 1968.
[17] s.134(2).

by judgment or settlement, no order can be made even though the victim can still show loss. In *Hammertons Cars Ltd v London Borough of Redbridge*[18]:

> The complainant bought a car described as "in perfect condition". It was not. He settled an action against the sellers on the basis that he paid his own legal costs of £170 and expert's fee of £25. When the sellers were convicted under the Trade Descriptions Act he was awarded £195 compensation by the justices. The dealer successfully appealed against the order to the Divisional Court.

Lord Widgery CJ, doubting whether in any case the section would cover such legal costs, said:

> "It seems to me to be abundantly clear that if the victim brings civil proceedings, and those civil proceedings are brought to an end, then they should be regarded as quite independent of the criminal proceedings and no compensation order should be made in respect of liabilities which arose, or might have arisen, in the civil proceedings."

3. BREACH OF STATUTORY DUTY

17.10 As has been seen earlier, frequently a consumer who has suffered loss will have a remedy flowing directly or indirectly from the civil or criminal law. As far as the civil law is concerned, the remedy may be for breach of contract, e.g. against a supplier of goods or services who has not fulfilled obligations imposed upon him by statute or the common law, or in tort for negligence or under the Consumer Protection Act 1987, e.g. against a manufacturer. Alternatively or additionally, where the supplier's activities involve a criminal offence resulting in a successful prosecution, the consumer may seek compensation under the 2000 Act discussed above.

However, a hiatus exists where the supplier has not broken a contract with the consumer, maybe because they are not in a contractual relationship; nor has he been negligent; nor does Pt 1 of the Consumer Protection Act 1987, apply, perhaps because the damage is too small; nor has the consumer recovered compensation, even though the supplier has committed a criminal offence, e.g. because no prosecution was brought. In such circumstances the consumer's last resort is to try to show that the supplier is liable in tort for breach of statutory duty.

If it were possible for such an action to be brought in every case where a supplier has failed to comply with its statutory duties, the consumers' position would be much more straightforward. In the absence of an award of compensation under the 2000 Act, they would be able to institute civil proceedings on this basis without concerning themselves with such questions as privity of contract with the supplier.

17.11 However, the courts when construing statutes have been reluctant to imply into them civil rights for the victim. The rationale seems to be that the legislation is for the protection of the public generally and is not intended to

---

[18] [1974] 2 All E.R. 216.

afford a civil remedy to individual members of the public. The reasoning is unconvincing. To draw an analogy from the contractual principles of offer and acceptance, where an offer is made to the world at large, contracts are formed only with those individuals who accept the offer; similarly where a duty is imposed on suppliers for the benefit of the public at large, it should be possible for those particular members of the public who suffer loss as a result of a breach of that duty to come forward and claim damages in a civil action founded upon that statutory duty.

Yet generally the courts are content to leave consumers to their separate civil rights. Thus in *Square v Model Farm Dairies (Bournemouth) Ltd*,[19] where the plaintiff alleged that contaminated milk sold in breach of the food legislation had made his family ill with typhoid fever, the Court of Appeal rejected his claim because he had a remedy under the Sale of Goods Act 1979. A comparable case is *Buckley v La Réserve*[20] where an action failed against a restaurant which, in contravention of the Food and Drugs Act 1955, sold food unfit for human consumption (the food was snails: legal symmetry would have been attained had the contamination of the snails resulted from ginger beer[21]). It is important to note that on the particular facts the plaintiff's civil rights would not have given him a remedy unless he could prove negligence, as he was taken to the restaurant as a guest, and had no contractual claim against the restaurant: nevertheless the court adopted the same stance as in the *Square* case.

17.12   Two cases involving defective cars also illustrate the courts' unhelpful attitude to consumers. In *Phillips v Britannia Hygienic Laundry Co*[22] the plaintiff failed to recover for injuries resulting from the defendants' breach of duties imposed by the antecedents to the Motor Vehicles (Construction and Use) Regulations.[23] Similarly a seller was not liable to a victim injured by a vehicle which the seller delivered in such a condition that its use on the road was unlawful, although he thereby committed an offence under the Road Traffic Act.[24]

The courts' restrictive interpretation leads to this principle in the consumer field: an action for breach of statutory duty has a chance of success only if the statute expressly states that a breach of the duty is actionable, e.g. s.41(1) of the Consumer Protection Act 1987[25]:

> An obligation imposed by safety regulations shall be a duty owed to any person who may be affected by a contravention of the obligation and, subject to any provision to the contrary in the regulations and to the defences and other incidents applying to actions for breach of statutory duty, a contravention of any such obligation shall be actionable accordingly.

---

[19] [1939] 2 K.B. 365.
[20] [1959] Crim. L.R. 451.
[21] See *Donoghue v Stevenson* [1932] A.C. 562 (see para.5.46 above).
[22] [1923] 2 K.B. 832.
[23] SI 1986/1078.
[24] *Badham v Lambs Ltd* [1946] K.B. 45.
[25] See para.16.25 above. For another example, see s.92(3) of the Consumer Credit Act 1974: entry to premises to recover possession of goods or land, see para.26.24 below.

Where a statute states the opposite, the position is equally clear. Where a statute is silent on the point, the presumption is that it gives no civil remedy. Such a presumption is strengthened where the statute expressly preserves other civil remedies, following the reasoning in *Square v Model Farm Dairies (Bournemouth) Ltd*,[26] for then Parliament is implicitly leaving the public to their general civil rights.

[26] See para.17.11 above.

Part III

ADMINISTRATIVE CONTROL

CHAPTER EIGHTEEN

"THEY'RE TRADING UNFAIRLY"

The civil and criminal sanctions discussed earlier in this book do a great deal **18.01**
to protect the consumer, but by themselves they are not enough. In particular:

(1) Industry is never static for long and the enterprising trader is likely to come up with new business practices. Some of these, while within the law, may be harmful to consumers and swift action may be needed to curtail them.

(2) There are a number of dishonest or inefficient traders who make large profits, e.g. by the delivery of shoddy goods. They may not be deterred by the occasional fine or award of damages. What the consumer really needs is a system whereby such traders can be restrained from trading altogether unless they mend their ways.

(3) The standards set by the law are minimum standards and the consumer can benefit if traders can be persuaded to undertake additional voluntary obligations.

(4) Neither the civil nor the criminal law achieves one of the most important aims of consumer protection—making consumers aware of their rights.

It is at this point that we meet the third weapon of consumer protection— **18.02**
administrative control. This involves a public body charged with the task of keeping the consumer scene under permanent review. The principal weapons of administrative control are to be found in the Enterprise Act 2002 (replacing the Fair Trading Act 1973 (the 1973 Act), see para.18.13 below), the Consumer Credit Act 1974 (see Chapters Nineteen to Twenty-Eight) and the Consumer Protection from Unfair Trading Regulations 2008 (the 2008 Regulations) (see para.18.36 below). For a further example of administrative control see Chapter Ten.

The scheme of this chapter is as follows:

(1) The Fair Trading Act 1973 will be considered first to put the current regime in historical perspective.

(2) Stop Now Orders will be briefly discussed, as their life was brief—from 2001 to 2003.

(3) The Enterprise Act 2002 will then be considered with its regime

dealing with both domestic and European Union infringements of the law; as well as the new 'enhanced consumer measures' added to the Enterprise Act by the Consumer Rights Act 2015 (CRA 2015).

(4) The Unfair Commercial Practices Directive 2005 and the 2008 Regulations, which have already had a significant impact on consumer protection, follow next.

(5) *The Business Protection from Misleading Marketing Regulations 2008*, will be discussed in the last section.

1. THE FAIR TRADING ACT 1973

18.03   The 1973 Act appeared out of the blue with no warning or consultation in the form of Green or White Papers.

Most of the Act did not break new ground inasmuch as broadly it consolidated, with some changes and improvements, the pre-existing law relating to competition. It gave the Director General of Fair Trading power to initiate subordinate legislation to protect the consumer by banning undesirable trade practices as and when they appeared (Pt II). It also enabled the Director General to bring into line individual rogue traders who regularly flouted their legal obligations (Pt III).

The essential difference between Pts II and III of the 1973 Act was that Pt II was concerned with undesirable *practices*, whereas Pt III was concerned with undesirable *traders*.

Part II—Adverse Consumer Trade Practices[1]

18.04   The point of Pt II was to refer consumer trade practices to the Consumer Protection Advisory Committee (the CPAC). A reference under s.14 could be made by the Director General or any Minister. The CPAC considered "whether a consumer trade practice specified in the reference adversely affects the economic interest of consumers".

The Secretary of State could make an order giving effect to the proposals. The intention and expectation was that it would be possible to identify new abuses at an early stage and to squash the practice before it mushroomed.

Three Orders

18.05   Only three orders were made and then Pt II was repealed by the Enterprise Act 2002.

(1) The Consumer Transactions (Restrictions on Statements) Order 1976 (SI 1976/1813) attacked the continuing use of void exemption clauses (e.g. "No money back on sale goods"). It also compelled retailers and manufacturers who chose to give guarantees or war-

---

[1] See early editions of this book for a detailed analysis of Pts II and III.

ranties with their goods to state that these did not affect the buyers' statutory rights.

(2) The Mail Order Transactions (Information) Order 1976 (SI 1976/1812) concerned suppliers requiring prepayment or deposits without specifying, or keeping to, delivery dates. This was revoked and its provisions incorporated in the Consumer Protection (Distance Selling) Regulations 2000 (SI 2000/2334) discussed in Chapter Six.

(3) The Business Advertisements (Disclosure) Order 1977 (SI 1977/1918) required business sellers to make it clear, in their advertisements to consumers, that they were traders to prevent them masquerading as private sellers.

Their replacements

The Consumer Transactions (Restrictions on Statements) Order 1976 and   **18.06**
The Business Advertisements (Disclosure) Order 1977 remained in force until they were revoked by the 2008 Regulations on 26 May 2008. However, the malpractices which they attacked continue to be offences.

The Consumer Transactions (Restrictions on Statements) Order 1976 has been replaced by provisions in the CRA 2015: reg.15(2A) deals with the guarantee aspect (see paras 5.05 and 5.06 above).[2] The other aspect of this Order is covered by reg.5(2)(a) and (4)(k) of the 2008 Regulations: a misleading action includes false information about "the consumer's rights". This is discussed in para.18.45 below.

The Business Advertisements (Disclosure) Order 1977 has also been replaced by the 2008 Regulations. The black list of unfair practices in Sch.1 includes para.22:

Falsely claiming or creating the impression that the trader is not acting for purposes relating to his trade, business, craft or profession, or falsely representing oneself as a consumer.

This is an offence under reg.12.

Part III—Persistently Unfair Traders

During its 30 years' existence, until the repeal of Pt III by the Enterprise Act   **18.07**
2002, hundreds of assurances were obtained covering diverse activities. Used car dealers, home improvement firms, sellers of electrical goods and mail order businesses figured most prominently.

The first assurance in 1974 was typical in so far as it covered three improper practices, namely, Trade Descriptions Act offences, breaches of the Sale of Goods Act 1979 implied conditions and the non-delivery of goods paid for in advance.

---

[2] The 2008 Regulations Sch.2 para.97.

Section 34(1) required the Director General to try to obtain an assurance where a person had "persisted in a course of conduct" which was "unfair to consumers".

Proposals for reform

18.08   The Office of Fair Trading (OFT) in its 1996 consultation paper *Consumer Affairs Strategy* stated that it had "long argued for reform" of Pt III because its effectiveness was "widely recognised to be limited, as a result of both the time which it may take to conclude cases, and of the relatively weak sanctions available".

Finally in July 1999 the Department of Trade and Industry (DTI) published its wide-ranging White Paper, *Modern Markets: confident consumers* (Cm. 4410). It stated (para.7.5):

> • The level of criminal sanctions, and the risk of civil action by consumers, do not deter determined rogues who continue to carry on unlawful conduct where the profits outweigh the occasional judicial setback and where they can live with an adverse effect on their reputation. This problem is compounded by the time it takes to enforce some of the existing legislative provisions. This enables the rogue trader to keep ahead of the authorities.
>
> • There is no means of preventing a rogue trader from continuing to pose a threat to consumers by moving from one dishonest practice to another.

It proposed to amend the 1973 Act by empowering the courts "to grant injunctions against specific practices carried out by specific traders" and by extending to trading standards departments the powers under Pt III hitherto exercised by the OFT only. These reforms were effected by the Enterprise Act 2002.

2. STOP NOW ORDERS (SNORS)

18.09   Before the Government had found Parliamentary time to bring in its proposed reforms to Pt III of the 1973 Act Brussels intervened in the shape of Directive 98/27/EC on Injunctions for the protection of consumers' interests (the Injunctions Directive), which had to be transposed into UK law by 1 January 2001. It was implemented late by the Stop Now Orders (EC Directive) Regulations 2001,[3] which came into force on 1 June 2001.

Injunctions Directive

18.10   The Injunctions Directive and the Regulations were concerned only with EU legislation (as implemented by the Member States). Thus in the UK two separate systems ran in parallel until both were replaced by the Enterprise Act 2002—Stop Now Orders for "Community infringements" and Pt III for domestic infringements of "home grown" UK law.

---

[3] SI 2001/1422 (known as SNORs).

Its purpose is clearly explained in the DTI Consultation Paper (February 2000) on its implementation:

> The purpose of the Directive is to permit consumer protection bodies to apply to the courts or competent administrative authorities both in their own and in other Member States for orders to stop traders infringing the legislation implementing nine specific consumer protection directives where these infringements harm the collective interests of consumers. It is not intended as a means of seeking redress for individual consumers.

The Injunctions Directive listed nine Directives, but the Regulations added a tenth adopted after the Injunctions Directive. Others have been added since. They cover the following areas:

Doorstep selling

Consumer credit

Television broadcasting

Package travel

Medicines

Unfair terms

Timeshare

Distance selling

Sale of consumer goods and guarantees.

Electronic commerce

Air travel

Unfair commercial practices

Enforcement

For Community infringements the Pt III regime was replaced by new provisions set out in Sch.2 to the Regulations. The new procedures formed the model for those now in force under the Enterprise Act 2002 discussed below.   **18.11**

One major change was that enforcement was (and is) no longer limited to the OFT. "Qualified entities", both public bodies and others, could do so. The "public UK qualified entities" were specified in Sch.3 and included trading standards departments and statutory regulators (e.g. gas, water, rail) following the approach adopted by the Unfair Terms in Consumer Contracts Regulations 1999. The "lead body" to coordinate enforcement was the OFT.

In addition "other UK qualified entities" could be designated by   **18.12**
the DTI. As the Directive is concerned with enforcement throughout Europe, "Community qualified entities" could also bring proceedings in any Member State: they are listed in the Official Journal under art.4.3 of the Directive.

Two separate systems aimed at rectifying similar conduct by similar traders were confusing and onerous. As *Consumer reforms*,[4] an OFT consultation paper on the Enterprise Bill, stated, "Part 8 of the Enterprise Bill simplifies this structure by establishing a more consistent enforcement regime. This will enable injunctive action to be taken against traders who infringe a wider range of consumer protection legislation". We now turn to that regime.

3. THE ENTERPRISE ACT 2002

18.13 The Enterprise Act 2002 (the 2002 Act) is an immense piece of legislation covering both competition law (Competition Appeal Tribunal, mergers, market investigation references, cartels) and consumer law enforcement. We are concerned with the last item which is contained in Pt 8 of the 2002 Act and came into force on 20 June 2003.

We pointed out in para.18.12 that the new enforcement regime put in place by the 2002 Act is based on SNORs. However, with the repeal of Pt III of the 1973 Act[5] a similar framework applies to all UK legislation whether or not it emanated from Brussels.

There are inevitably some detailed differences, since the enforcement of EU infringements must comply with the Injunctions Directive, whereas the control of domestic infringements is not subject to such limitations.

Domestic infringements

18.14 A domestic infringement is defined by s.211 as follows:

(1) In this Part a domestic infringement is an act or omission which—

    (a) is done or made by a person in the course of a business,
    (b) falls within subsection (2), and
    (c) harms the collective interests of consumers in the United Kingdom.

(2) An act or omission falls within this subsection if it is of a description specified by the Secretary of State by order and consists of any of the following—

    (a) a contravention of an enactment which imposes a duty, prohibition or restriction enforceable by criminal proceedings;
    (b) an act done or omission made in breach of contract;
    (c) an act done or omission made in breach of a non-contractual duty owed to a person by virtue of an enactment or rule of law and enforceable by civil proceedings;
    (d) an act or omission in respect of which an enactment provides for a remedy or sanction enforceable by civil proceedings;
    (e) an act done or omission made by a person supplying or seeking to supply goods or services as a result of which an agreement or security relating to the supply is void or unenforceable to any extent;
    (f) an act or omission by which a person supplying or seeking to supply goods or services purports or attempts to exercise a right or remedy relating to

---

[4] OFT 502 (August 2002).
[5] Sch.26.

the supply in circumstances where the exercise of the right or remedy is restricted or excluded under or by virtue of an enactment;

(g) an act or omission by which a person supplying or seeking to supply goods or services purports or attempts to avoid (to any extent) liability relating to the supply in circumstances where such avoidance is restricted or prevented under an enactment.

There are three requirements: **18.15**

(1) The act or omission must be "in the course of a business", defined by s.210(8) to include a profession and undertaking "for gain or reward" or "otherwise than free of charge".

(2) It harms the collective interests of UK consumers. A "consumer", as defined by s.210(2), (3) and (4), is an individual to whom goods or services are (or are sought to be) supplied by a business. The individual must not be a business customer, although they may be setting up in business but not yet trading ("with a view to carrying on. . .").[6]

(3) It falls within the exhaustive list in s.211(2). For example, (a) covers safety offences,[7] (b) a breach of the terms as to quality, fitness, etc. in the CRA 2015 and (c) tortious liability under Pt I of the Consumer Protection Act 1987. Section 211(2) also requires the conduct to be "of a description specified by the Secretary of State by order". The specified list is a long one[8] and, in addition to more than fifty pieces of primary and secondary legislation, includes common law breaches too. This was to be expected, in view of the references to "breach of contract" and "enactment or rule of law" in s.211(2)(b) and (c).

Community infringements

Community infringements may result in enforcement in the UK or in another   **18.16**
state in the European Economic Area (EEA). As far as the UK is concerned, they are defined by s.212.

(1) In this Part a Community infringement is an act or omission which harms the collective interests of consumers and which—

(a) contravenes a listed Directive as given effect by the laws, regulations or administrative provisions of an EEA State, or

(b) contravenes such laws, regulations or administrative provisions which provide additional permitted protections.

(2) The laws, regulations or administrative provisions of an EEA State which give effect to a listed Directive provide additional permitted protections if—

---

[6] s.210(4)(b).
[7] See Chapter Sixteen.
[8] Enterprise Act 2002 (Pt 8 Domestic Infringements) Order 2003 (SI 2003/1593).

(a) they provide protection for consumers which is in addition to the minimum protection required by the Directive concerned, and

(b) such additional protection is permitted by that Directive.

(3) The Secretary of State may by order specify for the purposes of this section the law in the United Kingdom which—

(a) gives effect to the listed Directives;

(b) provides additional permitted protections.

"Consumer" in this context has a different meaning from that in s.211, for by s.210(6) it means "a person who is a consumer for the purposes of (a) the Injunctions Directive, and (b) the listed Directive concerned". A listed Directive is an EU Directive specified, wholly or partly, in Sch.13 to the 2002 Act. Consequently each Directive must be checked to see whether in a particular case "the collective interest of" such consumers is harmed.

Enforcers

18.17 We saw that enforcement of the SNORs was in hands of three types of "entities".[9] This pattern is repeated, though their names are changed to "enforcers" and the three types are differently constituted. Section 213 creates the new structure. A fourth type—CPC enforcers—was added in 2006.

General enforcers

18.18 There are three categories: the Competition and Markets Authority (CMA), every trading standards department in Great Britain (called a "weights and measures authority") and the Department of Enterprise, Trade and Investment in Northern Ireland.

Designated enforcers

18.19 The Secretary of State may designate a body by order, if he thinks that it "has as one of its purposes the protection of the collective interests of consumers". If that general precondition is satisfied, then he may choose "a public body only if he is satisfied that it is independent" or any other (private) body which "satisfies such criteria as [he] specifies by order".[10]

So far he has designated only public bodies as enforcers. They are the Civil Aviation Authority, the Information Commissioner, the Office of the Rail Regulator, the Gas and Electricity Markets Authority and the Director Generals of Telecommunications, of Water Services and of Gas and of Electricity Supply for Northern Ireland.[11] He has also issued guidance on the criteria for private bodies.

---

[9] See para.18.12 above.

[10] See s.213(2), (3) and (4). An order may designate an enforcer for all or only some infringements (s.213 (6)). cf. the "super-complaints" procedure for consumer bodies designated under s.11(5) to make a complaint to the Competition and Markets Authority e.g. Which?, Citizens Advice.

[11] SI 2003/1399.

Community enforcers

A Community enforcer is a "qualified entity" for the purposes of the **18.20**
Injunctions Directive as listed in the Official Journal under art.4.3, but not a
general or designated enforcer, so only enforcers from other EEA states may
be such.[12]

CPC enforcers

The EU Regulation on Consumer Protection Cooperation (Regulation (EC) **18.21**
No.2006/2004 as amended by the UCPD) (CPC) requires the creation of
a network of enforcement bodies across the EU to stamp out cross border
infringements. A new s.215 (5A) has been added by the Enterprise Act 2002
(Amendment) Regulations 2006 (SI 2006/3363) designating the CPC enforcers. They include the CAA, Financial Conduct Authority (FCA), Ofcom and
all the general enforcers (see above).

What can they enforce?

General enforcers can apply for an enforcement order in respect of any **18.22**
infringement, domestic or Community. Designated enforcers are limited
to infringements to which their designation relates. Community and CPC
enforcers may act only in respect of a Community infringement.[13]

Enforcement procedure

Coordination by Competition and Markets Authority

Because of the range of enforcers there is a danger of overlap and duplication **18.23**
of proceedings. By s.216 the CMA is given the lead role of coordinator. It
may direct that only itself or a specified enforcer may apply for an enforcement order. This power, though, does not extend to controlling Community
enforcers. (SNORs had similar provisions.)

Consultation and undertakings

Another replication of SNORs appears in s.214. Before applying for an order **18.24**
an enforcer must consult the business and the CMA to try to ensure that the
infringement ceases and is not repeated. The consultation period is normally
14 days, but seven days suffice in the case of an interim order and consultation may be dispensed with altogether, if the CMA thinks that there should
be no delay in applying to the court.

    As action in the courts is intended to be used as a last resort, under s.219
enforcers may accept an undertaking that the business will not "continue or
repeat the conduct" or "engage in such conduct in the course of his business
or another business".[14] The last two words are to prevent the culprit from

---

[12] See para.18.12 above, s.213(5).
[13] s.215(2), (3), (4) and (4A).
[14] s.219(4).

carrying on his malpractices by setting up or moving to a different business. If the business complies with the undertaking, that will be the end of the matter. The enforcer must notify the CMA of the undertaking, so that monitoring may take place. If the undertaking is broken, the courts are the next step.

Applications to the court

18.25 Applications for an enforcement order—the expression "Stop Now Orders" is obsolete—are made to the High Court or county court (or Court of Session or sheriff in Scotland).[15] Section 217 empowers the court to make an enforcement order.

> (1) This section applies if an application for an enforcement order is made under section 215 and the court finds that the person named in the application has engaged in conduct which constitutes the infringement.
> (2) This section also applies if such an application is made in relation to a Community infringement and the court finds that the person named in the application is likely to engage in conduct which constitutes the infringement.
> (3) If this section applies the court may make an enforcement order against the person.
> (4) In considering whether to make an enforcement order the court must have regard to whether the person named in the application—
>
> > (a) has given an undertaking under section 219 in respect of conduct such as is mentioned in subsection (3) of that section;
> > (b) has failed to comply with the undertaking."[16]

18.26 It can be seen from s.217(1) and (2) that an odd distinction is made between Community infringements and domestic ones. For a domestic infringement, which falls within s.217(1), the court must find that the defendant "has engaged" in the conduct. For a Community infringement, which falls within s.217(1) and (2), it is enough if the defendant "is likely" to do so. (This distinction also appears elsewhere in Pt 8.) The reason, it seems, is that the Government thought that the wording of the Injunctions Directive covered not merely past and present infringements but also future ones in that art.2.1(a) talks of "requiring the cessation *or prohibition* of any infringement" (emphasis supplied). We are not convinced, as the preamble and other articles do not suggest such a wide interpretation. In any case, for the sake of conformity, why not make domestic infringements all-embracing too? In practice, where no infringement has already taken place, it may be an impossible task for enforcers to find convincing evidence to prove this "likelihood".

Where "it is expedient that the conduct is prohibited or prevented . . . immediately", s.218 enables the court to make an interim order.

Finally, instead of making an order, the court may accept an undertaking.[17]

---

[15] s.215(5).
[16] See OFT Press Release 17/11, 23 June 2011: order against *Avora Tech Ltd* in Cardiff County Court for refusal to give refunds.
[17] s.217(9) and s.218(10).

What happens if a business fails to comply with an enforcement order or an undertaking given to the court? The usual sanction for such bold conduct ensues—it is contempt of court, so prison could be the culprit's resting place.

Companies and accessories

There are complex provisions in ss.222 and 223 where the business is a "body **18.27** corporate". They enable the court to make orders against "accessories" such as directors and managers and against members of a group of companies where, for example, two companies are subsidiaries of the same parent company. A "controller" may also be sanctioned, e.g. someone with at least a third of the voting power at any general meeting either personally or with "associates" (a broad list including "the spouse of a relative of the individual's spouse" and a business partner).[18] This should obviate the rogue's ruse of putting his business apparently in the hands of others, while in reality running it himself.

Information and guidance

The OFT (now the CMA) has always taken seriously its role of providing **18.28** information to consumers and business. Section 229(1A) continues the practice by imposing on the CMA a duty to publish advice and information "to explain the provisions" of Pt 8 and to indicate "how the Competition and Markets Authority expects such provisions to operate".[19]

Enhanced Consumer Measures

Schedule 7 to the CRA 2015 has amended Pt 8 of the 2002 Act to introduce **18.29** the option of so called "enhanced consumer measures" (ECMs). So, ss.217– 219 of the 2002 Act now provide that where a court makes an enforcement order or accepts an undertaking under Pt 8 of the 2002 Act it may also attach ECMs to such an enforcement order or undertaking, and where an enforcer (such as a trading standards officer) obtains an undertaking, such an undertaking can also include ECMs.

A new s.219A provides for three categories of ECM:

- The redress category;
- The compliance category; and
- The choice category.

The redress category aims to facilitate redress for consumers who suffer loss as a result of breaches of consumer law (e.g. compensation, a refund, or other

---

[18] s.222(3), (4), (10), (11) and (12).
[19] s.6 also permits the OFT to publish educational materials and support others providing information or advice.

remedies such as repair or replacement—see Chapter Eight). Where redress to individuals is not viable or proportionate (e.g. because consumers cannot be identified or can only be identified at a disproportionate cost) an ECM can require a trader to make a payment "in the collective interests of consumers" (for example, to a consumer charity).

18.30   The compliance category is concerned with measures aimed at preventing or reducing the risk of traders committing future breaches of the law, so the focus is preventive. So, e.g., a trader might be required to give a member of staff responsibility for supervising particular matters and to improve staff training, to eradicate a pattern of pressure selling that violates the 2008 Regulations—see above.

The choice category includes measures to help consumers to make more effective choices between traders, e.g. requiring a trader to advertise the fact that it had breached some consumer protection law, and to explain the steps taken to address this, i.e. to stop it happening in future.

Under the new s.219B ((a) & (b)) it is provided that ECMs can only be used where they are just and reasonable, this taking into account the likely benefit of the measures to consumers, the costs likely to be incurred by the subject of the enforcement order or undertaking, and the likely cost to consumers of obtaining the benefit of the measures.

It is likely that firms will frequently contest the proportionality of ECMs (probably at the earliest stage), so this will be likely to act as a brake on some proposals, and the above test may ultimately be much argued over, perhaps ultimately in the courts. At the same time, in practice, it is likely that enforcers and traders will often negotiate their way to an informal conclusion and agreed course of action.

18.31   Use of ECMs is open to all public enforcers under Pt 8 of the 2002 Act. Again, this includes:

> The Competition and Markets Authority,
>
> Trading Standards Services in Great Britain,
>
> The Department for Enterprise, Trade and Investment in Northern Ireland,
>
> The Civil Aviation Authority,
>
> The Northern Ireland Authority for Utility Regulation,
>
> Ofcom,
>
> Ofwat,
>
> Ofgem,
>
> Phonepay Plus,
>
> The Information Commissioner,
>
> The Office of Rail Regulation,
>
> The Financial Conduct Authority,
>
> Community enforcers under the Injunctions Directive,

The Secretary of State for Health, Department of Health, Social Services and Public Safety in Northern Ireland.

Also, it is provided that subject to certain safeguards, provision can be made to extend the use of the ECMs to private designated enforcers—the only such body being Which?.

For useful guidance on the ECMs, in this case aimed generally at enforcers, mainly Trading Standards Authorities, but also dealing with the general position), see the Department for Business, Innovation & Skills (BIS), Enhanced Consumer Measures, Guidance for enforcers of consumer law May 2015.

4. Unfair Commercial Practices Directive

Background to the Directive

We have already mentioned the EU Unfair Commercial Practices Directive[20]   **18.32** earlier in this chapter. The general principle of a "duty to trade fairly", though it can be found in a number of European and other jurisdictions, has hitherto had no place in English law. We noted in Chapter Eleven the proposal floated by Lord Borrie in 1980 that a "general statutory duty to trade fairly in consumer transactions" should be introduced via codes of practice and saw that the OFT's support for that proposal was reluctantly removed in 1990 as "over-ambitious".[21]

We observed that, though the UK initiatives came to nought, the European Commission had picked up the torch in June 2003 with a proposed Directive on Unfair Commercial Practices. Within two years the proposal had been adopted as Directive 2005/29/EC "concerning unfair business-to-consumer practices in the internal market" (the Unfair Commercial Practices Directive or UCPD, as we shall call it).

Before considering the 2008 Regulations, which transposed the UCPD into UK law, we shall make some preliminary points on the UCPD to explain the provenance and approach of the 2008 Regulations and comment upon the DTI's approach to implementation.

Purpose

The 25 Preambles to the UCPD explain its general purposes and the reasons   **18.33** for the particular articles. Preambles (3), (4) and (6) focus on generalities:

> (3) The laws of the Member States relating to unfair commercial practices show marked differences which can generate appreciable distortions of competition and obstacles to the smooth functioning of the internal market. In the field of advertising, Council Directive 84/450/EEC of 10 September 1984 concerning misleading and comparative advertising establishes minimum

---

[20] Directive 2005/29/EC of 11 May 2005.
[21] See para.11.09 above.

criteria for harmonising legislation on misleading advertising, but does not prevent the Member States from retaining or adopting measures which provide more extensive protection for consumers. As a result, Member States' provisions on misleading advertising diverge significantly.

(4) These disparities cause uncertainty as to which national rules apply to unfair commercial practices harming consumers' economic interests and create many barriers affecting business and consumers. These barriers increase the cost to business of exercising internal market freedoms, in particular when businesses wish to engage in cross border marketing, advertising campaigns and sales promotions. Such barriers also make consumers uncertain of their rights and undermine their confidence in the internal market.

(6) This Directive therefore approximates the laws of the Member States on unfair commercial practices, including unfair advertising, which directly harm consumers' economic interests and thereby indirectly harm the economic interests of legitimate competitors. In line with the principle of proportionality, this Directive protects consumers from the consequences of such unfair commercial practices where they are material but recognises that in some cases the impact on consumers may be negligible. It neither covers nor affects the national laws on unfair commercial practices which harm only competitors' economic interests or which relate to a transaction between traders; taking full account of the principle of subsidiarity, Member States will continue to be able to regulate such practices, in conformity with Community law, if they choose to do so. Nor does this Directive cover or affect the provisions of Directive 84/450/EEC on advertising which misleads business but which is not misleading for consumers and on comparative advertising. Further, this Directive does not affect accepted advertising and marketing practices, such as legitimate product placement, brand differentiation or the offering of incentives which may legitimately affect consumers' perceptions of products and influence their behaviour without impairing the consumer's ability to make an informed decision.

It can be seen from the above that the UCPD is not confined to the harmonisation of the law on unfair commercial practices, but also amends Directive 84/450/EEC on Misleading and Comparative Advertising. This was replaced by Directive 2006/114/EC which we shall consider in Section 6 of this chapter.

18.34 A number of points may be gleaned from the Preambles:

(1) The UCPD aims to eliminate distortions of the internal market caused by different laws on unfair trading.

(2) It is concerned with practices which "directly harm consumers' economic interests" (Preambles (4) and (6)) rather than "only competitors' economic interests" (Preamble (6)). Preamble 7 elaborates this point by stating that the UCPD "addresses commercial practices directly related to consumers' transactional decisions in relation to products".

(3) This is a framework directive creating—to use that vogue expression—principles-based legislation, so that practices are regulated where "the consequences . . . are material", not merely "negligible" (Preamble (6)). We shall see this moderate approach when we consider the DTI's proposals on enforcement.

(4) Another important result of the framework approach is that it simplifies matters for consumers and businesses alike. As Preamble (12) puts it, they "will be able to rely on a single regulatory framework based on clearly defined legal concepts regulating all aspects of unfair commercial practices across the EU". Thus "it is necessary to replace Member States' existing, divergent general clauses and legal principles" (Preamble (13)).

DTI's consultation programme

The DTI accepted that the UCPD would probably involve the repeal of existing UK law in its *Consultation on a draft EU Directive* (July 2003, p.39): **18.35**

> Transposition of the framework Directive in the UK may present an opportunity to deregulate some of the existing body of UK regulations . . . Domestic legislation which implements existing EU directives may remain, but other sectoral provisions that go beyond or conflict with the provisions of the framework Directive may need to be removed.

In December 2005 it issued a consultation paper on the implementation of the UCPD and published a Summary of Responses in June 2006. *The Government Response to the Consultation Paper on Implementing the Unfair Commercial Practices Directive* ("the *Government Response*") was issued in December 2006. It acknowledged that it "committed itself to simplifying existing laws wherever sensible and appropriate in order to establish a modern and robust fair trading framework." The full list of the laws affected is set out in Schs 2, 3 and 4 to the 2008 Regulations, the most notable statutes to disappear were most of the Trade Descriptions Act 1968 and Pt III of the Consumer Protection Act 1987 as we saw in Chapters Fourteen and Fifteen.

UK implementation

Article 19 gives the deadlines to which Member States must adhere. They must "adopt and publish" the necessary regulations by 12 June 2007 and bring them into force by 12 December 2007. Not for the first time the DTI failed to meet its obligations on time. The 2008 Regulations came into force on 26 May 2008. **18.36**

Before commenting on the articles, we cannot but quote the conclusion reached in the DTI's December 2006 consultation paper (p.3):

> The coming into force of the UCPD will mark a new era in UK fair trading history. The UCPD will allow enforcers to tackle those practices that are unfair but not currently unlawful, taking either civil or criminal enforcement action as appropriate. Simplification and modernisation of the existing framework will also make the law easier for its users—business, consumers and enforcers—to understand and apply. The Government is confident that the wide-ranging changes set out below will help it meet its objective of

raising the UK's consumer protection regime to the level of the best in the world.[22]

We earnestly hope that such an ambitious objective can be attained. Certainly the UCPD is a major step on that journey.

5. THE CONSUMER PROTECTION REGULATIONS

Introduction

18.37 The UCPD was implemented by the 2008 Regulations. The 2008 Regulations broadly adopt a "copy out" approach making it unlikely that the EU Commission will bring proceedings in the ECJ claiming (as they did, unsuccessfully, in relation to the Product Liability Directive: see para.5.39 above) that the transposition into UK law is inaccurate.

The OFT (now CMA) have published two guides to the 2008 Regulations on their website. The better, more detailed one is *Guidance on the Consumer Protection from Unfair Trading Regulations* (May 2008, 84pp). It states that it is "principally intended to help traders to comply" with the 2008 Regulations and contains many useful examples of the types of commercial practices which may be unfair or permissible. The other one, described as a *Basic Guide for Business* (Aug 2008), is just that: its 22 pages are in large print, contain many illustrations and deal mainly with the black list in Sch.1.[23]

Before turning to the various regulations which control commercial malpractices, we draw attention to reg.2 (the interpretation provision) which contains the definitions of the essential words and phrases, e.g. average consumer, commercial practice, consumer, material information, product, professional diligence and transactional decision.[24]

When is a practice unfair?

18.38 The attack on "unfair commercial practices" is launched succinctly by reg.3(1): they "are prohibited". They may be divided into six categories of which the last four below are specified in reg.3(4):

(1) the general prohibition: reg.3(3);

(2) promotion by a code owner: reg.4;

(3) misleading actions: reg.5;

---

[22] In 2003 with that same "best in the world" aim, the DTI commissioned a study from Brunel University School of Law (Geoffrey Woodroffe and Dimitrios Giannoulopoulos) comparing the consumer protection laws and organisations of the G7 Countries, Australia, Canada and Norway (including the duty to trade fairly).

[23] See also, M. Koutsias and C. Willett, "UK Implementation of the Unfair Commercial Practices Directive", in O. Akseli, A. Garde and W. Van Boom, Experiencing Unfair Commercial Practices, Ashgate, 2014, 21–43 pp

[24] See *R. v Scottish and Southern Energy Plc* [2012] EWCA Civ 539 for the definition of "trader".

(4) misleading omissions: reg.6;

(5) aggressive practices: reg.7; and

(6) the black list in Sch.1.

What is a "commercial practice"? It is widely defined in reg.2(1) and means "any act, omission, course of conduct, representation or commercial communication (including advertising or marketing)". It must be directly connected with the supply of a product "to or from" consumers, whether occurring before, during or after a transaction. Thus it will apply where a consumer, who is selling a solid gold necklace to a cash-for-gold firm,[25] is told that it is only gold plated and so receives a very low price.

(1) General prohibition

Regulation 3(3) is as follows: **18.39**

> A commercial practice is unfair if—
>
>   (a) it contravenes the requirements of professional diligence; and
>   (b) it materially distorts or is likely to materially distort the economic behaviour of the average consumer with regard to the product.

This is a general "catch-all" provision in contrast to the other five varieties which are specific types with detailed lists of matters or factors to be taken into account.

(a) "Professional diligence" is defined as "the standard of special skill and care which a trader may reasonably be expected to exercise towards consumers", commensurate with honest market practice and good faith. The meaning is essentially similar to the duty imposed on suppliers of services under English law,[26] though here the regulation relates to the supply of a "product" meaning "any goods or service and includes immovable property".

(b) Who is the "average consumer"? "Consumer" has the usual meaning to be found in recent EU legislation: any "individual . . . . acting for purposes which are outside his business": so companies are excluded, as are all traders of any type. What does "average" add? "Average consumer" is defined by reg.2(2) as "reasonably well informed, reasonably observant and circumspect".

This objective test is modified by reg.2(4) where "the practice is directed to a particular group", when the "average consumer shall be read as referring to the average member of that group". It is also modified by reg.2(5) where the group comprises "particularly vulnerable" consumers "because of their mental or physical infirmity, age or credulity in a way which the trader could

---

[25] See *Which?* (February 2010): "Cash for Your Gold".
[26] See para.6.36 above.

be reasonably be expected to foresee". The supply of wheelchairs or stair lifts comes to mind, or the repair of roofs or front drives where unsuspecting elderly people are preyed upon by itinerant rogues.

OFT v Purely Creative Ltd[27]

18.40   "Average consumer", "material information" and "transactional decision" were all given the benefit of judicial interpretation in the first substantive case in the UK courts on the 2008 Regulations. *The Office of Fair Trading v Purely Creative Ltd* also concerned many other aspects of the 2008 Regulations which we discuss below. The case started in the High Court, progressed to the Court of Appeal and finished in the European Court of Justice.

18.41   **High Court**[28]   The OFT sought an enforcement order under s.215 of the 2002 Act to prevent the defendants (P) from distributing promotions to consumers in breach of the 2008 Regulations. The promotions related to prizes or awards to be claimed by consumers at some cost to themselves. The OFT claimed that the practices were prohibited by reg.3(1) as "unfair commercial practices". They were "unfair" because they were "misleading actions" or "misleading omissions" within regs 5 and 6 or "listed in Schedule 1" (see reg.3(4)(a)(b) and (d)). Paragraph 31 of Sch.1 is concerned with winning prizes.
Briggs J held as follows.

> (1) P were in breach of para.31 of Sch.1. He stated at para.45: "The critical requirement in proving any breach of Paragraph 31 is that a false impression has been created." The use of the words "win" or "prize" is not essential; whether a communication conveys that impression should take into account "not only the words used, but its layout and get-up" (at para.52).
>
> He stressed that in interpreting domestic regulations implementing EU Directives it is "neither a matter of grammars nor dictionaries nor . . . the use of those phrases . . . in national law . . . The primary recourse of the national court is to the jurisprudence of the ECJ".
>
> (2) Consideration of regs 5 and 6 required the interpretation of "average consumer", as the question posed in reg.5(2)(b) and reg.6(1) is whether the misleading action or omission "causes or is likely to cause the average consumer to take a transactional decision he would not otherwise have taken". Briggs J commented at para.62 that the Unfair Commercial Practices Directive protects "consumers who take reasonable care of themselves, rather than the ignorant, the careless or the over-hasty consumer".

---

[27] [2011] EWCA Civ 920; [2012] 1 C.M.L.R. 21.
[28] [2011] EWHC 106 (Ch).

"Transactional decision", defined in reg.2(1), includes "any decision with an economic consequence, even if it was a decision between doing nothing or responding to a promotion" by some method (Briggs J at para.68).

What is the meaning of "cause or is likely to cause"? It is equivalent to the English standard of the balance of probabilities.

(3) Regulation 6 required Briggs J to analyse the phrase "material information" which is defined by reg.6(3)(a) as " the information which the average consumer needs . . . to take an informed transactional decision". Stressing the concept of "need", he stated at para.74: "The question is not whether the omitted information would assist, or be relevant, but whether its provision is necessary to enable the average consumer to take an informed transactional decision."

The court concluded that P's promotions contravened the Regulations and that an enforcement order should be made.

Court of Appeal[29] Both parties appealed against the decision of Briggs J **18.42** discussed above. The company argued that their undertaking to the court was too wide and should be more limited. The OFT contended that it was too narrow. Thus the broad effect of the appeal and cross appeal would be to limit or widen the scope of para.31 of Sch.1 to the Regulations and of para.31 of Annex 1 to Directive 2005/29/EC.

The OFT also argued that, if the court were unwilling to grant the OFT's cross appeal, it should dismiss the appeal, stay the cross appeal and refer the interpretation of para.31 to the European Court of Justice.

The Court of Appeal held that the appeal and cross appeal be stayed and that questions on the interpretation of para.31 be referred to the ECJ.

The court was impressed by the fact that

"there is no judgment of any court of any Member State on the proper interpretation of paragraph 31 of the Directive or its various national equivalents. In addition the translations of the various provisions enacted by each Member State to give effect to paragraph 31 of the Directive display a divergence indicative of doubt as to what that true interpretation is. As another of the purposes of the Directive, clearly expressed in recitals 6 and 12 and article 5 quoted in paragraph 2 above, is to harmonise the laws of the Member States these translations indicate that that purpose may require a decision of the Court of Justice of the European Union." (para 17).

It would have dismissed the company's appeal if that were the only issue (para.14).

---

[29] [2011] EWCA Civ 920.

18.43 **ECJ**[30] The European Court of Justice issued a ruling on 18 October 2012 which confirms the OFT position that prizes must be genuine and not involve people being hit with additional costs to find out what they have won or to claim it. The judgment makes it clear that it is not acceptable for businesses to hide behind providing one route to claim a prize that is free, if the other ways of claiming the prize incur a cost.

> "Descriptions of prizes must also be clear so people understand what it is they are winning. But importantly, traders should not exploit the excitement consumers justifiably feel when told they have won a prize in order to make money."[31]

(2) Promotion by code owners

18.44 Codes of conduct are given special treatment by the 2008 Regulations. Regulation 4 states:

> The promotion of any unfair commercial practice by a code owner in a code of conduct is prohibited.

Clearly CMA and TSI Approved codes, which we discussed in Chapter Eleven, should not contain such material. However, one can imagine some traders masquerading as "professional" people—some funeral directors and used car dealers fit this category—and getting together to form an association with a code of practice: this will be of dubious value to consumers if it contains provisions such as exemption clauses which, though unreasonable and unfair, consumers believe to be valid merely because they appear in a code.

(3) Misleading actions

18.45 Misleading practices fall into two categories—misleading actions (reg.5) and misleading omissions (reg.6). As we saw in para.18.38 above, another type of unfair practice is an aggressive one (reg.7).

The common feature of all three varieties is that they cause the consumer "to take a transactional decision he would not have taken otherwise". A "transactional decision" is defined in reg.2(1); e.g. whether or on what terms to purchase, pay for or dispose of a product.

Would the consumer have made a different decision if not misled or pressured?

18.46 A commercial practice is a "misleading action" within reg.5(1) if it satisfies the conditions in para.5(2), i.e. "it contains false information and is therefore untruthful" or deceives or is likely to deceive the average consumer" in relation to a list (a) to (k) set out in reg.5(4).[32] This is so "even if the information is factually correct".

---

[30] [2012] EUECJ C-428/11 (18 October 2011).

[31] OFT Press Statement 93/12, 18 October 2012.

[32] See *The Office of Fair Trading v Ashbourne Management Services Ltd* [2011] EWHC 1237 (Ch).

The list (a) to (k) in reg.5(4) includes:

(b) the main characteristics of the product;

(e) the nature of the sales process;

(f) a statement or symbol about sponsorship or approval of the trader or product;

(g) the price[33];

(i) service, repair, etc.;

(j) the nature, attributes and rights of the trader; and

(k) the consumer's rights or risks.

The "main characteristics" in para.4(b) are defined in reg.5(5) which contains another non-exhaustive long list (a) to (r) including:

(a) availability;

(e) composition;

(f) accessories;

(i) method and date of manufacture;

(k) delivery;

(l) fitness for purpose;

(n) quantity;

(o) specification; and

(p) geographical origin.

Readers familiar with the Trade Descriptions Act 1968 (the 1968 Act) will **18.47** recollect that almost all of the ten matters specified in the s.2(1) of the 1968 Act) (which defined a "trade description" of goods) appear in the more extensive lists mentioned above.

Paragraph 4(j) ("nature, attributes. . .") is elaborated in reg.5(6) with yet another list (a) to (h) including identity, qualifications, affiliations and awards.

The list in reg.5(4) contains a third matter where a cross-reference is necessary, although para.4(k) does not specifically mention this. Regulation 5(7) amplifies the meaning of "consumer rights": these "include rights the consumer may have under ss.19 and 23 or 24 of the CRA 2015.", i.e. the rights to refund, repair, replacement and price reduction (discussed in paras 8.19–8.46 above). Thus it continues to be an offence for a trader to state "No refunds",

---

[33] See BIS Pricing Practices Guide URN/1312 (November 2010).

"No money back on sale goods" or "No exchanges, credit notes only"; while it is also now an offence to make statements denying that consumers are entitled to repair, replacement or price reduction.

Our last comment on reg.5 concerns two different types of misleading action set out in reg.5(3)(a) and (b). The first concerns marketing which creates confusion with a competitor's products or trade marks. The second is another code of conduct provision: it concerns a trader's failure to comply with a firm and verifiable commitment in a code by which he is bound.

(4) Misleading omissions

18.48   Regulation 6 deals with "misleading omissions" and is concerned with the omission or hiding of "material information" rather than giving false information.

"Material information" means by reg.6(3) information which the average consumer needs to take an informed decision. Information which is unclear or unintelligible may be treated as misleading, so as with the CRA 2015 unfair terms regime (see para.10.35 above) plain and intelligible language is crucial for suppliers.

Special requirements are set out in reg.6(4) where the supplier makes an "invitation to purchase", e.g. name and address of the trader, price, delivery charges, cancellation rights. "Invitation to purchase" means a commercial communication which indicates characteristics of the product and the price appropriately and enables the consumer to make a purchase. What is "appropriate" will depend on the type of transaction, e.g. goods in a window or on a shelf of a shop, internet supplies of goods or services such as travel. The expression presumably has its usual contractual meaning as something leading to an offer (see para.6.16 above): i.e. an invitation to treat.

(5) Aggressive practices

18.49   Regulation 7 deals with "aggressive commercial practices". The question here is whether freedom of choice is impaired by "harassment, coercion or undue influence". Regulation 7(2) lists various factors to be taken into account in relation to harassment, etc. For example, "timing, location, nature or persistence" are relevant; so pushy evening telephone calls from utilities or telecommunications companies can be controlled. The exploitation of misfortune or grave circumstances impairing the consumer's judgment are relevant too, e.g. pressuring the recently redundant or bereaved.

(6) Schedule 1 black list

18.50   Regulation 3(4)(d) states that a practice is unfair, if "it is listed in Schedule 1". Preamble (17) to the UCPD emphasised that it is "the full list . . . and those are the only" practices deemed to be unfair. In case the point has been missed, Sch.1 itself is headed "COMMERCIAL PRACTICES WHICH ARE IN ALL CIRCUMSTANCES CONSIDERED UNFAIR". This contrasts with the "grey list" approach adopted by the CRA 2015 unfair terms regime where

Sch.2 contains an "Indicative and non-exhaustive list of terms which may be regarded as unfair" (see para.10.47 above).

Schedule 1 consists of 31 practices. We mention a few examples, following the numbering in the schedule.

1 and 3: false claims about codes of conduct;

5: bait advertising[34];

6: bait and switch;

12: inaccurate claims about risk to personal security;

14: pyramid schemes;

15: closing down sales;

17: false claims about curing illnesses;

20: "free" products;

21: invoices for unordered goods;

26: persistent cold calling by telephone, fax, email, etc.;

28: advertisements aimed at children; and

31: winning prizes.[35]

Offences and defences

Regulation 8 applies to the general prohibition under reg.3(3). This is not a **18.51** strict liability offence. Does the defendant "knowingly or recklessly" engage in the practice?

Regulations 9 to 12 impose strict liability: "A trader is guilty of an offence if he engages . . .". They apply to offences under regs 5 to 7 and Sch.1. There are two exceptions. Regulation 9 does not apply to reg.5(3)(b) (codes) and reg.12 does not apply to Sch.1 paras 11 and 28 (advertisements). Although no offences are committed in these exceptional cases, enforcement proceedings may be brought under Pt 8 of the 2002 Act, which we discussed earlier in this chapter.

Regulations 13 to 18 are similar to the equivalent provisions of the 1968 Act which have not been repealed. Readers are referred to the explanation of these in Chapter Fourteen:

Regulation 13 the usual penalties: fines and prison.[36]

Regulation 14: time limits for prosecution.

Regulation 15: offences by bodies corporate.

---

[34] See *The Office of Fair Trading v Ashbourne Management Services Ltd* [2011] EWHC 1237 (Ch).

[35] See *The Office of Fair Trading v Purely Creative Ltd* [2011] EWCA Civ 920; [2012] 1 C.M.L.R. 21.

[36] Trader "jailed for car clocking": OFT press release 112/12, 22 November 2012.

Regulation 16: act or default of another person.

Regulation 17: the due diligence defence.

Regulation 18: the defence of innocent publication of advertisements.

Enforcement

18.52 Again readers are referred to Chapter Fourteen for an explanation.

Regulation 19 imposes a duty of enforcement on every "enforcement officer" (defined in reg.2(1)).

Regulations 20 to 25 cover related matters, e.g. powers to make test purchases and powers of entry.

Regulations 26 and 27 concern amendments to the 2002 Act. Regulation 27 is included to comply with art.12(a) of the UCPD, and adds s.218A to the 2002 Act. Where an application is made for an enforcement order in respect of a Community infringement in relation to the UCPD, the court may require evidence to substantiate the accuracy of a factual claim.

The Schedules

Schedule 1

18.53 This contains the black list of banned practices.

Schedule 2

18.54 This contains amendments to Acts (Pt 1) and Regulations and Orders (Pt 2). (All of the changes mentioned below are dealt with in detail elsewhere in this book.)

Part 1 includes the repeal of most of the 1968 Act (including ss.1 and 14). Part III of the Consumer Protection Act 1987 is also repealed; pricing is now covered by reg.5(4)(g). Section 10(2) of the 2002 Act is repealed too taking with it the two remaining orders made under Pt II of the 1973 Act: the Consumer Transactions (Restrictions on Statements) Order 1976 (SI 1976/1813) and the Business Advertisements (Disclosure) Order 1977 (SI 1977/1918) are unnecessary in view of reg.5(4)(k) and 5(7) and Sch.2, para.97, and Sch.1, para.22, respectively.

Part 2 comprises revocations of and amendments to Regulations and Orders. These include the Control of Misleading Advertisements Regulations 1988 (SI 1988/915).

Schedule 3

18.55 This contains "Transitional and Saving Provisions". For example, para.5 preserves the Price Indication (Bureaux de Change) (No.2) Regulations 1992 despite the repeal of Pt III of the Consumer Protection Act 1987 (see para.15.07 above).

Schedule 4

This contains a list of all the "Repeals and Revocations".   **18.56**

6. MISLEADING ADVERTISEMENTS

Changing of the guard

The 2008 Regulations discussed in the last section introduced a new regime   **18.57**
for the regulation of misleading advertisements. Previously the enforcement
powers of the OFT emanated from the Control of Misleading Advertisement
Regulations 1988 (the 1988 Regulations)[37] which implemented the 1984 EU
Misleading Advertising Directive[38]; in their amended form they covered
comparative advertising too.

Business Protection Regulations

The 1988 Regulations were revoked by the 2008 Regulations[39] and replaced   **18.58**
by the Business Protection from Misleading Marketing Regulations 2008[40]
(the BPRs) which came into force on May 26, 2008 (the same day as
the 2008 Regulations). They consolidate the 1988 Regulations and their
various amendments and so deal with both misleading and comparative
advertising.

There is one major difference between the old and the new regulations: as the title of the BPRs indicates, they are for the protection
of business only, not of consumers. This can be seen from reg.3(2)(a)
which states that advertising is misleading which deceives "*the traders* to
whom it is addressed" (emphasis supplied) whereas reg.5(2)(a) of the 2008
Regulations refer to "the average consumer". Regulation 3(2)(b) underlines
the business limitation by requiring the advertising "to injure a competitor". There is, though, one significant similarity between reg.5 of the 2008
Regulations[41] and reg.3 of the BPRs: the lists of relevant matters are almost
identical.

In view of their application to business-to-business transactions only we
shall confine ourselves to those few remarks on the BPRs, although readers
may find it helpful to consult earlier editions of this book which discuss the
similar 1988 Regulations more fully.

The 2008 Regulations

Following the revocation of the 1988 Regulations and the repeal of other   **18.59**
legislation which dealt with advertising such as the 1968 Act and the pricing

---

[37] SI 1988/915, amended by SI 2000/914.
[38] 84/450 O.J. L250/17.
[39] Sch.2 para.81.
[40] SI 2008/1276.
[41] See para.18.46 above.

provisions of Part III of the Consumer Protection Act 1987, the statutory control of advertising to consumers depends upon the 2008 Regulations.

We discussed the 2008 Regulations in the previous section, but highlight below some of the points already covered which relate to advertising:

(1) The definition of "commercial practice" specifically includes "advertising and marketing".

(2) "Misleading actions" and "misleading omissions" in regs.5(1) and 6(1) clearly cover advertising as they both refer initially to "a commercial practice".

(3) The same is true of "aggressive commercial practices" in reg.7(1).

(4) Many of the banned practices in Sch.1 inevitably involve advertisements in that they talk about "claiming", "falsely stating", "promoting", "falsely claiming", etc. Two practices are noteworthy in the list:

> 11. "Using editorial content . . .."(advertorial).
> 28. "Including in an advertisement . . .."

Advertising Standards Authority and self-regulation

18.60 The Advertising Standards Authority (ASA) has made it clear that, in dealing with complaints, it will have regard to the 2008 Regulations. How does self-regulation fit into the regulatory framework?

The ASA was established in 1962 to provide independent supervision of the industry's self-regulatory arrangements through a monitoring programme and investigation of complaints. The first Code was published in 1961 and modelled on the 1937 International Code of Advertising Practice. It is kept under continuous review and amendment by the Committee of Advertising Practice (CAP). The Code applies to advertisements in newspapers, magazines, posters, brochures, leaflets and other printed publications, for the public, cinema commercials and viewdata services. The most recent code is called the "Non-broadcast British Code of Advertising, Sales Promotion and Direct Marketing" and takes account of new media advertising such as email.

18.61 A separate system operates in relation to broadcasting. The Broadcasting Act 1990 imposed a duty on the Independent Television Commission and the Radio Authority to draw up and enforce codes governing standards and practice in advertising and programme sponsorship. In December 2003 the regulatory regime changed when the Office of Communications (Ofcom) took over the functions of these bodies under the Communications Act 2003.

In 2004 Ofcom contracted out its day-to-day monitoring functions to the ASA.[42] This "co-regulation" has simplified matters for complainants and

---

[42] The Contracting Out (Functions Relating to Broadcast Advertising) and Specification of Relevant Functions Order 2004 (SI 2004/1975).

advertisers alike, since the ASA is now responsible for ensuring that both non-broadcast advertisements and broadcast advertisements comply with the relevant codes. The Broadcasting Committee of Advertising Practice (BCAP) writes and keeps under review the UK Code of Broadcast Advertising.

Part IV

CREDIT TRANSACTIONS

CHAPTER NINETEEN

THE BACKGROUND TO CONSUMER CREDIT

1. INTRODUCTION

There has been a dramatic increase in consumer credit in the last 50 years—both in this country and in other Western industrialised countries. By far the greatest area is house purchase but there are many others including furniture, electrical appliances, clothing, vehicles, holidays and home improvements. The Crowther Committee Report on Consumer Credit revealed that in 1966 the amount of medium- and long-term credit extended totalled £3,692,000,000 (house purchase credit accounted for approximately 45 per cent of this figure). At the end of the year the total outstanding was £9,684,000,000, of which some 80 per cent was attributable to houses and flats. Forty years later, a staggering £1.25 trillion was outstanding at the end of 2006.

    The Crowther Committee clearly realised that:

> The use of consumer credit . . . enables individuals to enjoy the services of consumer durable goods sooner than they otherwise would and in a period of inflation offers them a real prospect of acquiring them more cheaply. Consumers in general are able to obtain a more satisfying "basket" of goods and services with the same income. Thus consumer credit may be said to enhance consumer satisfaction. Furthermore, some individuals, who lack the self-discipline to save up for the purchase of a durable consumer good but are nevertheless unlikely to break their contract with a creditor, are able to buy a durable consumer good which might otherwise never be theirs.[1]

The situation described above has its corresponding dangers and these are two-fold. First, borrowers may be tempted to overstretch their resources—either through bad economic planning or because they do not appreciate the full extent of their obligations. Secondly, some lenders might be tempted to "cash in" on the attractions of consumer credit by inducing borrowers (some of whom may already be under severe financial stress) to sign agreements which are one-sided and impose unduly onerous obligations.

    Until the passing of the Consumer Credit Act 1974 (the 1974 Act) the law developed in a fragmentary and piecemeal fashion—following rather than leading, checking abuses after they had come to light rather than laying down ground rules in advance. Thus:

19.01

19.02

---

[1] Cmnd.4596, p.118.

(1) The Bills of Sale Acts 1878 to 1882 were passed to deal with (inter alia) mortgages of personal property where the borrower retained possession.

(2) The Moneylenders Acts 1900 to 1927 were passed to regulate the activities of certain moneylenders (but not banks).

(3) The Pawnbrokers Acts 1872 to 1960 regulated the activities of pawnbrokers.

(4) The Hire-Purchase Act 1965 regulated hire-purchase agreements where the hire-purchase price did not exceed £2,000 and where the hirer was not a body corporate. (This limit was increased to £7,500 in 1983.)

19.03 The unsatisfactory nature of this fragmentary approach can be seen by looking at money-lending. If the lender happened to be a bank, the Moneylenders Acts did not apply at all, even though the borrower may have been an inexperienced private individual and the contract may have been a harsh one on the particular facts. On the other hand, if the lender was within the provisions of the Act the full rigours of the Act were applied, even though the borrower was a large public company well able to look after itself. Again, as new forms of credit developed (e.g. credit cards) the absence of any regulatory machinery meant that there was virtually no effective control at all. All this was changed by the 1974 Act which is probably the most comprehensive and sophisticated Act of its kind in the Western world.

The Act was designed to sweep away the piecemeal controls listed above and to replace them with a single code governing all forms of lending. The only pieces of legislation which remain unrepealed are the Bills of Sale Acts 1878 to 1882—the reason is that the 1974 Act does not regulate mortgages of personal property. A suggestion made by the Crowther Committee that the Government should introduce a Lending and Security Act was not implemented.

2. CONSUMER CREDIT ACT 2006 AMENDMENTS

19.04 Government concern at over-indebtedness led in 2001 to a review of the 1974 Act focussing on the financial limit, licensing, information disclosure, early settlement, consumer redress and, last but not least, unfair credit transactions. This then led to the publication in December 2003 of the White Paper *Fair, Clear and Competitive—The Consumer Credit Market in the 21st Century*.

Those areas not requiring primary legislation—e.g. advertising, pre-contractual disclosure, early settlement calculations—were immediately reformed in 2004 by a series of statutory instruments. However, primary legislation was needed for the reform of the other areas—financial limit, licensing, unfair credit relationships and consumer redress—and in due course the Consumer Credit Act 2006 (the 2006 Act) was passed. It came into force gradually as ordered by statutory instruments under s.71.

The Consumer Credit Directive 2008 is considered below (para.19.13); we shall call it the CCD.

Finally before turning to an analysis of the 1974 Act one point must be stressed. The 2006 Act is not a free standing statute: its effect is to *amend* the 1974 Act. Similarly the statutory instruments implementing CCD also amend the 1974 Act. In Part IV of this book a reference to "the Act" is a reference to the 1974 Act (as amended) and a reference to a section is to that section in the Act.

3. CONSUMER CREDIT ACT 1974—PRELIMINARY POINTS

The scope and effect of the Consumer Credit Act will be examined in detail in **19.05** the next eight chapters. In the remainder of this chapter it is proposed to deal with ten preliminary matters.

(1) The Act originally contained no definition of the word "consumer". We have already seen that under the Consumer Rights Act 2015 (CRA 2015) the term "consumer"[2] means a private consumer as opposed to a business consumer. *The Consumer Credit Act 1974 is not limited in this way.*

In one major type of agreement—consumer hire—the Act provides control where the hirer is an "individual" but the definition of this term is not what one might expect. The original definition has been narrowed by s.1 of the 2006 Act. Section 189(1) now reads:

"individual" includes—

    (a) a partnership consisting of two or three persons not all of whom are bodies corporate; and

    (b) an unincorporated body of persons which does not consist entirely of bodies corporate and is not a partnership;

This is a major change made by the 2006 Act, for now only partnerships of two or three people are protected whereas before there was no limit on their size. As before, sole proprietors of a business are covered but not companies. Thus many small traders are still protected just as much as the private individual.

Now where agreements are covered by the CCD amendments, "consumers" are protected.[3]

(2) Another change, and even more drastic, is the abolition of the financial limit (previously £25,000). However, many provisions in agreements regulated pursuant to the CCD do not apply where the credit exceeds £60,260.

(3) Section 189 adopts the very helpful practice of drawing together all the definitions which appear throughout the Act. Section 189(1) contains no less than 177 definitions. Some are defined in the section itself. In other cases s.189 refers to the section where the definition is to be found, e.g.:

"exempt agreement" means an agreement specified in or under section 16.

---

[2] s.2(3) of the CRA 2015.
[3] See para.19.17 below.

19.06   It is vitally important to refer constantly to s.189 because words are often used in unexpected ways. Thus, for example, the definition of the word "surety" is wide enough to include the principal debtor (unless the context otherwise requires).

(4) Another helpful innovation[4] is Sch.2 which contains 24 worked examples showing the use of the new terminology. Section 188(3), however, provides that:

> In the case of conflict between Schedule 2 and any other provision of this Act that other provision shall prevail.

(5) Although the Act is a long one, a very large part of the detail is contained in regulations. They cover such matters as the total charge for credit, regulated and exempt agreements, advertisements, documentation, disclosure of information and rebate for early settlement.

(6) The control provided by the Act is two-fold:

(a) Regulation of business activity—notably through the system administered by the Financial Conduct Authority (FCA).[5]

(b) Regulation of individual agreements.

19.07   (7) The Act provides various civil and criminal sanctions, as well as the administrative sanctions in ss.29 and 32 (non-renewal, suspension and revocation of a licence). The criminal sanctions are usefully collected together in Sch.1. Section 170(1) provides that:

> A breach of any requirement made (otherwise than by any court) by or under this Act shall incur no civil or criminal sanction as being such a breach except to the extent (if any) expressly provided for under this Act.

Thus no action can be brought for breach of statutory duty. Such claims or defences are shut out by s.170(1). Presumably the criminal court would still be able to award compensation under the Powers of Criminal Courts (Sentencing) Act 2000.[6] The section does not affect the power of the court to grant an injunction (s.170(3)).

(8) As one might expect, the statutory rights enjoyed by the debtor, the hirer, a surety or a relative[7] cannot in any way be cut down or fettered by the agreement.[8]

(9) One of the features of the Act is that certain steps can only be taken if the court or the FCA makes an order to that effect. An example of the former is

---

[4] The Government introduced another helpful practice under which all Government Bills are accompanied by explanatory notes. They are available for the 2006 Act.
[5] See para.21.02 below.
[6] See para.17.03 above.
[7] See para.19.10 below.
[8] See s.173(1) and (2).

the enforcement of an agreement which has not been properly executed.[9] An example of the latter is the enforcement of an agreement made by a creditor or owner while it was unlicensed. In either case s.173(3) provides that consent of the debtor or hirer "given at that time" shall be as effective as an order. The words "given at that time" presumably refer to the time of enforcement so that a provision for consent in the contract would not be effective. Clearly the court would examine the facts very carefully to ensure that there was real consent.

(10) It may be useful to end this chapter by setting out a few important definitions which will be met from time to time in the next eight chapters.

Hire-purchase agreement

A hire-purchase agreement is defined as an agreement under which goods are **19.08** bailed[10] in return for periodical payments by the bailee and the property in the goods will pass to the bailee if the terms of the agreement are complied with and one or more of the following occur:

(i) the exercise of an option to purchase by the bailee; or

(ii) the doing of any other specified act by any party to the agreement; or

(iii) the happening of any other specified event.

Conditional and credit sale agreements

A *conditional sale* agreement is an agreement for the sale of goods or land **19.09** under which the purchase price or part of it is payable by instalments and the property in the goods or land is to remain with the seller (notwithstanding that the buyer is to be in possession of the goods or land) until such conditions as to the payment of instalments or likewise as may be specified in the agreement are fulfilled.

If, however, there is a straight sale of goods on credit terms the property will usually pass to the buyer immediately under s.18, r.1 of the Sale of Goods Act 1979 and the agreement will be a *credit sale* agreement, *not* a conditional sale agreement.

Thus the crucial difference is whether the property passes to the buyer when the contract is made (credit sale) or at a later stage (conditional sale).

The term "property" is used to mean ownership.

Relative

Relative means husband, wife, brother, sister, uncle, aunt, nephew, niece, **19.10** lineal ancestor or lineal descendant. Relationship by marriage is also included and the reference to "husband or wife" includes a former or a reputed spouse.

---

[9] See para.22.02 below.
[10] Goods are "bailed" if one person ("the bailor") transfers possession to another ("the bailee") for a specific purpose. See CRA 2015 s.7.

Associate

19.11   The associate of an individual means (i) a relative, and (ii) a partner, or the relative of a partner, of that individual.

"Restricted-use" and "unrestricted-use"

19.12   These terms are defined in s.11 and are largely self-explanatory. If the debtor can actually use the credit in any way he wishes the agreement will be an "unrestricted-use" agreement, even though certain uses would constitute a breach of contract. Thus a loan paid by the lender to the borrower would be an unrestricted-use agreement. On the other hand, a hire-purchase agreement, a sale on deferred terms or a loan where the money goes straight from the lender to a third party (e.g. the supplier of goods or services) will be a restricted-use agreement. We shall meet the distinction at several points in the following chapters.

4. THE CONSUMER CREDIT DIRECTIVE 2008

Introduction

19.13   After 40 years of calm with comparatively few changes the 1974 Act is passing through a period of change, improving consumer protection but making business more complex for lenders and consumer advisers alike. Having come to grips with the amendments made by the 2006 Act (discussed at various points in Chapters Nineteen to Twenty-Six) they then had to apply their minds to Directive 2008/48/EC "on credit agreements for consumers and repealing Council directive 87/102/EEC" (the Consumer Credit Directive or CCD, as it is known).

Preamble to the CCD

19.14   The justification for Brussels' intervention again in this area is set out in the Preambles to the Directive. Preamble (3) points to "substantial differences between the laws of Member States". This situation "in some cases leads to distortions of competition among creditors in the Community" (Preamble (4)). Preamble (6) asserts:

> "The development of a more transparent and efficient credit market within the area without internal frontiers is vital in order to promote the development of cross-border activities."

This is a maximum Directive for the reasons given in Preamble (9):

> "Full harmonisation is necessary in order to ensure that all consumers in the Community enjoy a high and equivalent level of protection of their interests and to create a genuine internal market. Member States should therefore not be allowed to maintain or introduce national provisions other than those laid down in this Directive. However, such restriction should only apply where there are provisions harmonised in this Directive. Where no such harmonised provi-

sions exist, Member States should remain free to maintain or introduce national legislation."

Some CCD Articles

The UK regulations implementing the CCD were made by various statutory instruments, which we discuss in the later chapters. Meanwhile we shall comment briefly on some of the articles of the CCD. **19.15**

Article 2: Scope

A list of 12 exceptions appears in art.2.1, some of which are currently regulated by the Act, e.g. second mortgages, hire agreements. The existing legislation on hire agreements remains in place. Article 2.2(c) exempts agreements for a total amount of credit exceeding EUR 75,000 (£60,260 as transposed into UK law). **19.16**

Article 3: Definitions

Amongst the 14 definitions is "consumer": "a natural person . . . acting for purposes which are outside his trade, business or profession" in contrast to the 1974 Act where "individual" includes some businesses (see para.19.05 above). **19.17**

Article 5: Pre-contractual information

A list of 19 items appears in art.5.1. It includes all the obvious matters and is similar to current UK regulations. The most novel is the requirement by art.5(1) to provide the information "by means of the Standard European Consumer Credit Information Form" (SECCI) set out in Annex II. **19.18**

An additional duty is imposed on creditors by art.5.6 to "provide adequate explanations to the consumer" to enable them to assess whether the proposal is "adapted to his needs and to his financial situation" and by explaining various matters, e.g. the pre-contractual information, the consequences of default.

Article 8: Creditworthiness

The above explanation ties in neatly with art.8. The creditor must assess the consumer's creditworthiness on information from the consumer, a database or elsewhere. These provisions together may well prevent people borrowing beyond their means, and lead to more debtors becoming responsible borrowers. **19.19**

Article 9: Database access

A new right for debtors is given by art.9.2. If a creditor rejects an application for credit, it must inform the consumer "immediately and without charge of the result" of any database search, e.g. of a credit reference agency. **19.20**

Article 10: Information in agreements

19.21   Article 10.2 contains a list of 21 pieces of information to be included in the agreements themselves. (Overdrafts are treated separately in art.10.5.) The provisions are less prescriptive and detailed than those of the Act, e.g. no boxes for signature.

Article 14: Withdrawal

19.22   Although the Act gives a five-day cancellation right in limited circumstances, art.14.1 allows a debtor "to withdraw from the credit agreement without giving any reason" within 14 days.

Article 16: Early repayment

19.23   The difference between the early settlement provisions in s.94 of the Act (para.26.13 below) and art.16.1 is that the CCD permits *partial* early repayment.

Article 21: Intermediaries

19.24   By art.21 intermediaries must (a) in advertising indicate whether they are independent or work exclusively for one or more creditors and (b) disclose the fee payable for their services.

Summary

19.25   Some of the changes enhance consumer protection, but perhaps at the cost of excessive complexity.

We now have three systems in place: (1) agreements regulated by the Act as amended by statutory instruments to implement the Directive; (2) agreements outside the Directive but regulated by the Act in its pre-2011 state: agreements secured on land, hire agreements; (3) unregulated agreements, e.g. because they are entirely exempt.

The statutory instruments, most of which came into force on 1 February 2011, are as follows:

> The Consumer Credit (EU Directive) Regulations 2010 (SI 2010/1010)
> The Consumer Credit (Total Charge for Credit) Regulations 2010 (SI 2010/1011) (amended by SI 2012/1745)
> The Consumer Credit (Disclosure of Information) Regulations 2010 (SI 2010/1013)
> The Consumer Credit (Agreements) Regulations 2010 (SI 2010/1014)
> The Consumer Credit (Amendment) Regulations 2010 (SI 2010/1969)
> The Consumer Credit (Advertisements) Regulations 2010 (SI 2010/1970).

CHAPTER TWENTY

"WHAT AGREEMENTS ARE CAUGHT BY THE ACT?"

We have already seen that the scope of the Act is very wide. In this chapter   **20.01**
it is proposed to work through the very intricate provisions of the Act and
Regulations to find out the precise extent of control. The scheme of this
chapter is as follows:

1. Regulated agreements

2. Partially regulated agreements

3. Exempt agreements

4. Linked transactions

1. REGULATED AGREEMENTS

Most of the statutory controls only apply to a "regulated agreement".   **20.02**
In order to find out whether an agreement is regulated it is necessary to
consider both the provisions of the Consumer Credit Act 1974 and the
Financial Services and Markets Act 2000 (Regulated Activities) Order
2001 (SI 2001/544), as amended. There are consequently two stages to
consider:

(1) Does the agreement come within the definition of "consumer credit
agreement" in s.8 or "consumer hire agreement" in s.15? If the
answer is "no", the agreement cannot be a regulated agreement.

(2) If the answer to (1) above is "yes", then by ss.8(3) and 15(2) any such
agreement *is* a regulated agreement unless it is an exempt agreement.
The concept of "exempt agreement" is fleshed out in Chapters 14A
and 14B of the Financial Services and Markets Act 2000 (Regulated
Activities) Order 2001, as amended, which is dealt with later in this
chapter.[1]

Consumer credit agreement

Let us start by listing the many types of agreement which can come within   **20.03**
this term. They include:

---

[1] See para.20.15 below.

    (a) Hire-Purchase.

    (b) Conditional Sale.

    (c) Credit sale.

    (d) Personal loan.

    (e) Overdraft.

    (f) Loan secured by land mortgage.

    (g) Credit card.

    (h) Pawns.

    (i) Store cards.

Section 8(1) (as amended) defines a consumer credit agreement as an agreement whereby one person (the creditor)[2] provides an individual (the debtor) with credit of any amount. Five points are worthy of note:

    (i) There must be an "agreement". Thus where a sale is for cash and on delivery of the goods the buyer asks for time to pay, the granting of "credit" would not amount to an "agreement" unless it formed part of a separate bargain—as, for example, where the borrower agrees to pay interest on the outstanding amount.

    (ii) The creditor can be an "individual" or a body corporate, but the debtor must be an "individual" or "consumer".[3]

    (iii) The Act draws a sharp distinction between the "credit" and the "total charge for credit". The term "*credit*" includes a cash loan and any form of financial accommodation[4] and clearly refers to the loan, etc., itself. The term "total charge for credit" refers to interest and other charges.[5] Section 9(4) provides that:

        An item entering into the total charge for credit shall not be treated as credit even though time is allowed for payment.

    (iv) As an illustration of the above principles s.9(3) defines the "credit" in a hire-purchase agreement as the total price of the goods less (a) the deposit (if any), and (b) the total charge for credit.

Example

20.04   A finance house C agrees to let a Porsche car on hire-purchase to D (an individual). The total price is £27,000; this includes a down payment of £5,000 and

---

[2] "Creditor" include an assignee: *Jones v Link Financial Ltd* [2012] EWHC 2402 (QB).
[3] See para.19.05 above.
[4] s.9(3). For a recent example, see *Dimond v Lovell* [2002] 1 A.C. 384. Some 40,000 road traffic cases were stayed while this case made its slow progress through the courts.
[5] See para.20.16 below.

a total charge for credit of £3,000. When these two items are deducted from the price (£27,000–£8,000) one is left with credit of £19,000.[6]

(v) With the removal of the statutory ceiling of £25,000 it is usually unnecessary to calculate the "credit" to decide whether an agreement with a consumer is regulated. However, there is still such a ceiling for business debtors and hirers (para.20.15 below).

Three cases

The distinction between "credit" and "the total charge for credit" can be **20.05** crucial for the creditor. If the credit figure in the agreement wrongly includes an item which forms part of the total charge for credit, the agreement will be "not properly executed" and unenforceable by the creditor. The point has arisen in three recent cases; in two of them the creditor came to grief.

In *Wilson v First County Ltd (No.2)*[7] Mrs Wilson agreed to pay a £250 **20.06** document fee as part of a credit transaction. The agreement included this item as part of the credit but the Court of Appeal ruled that it formed part of the total charge for credit. The agreement was therefore unenforceable.

In *Watchtower Investments Ltd v Payne*[8] the creditor paid over an amount **20.07** after deducting a sum which was used to clear arrears under an earlier mortgage. This was one of the objects of the transaction and on that basis the deducted amount formed part of the credit.

In *McGinn v Grangewood Securities*[9] the facts were similar to those in **20.08** *Watchtower*, except that the clearance of the arrears was not one of the objects of the transaction. Accordingly the Court of Appeal distinguished the earlier case and held that the agreement had wrongly included the deducted amount in the "credit"—with the same result as in *Wilson*.

Fixed and running-account credit

The term "consumer credit agreement" is subdivided into "fixed-sum credit" **20.09** and "running-account credit"—the distinction is important in deciding whether an agreement is regulated or exempt[10] and for certain other purposes. Section 10(1)(a) tells us that

> running-account credit is a facility under a personal credit agreement whereby the debtor is enabled to receive from time to time (whether in his own person or by another person) from the creditor or a third party cash, goods and services (or any of them) to an amount or value such that, taking into account payments

---

[6] See *Humberclyde Finance v Thompson* [1997] C.C.L.R. 23 where the debtor paid a "payment waiver premium" under a clause extinguishing his liability if he died. The finance company claimed that this payment brought the "credit" above the statutory ceiling. The claim was rejected; the premium formed part of the "total charge for credit" and was not part of the "credit".

[7] [2001] EWCA Civ 663. Followed in *Southern Pacific Personal Loans Ltd v Walker* [2010] UKSC 32: broker's fee part of total charge for credit.

[8] [2001] EWCA Civ 1159. See also *Southern Pacific Mortgage Ltd v Heath* [2009] EWCA Civ 1135.

[9] [2002] EWCA Civ 522.

[10] See para.20.15 below, subpara.(6).

made by or to the credit of the debtor, the credit limit (if any) is not at any time exceeded.

The two most common examples of running-account credit are bank over-drafts and store cards.

Debtor-creditor-supplier (D-C-S) agreements and debtor-creditor (D-C) agreements

20.10 These terms are defined in ss.12 and 13. It is necessary to mention them at this point because a knowledge of them is vital when considering the all important question of whether the agreement is *regulated* or *exempt*.[11] The distinction between D-C-S and D-C turns on the relationship between the supplier of the credit and the supplier of the land, goods or services. The effect of ss.12 and 13 can be summarised as follows:

   (i) If the supplier of the credit and the supplier of the goods, etc., is *the same person*, then it is D-C-S. Examples include hire purchase, credit sale, and sale of land where the seller agrees to leave the price out-standing. This can be referred to as "two-party D-C-S".

   (ii) If the supplier of credit and the supplier of the goods, etc., are *different* but work together under *"arrangements"*, then again it is D-C-S. Thus, a credit card company has "arrangements" with its approved suppliers and a finance company might have "arrangements" with a car dealer whereby they would provide loans to finance sales made by him to customers. In both these cases the credit contract would be a D-C-S agreement. This can be referred to as "three-party D-C-S".

   (iii) If there are no such arrangements, the agreement is a D-C agreement. Thus if a customer borrows £4,000 from his bank to pay for central heating or a holiday or to finance his business, this is a D-C agreement.

   (iv) If an agreement is made to refinance an existing indebtedness, whether to the creditor or any other person, then again it is D-C.

As already stated the distinction is critical on the "regulated or exempt" point—we shall see that under a D-C-S agreement the critical factor is the number of instalments, whereas under a D-C agreement the critical factor is the annual percentage rate of charge for credit. The distinction is also important for other purposes, including joint responsibility of supplier and creditor in cancellation cases[12] and under s.75.[13]

---

[11] See para.20.15 below.
[12] See para.23.14 below.
[13] See para.24.06 below. This is a vital provision in relation to credit cards.

Consumer hire agreement

The second type of agreement to which the Act applies is a consumer hire   **20.11**
agreement. Clearly, this type of agreement is less important than the consumer credit agreement, but it is worth remembering that it covers not only
the domestic hiring of, e.g. a television set, but also the commercial hiring of,
e.g. equipment. Section 15 makes it clear that there are five elements:

(a) a bailment of goods

(b) by one person (the owner)

(c) to an individual (the hirer), provided that

(d) it is not hire-purchase, and

(e) it is capable of lasting for more than three months.[14]

2. PARTIALLY REGULATED AGREEMENTS

As already stated, the all important distinction is between *regulated* and *exempt*   **20.12**
agreements. Before considering the nature of exempt agreements it might be
useful to mention two types of agreement which are regulated in part only.

Non-commercial agreements

By s.189 a non-commercial agreement is an agreement not made by the credi-   **20.13**
tor or owner in the course of a business carried on by him. It is important to
notice the words "*a* business". If, for example, a manufacturer made loans to
his employees to enable them to buy season tickets or houses, the loans *would*
be made in the course of *a* business (even though it was not a consumer credit
or consumer hire business) and accordingly it would not be "non-commercial".
If, however, the agreement is non-commercial then a number of specific provisions do not apply. The most important area is formalities and cancellation.[15]

Small agreements

A small agreement is defined in s.17 as either: **20.14**

(a) a regulated consumer credit agreement for credit not exceeding £50, other
than a hire-purchase or conditional sale agreement[16]; or
(b) a regulated consumer hire agreement which does not require the hirer to
make payments exceeding £50.

There is a further condition, namely, that the agreement is unsecured or
secured by a guarantee or indemnity only. Not surprisingly, s.17(3) blocks

---

[14] The critical period is the duration of the bailment and not the duration of the payment obligation: *Clark v Ardington Electrical Services* [2002] EWCA Civ 510.
[15] See s.74(1)(a) and ss.77–79.
[16] See paras 19.08–19.09 above.

attempts to split up a transaction into a series of small agreements by providing that in such a case each small agreement shall be treated as a regulated non-small agreement.

Small debtor-creditor-supplier agreements for restricted-use credit are exempt from most of the provisions relating to formalities and cancellation.[17]

3. Exempt Agreements

20.15   Having decided that an agreement is a consumer credit or consumer hire agreement, we must now decide whether it is taken out of control by one of the exemptions. These are to be found in arts 60C to 60H in Pt 14A of the Financial Services and Markets Act 2000 (Regulated Activities) Order 2001, as amended (the 2001 Order) (for consumer credit agreements). We must note from the outset that the definitions of exempt agreements are complicated and cannot be discussed in full here. With regard to consumer credit agreements, there are seven broad categories of exemptions:

(1) Exemptions relating to the nature of the agreement (reg.60C): this category is essentially concerned with agreements where the borrower is wholly or predominantly acting for the purpose of a business carried on by the borrower and the credit exceeds £25,000. The exemption also applies if the credit is £25,000 or less but the borrower is wholly acted for business purposes and the agreement relates to a "Green Deal" plan (see reg.60LB).

(2) Exemption relating to purchase of land for non-residential purposes (reg.60D): this exemption applies where less than 40 per cent of the land acquired is used or intended to be used as a dwelling, with the total size of the land based on the aggregate of the floor space (in case of multi-story dwellings).

(3) Exemption relating to the nature of the lender (reg.60E): This exemption covers agreements in relation to the purchase of land where the lender is a local authority or a person specified by the Financial Conduct Authority (FCA) from the list of lenders in reg.60E(3). It also covers agreements secured by a mortgage on land to be used for a dwelling where the lender is a housing authority.[18]

(4) Exemption relating to the number of payments to be made (reg.60F): This exemption applies to a variety of borrower-lender-supplier (BLS) agreements (a term now used in place of the old "debtor-creditor-supplier" one still used elsewhere). It covers

---

[17] See paras 22.13 and 23.18 below.
[18] Defined in reg.60E(7).

      (i) a BLS agreement for a fixed sum, with the number of payments no more than 12 and all payments to be made within a 12-month period or less;

     (ii) a BLS agreement for running-account credit where the whole amount of credit is provided for a period of three months or less and has to be repaid in one sum;

    (iii) a BLS financing the purchase of land with the number of payments to be made is no more than four. In all cases, there is an additional requirement that the credit is either secured on land or provided without interest or other charges (but not conditional sale or hire-purchase agreements). Further exemptions in this category relate to BLS agreements to finance insurance premiums in respect of land.

(5) Exemption relating to the total charge of credit (reg.60G): there are a number of agreements within this category, including:

      (i) a borrower-lender agreement where the lender is a credit-union and where the total charge does not exceed 42.6 per cent,[19] and

     (ii) some borrower-lender agreements not offered to the public generally where the only charge for the credit is interest which does not exceed one percent above the highest base-rate published by the banks listed in reg.60G(7).

(6) Exemptions relating to the nature of the borrower (reg.60H): this category covers agreements where a borrower is an individual and the agreement is either secured on land or exceeds £60,260 and for a purpose not related to land, and the borrower has made a declaration agreeing to forgo the protection and remedies that would be available if the agreement were a regulated agreement, provided that this complies with the relevant FCA rules (so-called "high net-worth" borrowers).

(7) A credit agreement entered into after 21 March 2016 if it is an agreement within the scope of art.3(1) of the Mortgages Directive (reg.60HA).[20]

We also note that there are some exemptions in respect of regulated hire agreements in arts 60N to 60Q of Pt 14B of the 2001 Order.

---

[19] Additional qualifications apply to agreements of this type entered into before 21 March 2016 (reg.60G(2A)(c)).

[20] Article 3(1) of the Directive (2014/17/EU) covers "credit agreements which are secured either by a mortgage or by another comparable security commonly used in a Member State on residential immovable property or secured by a right related to residential immovable property; and credit agreements the purpose of which is to acquire or retain property rights in land or in an existing or projected building."

The total charge for credit (TCC)

20.16 We have already met this term on several occasions and it is now necessary to examine it more closely. It is vitally important for a number of reasons, including the following:

(a) Any sum forming part of the total charge for credit does not form part of the credit.[21]

(b) One of the cardinal principles of the Act is to give the debtor information on various matters and one such matter is the "true cost of borrowing".[22]

In the past, the total charge for credit is dealt with in the Consumer Credit (Total Charge for Credit) Regulations 2010 as amended by the Consumer Credit (Total Charge for Credit) (Amendment) Regulations 2012.[23] However, the relevant rules are now found in the FCA's rule book[24] which now determines the meaning of "total charge for credit".[25] The detail can be found in the Consumer Credit Sourcebook at Chapter 15 and Appendices 1.1–1.4 ("CONC").

Items included

20.17 CONC App.1.2.3(1) provides that the TCC is "the total cost of credit to the borrower" as specified In CONC App.1.2.3. The TCC therefore includes (a) any fee or charge payable by the borrower to a credit broker in connection with the agreement; (b) the costs of maintaining an account recording both payment transactions and drawdowns; (c) the costs of using a means of payment for both payment transactions and drawdowns; and (d) other costs relating to payment transactions.

Items excluded

20.18 Among items excluded are the following: (a) sums payable on default, (b) sums which would be payable in any event even if it were a cash transaction (e.g. installation charges).[26]

Annual percentage rate (APR)

20.19 CONC App 1.2.6 contains a highly complex equation which takes in the credit, the instalments and the relevant outstanding periods. The creditor must work out the rate in a way which will satisfy the equation. CONC App 1.2.6 (3)(f) requires the rate to be calculated to one decimal place—but on the

---

[21] s.9(3) at para.20.03 above.
[22] s.20.
[23] SI 2010/1011 and SI 2012/1745.
[24] reg.60M of the 2001 Order, as amended.
[25] reg.60L(1) of the 2001 Order, as amended.
[26] CONC App.1.2.3(5).

basis of rounding up if the second decimal place is five or greater (so that a rate of 12.26 per cent becomes 12.3 per cent).

Assumptions

The above explanation presupposes that all the items are constant and known **20.20** at the date of the agreement. In practice this may not be so and CONC App 1.2.5 recognises this by making 15 assumptions set out in that paragraph. For example, a provision giving the creditor the right to increase the interest must generally be disregarded (para (b)). In the case of an overdraft, it is assumed that the total amount of credit is drawn down in full and for the entire duration of the agreement, which if unknown will be three months (paras (i) and (j)). The credit limit is assumed to be £1,200 in the case of running account credit, e.g. credit cards (para (o)).

Land

CONC App 1.1 deals with certain agreements secured on land. **20.21**

4. LINKED TRANSACTIONS

Having examined the crucial distinction between regulated and exempt **20.22** agreements, it is necessary to end this chapter with a brief mention of linked transactions, i.e. transactions which are linked to an actual or prospective regulated agreement. The term "linked transaction" is important for a variety of reasons, including withdrawal, cancellation, early settlement and unfair relationships. It is clear from s.19 that an agreement for security will not be a linked agreement but, subject to this, the following are included:

(1) A transaction entered into in compliance with a term of the principal agreement, e.g. "the debtor shall insure his life with XYZ insurance company and shall enter into a maintenance contract with Eezikleen Ltd".

(2) A transaction to be financed by a debtor-creditor-supplier agreement. Thus where the supplier of a car and the supplier of the credit have "arrangements", the sale of the car is "linked" to the loan contract, so that cancellation of the latter will also cancel the former.[27]

(3) A transaction entered into by the debtor, hirer or a relative at the suggestion of the creditor, owner, an associate of his[28] or a person negotiating the principal agreement.

Regulations have been made[29] whereby certain types of linked agreement

---

[27] s.69(1).
[28] See para.19.11 above.
[29] Consumer Credit (Linked Transactions) (Exemptions) Regulations 1983 (SI 1983/1560).

are excluded from the provisions of the Act relating to effectiveness,[30] cancellation and early settlement. The excepted classes are:

(1) Contracts of insurance.

(2) Guarantees of goods.

(3) Agreements for the operation of a deposit and/or current account.

---

[30] In general a linked agreement is ineffective until the main agreement is made (s.19(3)).

CHAPTER TWENTY-ONE

CONTROL OF BUSINESS ACTIVITIES

We have already seen that the Consumer Credit Act controls business activi- **21.01** ties as well as individual agreements. It is clear that business control is of very great benefit to the consumer. It should help to ensure that the other party to the transaction is a reputable trader and that the consumer is not pressurised into a transaction by misleading advertising or other undesirable business practices. In this chapter it is proposed to consider this aspect of consumer protection under three main headings, namely:

1. Financial Conduct Authority authorisation.

2. Advertising.

3. Canvassing.

1. FINANCIAL CONDUCT AUTHORITY AUTHORISATION

From the coming into force of the 1974 Act until April 2014 the regulation of **21.02** the consumer credit industry by the licensing system was carried out by the Office of Fair Trading (OFT). Then in April 2014 this function was transferred to the Financial Conduct Authority (FCA).[1] The system is now called "authorisation".

The FCA Annual Report and Accounts 2014/15 points out that it now regulates 73,000 firms. To cope with the interregnum between the OFT and FCA regimes the FCA introduced "interim permission" for firms previously regulated by the OFT: "about 50,000" firms registered according to that Report.

There are now two types of permission—"full" and "limited". Firms applying for full permission must meet more conditions for authorisation and will be subject to more checks and monitoring.

Who needs authorisation?

The following activities require *full* permission: **21.03**

- consumer credit lending (e.g. personal loans, credit cards, hire-purchase);

---

[1] The Financial Services Authority was renamed the Financial Conduct Authority by s.1A of the Financial Services and Markets Act 2000 (FSMA 2000).

- credit broking:

    —where the main business is introducing consumers to lenders; or
    —where the supply of goods or services is in the consumer's home;

- debt adjusting and debt counseling;

- debt administration and debt collecting;

- credit reference agency;

- credit information services;

- peer-to-peer lending.

Only *limited* permission is required for:

- lending:

    —where the main business is sale of goods or non-financial services, not hire-purchase or conditional sale and no interest or charges;

- credit broking:

    —for hire-purchase or hire;
    —for Green Deal;
    —where the main business is sale of goods or non- financial services and it is a secondary activity to finance such purchases, e.g. car dealers;

- consumer hire;

- not-for-profit bodies:

    —debt adjusting, debt counselling and credit information services, e.g. CABx;

- local authorities.

Conduct

21.04 The FCA may make *rules*, which are legally binding, and publish non-binding *guidance* on possible ways for a firm to comply with the rules. The rules and guidance are set out in the FCA Handbook. A useful publication is the FCA "Guide for consumer credit firms". Also accessible on its website *http://www.fca.org.uk* is a step-by-step video guide on how to complete its online application form.

An important role of the FCA is the monitoring and supervision of authorised firms. We describe below three significant aspects of creditors' expected conduct.

(1) Approved firms

The OFT required a licensee to be "a fit person" to engage in credit activities. **21.05**
The FCA similarly requires each authorised business to have "an approved
person" to perform such activities. Such persons must be fit and proper to
perform their functions. Relevant criteria are honesty, integrity and reputa-
tion, financial soundness, and competence and capability. They must comply
with the FCA Statements of Principle and Code of Practice for Approved
Persons.

(2) CONC

The rules and guidance are primarily in the Consumer Credit Sourcebook **21.06**
(CONC). Many of the obligations are based on the existing standards to be
found in the Act, related statutory instruments and OFT guidance. There
are, however, new rules on credit broking and on High-Cost Short-Term
Credit (HCSTC), the latter following adverse publicity on the trading terms
of pay day lenders such as Wonga—now there is a cap on interest of 0.8 per
cent per day and interest and fees in total must not exceed 100 per cent of
the loan.

(3) TCF

"Treating customers fairly" (TCF) is a precept to be found amongst the 11 **21.07**
Principles of Business (PRIN) in the FCA Handbook which underpin the
high-level standards expected of all firms. Principle 6 states:

> Customers' interests—A firm must pay due regard to the interests of its custom-
> ers and treat them fairly.

Sanctions for non-compliance

There are two main sanctions against a business conducting regulated credit **21.08**
activities without permission. Agreements made in such circumstances are
unenforceable[2] by the credit business. The consumer may recover any
money or property transferred and may also recover compensation for resulting loss (s.26A of FSMA 2000).

The second sanction is criminal. It is an offence to carry on a credit-
related activity without permission. The business may be fined and anyone
guilty of an offence may be imprisoned for up to a year on summary
conviction or up to two years if convicted on indictment (s.23 of FSMA
2000).

The FCA may also withdraw authorisation, suspend firms or ban individuals from undertaking regulated activities or apply to the court for injunctions
or restitution orders.

---

[2] A "not properly executed" agreement is also unenforceable: see s.65 of the Act.

2. ADVERTISEMENTS AND QUOTATIONS

21.09   We have already seen that the very nature of credit carries the danger that the consumer may over commit himself. The likelihood of this is greatly increased if the creditor is allowed to exhibit a misleading advertisement with words like "five years to pay" in bold type and a very high interest charge tucked away in the small print.

Advertising controls are clearly required and are contained in two sets of statutory provisions—ss.43 to 47, which include a number of enabling powers, and the Consumer Credit (Advertisements) Regulations 2010.[3]

Advertisements and the consumer

21.10   Before embarking on a brief examination of the scope and content of advertisement regulation it may be relevant to consider what rights accrue to consumers as a result of a defective advertisement. There are three overlapping possibilities:

(1) If they are induced by a misleading advertisement to make a contract with the advertiser, they may have a civil claim under the general law for misrepresentation or for negligence.[4]

(2) If an advertisement contravenes the Act, the regulations or other legislation, the criminal court can exercise its general power to award compensation.[5]

(3) There is the ever-present possibility of a complaint to the FCA which could, in the last resort, lead to the suspension or revocation of a licence.

Scope of advertisement control

21.11   The advertising provisions stand apart from the rest of the Act; in some respects the controls are wider and in some narrower. Thus:

(1) The controls are not restricted to "regulated agreements" (see para.20.02 above). On the other hand, the controls will not apply if the advertisement indicates that the credit is only available to a body corporate (see s.43(3)(b)).

(2) The effect of the Consumer Credit (Exempt Advertisements) Order 1985 (SI 1985/621 (as amended)) is to take many—but not all—types of exempt agreements outside the advertising controls.

(3) When we turn to the Advertisements Regulations themselves, we

---

[3] SI 2010/1970, replacing the Consumer Credit (Advertisement) Regulations 2004 (SI 2004/1484) which continue to apply to land loans.
[4] See Chapters Three and Eight.
[5] See Chapter Seventeen.

find one of the few distinctions between private and business trans-actions. These Regulations will not apply to an advertisement which (1) expressly or by implication states that credit is available for the purposes of a person's business, and (2) does not indicate that the credit is available for non-business purposes (see reg.11).

The definitions

It is clear from s.189 that the concept of "advertisement" is extremely wide **21.12** and is not confined to visual forms. It can therefore include anything from a catalogue or brochure to films, radio and television commercials, inter-net, telephone and even sales patter. It is also important to note that "the advertiser" is not necessarily the person who causes the advertisement to be inserted; it is the person who is indicated in the advertisement as willing to provide the credit or credit brokerage facilities.

False advertisements

By s.46 an offence is committed if an advertisement is false or misleading **21.13** in a material respect. Thus an "APR nil" advertisement has been held to be false where the trader made a hidden charge by giving a lower part-exchange allowance to instalment buyers than to cash buyers.[6] Similarly, the Rover company was convicted when, in large print, they gave £595 as the price of a new Metro while adding (in very small print at the bottom) that an extra £480 was payable for twelve months' road tax, number plates and delivery to the dealer.[7]

The Advertisements Regulations 2010

The Regulations[8] deal in considerable detail with the form and content of **21.14** advertisements. Thus they must:

(a) use plain and intelligible language;

(b) be easily legible or clearly audible;

(c) specify the name of the advertiser (reg.3).

Representative example

Where an advertisement includes a rate of interest or amount relating to the **21.15** cost of credit, by reg.4(1) it must also include (a) a "representative" example, and (b) a postal address with some exceptions, e.g. television, on a dealer's premises.

---

[6] *Metsoja v H Norman Pitt & Co Ltd* (1989) 153 J.P.N. 630.
[7] *Rover Group Ltd v Sumner* [1995] C.C.L.R. 1 Chester Crown Court.
[8] SI 2010/1970.

In most cases the example must contain the information specified in reg.5, e.g.:

- rate of interest;

- amount of credit;

- representative APR;

- duration of agreement;

- total amount and amount of each instalment.

The "representative APR" is the APR which the advertiser would reasonably expect to apply to at least 51 per cent of the resultant agreements (reg.1(3)). All the items must be given equal prominence.

Banned expressions

21.16 Certain expressions (or similar ones) are banned or may be used only in limited circumstances. They are listed in reg.10:

- overdraft;

- interest free;

- no deposit;

- loan guaranteed, pre-approved;

- gift, present.

3. CANVASSING

21.17 Section 49 follows the precedent set by the Moneylenders Acts by prohibiting the canvassing of debtor-creditor agreements (e.g. personal loans) off-trade premises.

When is an offence committed?

21.18 The canvasser must be an individual and must solicit the debtor into the making of a regulated agreement by making oral representations to the debtor, or to any other individual, during a visit by the canvasser to non-trade premises. The visit must have been for the purpose of making such oral representations, so that a crime is not committed if one individual makes representations to another individual while they are both guests at a party. On the other hand, a social visit can be caught if the underlying intention was to make representations leading to the debtor-creditor agreement.

Previous request

No offence is committed if the visit was in response to a request made on a **21.19**
previous occasion, provided that the request was in writing signed by or on
behalf of the person making it.[9] Presumably the person making the request
need not be the debtor.

Trade premises

For *this* purpose the term "trade premises" is defined[10] as any premises **21.20**
where a business is carried on (whether on a permanent or temporary basis)
by (a) the creditor or owner, (b) the supplier, (c) the canvasser's employer, or
(d) the debtor.

Circulars to minors

Minors (persons under 18) are particularly vulnerable to blandishments of **21.21**
"easy credit" and accordingly s.50(1) makes it an offence for a person, with
a view to financial gain, to send to a minor any document inviting him or her
to (a) borrow money, (b) obtain goods on credit or hire, (c) obtain services
on credit, or (d) apply for information or advice on borrowing money or
otherwise obtaining credit or hiring goods.[11] A defence is available where
the person sending the circular did not know and had no reasonable cause to
suspect that the addressee was a minor (s.50(2)) but the following subsection
makes this defence somewhat difficult to raise if the document is sent to a
school! Any such offence will not invalidate any resulting agreement[12] and
such an agreement will be governed by a combination of common law rules,
the Minors Contracts Act 1987, s.3 of the Sale of Goods Act 1979 and the
Act.

---

[9] s.48(1)(b) and 49(2).
[10] cf. cancellation at para.23.07 below.
[11] For an unsuccessful prosecution, see *Alliance & Leicester Building Society v Babbs* [1993]
C.C.L.R. 77 DC.
[12] s.170(1) at para.19.07 above.

CHAPTER TWENTY-TWO

"I CAN'T REMEMBER WHAT I SIGNED"

In the previous chapter we examined vitally important provisions relating to **22.01** the control of business activities.

We now turn to the other main form of control—the regulation of individual agreements. The law is to be found in Pts V to IX of the Act and much of it is modelled on the previous hire-purchase legislation. This chapter is concerned with formalities and copies.[1] The object of the legislation is to make sure that the debtor or hirer are made aware of their rights and obligations and that they can obtain further information if, for example, they failed to keep a record of their payments. Once again a large amount of the detail is contained in regulations.

Sanctions for non-compliance

The sanctions are potentially severe. If the creditor or owner fails to comply **22.02** with the various formalities, the agreement is said to be *"not properly executed"*. By s.65 the creditor or owner cannot enforce such an agreement against the debtor or hirer unless (a) the court makes an enforcement order,[2] or (b) the debtor or hirer consents to enforcement (s.173(3)).[3] What happens if the creditor or owner, in defiance of s.65, enforces the agreement by retaking the goods? If the repossession amounts to the tort of trespass or conversion, the creditor or owner will be liable for this. If, however, the repossession is only unlawful because it contravenes s.65, it seems that the only remedy of the debtor or hirer is to apply for a mandatory injunction to restore the status quo.[4]

The purpose of the sanctions is to put the creditor or owner at a disadvantage if they do not comply with the rules designed for the protection of the consumer. The agreement is not invalidated[5]: it becomes *unenforceable by the creditor or owner* without an order of the court.[6] From the point of view of the debtor or hirer it is still valid and fully enforceable. For example, if goods held under a hire-purchase agreement are defective, the debtor can bring a claim under the Consumer Rights Act 2015 (CRA 2015) even though

---

[1] ss.58–65 and 77–80.
[2] See para.26.06 below.
[3] See para.19.07 above.
[4] As above.
[5] *R. v Modupe* [1991] C.C.L.R. 29 CA (total price omitted; liability to repay continued, though unenforceable). See also *McGuffick v Royal Bank of Scotland* [2009] EWHC 2386 (Comm): the agreement is not void.
[6] The court has a wide discretion—see s.127 at para.26.06 below.

the agreement is "improperly executed". Further, a dishonest hirer can be prosecuted for seeking to evade an "existing liability", even though the "liability" is unenforceable without a court order under s.65.[7]

Creditworthiness and explanations

22.03 To combat over-indebtedness, which typified and contributed to the economic disaster of the previous decade, two complementary provisions were introduced in 2011. Their aim is to ensure that creditors check and borrowers are made aware of the financial effect of granting credit in each particular case.

Creditworthiness check[8]

22.04 Section 55B(1) and (2) compels creditors to assess debtors' creditworthiness before making an agreement or "significantly" increasing the amount of credit or a credit limit. The assessment "must be based on sufficient information" obtained from the debtor (where appropriate) and a credit reference agency (where necessary).

Explanations[9]

22.05 Again before making an agreement s.55A(1) makes creditors provide debtors "with an adequate explanation" of the matters referred to in subs.(2):

(a) the features of the agreement which may make the credit unsuitable;

(b) what the debtor must pay periodically and in total;

(c) the features which have "a significant adverse effect ... which the debtor is unlikely to foresee";

(d) the main consequences of a failure to pay on time, e.g. legal action, repossession of their home; and

(e) the right of withdrawal and its effects.

Creditors must also advise debtors to consider the information (and where disclosed in person, that they can take it away) and how to ask for further explanation, and must give them an opportunity to ask questions about the agreement.

The purpose of these provisions is to help debtors to understand properly the transaction on which they are about to embark so that they will proceed only when fully informed of its effect and suitability.

Two final points should be noted. Usually the advice and information may be given orally or in writing (subss.(3) and (4)). Where a credit intermediary has complied with the above provisions, the creditor is not liable (subs.(5)).

---

[7] *R. v Modupe* [1991] C.C.L.R. 29 CA.
[8] reg.5 of SI 2010/1010. Land and pawns are excluded.
[9] reg.3 of SI 2010/1010. Land, pawns (mainly) and credit of £60,260+ excluded.

Pre-contractual information: 2004 Regulations

As part of the policy outlined above, s.55 enables regulations to be made **22.06** whereby specified information must be disclosed to the prospective debtor or hirer before a regulated agreement is made. The Consumer Credit (Disclosure of Information) Regulations 2004[10] state that the information is the same as that required in the agreement itself and specified in the 1983 Regulations[11] discussed in para.22.13 below.

The 2004 Regulations will now apply to fewer agreements as the Consumer Credit (Disclosure of Information) Regulations 2010 discussed below will generally apply instead (with some exceptions).

Disclosure Regulations 2010

The Consumer Credit (Disclosure of Information) Regulations 2010 (SI **22.07** 2010/1013) came into force on 1 January 2011. By reg.2 they apply to all regulated consumer credit agreements except land mortgages within s.58 (see para.22.11 below), certain non-business overdrafts, credit of £60,260+, land mortgages and business credit.

Information

Regulation 3(2) requires creditors to disclose "in good time before the agree- **22.08** ment is made" a list of 22 items set out in reg.3(4), which is similar to that required in the agreement itself, e.g. type of credit, interest rate, amount and frequency of instalments.

Different requirements are specified for the following types of agreement:

- reg.4   telephone contracts;
- reg.5   non-telephone distance contracts;
- reg.6   distance business contracts;
- reg.9   pawn agreements;
- reg.10   overdraft agreements; and
- reg.12   modifying agreements.

SECCI Form

The information must be disclosed by the form contained in Sch.1 known as **22.09** the PCI or SECCI (Standard European Consumer Credit) form (reg.8(1)). The information must be "clear and easily legible", but the asterisk, notes, gridlines and boxes may be deleted or omitted (reg.8(3)).

---

[10] SI 2004/1481.
[11] SI 1983/1553.

Credit intermediaries[12]

22.10 Another piece of information, which must be disclosed to the debtor before the agreement is made, relates to any "financial consideration" (e.g. commission, fees) payable to a "credit intermediary". This new provision appears in s.160A.

This person is defined in subs.(1) and s.189(1) as someone who for a financial consideration—and not as a creditor—(a) recommends or makes available regulated consumer credit agreements (unless secured on land) to individuals; (b) assists them by undertaking other such preparatory work; or (c) enters into such agreements for creditors.

They must, in their advertising and documentation, indicate the extent to which they act independently and whether they work exclusively with a creditor. They must also disclose to debtors any fees payable to themselves by the debtors and agree them in writing (subss.(3) and (4)) and disclose the same information to creditors if the annual percentage rate (APR) is to be ascertained by them (subs.(5)).

Consideration period in land mortgage cases

22.11 We have already seen that many land mortgage cases are outside the main control provisions because the agreements are exempted under s.16 or by regulations.[13] If, however, the agreement is a regulated agreement, s.58 lays down a special pre-contractual period of reflection and isolation; the reason for this is that the post-contractual cancellation provisions do not apply to any agreement secured on land.[14]

In two cases, however, the special reflection rules do not apply, namely (a) a restricted-use agreement to finance the purchase of the mortgaged land, and (b) an agreement for a bridging loan in connection with the purchase of the mortgaged land or other land. In these two cases the debtor will have neither reflection rights nor cancellation rights.

22.12 Let us suppose that John, a moneylender, is prepared to lend George £20,000 on the security of George's house. The reflection and isolation rules can be summarised as follows:

(1) At least seven days before sending the agreement for signature, John must give to George a copy of the agreement (and of any document referred to therein) containing a notice in the prescribed form indicating George's right to withdraw from the transaction.[15]

(2) When seven days have elapsed, John can post the agreement for signature unless he has received a notice of withdrawal.[16]

---

[12] As above, reg.41.
[13] See para.20.15 above.
[14] s.67 at para.23.07 below.
[15] s.58(1) and 61(2). Thus a copy of the proposed mortgage would have to accompany the reflection copy which refers to it.
[16] s.61(2) and (4).

(3) John must not approach George in any way during the "*consideration period*" except at George's specific request. The consideration period begins when the "reflection copy" is sent[17] and ends seven days after the sending of the agreement for signature[18] or, if earlier, its return by George duly signed.

Regulations have now been made relating to the wording of the "reflection copy". The document must contain an explanatory box drawing attention to the right to withdraw. Finally the agreement itself[19] must contain a box pointing out the debtor's right to an earlier reflection copy.

The above requirements also apply to a regulated consumer hire agreement secured by land mortgage.

Formalities of the agreement itself

Sections 60 and 61 enable regulations to be made to ensure that the debtor **22.13** or hirer is made aware of his rights and duties, the amount and rate of the total charge for credit and the protection and remedies available to him under the Act. The detail is to be found in the Consumer Credit (Agreements) Regulations 1983 as regards agreements falling outside the 2010 Regulations discussed below. They specify the information which must be included, having regard to the particular type of agreement.[20] The 1983 Regulations (not surprisingly) require that the information should be easily legible and of a colour which is easily distinguishable from the colour of the paper.[21] They also specify the prominence to be given to particular parts of the agreement, and the place where the debtor or hirer must sign and the words to be contained in the signature box. The financial and related particulars (description of goods, deposit, credit,[22] cash price, APR, total charges, repayments, etc.) must be shown together as a whole and not interspersed with other information.

The Act itself lays down three broad requirements in s.61(1):

(a) a document in the prescribed form itself containing all the prescribed terms[23] and conforming to regulations under s.60(1) is signed in the prescribed manner both by the debtor or hirer and by or on behalf of the creditor or owner, and

(b) the document embodies all the terms of the agreement, other than implied terms, and

---

[17] See (1) above.

[18] See (2) above.

[19] Sch.2 to SI 2010/1014.

[20] regs 2–5 of SI 1983/1553. Amended from 31 May 2005 by the Consumer Credit (Agreements) (Amendment) Regulations 2004 (SI 2004/1482).

[21] reg.6(2).

[22] *Brophy v HFC Bank* [2011] EWCA Civ 67: credit card limit.

[23] See reg.6 of and Sch.6 to the Agreements Regulations for the meaning of this term. See *Carey v HSBC Bank Plc* [2009] EWHC 3417 (QB) for judicial guidance: see para.22.22 below. See also *Harrison v Link Financial Ltd* [2011] E.C.C. 26.

(c) the document is, when presented or sent to the debtor or hirer for signature, in such a state that all its terms are readily legible.

The wording of para.(a) makes it clear that the debtor or hirer must sign *personally*. It is also clear that a signature on a blank form, with the details filled in later, would not be sufficient.[24]

Agreements Regulations 2010

22.14 Having discussed the various statutory provisions put in place to ensure that debtors enter into regulated consumer agreements with their eyes open and can pull out, if they are uneasy with what they see—explanations, disclosure of information, the right of withdrawal—we now turn to the agreement itself. The form, content and signature requirements imposed by the Consumer Credit (Agreements) Regulations 2010[25] came into force from 1 February 2011 like the other changes implementing Directive 2008/48/EC. They bear a close resemblance to the 1983 Regulations, which apply instead to agreements excluded from the 2010 Regulations by reg.2(2) to (5): land mortgages, credit exceeding £60,260 and business credit.

Form and content

22.15 Regulation 3 states that agreements must contain the information set out in Sch.1 "in a clear and concise manner"—legibility and colour are mentioned as in the 1983 Regulations—as well as the statements about the protection and remedies of debtors in the Form in Sch.2, e.g. termination and protected goods in hire-purchase cases.[26] (Regulation 7 stresses that the Forms in Schs 2 and 3 must be reproduced "without any alteration", with minor exceptions.)

Credit for insurance premiums is dealt with in paras (6) and (7). Modifying, pawn and overdraft agreements are covered by regs 5, 6 and 8.

Signature

22.16 To be properly executed and to comply with s.61(1)(a) reg.4 provides that the agreements must contain "the prescribed terms" in Sch.1, be signed by the debtor in a special "space"[27] (e.g. a box) and by the creditors or their agents, and be dated. Regulation 4(5) recognises electronic communication.

Copies

22.17 Clearly debtors need to know what they have signed and the precise terms of the agreement. These requirements have been in place for decades under ss.62 and 63 and continue in force in a limited way (see below). However, new

---

[24] Consider *Eastern Distributors v Goldring* [1957] Q.B. 600, a decision on a slightly different provision in the Hire-Purchase Act 1938.
[25] SI 2010/1014.
[26] See paras 23.19 and 26.27 below.
[27] See *Bassano v Toft* [2014] EWHC 377 (QB): online agreement.

provisions (enacted to comply with the 2008 Directive) appear in ss.55C and 61A which we shall explain first.

New provisions

A debtor may wish to peruse in advance the terms of a prospective agreement. On receipt of a request for such an advance copy s.55C(1) states that the creditor must give it "without delay". There are the usual exceptions: land, £60,260+, business loans and pawns.[28]

22.18

Section 61A deals with copies of the agreement itself. The creditor must give a copy of the executed agreement, and any document referred to in it, to the debtor, unless a copy of the unexecuted agreement in identical terms has already been given to the debtor (ss.61A(1) and (2)). The section does not apply to the usual trio (land, £60,260+ and business) or to cancellable agreements.

Three final points need to be made. Sections 62 and 63 apply to the excluded trio. Section 61B contains special provisions about overdrafts. An agreement is "not properly executed" if these requirements are not observed (s.61A(5)).

Earlier provisions: excluded agreements

As we mentioned in the previous paragraph, ss.62 and 63 continue to apply to the agreements excluded from s.61A[29] and hire agreements.

22.19

The basic rule is that the debtor or hirer is always entitled to at least one copy of the agreement; in many cases he is entitled to two copies.

The provisions are complex but they can be conveniently divided into (a) cases where the agreement is presented to the debtor or hirer for signature, and (b) cases where it is sent for signature.

(a) In the vast majority of cases in practice the document *presented* to and signed by the debtor or hirer will be *"an unexecuted agreement"*, i.e. a document embodying the terms of a prospective agreement. In other words, the document is an offer by the debtor or hirer and there will be no concluded agreement until the document is signed by the creditor or owner thus accepting the offer. In this situation one copy must be given to the debtor or hirer immediately after signature[30] and, in addition, a copy of the executed agreement must be delivered or sent within seven days after the making of the agreement.[31]

In the less likely situation where the creditor or owner has already signed, signature by the debtor or hirer will convert the document into an *"executed agreement"*, i.e. a contract; in that situation a copy

---

[28] s.55C(4). See reg.6 of SI 2010/1010.
[29] As amended by regs 10 and 11 of SI 2010/1010.
[30] s.62(1).
[31] s.63(2).

of that agreement must be given there and then and no further copy is required.[32]

(b) Here the position is somewhat similar to that mentioned above. In all cases the agreement *sent* to the debtor or hirer for signature must be accompanied by a copy.[33] If the document becomes an "executed agreement" when signed, no further copy need be sent.[34] Usually, however, the signed document is an offer to the creditor or owner and will not become an "executed agreement" until it is signed by the creditor or owner. In that situation a copy of the executed agreement must be delivered or sent to the debtor or hirer within seven days of the making of the agreement.

22.20 Special provisions apply in cancellation cases.[35]

The form and contents of copies are dealt with in considerable detail in the Consumer Credit (Cancellation Notices and Copies of Documents) Regulations 1983.[36] A failure to comply with these formalities will mean that the agreement is "not properly executed" (see ss.62–65 read with s.182(2)) and the consequences for the creditor or owner can be very serious.[37]

The duty to supply a copy includes a duty to supply a copy of every other document referred to in the agreement. Read literally this would require the creditor or owner to supply a copy of the Act merely because the agreement referred to it. Fortunately the Regulations make it clear that this is not necessary.[38]

Post-contractual information

Additional information on request

22.21 The copy provisions are supplemented by ss.77 to 79 which, as already stated, are designed to assist the debtor or hirer who has failed to keep a record of his payments (alternatively, he may have mislaid either or both of the copies referred to above). In each of these cases the debtor or hirer may make a written request and send the sum of £1. To ensure that the creditor or owner is not put to unreasonable trouble, the sections require him to send to the debtor or hirer, within the prescribed period,[39] a copy of the executed agreement and a signed statement containing certain particulars (e.g. as to sums paid, due and payable) "according to the information to which it is practicable for him to refer". Further, to prevent the creditor or owner from being inundated with such requests, the information need not be given at all

---

[32] s.63(1) and (2)(a).
[33] s.62(2).
[34] s.63(2)(b).
[35] See para.23.10 below.
[36] SI 1983/1557.
[37] See para.22.02 above and para.26.06 below. See also *Carey* [2009] EWHC 3417 (QB) at para.22.13 below.
[38] reg.11(e) of SI 1983/1557.
[39] Twelve working days (reg.2 of SI 1983/1569).

if the request was made within one month of a previous request having been complied with.

Section 77 concerns fixed sum credit, s.78 running-account credit and s.79 hire agreements. In each case the creditor or owner "is not entitled, while the default continues, to enforce the agreement".

Hundreds of claims by creditors for arrears have been met by debtors, **22.22** advised by claims management companies (often on a fishing expedition) and solicitors, with the argument that the agreements are void and the debts have ceased to exist because the creditor has not given the required copies under s.77 to the debtor. This defence depends on the meaning of "not entitled . . . to enforce". (A similar problem arises where agreements are improperly executed and so under s.65(1) "enforceable . . . on an order of the court only".) The County Court cases had been stayed while awaiting the decision on a test case by the Commercial Court: *McGuffick v Royal Bank of Scotland.*[40] The court decided unsurprisingly that the agreement was not void. It remained valid and the debt continued to exist. Thus although the bank could not enforce the agreement until it had given the relevant copy, it was proper for it to report the debtor's liability to a credit reference agency.

Another test case (decided the following month) where again hundreds of County Court cases around the country were stayed pending its outcome is *Carey v HSBC Bank Plc.*[41] Here the question was about copies of credit card agreements under s.78. Must they be copies such as photocopies of the original agreements or will something else suffice provided it contains the required information? The answer is the latter. Judge Waksman QC, in view of the general importance of the issues before him, helpfully took the view that "the purpose of this judgment is to give general guidance" (para.2). In para.234 he set out a Summary of Findings as follows:

"(1) A creditor can satisfy its duty under s.78 by providing a reconstituted version of the executed agreement which may be from sources other than the actual signed agreement itself;

(2) The s.78 copy must contain the name and address of the debtor as it was at the time of the execution of the agreement. But the creditor can provide the name and address from whatever source it has of those details. It does not have to take them from the executed agreement itself;

(3) The creditor need not, in complying with s.78, provide a document which would comply (if signed) with the requirements of the Consumer Credit (Agreements) Regulations 1983 as to form, as at the date the agreement was made;

(4) If an agreement has been varied by the creditor under a unilateral power of variation, the creditor must still provide a copy of the original agreement, as well as the varied terms."

---

[40] [2009] EWHC 2386 (Comm).
[41] [2009] EWHC 3417 (QB). See also *Phoenix Recoveries (UK) Ltd v Kotecha* [2011] EWCA Civ 105: interest rate discrepancy—s.78 copy defective.

22.23   Judge Waksman QC also had to consider issues about the form and content of credit agreements themselves under s.61(1)(a)[42] and again gave general guidance by stating in para.173 "Agreed Principles" with which all the parties agreed:

> "(1) It is not sufficient for the piece of paper signed by the debtor merely to cross-refer to the Prescribed Terms without a copy of those terms being supplied to the debtor at the point of signature;
>
> (2) A document need not be a single piece of paper;
>
> (3) Whether several pieces of paper constitute one document is a question of substance not form. In particular a physical connection between several pieces of paper is not necessary in order for them to constitute one document;
>
> (4) Additionally, a physical connection (or one or more physical connections) between several pieces of paper does not necessarily constitute them as one document;
>
> (5) Accordingly, where the debtor's signature and the Prescribed Terms appear on separate pieces of paper, the question of whether those pieces of paper together constitute one document is a question of substance and not form."

22.24   Following these cases in November and December 2009, the Office of Fair Trading (OFT) published draft guidance on the application of ss.77–79. In a press release of 27 January 2010 (05/10) the OFT said:

> "There has been a great deal of confusion over the meaning of these sections with many borrowers being misled into thinking they can get their debt written off.
>   This guidance is to clarify the legal position and the OFT view on standards expected of the industry, and to make consumers aware that they may be at risk if they seek to use these sections to avoid paying legitimately owed debts."

We warmly support the OFT's comments in view of the questionable activities of some credit management companies, since they charge for the advice and conciliation which would be available free of charge from CABx, money advice centres and trade associations such as the Finance and Leasing Association and mislead consumers into believing that their financial commitments can easily (if not cheaply) be avoided or reduced.

Statement of account

22.25   A new right, given to debtors by s.77B,[43] allows them to request a statement of account not more than once a month showing details of instalment payments. It applies to fixed sum credit of fixed duration repayable by instalments, e.g. a personal loan repayable monthly over five years.

---

[42] See para.22.17 above.
[43] reg.26 of SI 2010/1010.

The request may be written or oral and the creditor must reply "as soon as reasonably practicable" free of charge. The statement must include a table showing details of each instalment due.

The usual exclusions apply: land, £60,260+, business credit and pawns.

Additional information without request

In the case of a running-account credit agreement, other than a small **22.26** agreement,[44] the creditor must send to the debtor periodic statements at least once a year containing the information required by regulations.[45] Similar provisions in relation to fixed-sum credit agreements now appear in s.77A (added by the Consumer Credit Act 2006); the form and content of the statements are given in the Consumer Credit (Information Requirements and Duration of Charges) Regulations 2007 (SI 2007/1167) (the 2007 Regulations).

In *J P Morgan Chase Bank NA v Northern Rock (Asset Management) Plc*[46] the court considered the time limits for giving a statement. It decided that a statement not complying with the 2007 Regulations was not a statement given under s.77A.

Interest rate changes

Section 78A provides that where there is to be a variation in the rate of inter- **22.27** est, the creditor must inform the debtor in writing in advance of the matters mentioned in subs.(3), e.g. the variation in the rate and any effect on the amount, number and frequency of payments. Its application is more limited in the case of most overdrafts and there are two exclusions, i.e. unauthorised overdrafts and land mortgages.[47]

Assignment of debts

Where creditors sell the benefit of their credit agreements to a third party, **22.28** s.82A provides that their debtors must be notified of the assignment of the debts by the assignee, unless the creditor/assignor agrees to do so.

Information as to the whereabouts of the goods

So far all the provisions have required information to be given *by* the creditor **22.29** or owner, but s.80 is concerned with the reverse situation. It provides that where a regulated agreement requires the debtor or hirer to keep goods in his possession or control, he must, within seven working days after receiving a written request from the creditor or owner, tell them where the goods are. If

---

[44] See para.20.14 above.
[45] s.78(4) and SI 1983/1570 which deal with form, contents and time-limits (as amended by the 2006 Act: new s.78(4A)).
[46] [2014] EWHC 291 (Ch).
[47] subss.(4) to (6).

the information is not given within 21 days of receiving the request the debtor or hirer commits an offence.

Guarantees

22.30 Formality and copy provisions also apply to guarantees of regulated agreements.[48]

Electronic agreements

22.31 The Consumer Credit (Electronic Communications) Order 2004[49] enables regulated agreements to be made electronically and notices, copies and statements to be given in the same way.

---

[48] See ss.105–110 and SI 1983/1556.
[49] SI 2004/3236. In force 31 May 2005.

CHAPTER TWENTY-THREE

"CAN I GET OUT OF THE AGREEMENT?"

We have seen that a debtor or hirer may commit himself too heavily (perhaps **23.01** aided by an over-enthusiastic salesman). In this chapter we shall consider his right to resile from a regulated agreement and the financial consequences of his doing so. The subject will be considered under four headings, namely:

1. Withdrawal

2. Rescission and Repudiation

3. Cancellation

4. Termination

The above topics must be distinguished from the problem which arises where the consumer wants to perform the agreement ahead of time. Early settlement is considered at para.26.13 below.

1. WITHDRAWAL

Prospective agreement: s.57

On general contractual principles a prospective debtor or hirer can with- **23.02** draw from the transaction at any time before the offer has been accepted by revoking it. In the case of a regulated agreement this position is strengthened by s.59(1) which provides that an agreement is void if it binds a person to enter, as prospective debtor or hirer, into a prospective regulated agreement.

Section 57, which deals with withdrawal from a prospective agreement, provides that no special form of wording is required[1] and the notice of withdrawal can be written or oral. Two important points should be noted:

(1) The list of persons to whom notice of withdrawal can be given is surprisingly wide. It includes not only the credit-broker or supplier but also "any person who, in the course of a business carried on by him, acts on behalf of the debtor or hirer in any negotiations for the agreement."[2] Thus if, for example, the prospective debtor had

---

[1] s.57(2).
[2] s.57(3).

instructed a solicitor to negotiate on his behalf, a notice given by him to that solicitor would be sufficient. Such a deemed agent is under a deemed contractual duty to transmit the notice to his deemed principal (the creditor or owner) forthwith.[3]

(2) Withdrawal has the same effect as cancellation.[4] Thus, (a) the prospective debtor or hirer can recover all payments made to the creditor or owner (e.g. a pre-contract deposit, or a payment made for a survey of the house); (b) the withdrawal will also terminate any linked transaction and sums paid under it become repayable; (c) under a three-party D-C-S agreement[5] the creditor and the supplier are jointly liable[6] to repay the sums paid by the debtor; and (d) the prospective debtor or hirer will have a lien over the goods until sums repayable have been repaid.[7]

One final point: the Act does not cut down the general rule that the revocation of an offer must be communicated to the offeree before acceptance. Thus if the consumer uses the post he runs the risk that his letter of withdrawal will be lost in the post or will not reach the creditor or owner until after their acceptance. In both of these cases the withdrawal is ineffective.

Right of Withdrawal from Consumer Credit Agreement: s.66A

23.03   The Act has been amended to give a new right of withdrawal which complements s.57. Debtors will now have time to reflect on regulated consumer credit agreements and "withdraw" from them "without giving any reason", even though the agreement has already been made (s.66A(1)). The two provisions are not meant to overlap.

Similarly the right given by s.66A will apply to credit agreements and takes priority, where otherwise there would have been a conflict with the cancellation rights given by s.67 of the Act.[8]

Where and how to withdraw

23.04   The debtor must give notice within 14 days of "the relevant day", of which there are four varieties set out in subs.(3), e.g. the day after the day on which the agreement is made.

Where notice is given by fax, electronically (e.g. email) or by post, it is regarded as having been received by the creditor when it was sent or posted.[9]

---

[3] s.175.
[4] s.57(1).
[5] See para.20.10 above.
[6] See, e.g., s.75, at para.24.06 below.
[7] The consequences of cancellation are considered in more detail in paras 23.12–23.14 below.
[8] s.67(2).
[9] s.66A(5) and (6).

Effects of withdrawal

After withdrawal by subs.(7) the agreement is treated "as if it had never been **23.05** entered into" (it is void), as is an "ancillary service" relating to the credit agreement and provided by the creditor or a third party by agreement with the creditor, e.g. insurance.[10] However, a contract for the supply of goods or services is not affected, though financed by the agreement. Within 30 days of withdrawal the debtor must repay the credit and any interest, but not any charges or fees.[11]

Hire-purchase, conditional sale and credit sale agreements pose special problems in relation to the passing of title to the goods. Under a hire-purchase agreement the title usually passes when debtors exercise their option to purchase and pay the option fee. Section 66A(11) provides that title will pass when the debtor repays the credit and interest.

There are a number of familiar exclusions set out in s.66A(14), where the new right of withdrawal is not available: credit exceeding £60,260 and three types of land agreement.

2. RESCISSION AND REPUDIATION

Again on general contractual principles a debtor or hirer may have a right to **23.06** rescind an agreement for misrepresentation or to treat it as repudiated by a breach by the creditor or owner. One example of this is considered in the next chapter. The deemed agency provisions referred to above also apply to rescission.[12] The principal distinction between rescission and accepting a repudiation is that the former is retrospective and the innocent party is treated as if the agreement had never been made. In the latter case obligations arising before the acceptance of repudiation remain enforceable, although they can usually be reduced or extinguished by a claim for damages.

3. CANCELLATION

In addition to the right of withdrawal, there is a cancellation right available **23.07** under ss.67 to 73 of the Act which is considered below. This s.67 right is not available where the s.66A right of withdrawal applies (see para.23.03 above). The cancellation rights under the Regulations will not apply if the consumer has cancellation rights under the rules discussed below.

The object of the cancellation provisions in ss.67 to 73 is clear enough—to give the debtor or hirer a chance for second thoughts (i.e. a "cooling-off period") in a case where he may have been pressurised by a doorstep salesman into signing an agreement. The matter can be considered under the following headings:

---

[10] s.66A(13).
[11] s.66A(9) and (10).
[12] s.102.

(1) What agreements are cancellable?

(2) The copy provisions.

(3) The time for cancellation.

(4) How is cancellation effected?

(5) Effect of cancellation.

(6) Duty to return goods.

(7) The part-exchange allowance.

(1) What agreements are cancellable?

23.08 A regulated consumer credit or hire agreement is cancellable if two conditions are satisfied, namely, (a) oral representations were made by or on behalf of the negotiator in the presence of the debtor or hirer[13]; *and* (b) the unexecuted agreement was not signed by the debtor or hirer at premises where a business was carried on by (i) the creditor or owner, (ii) any party to a linked transaction (other than the debtor or hirer or a relative of his), or (iii) the negotiator in any antecedent negotiations.

Let us suppose that John, a trader, goes to a car dealer to buy a new car. The transaction is financed by a loan from a finance company who require John to take out a life policy with an insurance company. The car dealer (the negotiator) makes oral representations in John's presence. If John signs the agreement at the office of the dealer, finance company or insurance company, he will have no right of cancellation. On the other hand, if he signs at his own home, or at his own business premises, then cancellation is available. Thus, the definition of business premises does *not* include the business premises of the debtor or hirer.[14] The place where the representations were made is immaterial. They must, however, have been made in the *presence* of the debtor or hirer. Representations made on the telephone would not give cancellation rights. If no oral representations were made at all (e.g. a mail-order purchase) there is no right of cancellation.

23.09 In the case of land transactions the concept of post-contractual cancellation can result in considerable administrative problems. Accordingly, the cancellation provisions do not apply to (a) an agreement secured on land, (b) a restricted-use agreement to finance the purchase of land, or (c) a bridging loan in connection with the purchase of land. It will be recalled that in case (a) above the prospective debtor or hirer will have a pre-contractual period of reflection and isolation.[15]

Two other types of agreement are not cancellable. They are (a) a non-

---

[13] See *Moorgate Services Ltd v Kabir*, *The Times*, 25 April 1995 CA.
[14] Contrast the canvassing rules, see para.21.17 above.
[15] See para.22.11 above.

commercial agreement,[16] and (b) a "small" debtor-creditor-supplier agreement for restricted-use credit.[17]

(2) The copy provisions

The basic rules in ss.62 and 63[18] are modified in three respects by s.64. Thus: **23.10**

    (a) each copy must contain a notice in the prescribed form indicating the right of cancellation, how and when it is exercisable and the name and address of a person to whom notice of cancellation may be given[19];

    (b) in cases where a second copy is required it must be sent *by an appropriate method*[20];

    (c) in cases where a second copy is not required a notice, containing the information mentioned in (a) above, must be sent by an appropriate method to the debtor or hirer within seven days of the making of the agreement.[21]

Exemptions

The Financial Conduct Authority (FCA) can grant exemption from the **23.11** duty to send a cancellation notice in certain specified cases if satisfied that this requirement can be dispensed with without prejudicing the interests of debtors or hirers (see s.64(4) and the Consumer Credit (Notice of Cancellation Rights) (Exemptions) Regulations 1983).[22]

(3) The time for cancellation

The cancellation period starts when the debtor or hirer signs the unexecuted **23.12** agreement and ends five days after the debtor or hirer *receives* the statutory second copy or notice.[23] Thus, if the second copy is received on a Friday the cancellation period runs out at midnight on the following Wednesday. If the second copy is delayed in the post the cancellation period will, to that extent, be prolonged since the period only starts to melt away when the debtor or hirer *receives* the second copy.

    What happens if the second copy is not received at all and the creditor or owner then sends a further copy? Alternatively, what happens if the second copy or notice is sent off more than seven days after the making of the agreement? The wording of the Act is ambiguous. If the third copy or the late

---

[16] s.74(1)(a).
[17] s.74(2).
[18] See para.22.17 above.
[19] s.64(1)(a) read with the Consumer Credit (Cancellation Notices and Copies of Documents) Regulations 1983 (SI 1983/1557).
[20] s.63(3).
[21] s.64(1)(b).
[22] SI 1983/1558.
[23] s.68.

copy could be regarded as given "under" s.63, then it would start the five-day period running. On the other hand it could be argued that a notice is only given "under" s.63 if it is posted within seven days; if this is correct then the effect of delay or non-receipt would be that the right of cancellation would remain permanently available. This seems so absurd that the court is likely to prefer the former view.

(4) How is cancellation effected?

23.13   By s.69 the agreement can be cancelled if the debtor or hirer serves a notice of cancellation on (a) the creditor or owner, (b) the person specified in the copy or notice, or (c) the agent of the creditor or owner (including his deemed agent).[24] No special form of wording is required but it is clear from the definition of "notice"[25] that it must be in writing. If it is posted it takes effect as from the date of posting and the mere fact that it is not received by the creditor or owner is immaterial (this is in marked contrast to the second copy or notice which only triggers the count-down of the cancellation period when it is received).[26] The Regulations require that the second copy or the notice (see (2) above) must include a cancellation form which the debtor or hirer can use to cancel the agreement.[27]

(5) Effect of cancellation

23.14   Subject to two exceptions the general effect of cancellation is to treat the agreement, and most linked transactions,[28] as if it had never been made.[29] Thus the debtor or hirer can recover his payments and is discharged from liability to make further payments. In the case of a three-party D-C-S agreement[30] for restricted-use credit the creditor and supplier are jointly and severally liable to repay sums paid by the debtor or a relative. The debtor, hirer or relative has a lien over the goods until repayable sums are repaid to him. Thus, if Albert paid a £500 deposit to buy a £5,000 car and the remaining £4,500 was paid by a creditor who had "arrangements" with the seller, the effect of a cancellation of the loan agreement would be that (a) the sale contract, as a linked transaction, would also be cancelled, (b) the seller and creditor would be jointly and severally liable to repay the £500 to Albert, and (c) if the £4,500 were paid direct to the supplier he would have to repay it to the creditor.[31]

---

[24] See para.23.02 above.
[25] s.189.
[26] Notice of cancellation (effective when posted) can also be contrasted with s.57 notice of withdrawal—see para.23.02 above.
[27] SI 1983/1557 regs 5 and 6 and Pts IV and VI of the Schedule.
[28] By SI 1983/1560 certain linked transactions (insurance, guarantee of goods, deposit accounts and current accounts) will survive the cancellation of the main agreement.
[29] s.69(4).
[30] See para.20.10 above.
[31] s.70(1)(c).

Two exceptions

(1) The first exception is in s.70(2) and deals with a debtor-creditor-supplier **23.15**
agreement for restricted-use credit to finance (a) the doing of work or supply
of goods to meet an emergency, or (b) the supply of goods which have
become incorporated in any land or thing before service of the notice of cancellation. Since the debtor is unable to return the goods, it would clearly be
wrong to allow him to avoid payment simply by serving a notice of cancellation. Accordingly, in this type of case the cancellation will wipe out the credit
part of the agreement but the debtor will remain liable to pay the cash price
for the goods or work.

(2) The second exception is to be found in s.71 and it deals with a case
where the credit has already been advanced by the creditor before the expiry
of the cancellation period. Here the strict application of the cancellation
provisions would cause hardship. On the one hand, since the agreement is
treated as never having been made, the creditor might be able to bring an
action to recover money lent. On the other hand the debtor might try to avoid
all liability in reliance on s.70(1)(b) which provides that any sum payable by
the debtor or his relative shall cease to be payable. To deal with these problems s.71 starts by providing that cancellation of a regulated consumer credit
agreement (other than a debtor-creditor-supplier agreement for restricted-use
credit) shall not destroy the obligation to repay the credit and interest. The
words in brackets are inserted because, as we have seen, this type of transaction does not raise the type of problem at which s.71 is aimed—the supplier
merely repays the credit to the creditor. The section then goes on to provide
a complex formula. First of all it provides that if the whole or part of the
credit is repaid within one month of cancellation, or not later than the first
instalment repayment date, no interest is chargeable on the amount repaid. In
other words, the consumer will have had the use of the money interest-free. It
then goes on to deal with credit which is repayable by instalments where any
part of the credit is still outstanding after the first repayment date. In such a
case the creditor must serve a notice[32] recalculating the instalments over a
period starting when this notice is served and ending with the final contractual repayment date. This shortening of the repayment period will often mean
larger instalments.

(6) Duty to return goods

Let us remind ourselves at this point of the distinction between debtor- **23.16**
creditor-supplier agreements and debtor-creditor agreements:

(a) Where the debtor under a debtor-creditor agreement uses the credit
to buy goods, the sale contract is *not* a linked transaction and is not
affected by cancellation of the credit agreement.

(b) In the case of a debtor-creditor-supplier agreement the supply of

---

[32] See SI 1983/1559 which sets out the form of the request.

the goods is either an integral part of the credit agreement itself (e.g. hire-purchase) or a linked transaction under s.19 which is cancelled along with the credit agreement. In either case the debtor will have to restore the goods to the other party under the rules set out below.

23.17 Section 72 deals with a case where a debtor-creditor-supplier agreement for restricted-use credit, a consumer hire agreement or a linked transaction (to which the debtor, hirer or a relative is a party) is cancelled after the debtor, hirer or relative has obtained possession. In such a case the possessor is under a duty to restore the goods to the person from whom he got them and in the meantime to retain possession and to take reasonable care. The duty to restore the goods is merely a duty to redeliver them at *his own* premises on receiving a written request from the other party. The duty is also discharged if the possessor delivers the goods (whether at his own premises or elsewhere) to any person to whom a notice of cancellation could have been sent other than the "deemed agent".[33] Alternatively, he can send the goods to such a person, but in this case he must take reasonable care to see that they are received by the other party and are not damaged in transit. The duty to take reasonable care comes to an end 21 days from cancellation, unless within that time the possessor has received a written request for redelivery and has unreasonably failed to comply with it.

There is, however, a sting in the tail. The duty to restore does not apply to emergency or incorporation cases where, as we have seen, the debtor remains liable to pay the price.[34] Nor does it apply to perishable goods, nor to goods which by their nature are consumed by use and were so consumed before cancellation—a classic case of having one's cake and not having to pay for it![35]

Any breach of s.72 is actionable as a breach of statutory duty.

(7) The part-exchange allowance

23.18 Section 73 deals with a case where, as part of a cancelled agreement, the negotiator agreed to take goods in part exchange and those goods have been delivered to him. The effect of s.73(2) is to give the debtor or hirer a right to recover the part-exchange allowance from the negotiator, unless within 10 days of cancellation the goods were returned to the debtor or hirer in substantially the same condition. If the negotiator was the supplier in a three-party debtor-creditor-supplier agreement, the negotiator and the creditor are jointly and severally liable to repay the allowance, and the lien of the debtor or hirer[36] extends to cover the return of the goods (during the 10-day period) or the part-exchange allowance.

---

[33] See para.23.13 above.
[34] s.69(2)(b) at para.23.15 above.
[35] Thus the hirer of a motor vehicle would not have to pay for petrol consumed before cancellation.
[36] See para.23.14 above.

4. TERMINATION

If there is no right of withdrawal, rescission or cancellation the final possibil- **23.19**
ity (apart from any contractual right of termination) is a right of termination
under ss.98A and 99 to 101. These are limited in scope; s.98A applies to open-
end agreements and ss.99 and 100 apply to regulated hire-purchase and conditional sale agreements only, while s.101 relates to regulated consumer hire
agreements. In either case the statutory rights cannot be cut down by agreement; on the other hand if the agreement is more favourable to the debtor or
hirer they can take advantage of it.

Open-ended agreements

An "open-ended agreement" is defined by s.189 as "of no fixed duration", **23.20**
e.g. a credit card.

By debtors

By s.98A(1) a debtor may terminate such regulated agreements "free of **23.21**
charge at any time" by a notice "not exceeding one month". It need not be in
writing, unless the creditor so requires (subs.(2)).

By creditors[37]

When the agreement provides for its termination, the creditor must give at **23.22**
least two months' written notice (subs.(3)).

However, if it is a question only of the right to draw on credit, the creditor
may terminate or suspend this by written notice before or, if impracticable,
immediately afterwards. The notice must give reasons "objectively justified",
e.g. unauthorised use (subss.(4) to (6)).

Exclusions

These provisions do not apply to authorised overdrafts, unauthorised over- **23.23**
drafts on current accounts or land mortgages (subs.(8)).

Hire-purchase and conditional sale

Sections 99 and 100 give debtors the right to terminate a hire-purchase or **23.24**
conditional sale agreement at any time before the last instalment falls due. It
can be exercised by giving notice to any person who is entitled or authorised
to receive payments. However, there are two cases in which the right to terminate is not available. The first is where, under a conditional sale agreement
relating to land, title has passed to the buyer. The second is where, under a
conditional sale of goods, the property has become vested in the buyer and
has then been transferred to a third person, e.g. a sub-buyer.

Termination only operates for the future, so that sums which have *accrued*

---

[37] s.98 has comparable provisions about fixed period agreements.

due remain payable.[38] The effect of termination may well be to leave the creditor with heavily depreciated goods. In order to provide some measure of compensation, s.100(1) requires the debtor to pay such further sum (if any) as will bring the total payments up to *one-half* of the total price. If, however, in any action the court is satisfied that a smaller sum is adequate to cover the creditor's loss, the court may order such smaller sum to be paid. This could clearly be relevant if, for example, a hirer acquired a car on hire-purchase and then wished to terminate the agreement after only a few weeks' use. He would presumably tender a sum falling far short of one-half, leaving it to the creditor to take court proceedings. The court has no discretion with regard to sums which have already accrued due.

The debtor may also have to pay damages if he is in breach of an obligation to take reasonable care of the goods[39] and he must allow the creditor to retake them.[40]

If the creditor agrees to carry out any installation and if the cost of the installation forms part of the total price, it is clearly reasonable that he should be paid for this in full. Accordingly, the reference to one-half is a reference to the installation charge in full and one-half of the balance.[41]

Example

23.25   A television set is let out on hire-purchase at a price of £300, including a £30 installation charge. The debtor pays a £50 deposit and one instalment of £10 is outstanding. He now wishes to terminate the agreement. He must first of all pay the £10. Then (unless otherwise ordered) he must bring his payments up to one-half of the total price:

$$\text{one half} = £30 + \frac{270}{5} \quad = \quad £165$$

$$\text{less sums paid and due} \quad = \quad 60$$

$$\text{further sum payable}[42] \quad = \quad £105$$

Consumer hire

23.26   Section 101 gives the hirer a non-excludable right to terminate the agreement, but the earliest termination date is 18 months after the making of the agreement (unless the contract provides for an earlier termination date).[43] Once again termination only operates for the future and sums which have accrued due are not affected. The hirer must give a termination notice equal to the shortest payment interval, or three months, whichever is less. Thus, if rentals are payable monthly, the hirer can end the agreement by giving one month's notice at the end of month 17.

---

[38] s.99(2).
[39] s.100(4).
[40] s.100(5).
[41] s.100(2).
[42] s.100(1).
[43] s.101(3).

The exercise of a right of termination can often cause financial problems to the owner, especially where the owner leases out commercial equipment. Accordingly, s.101(7) provides that in three cases the statutory right of termination is not available at all. These are:

(a) where the total payments (disregarding sums payable on breach) exceed £1,500 in any one year;

(b) where goods are let out for the hirer's business and were selected by the hirer and acquired by the owner, at the hirer's request, from a third party;

(c) any agreement where the hirer requires the goods to relet them in the course of a business.

Apart from these special cases the FCA has a general power to exclude the operation of s.101 from agreements made by a particular trader[44] or within a specified description.[45]

The section does not mention damages for failure to take reasonable care but on principle the hirer owes a duty of reasonable care as a bailee at common law and will be liable to pay damages for breach of that duty.

[44] See s.101(8) as amended by the Consumer Credit (Increase of Monetary Amounts) Order 1983 (SI 1983/1571).
[45] s.101(8A): inserted by s.63 of the Consumer Credit Act 2006.

CHAPTER TWENTY-FOUR

"THE GOODS ARE DEFECTIVE"

In Pt I of this book we considered the terms implied by the Consumer **24.01**
Rights Act 2015 (CRA 2015). In this chapter we shall consider these problems again in the context of credit transactions. The basic point can be
made very briefly at the outset—the differences between cash and credit
transactions are very slight. It is proposed to consider this topic under five
headings and for convenience the term "connected lender" will be used in
preference to "creditor with whom the supplier had arrangements". The five
headings are:

1. Cash sale—unconnected lender

2. Cash sale—connected lender

3. Credit sale and conditional sale

4. Hire-purchase

5. Hire

1. CASH SALE—UNCONNECTED LENDER

Let us suppose that Robert borrows money from his bank and uses it to buy **24.02**
a car which proves to be defective. The loan is a debtor-creditor agreement.
As between seller and buyer, the position is governed by the CRA 2015.
These matters have been fully discussed in Chapters Three, Four and Eight.
Alternatively, if the seller was guilty of misrepresentation Robert may be
entitled to rescind the contract or to claim damages.[1] As between Robert and
his bank the bank are not affected by any breach of contract on the part of
the seller. It follows that Robert will have to continue to repay the loan and
his sole remedy is against the seller. If he cannot afford the repayments his
only right as against the bank is to wait for an arrears notice and a notice of
default[2] or for proceedings to enforce the loan agreement and then apply to
the court for a time order.[3]

---

[1] See para.8.03 above.
[2] See paras 26.19 and 26.21 below.
[3] See para.26.18 below.

2. CASH SALE—CONNECTED LENDER

24.03   Let us now suppose that the seller introduces Robert to a finance company with whom the seller has arrangements. The finance company makes a loan to Robert to finance the sale. This is a three-party debtor-creditor-supplier agreement. As between Robert and the seller, the position is exactly the same as in the previous example. As regards the position between Robert and the finance company there are two overlapping provisions of considerable practical importance which may enable Robert to hold the finance company responsible for the seller's default.

Section 56

24.04   The first provision is s.56 of the Consumer Credit Act which applies (inter alia) to antecedent negotiations with the debtor conducted by the supplier in relation to a transaction financed by a debtor-creditor-supplier agreement.[4] The key provision is s.56(2) which reads as follows:

> Negotiations with the debtor . . . shall be deemed to be conducted by the negotiator in the capacity of agent of the creditor as well as in his actual capacity.

In other words, if the seller made a misrepresentation (e.g. as to credit terms[5] or the quality of the goods), he will have made it as *agent* for the finance company. Thus Robert could bring proceedings against the finance company, or he could merely discontinue his payments, wait to be sued and then counterclaim. It remains to add that s.56(3) makes void a clause (a) purporting to make the negotiator the agent of the dealer, or (b) relieving a person from liability for acts or omissions of any person acting as, or on behalf of, a negotiator.

24.05   Section 56 can be regarded as an exception to the general rule that the dealer is not an agent of the creditor—even if he carries a stock of the creditor's finance application forms.[6] It should also be noted that s.56 is not limited to defects in the goods but applies to all negotiations.

Suppose that H takes a car on hire-purchase from F1. Before completing his payments he takes it to a dealer D and agrees to sell it to D in part exchange for another car owned by D. D sells the new car to a linked finance company F2 who then let it out to H. D promises H to pay off the balance owing to F1 but fails to do so and becomes insolvent. By s.56 the promise by D was made as agent of F2; accordingly if F1 sues he can claim an indemnity from F2.[7]

---

[4] s.56(1)(c).

[5] *Scotland v British Credit Trust Ltd* [2014] EWCA Civ 790.

[6] The leading case is *Branwhite v Worcester Works Finance Co* [1969] 1 A.C. 552. See also *Woodchester Equipment (Leasing) Ltd v British Association of Canned and Preserved Food Importers and Distributors* [1995] C.C.L.R. 51 CA.

[7] *Forthright Finance v Ingate* [1997] C.C.L.R. 95 CA.

Section 75

The second provision affecting three-party debtor-creditor-supplier agreements is s.75. This is a vital provision for consumers, where a supplier of goods or services refuses to meet its obligations under the contract or becomes insolvent. In this situation it is provided that: **24.06**

> (1) if the debtor under a debtor-creditor-supplier agreement falling within section 12(b) or (c) has . . . any claim against the supplier in respect of a misrepresentation or breach of contract, he shall have a like claim against the creditor, who, with the supplier, shall accordingly be jointly and severally liable to the debtor.

Subsection (3)[8] lays down three limitations.

> Subsection (1) does not apply to a claim—
>
> (a) under a non-commercial agreement,
> (b) so far as the claim relates to any single item to which the supplier has attached a cash price[9] not exceeding £100 or more than £30,000, or
> (c) under a debtor-creditor-supplier agreement for running-account credit—
>> (i) which provides for the making of payment by the debtor in relation to specified periods which, in the case of an agreement which is not secured on land, do not exceed three months, and
>> (ii) which requires that the number of payments to be made by the debtor in repayments of the whole amount of the credit provided in each such period shall not exceed one.

As already stated there is substantial overlap between ss.56 and 75. If the "negotiator" makes a misrepresentation, the buyer/borrower may well have a claim against the creditor under either section. In two respects, however, s.56 is wider; it is not limited to three-party D-C-S agreements and it is not subject to the s.75 upper and lower limits.[10] **24.07**

The real importance of s.75(1) lies in the words "or breach of contract". It means that the creditor will be liable not merely for the misrepresentation or for breach of express terms but also for breach of the *implied* terms, e.g. under the CRA 2015.[11] This seems reasonable enough; finance companies who finance the transaction by letting the goods out on hire-purchase have been responsible for the quality of the goods ever since 1938. The effect of s.75 is to place them in basically the same position if they choose to finance the transaction by means of a connected loan. From the debtor's point of view the effect of s.75 can be very favourable. In an extreme case he might have a claim against a solvent finance company whereas a person buying with his own money, or with money borrowed from an unconnected lender, would only have had a claim against an insolvent seller.

It will be appreciated that the amount of the claim can be far greater than

---

[8] As amended by the Consumer Credit (Increase of Monetary Limits) Order 1983 (SI 1983/1878).
[9] This is the cash price of the item, *not* the credit advanced.
[10] See above.
[11] See Chapters Three and Four.

the amount of the credit. Nor is the creditor only secondarily liable—the liability is "joint and several", so that the debtor may pursue the creditor *before* the supplier if he wishes.

Unless the supplier is insolvent, the creditor will not be saddled with ultimate liability, for as between creditor and supplier the creditor is entitled to join the supplier as a party to the proceedings and to claim an indemnity from him.[12]

Credit cards

24.08   In the example above[13] we took the case of a car buyer, connected lender and dealer. Another situation where s.75 is highly relevant is in relation to buyer, credit card company and approved supplier. If goods bought with a credit card prove to be defective and cause enormous damage (e.g. death or personal injury or damage to property, including buildings), the buyer (or his personal representatives) will have a claim against the credit card company for the full amount of the damage.

The precise legal effect of a renewable credit card still remains to be decided—is it a standing offer or a single contract or a new contract at each renewal?[14] One further point has been decided: a credit card payment by the consumer gives him an absolute discharge and he cannot be made to pay again, if the credit card company becomes insolvent before it has paid the retailer.[15]

24.09   As a modern example of s.75 in operation, many holiday-makers used credit cards to book holidays with tour operators which went into liquidation before the holidays had been completed. The credit card companies wrongly resisted s.75 claims against them on the ground that the holiday-makers should look to the special fund set up by the tour operators. Similarly a buyer placing a deposit when ordering, say, furniture, curtains or domestic electrical equipment would be well advised to pay by credit card; then if the retailer goes bust, the buyer can recover the deposit from the credit card company.

Problems may arise when booking a package holiday through a travel agent. The Office of Fair Trading (OFT) took the view in its paper, *Connected Lender Liability* (March 1994) that s.75 will apply even though the payment is made directly to the travel agent, where he is acting as agent for the tour operator.[16] While we support this view, we urge consumers to pay the tour operator itself; without doubt the tour operator will then be "the supplier" within the meaning of s.75(1).

24.10   As part of an aggressive sales campaign a credit card company C2 may persuade a customer of C1 to surrender his card and take a C2 card instead. This can raise a problem of timing. Consider the following scenario:

---

[12] s.75(2) and (5).
[13] See para.24.03 above.
[14] We prefer the third view.
[15] *Re Charge Card Services* [1988] 3 W.L.R. 764.
[16] He usually is: see para.7.01 above.

January	consumer with card company X orders goods and pays by card
February	consumer switches to card company Y
March	the goods are delivered and are defective.

On these facts, some companies in the position of X are refusing to pay a s.75 claim (see para.24.06 above) on the ground that the card has been surrendered. We believe that this argument can be successfully attacked; the use of the X card in January crystallised a potential claim against that company.

Credit cards abroad

A related matter is the use of a credit card abroad. We stated in previous editions that we agreed with the OFT that s.75 applies to overseas transactions by a UK-based cardholder.[17] This was disputed by (among others) Lloyds TSB and Tesco Personal Finance. The OFT sensibly thought it desirable to have the point tested in court and in *Office of Fair Trading v Lloyds TSB Bank Plc*[18] the House of Lords, unanimously affirming the decision of the Court of Appeal, decided the issue in the OFT's favour.   **24.11**

One further point arises—which system of law will the English courts apply when the supply contract was made abroad? Suppose Sarah buys an expensive watch in Vietnam using Mastercard. On her return she discovers that it is faulty or, even worse, a pirated copy worth a few pounds. Her "like claim" against the creditor in England will presumably be based on Vietnamese law as the proper or applicable law of the contract, since "her claim against the supplier" for breach of contract would be governed by that law if she had brought her claim in Vietnam. This effect of s.75 appears not to have been decided by the courts. Regrettably for consumers, we consider that the English court would require expert evidence on Vietnamese law to learn whether her claim would have succeeded abroad. If the claim involved an EU country, the problem would be less complicated since the same rules about goods being in conformity with the contract and remedies apply by virtue of the EU Directive 1999/44/EC "on certain aspects of the sale of consumer goods and associated guarantees" (see para.8.30 above).

Some further points on s.75

Clearly s.75 is of great importance to consumers (even though in 1983 the lower cash limit in s.75(3) was raised from £30 to £100, thereby taking many credit transactions outside the s.75 protection). It must however be appreciated that s.75 can only be used by the consumer if the relevant credit agreement was a "regulated agreement" (see para.20.02 above). If, for example, they book a holiday and pay with an American Express *charge* card, the credit agreement is within the "single repayment" exemption (see para.20.15 above, subpara.(4)); accordingly it is not a regulated agreement and s.75 will not help   **24.12**

---

[17] *Connected Lender Liability*, pp.26–28. See also *Connected Lender Liability—A Second Report* (OFT, May 1995).
[18] [2007] UKHL 48.

the consumer. Debit cards are not covered either, as no credit is provided, but a scheme called "Chargeback" may help for goods costing less than £100.[19]

It is also important to note that a consumer who has a claim against the supplier has "a like claim" against the creditor. In a Scottish case[20] *United Dominions Trust Ltd v Taylor* it was held that a breach of the sale contract gives the consumer a right to rescind not only that contract but also the connected loan contract.

24.13   We argued in previous editions that this reasoning cannot be correct since the two claims are not identical. The court could have reached the same (and correct) result by a different route—namely by allowing the consumer to sue the supplier and the creditor for the return of the price of the goods which he had rejected. In a recent appeal case from Scotland *Durkin v DSG Retail Ltd*[21] the Supreme Court reached the same conclusion as ourselves and disapproved *United Dominions Trust Ltd v Taylor*.

> Mr Durkin (D) appealed to the Supreme Court against a decision of the Scottish Inner House of the Court of Session that he was not entitled to rescind a credit agreement with HFC Bank, the second respondent (H), to finance the purchase of a computer from the retailer DSG (PC World).
>
> In 1998 D paid a deposit of £50 to DSG and funded the balance of £1,449 from a debtor-creditor-supplier agreement with H. He was told by DSG that he could return it if it did not meet his needs. Next day he tried to return it, as it was unsuitable, but DSG refused to accept his rejection and did not cancel the credit agreement. He informed H that he had rescinded both the sale contract and the credit agreement and made no further payments. H then issued a default notice and informed credit reference agencies (CRAs) of the default without making any enquiries.
>
> In 2004 D claimed damages from H under three heads of loss: (a) damage to his financial credit, (b) loss from interest charges by his inability to exploit offers of 0% credit and (c) loss of a capital gain arising from his inability to put down a deposit on a Spanish property. He relied on s.75. The sheriff held that (1) s.75 enabled D to rescind both the sale and credit agreements; (2) H had breached their duty of care to D in respect of its representations to the CRAs and awarded (a) £8,000, (b) £6,880, and (c) £101,794.
>
> H succeeded in their appeal to the Inner House on s.75, the duty of care and heads (b) and (c) of the damages. D appealed to the Supreme Court. The questions were whether (1) D had rescinded the credit agreement; (2) H had breached a duty of care; (3) such breach caused loss in excess of £8,000.

24.14   The Supreme Court held:

> (1) The Inner House was correct to hold that s.75 did not give D the right to rescind the credit agreement as well as the contract of sale; the rescission of the sale agreement excused the consumer from further performance and entitled him to damages against DSG.

---

[19] Some banks subscribe—it applies to Visa, Maestro and Amex debit cards.
[20] (1980) S.L.T. (Sh.Ct.) 18.
[21] [2014] UKSC 21.

However, the law implied into D-C-S credit agreements under s.12(b) a term making them conditional upon the survival of the supply agreement. The debtor, on rescinding the supply agreement for breach of contract, could also rescind the credit agreement by invoking that condition. D was thus entitled to rescind the credit agreement at common law.

(2) H had broken its duty of care to D by notifying the CRAs of a default without checking that the credit agreement was still enforceable, for they then knew of D's assertion that the credit agreement had been rescinded.

(3) H did not contest the £8,000 award. However, the Inner House's decision would stand that there was insufficient evidence to support the other claims in excess of £8.000.

We urge consumers to take full advantage of their legal rights by using credit cards when making substantial purchases of goods or services.

Linked credit agreements—s.75A

Section 75A was added by SI 2010/1010 to supplement s.75(1). It applies where s.75(1) does not apply and only in the conditions specified in s.75A(1) and (2):   **24.15**

(1) If the debtor under a linked credit agreement has a claim against the supplier in respect of a breach of contract the debtor may pursue that claim against the creditor where any of the conditions in subs.(2) are met.

(2) The conditions in subs.(1) are—

    (a) that the supplier cannot be traced,
    (b) that the debtor has contacted the supplier but the supplier has not responded,
    (c) that the supplier is insolvent, or
    (d) that the debtor has taken reasonable steps to pursue his claim against the supplier but has not obtained satisfaction for his claim.

In contrast to s.75(1) debtors cannot choose between the supplier and the creditor when making their initial claim: the creditor's liability comes into play only when one of the conditions in s.75A(2) is satisfied. Further, the claim must relate to a "breach of contract" but not misrepresentation.

Section 75A(3) and (4) make it clear that the debtor need not have resorted to litigation, but the creditor's liability ceases once the claim against the supplier is settled.   **24.16**

"Linked credit agreement" is defined in s.75A(5). It must "serve exclusively to finance" the supply of "specific" goods or services, where either they are "explicitly specified" in the agreement or the creditor uses the services of the supplier in the preparation or making of the agreement.

By s.75A(6) the following are excluded:

(a) the cash value of the goods or services is £30,000 or less;

(b) the credit exceeds £60,260; and

(c) the agreement is "wholly or predominantly" for the debtor's business.

3. CREDIT SALE AND CONDITIONAL SALE

24.17   A dealer may sell goods and allow the customer to pay by instalments. If nothing is said about the passing of property, it will pass as soon as the contract is made[22] and the sale will be a credit sale. If, however, the passing of property is postponed it will be a conditional sale.[23] In either case the obligations of the seller with regard to the goods are to be found in the CRA 2015. It will be recalled that a notification of purpose to a credit-broker will be as effective as if it had been notified to the seller.[24]

4. HIRE-PURCHASE

24.18   In the case of a hire purchase agreement (*whether or not it is regulated* by the Consumer Credit Act) the implied obligations with regard to the goods are contained in the CRA 2015.[25] The terms are virtually identical to those for the sale of goods and they include notification of purpose to a credit-broker.[26]

In practice, the dealer will frequently sell the goods to a finance company, which will then let the goods out on hire-purchase. If the hire-purchase agreement is a regulated agreement the dealer will be a "credit-broker" or "negotiator" and s.56[27] will apply. In other words, any representations made by the dealer are treated as made as agent for the finance company as well as in his personal capacity. Thus, the debtor has two concurrent remedies; he can bring a claim against the finance company which is bound by the dealer's representations. He can also bring a claim against the dealer, either in negligence[28] or on the basis of a collateral contract.[29]

---

[22] See para.19.09 above.
[23] See para.19.09 above.
[24] See CRA 2015 s.10(2)(c).
[25] See CRA 2015 ss.9–17.
[26] See CRA 2015 s.10(2)(c).
[27] See para.24.04 above.
[28] *Hedley Byrne & Co Ltd v Heller and Partners Ltd* [1964] A.C. 465. There can also be liability without any statement under the general law of negligence which was discussed in Chapter Five.
[29] *Andrews v Hopkinson* [1957] 1 Q.B. 229 (see para.3.20 above). The dealer was also liable in negligence. See fn.28 above.

5. HIRE

The statutory implied terms have already been considered[30] and the law is **24.19** not affected in any way by the Consumer Credit Act. Section 56[31] does not apply and there is no rule of law that the dealer is to be regarded as the agent of the finance company; in many cases this will not be so. If, however, the documentation used by the finance company misleads a consumer into thinking that he is dealing with the dealer, the finance company may be estopped from denying that the dealer's sales staff had authority to speak on its behalf. In such a case statements made by the sales staff will bind the finance company.[32]

---

[30] See Chapter Four.
[31] See para.24.04 above.
[32] *Lease Management Services v Purnell Secretarial Services, Canon (South West) Third Party, The Times*, 1 April 1994 CA.

CHAPTER TWENTY-FIVE

"I HAVE LOST MY CREDIT CARD"

The credit token, and especially the credit card, is of great importance as a **25.01** form of consumer credit and the 1974 Act brings them within the ambit of control.

The Act contains a number of provisions relating to "credit tokens" and "credit token agreements" and these provisions will be considered in this chapter.

What is a credit token?

The term is defined in s.14(1) as "a card, check, voucher, coupon, stamp, **25.02** form, booklet or other document or thing given to an individual by a person carrying on a consumer credit business who undertakes":

(a) that on production of it (whether or not some other action is also required) he will supply cash, goods and services (or any of them) on credit, or

(b) that where, on the production of it to a third party (whether or not any other action is also required), the third party supplies cash, goods and services (or any of them), he will pay the third party for them (whether or not deducting any discount or commission) in return for payment to him by the individual.

Thus the term clearly includes credit cards and trading checks used in a form of credit known as "check trading". It does *not* include a cheque card, because the bank issuing a cheque card merely promises to honour cheques. Debit cards also fall outside the term, as the bank does not provide any credit. Nor does it cover trading stamps or free gift vouchers (e.g. on the back of a cereal packet), because the customer will not receive goods *on credit*.

Unsolicited credit tokens

Section 51 made it an offence "to give a person a credit token if he has not **25.03** asked for it". Although the section was repealed by art.20(15) of the Financial Services and Markets Act 2000 (Regulated Activities) (Amendment) (No 2) Order 2013,[1] it is saved with regard to a regulated credit agreement and continues to apply instead of reg.58(1)(b) of the Payment Services Regulations (which prohibits the sending of an "unsolicited payment instrument").[2]

---

[1] SI 2013/1881.
[2] The Payment Services Regulations 2009 (SI 2009/209). See reg.52(a) for the saving provision.

What is a credit token agreement?

25.04 By s.14(2) (read with s.189) it is a regulated consumer credit agreement for the provision of credit in connection with the use of a credit token. Thus the term will not apply to an agreement where, for example, the debtor is a body corporate or the agreement is exempt. It will be recalled that agreements involving the use of American Express charge cards are exempt agreements, because they are debtor-creditor-supplier agreements for running-account credit and the indebtedness over a period has to be discharged by a single payment.[3]

Modification of formalities

25.05 The formalities required for a regulated agreement were considered in Chapter Twenty. They are modified in two minor respects in the case of a credit token agreement. The first relates to the sending of the second copy; by s.63(4) it need not be given within seven days following the making of the agreement if it is given before or at the time when the credit token is given to the debtor. The second relates to the notice setting out cancellation rights; by s.64(2) it need not be posted within seven days following the making of the agreement if it is posted to the debtor before the credit token is given to him, or if it is sent by post with the credit token.

Additional copies

25.06 Where, under the credit token agreement, the creditor issues a new token to the debtor he must at the same time give the debtor a copy of the executed agreement (if any) and of any document referred to in it. Failure to do so has the usual consequences, i.e. the creditor cannot enforce the agreement while the default continues and, if it continues for one month, he commits an offence.[4] The section does not apply to a small agreement.[5]

Liability of debtor

25.07 We come now to the problem which is likely to be the most troublesome one in practice—the extent of the debtor's liability if the token is used by someone else without the debtor's authority. This matter is primarily governed by ss.66 and 84. By s.66 the debtor under a credit token agreement is not liable for use made of the token by another person unless (a) the debtor had previously accepted the token, or (b) its use constituted an acceptance by him. The debtor accepts a credit token when he or a person authorised by him to use it under the terms of the agreement:

> (a) signs it, or

---

[3] See para.20.15 above, subpara.(4).
[4] s.85.
[5] As above.

(b) signs a receipt for it, or

(c) uses it.

If the token has been accepted under s.66 we can turn to s.84 to consider the debtor's liability for its misuse by someone else. The provisions of this section can be summarised as follows: **25.08**

(1) The underlying principle is that the debtor should give notice of the loss or misuse as soon as possible. Accordingly, the credit token agreement must contain, in the prescribed manner,[6] particulars of the name, address and telephone number of a person to whom notice of loss, etc., can be given. If the agreement does not contain this information the debtor will not be liable for misuse at all.[7]

(2) The debtor is not liable for any loss arising after the creditor has been given written or oral notice that the token has been lost or stolen or is otherwise liable to misuse.[8] The notice takes effect when received, but if it is given orally the agreement may provide that it is not effective unless confirmed in writing within seven days.[9]

(3) Subject to (2) above, the debtor's liability depends on the person by whom the token was misused. If it was misused by a person who acquired possession of the token with the debtor's consent, he is liable *without limit*.[10] In other cases (e.g. loss or theft) his liability is limited to £50,[11] or the credit limit if lower, for misuse in a period beginning when the token ceased to be in the possession of an authorised person and ending when the token is once again in the possession of an authorised person.[12]

Thus the moral is clear: the onus is on the debtor to notify the loss to the creditor without delay.

Cancellation

If the debtor cancels a credit token agreement he can only recover a sum paid for the token, and he will only cease to be liable for such a sum, if the token has been returned to the creditor or surrendered to a supplier.[13] **25.09**

---

[6] i.e. prominently and so as to be easily legible (see reg.2 of the Consumer Credit (Credit-Token Agreements) Regulations 1983 (SI 1983/1555)).
[7] s.84(4).
[8] s.84(3).
[9] s.84(5).
[10] s.84(2).
[11] See art.3 of and the Schedule to the Consumer Credit (Further Increase of Monetary Amounts) (Amendment) Order 1998.
[12] s.84(1).
[13] s.70(5).

Some further points on misuse

25.10 There has been recurring publicity concerning the enormous losses sustained
by credit card companies through credit card frauds—. The increasing popularity of on-line transactions involving "cardholder not present" transactions
has contributed to this. Consumers should take care when using their credit
card on-line or when ordering goods or services at a distance. In any event the
consumer should always check statements carefully and immediately report
any unauthorised transactions.

The use of "chip and pin" cards has led to a reduction in losses sustained by
credit card fraud. The increasing popularity of "contactless payment" cards
which do not require a user to enter his PIN for transactions of a low value
(up to £30 at the time of writing) might reverse this trend, of course.

Chapter Twenty-Six

"I CAN'T AFFORD TO PAY"

In practice there are two main areas where a debtor is likely to seek legal **26.01** advice. The first is where he is dissatisfied with the goods. This has been considered in Pt I of this book and also in Chapter Twenty-Three. The second is where, for one reason or another, he finds himself in difficulties with his payments. The legal adviser can approach the problem by asking a number of preliminary questions:

(1) Is there a contract at all?

If, for example, the document signed by the debtor was merely an offer, revo- **26.02** cation is possible before it has been accepted.[1]

(2) Is the contract voidable for misrepresentation?

If so, it can be rescinded and money recovered, if it is not too late.[2] **26.03**

(3) Has the debtor a claim for breach of contract against the creditor?

If so, he may be able to treat the contract as repudiated or have a claim for **26.04** damages which he can set against the instalments.[3]

(4) Is the agreement cancellable?

If so, the debtor may be able to serve a notice of cancellation under provi- **26.05** sions which have already been discussed.[4]

(5) Was the agreement "improperly executed"?

We have seen that if the creditor fails to comply with the statutory formalities **26.06** such as to contents, signature and copies (and pre-contractual reflection in certain land mortgage cases) the agreement can only be enforced against the debtor or hirer on an order of the court[5] or with the consent of the debtor or hirer given at the time.[6]

One of the features of the legislation is the very wide power given to the

---

[1] See also ss.57 and 66A for the rights of withdrawal, see para.23.02 above.
[2] See para 8.07 above.
[3] See Chapter Eight.
[4] See para.23.04 above.
[5] s.65.
[6] s.173(3).

court to rewrite the agreement or to postpone its enforcement. If the creditor or owner brings proceedings for an enforcement order, the court must consider the degree of culpability for the defect and the prejudice (if any) which it has caused to any person.[7] The court can then do any of the following things:

(a) it may make an enforcement order;

(b) it may make a "time order" under s.129[8];

(c) it may modify the agreement as set out below and then make an enforcement order relating to the agreement as modified; or

(d) it may dismiss the application—but only if it considers it just to do so having regard to the matters mentioned above.[9]

Power to modify agreement and enforcement orders

26.07   Section 127(2)[10] provides that:

> If it appears to the court just to do so, it may in an enforcement order reduce or discharge any sum payable by the debtor or hirer or any surety, so as to compensate him for prejudice suffered as a result of the contravention in question.

We must also consider ss.135 and 136 which are not confined to proceedings for an enforcement order but apply to any order made by the court in relation to a regulated agreement. By s.135(1) an order may include a provision:

> (a) making the operation of any term of the order conditional on the doing of specified acts by any party to the proceedings;
> (b) suspending the operation of any term of the order either—
>
> > (i) until such time as the court subsequently directs, or
> > (ii) until the occurrence of a specified act or omission.

26.08   Section 136 gives the court a wide power to alter the agreement in consequence of a term of an order made under the Act. This can include a reduction in the rate of interest.[11]

These very wide powers cannot be used to suspend an order requiring a person to deliver up goods unless the court is satisfied that they are in that person's possession or control.[12] In the case of a consumer hire agreement the

---

[7] s.127(1).
[8] See para.26.18 below.
[9] s.127(1).
[10] s.127(3) to (5) provided that "the court shall not make an enforcement order" where certain provisions in ss.60–64 were not complied with. Section 15 of the Consumer Credit Act 2006 repeals ss.127(3) to (5) so that now the court *always* has discretion: Consumer Credit Act 2006 (Commencement No.2 and Transitional Provisions and Savings) Order 2007 (SI 2007/123). See early editions of this book for a discussion of the old law.
[11] *Southern and District Finance Plc v Barnes, The Times*, 19 April 1995 CA.
[12] s.135(2).

section cannot be used to extend the period for which the hirer is entitled to possession.[13]

We must also mention certain special powers available to the court in the case of hire-purchase and conditional sale agreements. These are considered later.[14]

Finally, the court has a general power under s.136 to amend any agreement or security in consequence of a term of the order.

The cases show that, as forecast in the Third Edition of this book, these **26.09** wide powers will only be exercised if the court feels that the debtor or hirer has been prejudiced by the failure to comply with the formalities. If the breach is only a technical one (e.g. the second copy sent a few days late) the court is likely to waive the breach entirely.[15]

What happens if the creditor or owner purports to terminate the agreement and repossesses the goods? If it involves entry on premises without the consent of the debtor or hirer there may be liability for breach of statutory duty.[16] Apart from this there may be very little that the debtor or hirer can do about it, because of the "no sanctions" rule in s.170.[17] The section does not however prevent the grant of an injunction[18] and it is just possible that a mandatory injunction could require the goods to be returned to the debtor or hirer. Apart from this, the only sanction is the ever-present administrative sanction of reporting the matter to the Financial Conduct Authority (FCA).

Despite the unenforceability of the agreement for defective formalities there **26.10** is no doubt that the creditor or owner can sue the debtor or hirer in tort if, for example, the debtor or hirer wrongly disposes of the goods[19] or can report the customer to a credit reference agency.[20] Similarly the sanction of not allowing enforcement of "the agreement" would not apply where, for example, the agreement has expired by effluxion of time so that the creditor or owner has a common law right to repossess which he can, it is thought, enforce by action.

In this chapter and elsewhere in Pt IV of this book there are numerous references to "the court". By s.141 any action by the creditor to enforce a regulated agreement must be brought in the county court. An attempt to gain an advantage by starting in the High Court may be struck out as an abuse of process.[21]

"The section infringes my human rights", says the finance company!

The Human Rights Act 1998 has spawned many ingenious arguments—but **26.11** few as remarkable as one involving consumer credit. In *Wilson v First County*

---

[13] s.135(3).
[14] See para.26.24 below.
[15] See *Nissan Finance UK v Lockhart* [1993] C.C.L.R. 39 CA, and contrast *National Guardian Mortgage Corp v Wilkes* [1993] C.C.L.R. 1: failure to supply the pre-contract copy (see para.22.18 above); prejudice to borrower; court reduced interest by 40 per cent.
[16] s.92(3).
[17] See para.19.04 above.
[18] s.170(3).
[19] See *Eastern Distributors Ltd v Goldring* [1957] 2 Q.B. 600.
[20] *McGuffick v Royal Bank of Scotland* [2009] EWHC 2386 (Comm).
[21] *Barclays Bank v Brooks* [1997] C.C.L.R. 60 QBD.

Trust (No.2)[22] a finance company sued a debtor who claimed that the agreement was "improperly executed" within s.61 and that by virtue of s.127(3) it was irredeemably unenforceable. The finance company boldly argued that this section violated their human rights and was therefore incompatible with the European Convention on Human Rights. They argued that (a) it denied them the right to a fair trial under art.6, and (b) it was an unlawful interference with their possessions under art.1 of the First Protocol. Amazingly these arguments succeeded in the Court of Appeal but the House of Lords disagreed. They ruled that (a) art.6 was solely concerned with procedural matters and s.127(3) was a matter of substance, and (2) even if the section infringed art.1 of the First Protocol, it was justified as a reasonable and proportionate response to a genuine social problem. The significance of this case disappeared with the repeal of s.127(3).

(6) Can the debtor terminate the agreement?

26.12 This has already been considered (see para.23.19 above).

(7) Can the debtor settle early and obtain a rebate?

26.13 The debtor may be able to find another source of credit which is less expensive. In the case of hire-purchase the debtor may be better advised to settle early, become the owner of the goods and re-sell them.[23] Section 94(1) gives the debtor a non-excludable right to complete the agreement ahead of time by notice to the creditor and on payment of all sums due, less any statutory rebate of the charge for credit.

Partial repayment

26.14 Until 2011 this right did not extend to partial repayment. This anomaly is rectified by s.94(3) and other consequential amendments made by SI 2010/1010.

 The debtor must give notice to the creditor—and notice under s.94 need no longer be written, unless the credit is secured on land[24]—and make payment before (i) the end of 28 days from the date of receipt of the notice by the creditor, or (ii) any later date specified in the notice.[25]

Creditor's compensation

26.15 Section 95A gives creditors a new right to compensation for early settlement, where the agreement provides for a fixed rate of interest for a period and the repayment exceeds £8,000 in any 12-month period. This right does not apply

---

[22] [2003] 3 W.L.R. 568 HL. A number of cases where unmeritorious debtors benefitted from s.127(3) or (4) led to their repeal: n.10 above.

[23] If the finance company gives an incorrect settlement figure, it may be estopped from claiming the true amount due if their mistake has caused the hirer to alter his position: *Lombard North Central v Stobart* [1990] C.C.L.R. 53 CA.

[24] s.94(6).

[25] s.94(4).

to a current account overdraft, to a payment from a payment protection insurance policy or to a loan on land.

The amount must be fair and objectively justified. It must not exceed one per cent of the repayment or the interest payable on such sum to the end of the agreement, whichever is the higher.[26]

Debtor's rebate

In calculating the total charge for credit the critical factor is the time during which the creditor will be kept out of his money. Accordingly, it is clearly reasonable to allow a rebate where the debtor pays off early, because the creditor will be able to earn fresh interest on the repaid amount. Section 95 enables regulations to be made for the calculation of this rebate, which will apply in any case of early settlement—whether by reason of re-financing, breach or for any other reason. How then is the rebate to be calculated? Three principles must be borne in mind: **26.16**

(a) the total charge for credit should be spread actuarially over the repayment period and the debtor should get a rebate corresponding to the proportion of the total charge for credit which would have accrued after the settlement date;

(b) where capital is being constantly repaid (as in the case of mortgages and hire-purchase agreements) the proportion will reflect the fact that the interest payable at the beginning of the agreement is much greater than it is at a later stage when the outstanding capital is much lower;

(c) a completely even actuarial spread would be unfair to the creditor because certain one-off expenses are incurred at the beginning of the transaction (legal fees, survey fees, stamp duty, etc.).

The calculation of the rebate is governed by the Consumer Credit (Early Settlement) Regulations 2004 (SI 2004/1483) (the 2004 Regulations).[27]

Regulation 4 incorporates an actuarial formula to be used in calculating the amount of the rebate. The formula in the 2004 Regulations is mind boggling and requires an actuary, or at least an accountant, to understand its application. Regulation 4(1) is as follows: **26.17**

> The amount of the rebate is the difference between the total amount of the repayments of credit that would fall due for payment after the settlement date if early settlement did not take place and the amount given by the following formula—

$$\sum_{i=1}^{m} A_i (1 + r)^{aj} - \sum_{i=1}^{n} B_j (1 + r)^{bj}$$

where:

A_i = the amount of the *ith* advance of credit,

---

[26] s.95(2) to (4).
[27] Amended by regs 77–84 of SI 2010/2010.

B_j = the amount of the *jth* repayment of credit,
r = the periodic rate equivalent of the APR/100,
m = the number of advances of credit made before the settlement date,
n = the number of repayments of credit made before the settlement date,
a_i = the time between the *ith* advance of credit and the settlement date, expressed in years and days, or whole weeks or months, as appropriate,
b_j = the time between the *jth* repayment of credit and the settlement date, expressed in years and days, or whole weeks or months, as appropriate, and
Σ represents the sum of all the terms indicated.

They reflect the principles set out above. Thus:

(1) They seek to meet point (c) above by allowing the settlement date (on which the rebate calculation depends) to be notionally deferred by one month (see reg.6).

(2) The Regulations also assist the creditor by allowing him to exclude from the rebate calculations (a) taxes and duties, and (b) sums payable or paid under a linked transaction.

Regulation 4A has a separate formula for partial repayment.

A debtor contemplating making an early settlement can ask the creditor to give him a statement containing the settlement figure.[28] If the creditor fails to comply within seven working days the usual sanctions will follow.[29] Similar provisions apply to partial repayment.[30]

(8) Time orders

26.18 If the debtor or hirer is unable to withdraw, rescind, cancel, terminate or settle early, and if all the formalities have been complied with, the next possibility is to apply for a "time order". Apart from s.127[31] the debtor or hirer can apply for a time order (a) after he has been served with a notice of default, or (b) where the creditor or owner brings proceedings to enforce a regulated agreement or any security or to recover possession of any goods or land to which a regulated agreement relates,[32] or (c) where the debtor or hirer has been given a notice of sums in arrears (see para.26.19 below), 14 days have elapsed and they have notified the creditor or owner of their intention to apply together with a proposal.[33]

In *Southern and District Finance v Barnes*[34] the Court of Appeal laid down the following guidelines:

---

[28] s.97. The contents of the statement and the calculation of the settlement date are contained in the Consumer Credit (Settlement Information) Regulations 1983 (SI 1983/1564) as amended by the 2004 Regulations.
[29] See para.22.02 above.
[30] s.97A.
[31] See para.26.07 above.
[32] s.129. See *First National Bank v Syed* [1991] C.C.L.R. 37 CA (debtor proposed instalments which would not even cover interest accruing; order refused).
[33] s.129A inserted by s.16 of the 2006 Act.
[34] [1995] C.C.L.R. 62 CA.

(1) The power to grant a time order only relates to "any sum owed"— but where a creditor brings a possession action the balance of the loan can be treated as "owed" and s.136 will apply to it.

(2) The court can only vary the terms of a regulated agreement under this section if:

    (a) the proposed amendment is truly a consequence of the term of the order; and

    (b) the making of the amendment is also just (see below).

(3) In any time order application the court must first consider whether it is just to make the order. This will involve a consideration of all the circumstances and the position of the creditor as well as that of the debtor.

(4) Any time order should normally be made for a stipulated period on account of temporary financial difficulty.

(5) The court must consider what instalments would be reasonable, both as regards amount and timing.

(6) If the rate of interest is altered, the court will bear in mind that (a) smaller instalments will result in a liability to pay interest on accumulated arrears, and (b) the payment period will be extended.

(7) If the full amount is due, the order will clearly affect the term of the loan, or the rate of interest, or both.

(8) If justice requires the making of a time order, the court should suspend any possession order while the time order is complied with.

In a recent case[35] involving an allegedly unfair contract term the House of Lords considered that debtors undoubtedly suffered a detriment by the ability of the court to enter judgment without considering their powers under s.129. However, this was not caused by the disputed contractual term but by the drafting of the Act in not requiring the provisions of s.129 to be brought to the notice of debtors. This lacuna should be filled when "information sheets" have to be given with arrears statements, to which we now turn.

Sums in arrears notices and information sheets

Sections 9 to 11 of the 2006 Act introduce new provisions to ensure that
  26.19
debtors and hirers are reminded of the fact that they are in arrears and at the same time given information to help them. These are ss.86B, 86C and 86D of the 1974 Act which contain the requirements about the new "notices of sums in arrears".

    Section 86B deals with fixed-sum credit and consumer hire agreements. The broad effect is that where the debtor or hirer is at least two payments in

---

[35] *Director General of Fair Trading v First National Bank* [2001] UKHL 52.

arrear, the creditor or owner must within 14 days give them an arrears notice. Section 86C imposes comparable requirements in respect of running-account credit agreements. Such notices must include "arrears information sheets". These are sheets which the Office of Fair Trading (OFT) must prepare under s.86A and "include information to help debtors and hirers who receive" arrears notices (s.86A(2)).

Three final points should be noted. (1) A creditor or owner not complying with these requirements cannot enforce the agreement or claim interest during the period of non-compliance (s.86D). (2) Regulations[36] contain the detail about the form and content of arrears notices and the information in information sheets, e.g. the legal consequences of non-payment, details of advice agencies. (3) Non-commercial agreements and small agreements fall outside these provisions.

Notice of default sums and interest

26.20 Another new notice is introduced by s.12 of the 2006 Act and inserted into the 1974 Act as s.86E. Where a debtor or hirer incurs a "default sum", the creditor or owner must give them a notice in the form, with the contents and within the period prescribed by the regulations mentioned in Chapter Twenty-Two. "Default sum" is defined in a new s.187A (inserted by s.18 of the 2006 Act) as "a sum other than interest payable in connection with a breach of the agreement by him".

The sanctions for non-compliance are similar to those in respect of arrears notices mentioned in para.26.19 above: the agreement is unenforceable and interest is not payable on the default sum, in this case for 28 days after the notice was given. Here again non-commercial and small agreements are not affected.

To prevent interest being charged as compound interest on default sums, a new s.86F is inserted by s.13 of the 2006 Act: interest is payable only if it is simple interest.

Default notice

26.21 The agreement may provide that, on default by the debtor or hirer, the creditor or owner shall become entitled to take certain action, e.g. to terminate the agreement, to demand early payment of any sum, to recover possession of any goods or land, to enforce any security or to treat any right conferred on the debtor or hirer (e.g. an option to purchase in the case of a hire-purchase agreement) as terminated, restricted or deferred. The effect of s.87 is that such a provision will not be enforceable unless the creditor or owner first serves on the debtor or hirer a notice of default in the prescribed form.[37] The notice must contain the following information[38]:

---

[36] SI 2007/1167: see para.22.26 above.
[37] See Consumer Credit (Enforcement Default and Termination Notices) Regulations 1983 (SI 1983/1561). Note that if the notice claims a sum larger than the amount owed by the debtor or hirer the notice is invalid: *Woodchester Lease Management Services Ltd v Swain & Co* [1999] 1 W.L.R. 263 CA.
[38] s.88 as amended by s.14 of the 2006 Act inserting ss.(4A). Also "14" was previously "7" days.

(a) it must specify the breach;

(b) if the breach is capable of remedy (e.g. default in payment) the notice must indicate what action has to be taken to remedy it and the date before which it must be done;

(c) if the breach is incapable of remedy (e.g. causing permanent damage to the goods) what compensation (if any) is required and the date before which it is to be paid;

(d) the consequences of non-compliance;

(e) a default information sheet; and

(f) in appropriate cases the restrictions on the creditor's right to repossess "protected goods" (see para.26.25 below).

The date in (b) and (c) above must be not earlier than 14 days after the service of the notice of default.[39]

Effect of default notice

If, before the specified date the debtor or hirer takes the steps specified in the notice, the default is treated as never having taken place.[40] Alternatively, as already stated, the debtor or hirer can apply under s.129 for a "time order". Such an order may contain either or both of the following provisions:

26.22

(a) that any sum owed by the debtor or hirer or any surety shall be payable at such times as the court, having regard to the means of the debtor or hirer and any surety, considers reasonable;

(b) that a breach by the debtor or hirer (other than the non-payment of money) shall be remedied within such period as the court may specify.

Effect of repossession

The Act does not specify what remedies are available if the creditor or owner repossesses the goods or land without a default notice. The section provides that the creditor or owner is not *entitled* to repossess, etc., without serving a notice of default. It may well be, therefore, that non-compliance could be actionable as trespass to goods or conversion or there might be a breach of the implied warranty for quiet possession. There may also be liability for breach of statutory duty if there is unauthorised entry on premises[41] and the "snatch-back" of protected goods[42] will lead to the severe sanctions set out in s.91.[43]

26.23

---

[39] See *Brandon v American Express Services Europe Ltd* [2011] EWCA Civ 1187.
[40] s.89.
[41] See para.26.25 below.
[42] See para.26.27 below.
[43] As above.

(9) Additional protection in hire-purchase and conditional sale cases

26.24 The notice of default provisions are backed up by four other provisions aimed at what is known as "snatch-back"—the repossession of goods or land without an order of the court.

Entry on premises

26.25 In the case of a regulated hire-purchase or conditional sale agreement the creditor or owner cannot enter any premises to repossess the goods without an order of the court.[44] Clearly, a contractual provision conferring such a right would be void[45] but a consent at the time of entry would be effective.[46]

Land

26.26 If the debtor is in breach under a conditional sale agreement relating to land the creditor cannot recover possession of the land from the debtor, nor from any person claiming under him, without an order of the court.[47] The point relating to the debtor's consent will be equally relevant here.

In both the above cases, s.92(3) does provide a sanction—any entry in contravention of either of these provisions is actionable as a breach of statutory duty.

Protected goods

26.27 In the case of hire-purchase and conditional sale it is clearly inequitable that the debtor, having paid a substantial part of the price, should have the goods snatched away (with no credit for his payments) merely because he gets into arrears. Accordingly, s.90 gives him protection if the debtor (a) is in breach, (b) has not terminated the agreement, (c) has paid to the creditor one-third or more of the total price, and (d) the property in the goods remains in the creditor. In such a case the goods are called *"protected goods"*. The creditor cannot recover possession of the goods from the debtor without an order of the court.

The Act imposes serious sanctions for contravention. By s.91 if goods are recovered by the creditor in contravention of s.90 the agreement, if not already terminated, will terminate, the debtor is released from all further liability and he can recover from the creditor all sums paid under the agreement. A number of points arise under this very important provision.

> (a) Where the agreement requires the creditor to carry out any installation work and the cost of this work forms part of the total price, then the fraction of one-third is calculated by taking the installation charge in full and adding one-third of the balance.[48] Thus, if the price

---

[44] s.92(1).
[45] s.173(1).
[46] s.173(3).
[47] s.92(2).
[48] s.90(2). Similar to s.100(2), see para.23.24 above.

of £300 includes an installation charge of £30 the fraction of one-third will be:

$$£30 + \frac{270}{3} = £120$$

(b) A dealer might be tempted to avoid the "protected goods" provisions in one of two ways. First of all there might be an agreement for a television set with a price of £250, of which £90 has been paid. If the customer then comes in for a £500 computer the dealer might say "let us cancel the original agreement and make a new one for both items (£750) with a credit for sums already paid (£90)". Secondly, if the original agreement (with payments exceeding one-third) related to a telescope and a camera, he might suggest that the telescope should be treated as fully paid up and that a new agreement should be made relating solely to the camera. In both cases the debtor starts inside s.90 and would end up outside it—because he has not paid one-third under the new agreement. To prevent such avoidance the effect of s.90(3) is to bring the new agreement within the section, even though one-third has not been paid.

Where the agreement provides that on default the hirer must pay default interest in addition to the hire-purchase price, the hirer can appropriate any payment towards the price (so as to gain protection under s.90). If he fails to do so, the creditor can appropriate. In one case[49] the creditor issued proceedings for possession and the summons showed that just over one-third of the price had been paid. He then sought to amend the summons by earmarking a small amount towards default interest. It was held that it was too late for him to do so.

(c) Repossession of the goods from the debtor without a court order kills the agreement. Thus, on the one hand, the debtor cannot claim the return of the goods[50] while on the other hand the creditor cannot breathe any fresh life into the agreement by returning the goods to the debtor.[51]

(d) Section 90 prohibits recovery of possession only "from the debtor". Thus, if the creditor seizes the goods which the debtor has abandoned the section is not infringed.[52] A similar principle would apply where the creditor seizes the goods from a third party to whom the debtor has purported to sell them.[53]

(e) A consent by the debtor given at the time is as effective as an order

[49] *Julian Hodge Bank Ltd v Hall* [1998] C.C.L.R. 14.
[50] *Carr v Broderick & Co Ltd* [1942] 2 K.B. 275.
[51] *Capital Finance Co Ltd v Bray* [1964] 1 W.L.R. 323.
[52] *Bentinck Ltd v Cromwell Engineering Co Ltd* [1971] 1 Q.B. 324.
[53] Consider *Eastern Distributors Ltd v Goldring* [1957] 2 Q.B. 600.

of the court[54] but the court is likely to examine the facts closely to make sure that there was a true and free consent.[55]

(f) If the debtor chooses to terminate under s.99,[56] the goods are not protected.

Relief against forfeiture

26.28 The court has a general power to grant relief against the forfeiture of a proprietary or possessory right (which could be relevant where, for example, the finance company sought to repossess after the debtor had paid most of the instalments). Such a power will only be exercised in exceptional circumstances.[57]

Additional powers of the court[58]

26.29 In any proceedings for an enforcement order, or for a time order, or in proceedings by the creditor to recover possession, the court may (in addition to its other powers) make (a) a return order, or (b) a transfer order.[59] A return order, as the name implies, requires the debtor to return the goods to the creditor. A transfer order is, in effect, a "split" order, in that it orders the debtor to return some of the goods to the creditor and it vests in the debtor the creditor's title to the remainder. This is subject to a ceiling set out in s.133(3), namely, that the maximum transferable to the debtor is found by deducting from the sum paid one-third of the unpaid balance. Thus, if the debtor had paid £80 out of a total price of £200, the court can vest in the debtor goods to the value of:

$$£80 - \left[\frac{200 - 80}{3} \right] = £40$$

In practice, the court frequently makes a return order and then exercises its powers under s.135 to suspend the operation of the order on condition that the debtor pays the balance by instalments fixed by the court.

(10) Additional protection in consumer hire cases

26.30 A number of provisions which are relevant to consumer hire have already been considered earlier in this chapter. They include s.65 (improperly executed agreements), s.87 (notice of default), s.92 (no entry on premises without court order) and s.129 (time orders). In addition, s.132 provides that where the owner recovers possession otherwise than by action the hirer may

---

[54] s.173(3).
[55] The matter could be raised if the debtor took proceedings alleging a breach of s.90 and denying his consent to the repossession. See *Chartered Trust Plc v Pitcher* [1988] R.T.R. 72 CA.
[56] See para.23.24 above.
[57] *Transag Haulage Ltd v Leyland Daf* (1994) 13 Tr.L.R. 361.
[58] The county court has exclusive jurisdiction over regulated agreements; see s.141 and *Sovereign Leasing v Ali* [1992] C.C.L.R. 1 (transfer of action started in High Court).
[59] s.133.

apply to the court for an order (a) extinguishing any further liability to make payments in whole or in part, or (b) requiring the owner to repay sums paid by the hirer in whole or in part. The court can also include such a provision when it makes an order for delivery to the owner. Such a power could be exercised where, for example, the hirer has paid a year's rental in advance and then finds it necessary to terminate the hiring after only a few weeks or where the owner retakes the goods following the hirer's default.

A hirer can also argue, in appropriate cases, that the owner had no right to terminate at all. The right to terminate depends primarily on the terms of the contract; if the termination clause is very precise it may be construed as exhaustive and as excluding the general common law right to terminate if the hirer commits a repudiatory breach.[60]

It will be recalled that the general power to make a "suspended" order under s.135 cannot extend the period for which the hirer is entitled to possession.[61]

(11) Appropriation of payments

A debtor or hirer may have two or more separate regulated agreements with the same creditor or owner. If he finds himself unable to pay a sum to cover all the sums due and sends a smaller amount, s.81 allows him, on making the payment, to appropriate it to one or more of the agreements in such proportions as he thinks fit. If he fails to appropriate at the time of payment, then s.81(2) may come into play. It provides that where one or more of the agreements is a hire-purchase, conditional sale, consumer hire or secured agreement, the payment shall be appropriated in the proportion which the sums *due* bear to each other.

26.31

Example

> £20 is due under a hire purchase agreement relating to a dishwasher and £10 is due under a hire agreement relating to a television set. The debtor sends a cheque for £12. If he fails to appropriate at the time of payment, £8 will go towards the dishwasher and £4 towards the television set.

26.32

Finally, if the debtor fails to appropriate in a case to which s.81(2) does *not* apply (e.g. if he has two debtor-creditor agreements with the same creditor) the general law will apply and the creditor will have the right of appropriation.

(12) Unfair relationships

Background

At the beginning of Pt IV of this book we referred in para.18.04 to the 2003 White Paper, *Fair, Clear and Competitive–the Consumer Credit Market in the 21st Century*. We noted that one of the areas of concern was unfair credit relationships, to which we now turn.

26.33

---

[60] *Eurocopy Rentals v McCann Fordyce* [1995] C.C.L.R. 4.
[61] See para.26.08 above.

The Act attempted to solve the problems faced by debtors, who had been unable to cope with credit transactions which they alleged were unfair, by using the powers given by ss.137 to 140. These provisions had been drafted very narrowly, so that the courts could not interfere, unless the credit bargain was "extortionate", i.e. it involved "grossly exorbitant" payments or "grossly contravenes ordinary principles of fair dealing". The absence of the words "grossly" would have given the judges greater room to manoeuvre, but as it was they were in a straitjacket and forced to give a restricted meaning to the expressions in the Act. (Readers may refer to the first seven editions of this book for a more detailed analysis of the old law.)

Criticism of sections 137 to 140

26.34 The White Paper listed a number of factors which had contributed to the ineffectiveness of the existing law:

(a) few cases had reached the courts because the qualifying hurdles were very high;

(b) the wording of the legislation was imprecise, resulting in a restrictive interpretation by the courts;

(c) the courts had focussed on interest rates under the agreement, whereas other terms (such as the level of security required, default charges and lack of transparency) were equally likely to cause detriment to consumers; and

(d) the courts had considered only the position as at the date of the agreement and had refused to take into account such matters as a power to vary the rate of interest from time to time.

Unfair relationships—the new test

26.35 The new s.140A of the Act enables the court to make an order under the new s.140B (see below) if it finds that the relationship between the creditor and the debtor arising out of a credit agreement, or that agreement taken with any related agreement, is unfair to the debtor. Such unfairness can result from one or more of the following factors:

(a) any of the terms of the agreement or of any related agreement (onerous charges and restrictions on termination rights are obvious examples);

(b) the way in which the creditor has exercised or enforced any of his rights under the agreement or any related agreement (heavy-handed enforcement comes to mind); and

(c) any other thing done (or not done) by, or on behalf of, the creditor (either before or after the making of the agreement or any related agreement). The bracketed words highlight an important difference between the new provisions and those which they replace. Sections 137 to 140 were only concerned with "the bargain" and not post-contractual matters.

The court can take into account all matters which it considers relevant, including acts done or not done by the creditor's associate or former associate. The debtor's age, financial circumstances, track record and business experience will no doubt be relevant—and so will any misleading statements and high-pressure sales techniques.

Powers of the court

The new s.140B (inserted by s.20 of the 2006 Act) contains a wide range of orders which may: **26.36**

    (a) require the repayment of any sum paid by the debtor or a surety;

    (b) require the creditor to do or not to do anything;

    (c) reduce or discharge any sum payable;

    (d) direct the return to a surety of any property provided as security;

    (e) set aside any duty imposed on the debtor or surety;

    (f) alter the terms of the agreement; and

    (g) direct accounts to be taken.

The Competitive Markets Authority (and now also the FCA) and two-tier enforcement—publication of guidance

A debtor seeking to challenge an agreement (and the changes set out above are designed to make this easier) can do so by (a) making an application to the county court, or (b) raising the matter in enforcement proceedings brought by the creditor or in any other proceedings in which such a challenge is relevant. The Competitive Markets Authority (CMA) and the FCA has no power to intervene in individual cases, but it has a general power under Pt 8 of the Enterprise Act 2002 to apply for an enforcement order where a trader commits a breach of duty which is harmful to the collective interests of consumers (a further example of this public/private enforcement dichotomy can be found with the unfair terms regime under the Consumer Rights Act 2015).   **26.37**

Three illustrative cases

Patel v Patel[62]
The dispute between two close family friends involved oral agreements for loans totalling £56,450, which by 1992 had risen to £207,465 after taking into account interest and repayments. It was then agreed that the interest would   **26.38**

---

[62] [2009] EWHC 3264 (QB).

accrue at 20 per cent per annum compounded monthly. No records were kept by the creditor (C) nor chasing documentation given to the debtor (D). C claimed, including interest, £4.5 million.

D's defences were that: (1) the arrangements were informal and no legally binding agreements had been made; (2) the court should make an order under s.140B to discharge or reduce the sum payable because their relationship was unfair.

Leggatt QC had no hesitation in accepting C's evidence as to the terms of the 1992 agreement, although it had been commercial madness for D to allow the debt to grow over many years at such a high rate of compound interest.

The court had to determine whether the relationship arising out of the agreement was unfair, not whether the credit agreement was unfair. Where the relationship was continuing, the determination had to be made at the date of the trial having regard to the entirety of the relationship and all potentially relevant matters.

On the facts the relationship was unfair taking into account the terms of the agreement and C's failure to provide any further calculation after 1992 or to keep any proper records. In considering what order to make the court had to consider what was proportionate having regard to the nature and degree of the unfairness. It was not fair to D to order him to pay more than £207,465 the sum outstanding in 1992.

Harrison v Black Horse Ltd

26.39   **High Court**[63]   Mr and Mrs Harrison's (H) claim related to payment protection insurance (PPI) taken out at the same time as a loan made to them by the defendant bank. The loan was £60,000 repayable over 23 years. The premium was £10,200, of which commission of 87 per cent was retained by the bank as intermediary, and covered five years only. The bank did not disclose the fact or amount of the commission.

H's claim was based, inter alia, on an unfair relationship between the parties.

The High Court held that the claim against the bank failed. Although the non-disclosure of the commission was a relevant factor, there was no misrepresentation or improper conduct by the bank. As to the length and cost of the PPI cover, H knew the PPI was optional and its cost relative to the loan and that it was for only five years. There was no unfair relationship.

26.40   **Court of Appeal**[64]   H appealed against the decision of the High Court. H argued that the commission was so egregious that it gave rise to a conflict of interest which it was the lender's duty to disclose.

The Court of Appeal, dismissing the appeal, held that there was no conflict of interest and the relationship was not unfair under s.140A.

---

[63] [2010] EWHC 3152 (QB).
[64] [2011] EWCA Civ 1128.

Tomlinson LJ stated at paras 58 and 59:

"The commission here is on any view quite startling and there will be many who regard it as unacceptable conduct on the part of lending institutions to have profited in this way. I struggle however to spell out of the mere size of the undisclosed commission an unfairness in the relationship between lender and borrower. Moreover the touchstone must in my view be the standard imposed by the regulatory authorities pursuant to their statutory duties, not resort to a visceral instinct that the relevant conduct is beyond the Pale. In that regard it is clear that the ICOB regime after due consultation and consideration does not require the disclosure of the receipt of commission. It would be an anomalous result if a lender was obliged to disclose receipt of a commission in order to escape a finding of unfairness under s.140A of the Act but yet not obliged to disclose it pursuant to the statutorily imposed regulatory framework under which it operates . . .

Nor do I think that the circle can be squared by arguing that a recommendation of suitability cannot be objective if given by a lender in receipt of a large commission. The judge rejected that submission on the facts of this case. There is also the obvious difficulty in deciding where the line is to be drawn. How large must the commission be before there is held to be a conflict of duty and interest? The cover was expensive but the lender was in the circumstances for the reasons I have given under no obligation to advise that the same cover could have been obtained more cheaply elsewhere. A seller is not ordinarily obliged to warn his buyer that his product is expensive when compared to other similar products and in my judgement it is telling that in this heavily regulated market no such obligation has been imposed. It was irrelevant to the Harrisons that the high price they were paying contained a substantial element of reward for Black Horse."

The court was fortified in its conclusions by the Financial Services Authority's report in March 2007 on consumer experiences in the general insurance markets and its policy statement of August 2010 which did not list non-disclosure of commission among the 15 common failings resulting in consumer detriment (see paras 61 and 62).

Plevin v Paragon Personal Finance Ltd ([2014] UKSC 61, on appeal from 2013 EWCA Civ 1658)

However, everything has changed since this recent decision. Mrs Plevin was **26.41** a 59-year-old college lecturer. She received an unsolicited leaflet from LLP Processing (UK) Ltd (LLP), an ICOB regulated broker, and following a demands and needs assessment conducted via telephone, LLP made a recommendation of PPI to her.

Paragon Personal Finance Ltd (Paragon) was one of a number of lenders on LLP's books. After signing the application form, Paragon telephoned Mrs Plevin and conducted a "*speak with*" call, the purpose of which was to comply with anti-money laundering regulations. There was no further assessment for Mrs Plevin's demands and needs during that call. Mrs Plevin subsequently entered into a credit agreement with Paragon on 21 March 2006 for a total amount of £39,780 which comprised a loan of £34,000 together with an upfront PPI premium of £5,780. Of the PPI premium, 71.8 per cent was taken in commission with LLP receiving £1,870 and Paragon retaining £2,280. Neither of the commission amounts were disclosed to Mrs Plevin.

26.42   First of all, in this case the Supreme Court found that the broker's failure
to properly assess the consumer's needs was not something that the lender
could be held responsible for, so it did not contribute to making the relationship unfair.

However, while the High Court and Court of Appeal had agreed with the
decision in *Harrison* above (i.e. that failure to disclose the broker's commission did not make the relationship unfair), the Supreme Court disagreed.
The Supreme Court took the view that *Harrison* was wrongly decided, and
overturned it, saying that the failure to disclose the broker's commission to
the customer did indeed make the relationship unfair.

See also the Financial Conduct Authority (FCA) statement on the
Plevin case, at *http://www.fca.org.uk/news/statement-plevin-paragon-personal-
finance-ltd.*

(13) Special Rules on High Cost Short Term Credit

26.43   Recently a special regime was introduced by the FCA to control the particular problem of High-Cost-Short-Term Credit (HCSTC), the most common
example of which being so called "payday lending". The regime contains
rules on advertising, pre-contractual information and fair treatment of customers after default, as well as a price cap and a rollover limit. For a fuller
explanation of all of this, see A. Fejos, "Achieving Safety and Affordability
in the UK Payday Loans Market" (2015) 38 (1) Journal of Consumer
Policy 181; Financial Conduct Authority (2014) *Detailed rules for the price
cap on high-cost short-term credit Including feedback on CP14/10 and final
rules,* Policy Statement, PS 14/16, November 2014; and Financial Conduct
Authority (2014) *Guide for Consumer Credit Firms,* London: Financial
Conduct Authority, *http://www.fca.org.uk/static/documents/consumer-credit-
being-regulated-guide.pdf.*

Here we shall focus on those rules that allow for direct control of the
amount that has to be paid. These are the rules on price caps (contained in
the Consumer Credit Source Book-CONC-5A), and those on rollover limits
(CONC 6.7.23R).

26.44   First, however, let us set out the type of agreements covered by these rules.
High-Cost Short-Term credit is defined as "a regulated credit agreement: (a)
which is a borrower-lender agreement or a peer-to-peer (P2P) agreement; (b)
in relation to which the annual percentage rate (APR) of charge is equal to
or exceeds 100 per cent; (c) either: (i) in relation to which a financial promotion indicates (by express words or otherwise) that the credit is to be provided
for any period up to a maximum of 12 months or otherwise indicates (by
express words or otherwise) that the credit is to be provided for a short term;
or (ii) under which the credit is due to be repaid or substantially repaid within
a maximum of 12 months of the date on which the credit is advanced; (d)
which is not secured by a mortgage, charge or pledge; and (e) which is not:
(i) a credit agreement in relation to which the lender is a community finance
organisation; or (ii) a home credit loan agreement, a bill of sale loan agreement or a borrower-lender agreement enabling a borrower to overdraw on a

current account or arising where the holder of a current account overdraws on the account without a pre-arranged overdraft or exceeds a pre-arranged overdraft limit" (FCA Handbook, Glossary).

Price Cap

There are three elements to the price cap: **26.45**

1) an initial cost cap, of 0.8 per cent per day of the outstanding principal (CONC 5A.2.3R);

2) a cap on default charges of £15 (CONC 5A.2.14R); and

3) all loan costs, including default fees and charges, are capped at 100 per cent of the amount borrowed ((CONC 5A.2.2R).

So, for example, a consumer who borrows £100 for 30 days, would pay a maximum of £24 during the agreed loan duration (rule 1), up to £15 in default charges (rule 2), and a maximum of £61 in other fees and charges, so that the total amount that would need to be repaid is no more than £200, this (following rule 3), being 100 per cent of the amount borrowed.

Rollover Limit

A key feature of HCSTC is the so called "roll-over" element. This means that   **26.46** the consumer pays off the interest and charges initially due, but the capital amount, which has not been paid off, "rolls-over" (with new interest and charges) beyond the original repayment period, into a new loan. This new loan is repayable over the same period, and on the same terms, as the initial loan.

In 2012 roughly 10 per cent of loans rolled over 4–6 times, around 5 per cent over 7–10 times. The OFT found an example of a loan rolling over 36 times (Office of Fair Trading, (2013) *Payday Lending Compliance Review, Final Report,* OFT 1481, March 2013).

To illustrate the potential detriment caused by rollovers, take a case where £100 is borrowed for 30 days at one per cent per day, amounting to £30 in interest. After 30 days, the consumer has paid the outstanding interest, the obligation to pay the principal is rolled-over, and has accrued another £30 interest. So even after only four rollovers, the total amount paid in capital and interest will be £250, instead of the initially planned £130. This figure ignores the likelihood of the extra fees and charges likely to be payable for a rollover, and also the practice of some lenders also to allow not only the principal sum to rollover, but also the interest, which could itself generate further compound interest payments.

The new regime restricts the numbers of permitted rollovers to two (CONC 6.7.23 R). This obviously significantly reduces the scope for consumer detriment. It is also important to note that this restriction does not only apply to "rollovers" in the strict sense that this concept has been understood and used in payday lending. "Rollovers" in this strict sense, involve the new loan being repayable over the same period, and on the same terms that had applied to the original loan. However, the new regime applies not only to this scenario, but to any form of refinancing, including where, for instance, the loan is refinanced on different terms (the outstanding loan amount being repackaged into a new loan, possibly with extra borrowing and/or being repayable over a longer period. This is a very important element in making the restriction on rollovers work in practice. It prevents firms getting around the rules by simply adopting some other form of refinancing, involving, e.g., some variation of the loan period or of the other terms and conditions (see CONC 6.7.17 R).

CHAPTER TWENTY-SEVEN

"I WANT TO SEE MY CREDIT FILE"

At the beginning of Chapter Nineteen we drew attention to the explosion of **27.01** credit business. A credit transaction can, of course, cause problems at both ends. The consumer may overreach himself and may plunge into debt. The creditor may supply goods or services on credit terms and then suffer substantial financial loss if the consumer fails to pay the sums due. To protect himself the creditor will frequently consult a credit reference agency[1] as to the financial standing of the prospective debtor. The activity of a "credit reference agency" is defined as "furnishing of persons with information relevant to the financial standing of individuals or relevant recipients of credit if the person has collected the information for that purpose".[2]

If the debtor then finds that his application for credit has been rejected, or has been granted on unfavourable terms, he may well suspect that the credit reference agency has passed on unfavourable information. The Act, as originally drafted, contained provisions—which stand apart from the remaining provisions of the Act—giving the debtor a right:

(1) to ask for details of any credit reference agency consulted by the creditor or credit-broker;

(2) to obtain a copy of his file from the agency; and

(3) to have errors corrected.

The limited right to seek information from a credit reference agency (see (2) **27.02** above) has been replaced by the much wider right of an individual to access personal data under the Data Protection Act 1998 (the 1998 Act). The 1998 Act (which was passed to give effect to an EU Directive) is not limited to computerised data; it also covers data which is "recorded as part of a relevant filing system"—a term which leaves considerable room for debate. From 25 May 2018, the new EU General Data Protection Regulation[3] will come into effect, which inter alia includes new rules governing the use of credit-referencing information (see art.22).

It is now proposed to conclude this part of the book by looking briefly at the three matters listed above. It can be said at the outset that a company

---

[1] Such an agency will require a licence under the Act—see s.145(1)(e).

[2] art.89B(1) of the Financial Services and Markets Act 2000 (Regulated Activities) Order 2001, as amended.

[3] Regulation 2016/679, (2016) OJ L119/1.

which keeps its own credit records of customers would not of itself be a credit reference agency; the reason is that the statutory controls only apply where the activities of the credit reference agency are carried on as a business (see s.145(8), as amended).

Duty to disclose name and address of agency

27.03 Section 157(A1) obliges creditors, when informing debtors of a decision to reject a credit application (when that decision was made on "the basis of information obtained" from a credit reference agency) to inform them unasked that the decision was based on such information and to provide them with particulars of the agency. Section 157(2A) and (4) sets out several exceptions.

In any other case s.157(1) entitles the debtor or hirer to make a written request to the creditor, owner or negotiator asking for the name and address of any credit reference agency to which the creditor, owner or negotiator applied for information as to his financial standing at any time during the antecedent negotiations. The creditor, etc., must then give him notice containing this information within seven working days of receiving the request (see s.157(1) and reg.3 of the Consumer Credit (Credit Reference Agency) Regulations 2000).[4] The debtor or hirer must, however, act quickly because the duty to supply the information does not arise where the request is received more than 28 days after the end of the antecedent negotiations (whether on the making of the regulated agreement or otherwise).[5]

27.04 In practice the consumer will often be dealing with a credit-broker (for example, with a car dealer who arranges to finance the transaction through the creditor). Accordingly any request is likely to come from the consumer to the credit-broker. The regulations seek to ensure that the credit-broker will be able to pass on to the consumer the names of the agency or agencies consulted by the creditor as well as the agencies which he himself consulted. Accordingly, they provide that the creditor must give this information to the credit-broker not later than the date on which he informs him that he is not willing to make a regulated agreement.[6] The credit-broker must then include this information in the s.157 notice which he gives to the debtor or hirer.[7]

A creditor, owner or negotiator who fails to give the notice within the seven-day period commits an offence (see s.157(3)).

Duty on agency to disclose filed information

27.05 We have seen that the information rights of an individual are now to be found in the Data Protection Act 1998 (1998 Act). Accordingly, s.158 of the 1974 Act now only applies to a "consumer" which is defined, for this purpose only,

---

[4] SI 2000/290. See also SI 1977/329.
[5] See s.157(2).
[6] reg.2 of the Consumer Credit (Conduct of Business) (Credit Reference Agencies) Regulations 1977 (SI 1977/330).
[7] reg.3 of the Consumer Credit (Conduct of Business) (Credit Reference Agencies) Regulations 1977 (SI 1977/330).

as a partnership of two or three persons or other unincorporated association. A consumer who suspects that a credit reference agency has information on him can make a written request for that information ("the file") together with a fee of £2. On receipt of the request and fee and such particulars as the agency may reasonably require to identify the file the agency must within seven working days supply a copy of the file together with a statement in the prescribed form[8] informing him of his rights under s.159 (as to which see below). It may well be that the file is not readily intelligible (perhaps because it is computerised). In any such case the consumer's right to a "copy of the file" is a right to a transcript reduced into plain English (see s.158(3)).

It may be, of course, that the agency has no file on the consumer; in that case they must give him notice of that fact but they need not return any fee paid (see s.158(3)).

An agency which contravenes any provision of s.158[9] commits an offence.

Rights of individual to obtain information under the 1998 Act

Under ss.7–9 of the 1998 Act an individual who makes a request in writing **27.06** and pays the appropriate fee has the following rights:

(1) The data controller must inform them whether any data relating to him or her is being processed.

(2) The data controller must also give a description of:

    (a) any relevant personal data;
    (b) the purposes for which it is being processed; and
    (c) the recipients or class of recipients to whom it is, or may be, disclosed.

(3) There must be communicated in intelligible form:

    (a) the information constituting the personal data; and
    (b) any information available to the data controller as to the source of that information.

(4) Where data is processed by automatic means to evaluate matters relating to them (e.g. reliability), and where this is the sole basis of any decision significantly affecting them (e.g. the grant or refusal of credit), the data controller must inform them as to the logic involved in that decision taking.

Where compliance with the request would involve information relating to a **27.07** third party the controller can refuse to comply with that request unless (a) the third party consents, or (b) it is reasonable to comply with that request even without such consent.

---

[8] reg.4 and Schs 1, 2 and 3 to the Consumer Credit (Credit Reference Agency) Regulations 2000 (SI 2000/290)
[9] See also s.160 which lays down an alternative procedure for "business consumers".

Where the data controller is a credit reference agency, s.9 provides that (a) the individual may limit the request to personal data relating to their financial standing (and the request is to be treated as limited in this way unless it shows a contrary intention), and (b) where the data controller is processing the data, the information must include a statement as to the rights available under s.159 (see below).

Correction of wrong information under the 1974 Act

27.08   A consumer may realise that the information disclosed under s.158 or the 1998 Act contains an entry which is incorrect—perhaps that he is an undischarged bankrupt or has an outstanding unsatisfied judgment against him. If the consumer considers that an entry is incorrect and that he is likely to be prejudiced if it is not corrected, he may give notice to the agency requiring them to remove the offending entry or to amend it (s.159(1)). The agency must then, within 28 days, send the consumer a notice stating that they have (a) removed the entry, (b) amended it, or (c) taken no action (see s.159(2)). In case (b) above the notice must include a copy of the amended entry.

27.09   If the notice is given under (b) or (c) above (or is not given at all within the 28-day period) the consumer is given a further right under s.159(3). In any such case he can, within 28 days, serve a further notice on the agency requiring it (a) to add to the file an accompanying notice of correction, not exceeding 200 words, drawn up by himself, and (b) to include a copy of it when furnishing information included in or based on that entry. On receiving this further notice the agency has a choice. It can either (a) comply with it and inform the consumer that it has done so, or (b) apply to the Information Commissioner (formerly the Data Protection Commissioner) on the grounds that "it would be improper for it to publish a notice of correction because it is incorrect, or unjustly defames any person, or is frivolous or scandalous, or is for any other reason unsuitable" (s.159(5)). Conversely, the consumer may apply to the Information Commissioner[10] on the ground that he has not received a correction notice within 28 days of requesting it. The Commissioner, after considering the relevant facts and the documentation,[11] can make such order as he thinks fit.

27.10   The consumer may have one further problem; the correction of an erroneous entry may be all very well for the future but what about the past? What can be done to correct damage which he may already have suffered as the result of the erroneous information having been passed on to an enquirer? The Regulations deal with this problem.[12] If the agency agrees to remove or amend an entry, or if it is ordered to do so by the Commissioner, the agency must notify each person to whom it furnished information relevant to the financial standing of the consumer at any time within six months before it

---

[10] Form CC 314/77 must be used for such an application.
[11] See SI 2000/290 which sets out the procedure to be followed.
[12] reg.5 of the SI 1977/330.

received a s.158 request, particulars and fee (see para.27.03 above). This must be done within 10 working days after the notice of removal or compliance or after the expiry of the compliance period specified by the Commissioner under s.159(5) (see para.27.09 above).

Further rights under the 1998 Act

The s.159 rights summarised above are supplemented by further rights under the 1998 Act. Thus: **27.11**

(1) Section 10 allows the individual to serve a notice on the data controller requiring him not to process (or to cease processing) any data on the ground that it would cause him unwarranted damage or distress. The controller must then within 21 days give a written notice stating that (a) he has complied or intends to do so, or (b) the extent to which he considers the request unjustified.

(2) By s.13 the individual can claim compensation for damage and distress (but not for distress on its own) if he suffers damage flowing from inaccuracy of the data or from unauthorised disclosure—subject in either case to a "reasonable care" defence.

(3) By s.14 the court can order rectification, erasure, destruction and notification to third parties.

From May 2018, the EU's General Data Protection Regulation is likely to replace the provisions of the Data Protection Act 1998. At the time of completing this edition, the new Regulation had only just been formally published, and the impact on UK law has not yet been fully determined.

COUNTY COURT PRECEDENTS

In the County Court at Bigtown   Case No.   **A1.01**

BETWEEN:

Robert Lowe   Claimant

and

New Antiques Ltd   Defendants

PARTICULARS OF CLAIM

1. By an oral agreement made between the Claimant and the Defendant on 1 December 2015 the Defendant sold to the Claimant a pair of antique vases for £1,400 and the Claimant paid that sum to the Defendant. Attached to these particulars is a copy of the receipt for purchase.

2. It was an implied condition of the sale that the Defendant had a right to sell the vases.

3. The Defendant was in breach of this implied condition because he had no right to sell. On or about 3 January 2016 the police seized the vases on the ground that they belonged to a Mr Jones and that they were stolen from him by an unknown person who had sold them to the Defendant.

4. The Defendant has refused to refund the £1,400 (or any part of it) to the Claimant.

5. By reason of the matters set out above the Claimant is entitled to the return of £1,400 as money paid for a consideration which has wholly failed.

6. The Claimant is also entitled to interest under section 69 of the County Courts Act 1984 at the rate of 8 per cent per annum from 1 December 2015 until today's date (£56) and further interest at the rate of 0.31p per day until judgment or earlier payment.

And the Claimant claims

(a) £1,400 and interest as set out above.

(b) Costs

In any event the amount of the claim for damages is limited to £10,000.
[I believe] [the claimant believes] that the facts stated in [this claim form] [these particulars of claim] are true.

In the County Court at Bigtown   Case No. **A1.02**

BETWEEN:

Geoffrey Woodroffe   Claimant

and

Reliable Karsales Ltd   Defendant

PARTICULARS OF CLAIM

1. By an agreement made in writing dated 1 November 2015 the Defendant sold to the Claimant a second-hand Bonecrusher car registration number M123 ABC at a price of £5,000, a copy of the sales receipt being attached to these particulars.

2. During the negotiations for the sale the Claimant was informed by one Lowe, an employee of the Defendant, that the engine was "good as new" and had done only 3,000 miles. This statement was an express term of the contract. Alternatively it was a misrepresentation which induced the Claimant to enter into the contract.

3. It was an implied condition of the contract that the car was of satisfactory quality and reasonably fit for the Claimant's purpose.

4. On or about 20 November 2015 the Claimant took the car to a garage for repair and was then informed that the engine had done 30,000 miles and that it was worn out and that it would cost £1,000 to replace.

5. The Defendant is accordingly in breach of the representation in paragraph 2 above and the express and implied terms under paragraphs 2 and 3 above.

6. The Claimant then wrote to the Defendant on 25 November 2015 rejecting the car by reason of the misrepresentation and/or the breaches of contract and claiming the return of his £5,000 but the Defendant refused and has continued to refuse to accept the rejection.

7. On 30 November 2015 the Claimant hired an alternative Screecher vehicle from Carhire Ltd and has paid a hire charge of £100 per week, a copy of the hire agreement being attached to these particulars.

8. The Claimant has not used the Bonecrusher car since giving notice of rejection and it has at all material times been available for collection by the Defendant.

9. The Claimant is entitled to rescind, and has rescinded, the contract by reason of the misrepresentation by the Defendant. Similarly the Claimant is entitled to treat, and has treated, the contract as discharged by the Defendant's breaches.

10. Alternatively, the Claimant is entitled to damages under section 2(1) of the Misrepresentation Act 1967 and/or under section 20 Consumer Rights Act 2015 in the sum of £3,000 (being the amount by which the price of £5,000 and the hire-charges of £2,000 exceed the current value of the car namely £4,000) plus further damages to cover additional hire charges of £100 per week until judgment or earlier payment.

11. Under section 69 of the County Courts Act 1984 the Claimant is also entitled to interest at such rate and for such period as the court thinks just.

And the claimant claims:

1. Under paragraph 9 £5,000;

2. Alternatively, under paragraph 10 damages for misrepresentation and/or for breach of contract;

3. Under paragraph 11 above interest under section 69 of the County Courts Act 1984.

4. Costs

In any event the amount of the claim for damages is limited to £10,000.
[I believe] [the claimant believes] that the facts stated in [this claim form] [these particulars of claim] are true.

In the County Court at Bigtown   Case No.   **A1.03**

BETWEEN:

John Lowe   Claimant

(A child, by Robert Lowe,
   his litigation friend)

and

Toy Importers Ltd   Defendants

PARTICULARS OF CLAIM

1. On 4 January 2016 Robert Lowe the father and litigation friend of the Claimant bought a catapult for the Claimant (then aged eight) from Rundown Stores Ltd a company now in liquidation.

2. The said Robert Lowe has been informed by the liquidator that Rundown Stores Ltd purchased all their catapults from the Defendants who imported them from Taiwan. Accordingly under section 2(2)(c) of the Consumer Protection Act 1987 the Defendants are liable for damage under the Act.

3. The catapult was defective within section 3 of the 1987 Act and when it was first used by the Claimant it broke and a piece entered his left eye.

PARTICULARS OF DEFECT

The moulded plastic which formed the catapult frame was too weak to withstand normal use by a child.

4. By reason of the defect the Claimant has suffered damage within section 5 of the 1987 Act.

PARTICULARS OF DAMAGE

The Claimant was born on 1 November 2008 and is now aged eight years. He suffered acute pain and suffering and underwent two operations in an unsuccessful attempt to save the sight of his left eye. Full particulars are set out in the medical report served with these Particulars of Claim.

PARTICULARS OF PAST AND FUTURE EXPENSES AND LOSSES

Full particulars are set out in the statement which is served with these Particulars of Claim.

5. The Claimant is also entitled to interest under section 69 of the County Courts Act 1984 for such periods and at such rate as the court thinks just.

And the claimant claims:

1. Under paragraphs 3 and 4—damages up to the sum of £25,000;

2. Under paragraph 5—interest under section 69 of the County Courts Act 1984.

3. Costs

[I believe] [the claimant believes] that the facts stated in [this claim form] [these particulars of claim] are true.

In the County Court at Bigtown   Case No.   **A1.04**

BETWEEN:

Robert Lowe   Claimant

and

Ghastly Holidays Ltd (1)   Defendants
Eesipay Ltd (2)

PARTICULARS OF CLAIM

1. By an agreement in writing ("the agreement") dated 10 January 2016 the First Defendant agreed to provide a skiing holiday for the Claimant and his wife and son, a copy of the relevant page in the brochure being attached to these particulars of claim.

2. The Claimant paid the sum of £2,000 for the holiday by means of a credit card issued by the Second Defendant under arrangements made between the First and Second Defendants. The agreement between the Claimant and the Second Defendant was therefore a fixed sum restricted use debtor-creditor-supplier agreement falling within section 75 of the Consumer Credit Act 1974. A copy of the Claimant's credit card account showing the payment made by the claimant through the Second Defendant to the First Defendant is attached to these particulars of claim.

3. It was an express term of the contract between the Claimant and the First Defendant that the Claimant and his family would stay at the Ski Palace Hotel which was described in the First Defendant's brochure as a "first class luxury hotel".

4. In breach of the said term the Claimant and his family were unable to stay at the Ski Palace Hotel because it was still in the course of construction. They were compelled to accept accommodation at the Backstreet Mews Hotel which was not a first class luxury hotel.

PARTICULARS

1. There was no bar.

2. There was no lift.

3. The walls were peeling.

4. The Claimant and his family were unable to sleep because of the noise from a nearby discotheque.

5. In consequence of the said breach the Claimant's holiday was ruined and he and his family came home more tired than when the holiday started.

6. The Claimant is entitled to the return of the £2,000 as money paid on a total failure of consideration or alternatively as damages for loss of enjoyment and mental distress.

7. The Claimant is also entitled to interest under Section 69 of the County Courts Act 1984 at such rate and for such period as the court thinks Wt.

And the Claimant claims against the First and Second Defendants jointly and severally:

1. Under paragraph 6 £2,000;

2. Under paragraph 7 interest under section 69 of the County Courts Act 1984.

3. Costs

In any event the amount of the claim for damages is limited to £10,000.
[I believe] [the claimant believes] that the facts stated in [this claim form] [these particulars of claim] are true.

In the County Court at Bigtown   Case No. **A1.05**

BETWEEN:

Rosemary Woodroffe   Claimant

and

Furnishings Ltd   Defendant

PARTICULARS OF CLAIMS

1. By a hire-purchase agreement ("the Agreement") in writing made on 1 November 2014 between the Claimant and the Defendant and bearing number 12345, a copy of which is attached to these Particulars, the Defendant supplied to the Claimant a suite of furniture at a hire-purchase price of £1,500. The Claimant signed the Agreement at the Defendant's store.

2. Under the terms of the agreement the Claimant paid a deposit of £300 and she agreed to pay the balance by twelve monthly instalments of £100 on the first day of each month. The agreement was a regulated consumer credit agreement within the Consumer Credit Act 1974 ("the Act").

3. The Claimant paid the first seven instalments and the goods became "protected" goods within section 90 of the Act. The total paid up sum is £1,000.

4. On 20 June 2015 the Claimant was made redundant and she failed to pay the instalment due on 1 July 2015.

5. On or about 10 September 2015 a driver employed by the Defendant knocked at the door of the Claimant's home and when the door was opened by the Claimant's husband the said driver and another man forced their way into the house and removed the suite. In doing so the Defendant was in breach of section 92(1) of the Act.

6. Under the Act the Claimant is entitled to damages for trespass and to the return of all her payments.

7. Under Section 69 of the County Courts Act 1984 the Claimant is also entitled to interest at such rate and of such period as the court thinks just.

And the Claimant claims against the Defendant:

1. Under Paragraph 6 £1,000 and damages for trespass not exceeding £10,000;

2. Under Paragraph 7 interest under section 69 of the County Courts Act 1984.

3. Costs

[I believe] [the claimant believes] that the facts stated in [this claim form] [these particulars of claim] are true.

JACKSON REFORMS

QOCS (Qualified one way costs shifting)

The amendments to the Civil Procedure Rules following the Jackson reforms **A1.06** introduced a system of qualified one-way costs shifting to replace the claimant's protection from adverse costs currently offered by ATE insurance and CFAs. The concern was that such insurance offered a licence to claimants to sue with very little risk as to costs. It will be available for all claimants whatever their means—there is to be no financial test to determine eligibility. QOCS applies only in personal injury claims and not, for example in professional negligence claims.

Under QOCS, if the claimant wins his action, the defendant pays both sets of costs. However, if the claimant loses QOCS protection will be lost only if the claim is found to be fraudulent, the claimant has failed to beat a defendant's CPR Part 36 offer to settle but only up to the value of damages awarded; or the case has been struck out where the claim discloses no reasonable cause of action or where it is otherwise an abuse of the court's process.

QOCS protection will also be lost in part, and subject to the court's permission, in two instances: first, if an otherwise successful claim includes an unsuccessful non-personal injury element (e.g. housing disrepair or costs of credit hire in arranging an alternative vehicle), and there is an order for costs against the claimant of that unsuccessful element, the claimant is liable for all the defendant's costs of that unsuccessful element to the extent that it is just and fair; and second, where the claim, or an element of it, is made for the financial benefit of someone other than the claimant (e.g. a credit hire claim in respect of the financing company), an order for the defendant's costs of the claim, or that element, may be made, and enforced, against that person/organisation.

Part 36

Defendants who do not accept a claimant's reasonable offer which they fail **A1.07** to beat at trial will be subject to an additional sanction equivalent to 10 per cent of the value of the claim or, for non-damages claims, 10 per cent of costs plus an extra 5 per cent of any costs awarded above £500,000. This cannot exceed £75,000 in either case. The object of this is to encourage parties to take Pt 36 more seriously.

Disclosure

A new rule on disclosure applies to all multi-track cases other than personal **A1.08** injury claims. In all other cases standard disclosure will apply.

Shortly before the first case management conference, each party will serve a report, describing the documents likely to be relevant to the matters in issue and their location, and estimating the broad range of costs that could result from standard disclosure. The court is able to direct the parties to agree a proposal on disclosure that enables the case to be tried fairly, based on a list of options available under a "menu" of disclosure options in the new rule:

CPR r.31.5(6):

"At the first or any subsequent case management conference, the court will decide, having regard to the overriding objective and the need to limit disclosure to that which is necessary to deal with the case justly, which of the following orders to make in relation to disclosure—

    (a) an order dispensing with disclosure;

    (b) an order that a party disclose the documents on which it relies, and at the same time request any specific disclosure it requires from any other party;

    (c) an order that directs, where practicable, the disclosure to be given by each party on an issue by issue basis;

    (d) an order that each party disclose any documents which it is reasonable to suppose may contain information which enables that party to advance its own case [or to damage that of any other party,] or which leads to an enquiry which has either of those consequences;

    (e) an order that a party give standard disclosure;

    (f) any other order in relation to disclosure that the court considers appropriate."

Evidence of witnesses

A1.09   CPR r.32.2 has been supplemented to emphasise the control the courts intend to impose over the evidence to be used at court:

CPR r.32.2(3):

"(3) The court may give directions—

    (a) identifying or limiting the issues to which factual evidence may be directed;

    (b) identifying the witnesses who may be called or whose evidence may be read; [or]

    (c) limiting the length [and] [or] format of witness statements."

Expert witnesses

A1.10   Parties will be required to give an estimate of the costs of their experts and the issues they intend to address. In addition, the court may lay down the issues to be addressed. A rule has been approved to make "hot-tubbing" an option under the Civil Procedure Rules. This practice involves both sides' expert witness appearing in court concurrently, with the judge asking each expert their views on a particular aspect of the expert evidence.

Case management

A1.11   New rules have been approved to improve judicial case management. All money cases will have to be issued online where they will initially be dealt with by the Northampton County Court. Once a defence is filed the case will then be transferred to Salford County Court for further directions before be distributed out to appropriate courts. If directions are needed from a judge the case will be transferred to the stated preferred court or the defendant's court, if the defendant is an individual and it is a money claim.

Standard case management directions for all types of common cases will be used where possible. Case management conferences will only be held where they would serve a useful purpose and will involve serious discussion about the issues in the case. Otherwise, the judge will, having seen the parties' proposed (ideally agreed) directions on paper, issue case management directions in writing. The entire timetable for an action will be drawn up as early as practicable in the action, subject to change if necessary.

There will be a change in the system of allocation of cases. The Allocation Questionnaire is abolished. It is replaced by a form called a directions questionnaire for SCT cases, is optional for FT cases and compulsory for MT cases. Other than in small claims cases, once the defence has been filed a court officer will provisionally decide which track the case will go into and will serve on the parties notice of proposed allocation. This notice will contain directions and a requirement for the parties to complete a directions questionnaire. In other words, the court will not now be waiting for an allocation questionnaire to be filed by the parties before making directions. The directions will be made first and only subject to variation, if necessary, on receipt of the directions questionnaire completed by the parties. Model directions will be available for the parties to scrutinise online. Specimen Directions are available at http://www.justice.gov.uk/courts/procedure-rules/civil/standard-directions. The directions handed down by the court can be challenge by parties (new CPR r.26.3) and the court has its usual discretion when hearing the question of reallocation.

New CPR r.26.3(1): **A1.12**

"If a defendant files a defence—

a court officer will provisionally decide the track which appears to be most suitable for the claim; and will serve on each party a notice of proposed allocation; the notice of proposed allocation will—

- specify any matter to be complied with by the date specified in the notice (*i.e. directions*);
- require the parties to file a completed directions questionnaire and serve copies on all other parties;
- state the address of the court or the court office to which the directions questionnaire must be returned;
- inform the parties how to obtain the directions questionnaire; and
- if a case appears suitable for allocation to the fast track or multi-track, require the parties to file proposed directions by the date specified in the notice."

Two Court of Appeal judges will consider any issues on the interpretation or application of the CPR.

The CPR will require courts to take a tougher approach to breaches of the rules. See, for example, the sanction for failing to file a response to the directions questionnaire (CPR r.26.3):

"(7A) If a claim is a designated money claim and a party does not comply with the notice served under rule 26.3(1) by the date specified)—

> the court will serve a further notice on that party requiring them to comply, within 7 days of service; and if that party fails to comply with the notice served under subparagraph (a), the party's statement of case *shall* be struck out without further order of the court."

So far as possible, judges should monitor (by phone or email) the parties' progress in terms of complying with orders, to pre-empt the need for sanctions. CPR r.3.9 (relief from sanctions) is simplified:

> "On an application for relief from any sanction imposed for a failure to comply with any rule, practice direction or court order, the court will consider all the circumstances of the case, so as to enable it to deal justly with the application, including the need—
>
> (a) *for litigation to be conducted efficiently and at proportionate cost; and*
> (b) to enforce compliance with rules, practice directions and orders."

The automatic stay of proceedings on request by both sides, or of the court's own initiative, is restored, after having been recently removed. CPR r.26.4(2):

> "(2) If all parties request a stay the proceedings will be stayed for one month and the court will notify the parties accordingly.
> (2A) If the court considers that such a stay would be appropriate, the court will direct that the proceedings, either in whole or in part, be stayed for one month, or for such other period as it considers appropriate."

Costs management

A1.13   New rules relating principally to multi-track cases have been introduced. To emphasise its importance, a new Section II is added to CPR Pt 3, dealing solely with costs management. Costs management involves each party, early in the proceedings, producing an estimate of how many hours are likely to be spent—and by which seniority of lawyer—on each stage of their action from pre-issue of the claim until trial. The budgets are then approved by a judge at a hearing, if proportionate to the remedy being sought. If not, the judge can amend them, for example by reducing the amount of hours to be spent on a particular task. Budgets may be updated during the life of the action. The case will then be managed by reference to the approved budgets and, when assessing the costs liability of the losing party, the court will generally adopt the finally approved budget.

Note the sanction at CPR r.3.14—in the absence of a From H budget, the costs are assumed to be the court fees only. Parties can agree their respective budgets, and the court cannot go behind that agreement. This means that if they agree, in a cosy sort of way, two huge budgets, the rules do not permit Court intervention. This seems likely either to be found to be a misreading of the rules, or to need early change. Note also that the Court cannot intervene in costs already incurred, save to say that they may not be incurred again, or possibly to limit the future costs quite severely in the interests of overall proportionality.

Further along, at the end of the case, and in general, an agreed or approved budget cannot be exceeded and can only be challenged on detailed assessment if a party can establish that there was "good reason" to exceed the budgeted amount for the work included in that budget. "Good reason" is undefined but some guidance may be obtained from *Sylvia Henry v Newsgroup Newspapers Ltd* [2013] EWCA Civ 19.

This Section and Practice Direction 3E apply to all multi-track cases commenced on or after 1 April 2013, except:

(a) cases in the Admiralty and Commercial Courts;

(b) such cases in the Chancery Division as the Chancellor of the High Court may direct; and

(c) such cases in the Technology and Construction Court and the Mercantile Courts as the President of the Queen's Bench Division may direct, unless the proceedings are the subject of fixed costs or scale costs or the court otherwise orders.

This Section and the Practice Direction 3E will apply to any other proceedings (including applications) where the court so orders.

It has also been decided that the new rules will not apply to Commercial cases worth more than £2m.

Costs capping

As part of the courts' increased powers to set budgets, the ability of the courts to impose costs-capping is increased. CPR r.3.19(5):   **A1.14**

> "The court may at any stage of proceedings make a costs capping order against all or any of the parties, if—
>
> (a) it is in the interests of justice to do so;
> (b) there is a substantial risk that without such an order costs will be disproportionately incurred; and
> (c) it is not satisfied that the risk in subparagraph (b) can be adequately controlled by–
>   (i) case management directions or orders made under Part 3; and detailed assessment of costs."

In considering whether to make a costs-capping order, the court will consider all the circumstances including:

> "(a) whether there is a substantial imbalance between the financial position of the parties;
> (b) whether the costs of determining the amount of the cap are likely to be proportionate to the overall costs of the litigation;
> (c) the stage which the proceedings have reached; and
> (d) the costs which have been incurred to date and the future costs." (Rule 3.19(6))

The parties do not have to wait for such an order; they can apply for one themselves (see CPR r.3.20).

Assessment streamlining

A1.15   This concerns the procedure for processing bills of costs in which the costs claimed are £75,000 or less, which will now be assessed by a judge who will make a provisional assessment of the amount of costs due to the receiving party. The costs of the assessment will be limited to not more than £1,500. If any party is dissatisfied with the assessment an oral hearing will be fixed. If the dissenting party achieves a result at the oral hearing which is better the provisional assessment the court will award costs accordingly.

These new arrangements apply to all detailed assessment proceedings commenced after 1 April 2013—not to bills in cases started after that date. Please check what the local arrangements are. The bills will be box work, but it is hoped that most Courts will in fact list them, so as to allow proper time for these matters to be dealt with (at least 60 minutes per bill to start with might seem reasonable). They are not like any other box work, but more like Stage 3 RTA protocol paper hearings—proper hearings, but simply not attended.

In assessing bills of costs generally, Lownds is not reversed, but the new wording of the rules is to be followed. This means that one first decides what work was reasonably done, then asks what a reasonable charge was, then steps back and applies proportionality.

Limiting costs on appeals

A1.16   This will apply where the decision under appeal was made in a no-costs or limited costs jurisdiction. The amendments enable the court at the outset of such an appeal to order that the costs be limited to the extent which the court specifies. The court will take into account the means of both parties; the circumstances of each case; and the need to facilitate access to justice before making any such order.

Docketing

A1.17   Jackson LJ advocated greater use of docketing, i.e. the assignment of a case to one judge throughout its life. This applies specifically to multi-track cases.

REGULATION (EC) NO 261/2004 OF THE EUROPEAN PARLIAMENT AND OF THE COUNCIL

of 11 February 2004

establishing common rules on compensation and assistance to passengers in the event of denied boarding and of cancellation or long delay of flights, and repealing Regulation (EEC) No 295/91

(Text with EEA relevance)

THE EUROPEAN PARLIAMENT AND THE COUNCIL OF THE EUROPEAN UNION,

Having regard to the Treaty establishing the European Community, and in particular Article 80(2) thereof,

Having regard to the proposal from the Commission,(1)

Having regard to the opinion of the European Economic and Social Committee,(2)

After consulting the Committee of the Regions,

Acting in accordance with the procedure laid down in Article 251 of the Treaty,(3) in the light of the joint

text approved by the Conciliation Committee on 1 December 2003,

A2.01

Whereas:

(1) Action by the Community in the field of air transport should aim, among other things, at ensuring a high level of protection for passengers. Moreover, full account should be taken of the requirements of consumer protection in general.

(2) Denied boarding and cancellation or long delay of flights cause serious trouble and inconvenience to passengers.

(3) While Council Regulation (EEC) No 295/91 of 4 February 1991 establishing common rules for a denied boarding compensation system in scheduled air transport (4) created basic protection for passengers, the number of passengers denied boarding against their

---

1   ()   OJ C 103 E, 30.4.2002, p.225 and OJ C 71 E, 25.3.2003, p.188.
2   ()   OJ C 241, 7.10.2002, p.29.
3   ()   Opinion of the European Parliament of 24 October 2002 (OJ C 300 E, 11.12.2003, p.443), Council Common Position of 18 March 2003 (OJ C 125 E, 27.5.2003, p.63) and Position of the European Parliament of 3 July 2003.

Legislative Resolution of the European Parliament of 18 December 2003 and Council Decision of 26 January 2004.
4   ()   OJ L 36, 8.2.1991, p.5.

will remains too high, as does that affected by cancellations without prior warning and that affected by long delays.

(4) The Community should therefore raise the standards of protection set by that Regulation both to strengthen the rights of passengers and to ensure that air carriers operate under harmonised conditions in a liberalised market.

(5) Since the distinction between scheduled and non-sched-uled air services is weakening, such protection should apply to passengers not only on scheduled but also on non-scheduled flights, including those forming part of package tours.

(6) The protection accorded to passengers departing from an airport located in a Member State should be extended to those leaving an airport located in a third country for one situated in a Member State, when a Community carrier operates the flight.

(7) In order to ensure the effective application of this Regulation, the obligations that it creates should rest with the operating air carrier who performs or intends to perform a flight, whether with owned aircraft, under dry or wet lease, or on any other basis.

(8) This Regulation should not restrict the rights of the operating air carrier to seek compensation from any person, including third parties, in accordance with the law applicable.

(9) The number of passengers denied boarding against their will should be reduced by requiring air carriers to call for volunteers to surrender their reservations, in exchange for benefits, instead of denying passengers boarding, and by fully compensating those finally denied boarding.

(10) Passengers denied boarding against their will should be able either to cancel their flights, with reimbursement of their tickets, or to continue them under satisfactory conditions, and should be adequately cared for while awaiting a later flight.

(11) Volunteers should also be able to cancel their flights, with reimbursement of their tickets, or continue them under satisfactory conditions, since they face difficulties of travel similar to those experienced by passengers denied boarding against their will.

(12) The trouble and inconvenience to passengers caused by cancellation of flights should also be reduced. This should be achieved by inducing carriers to inform passengers of cancellations before the scheduled time of departure and in addition to offer them reasonable re-routing, so that the passengers can make other arrangements. Air carriers should compensate passengers if they fail to do this, except when the cancellation occurs in extraordinary circumstances which could not have been avoided even if all reasonable measures had been taken.

(13) Passengers whose flights are cancelled should be able either to obtain reimbursement of their tickets or to obtain re-routing under satisfactory conditions, and should be

adequately cared for while awaiting a later flight.

(14) As under the Montreal Convention, obligations on operating air carriers should be limited or excluded in cases where an event has been caused by extraordinary circumstances which could not have been avoided even if all reasonable measures had been taken. Such circumstances may, in particular, occur in cases of political instability, meteorological conditions incompatible with the operation of the flight concerned, security risks, unexpected flight safety shortcomings and strikes that affect the operation of an operating air carrier.

(15) Extraordinary circumstances should be deemed to exist where the impact of an air traffic management decision in relation to a particular aircraft on a particular day gives rise to a long delay, an overnight delay, or the cancellation of one or more flights by that aircraft, even though all reasonable measures had been taken by the air carrier concerned to avoid the delays or cancellations.

(16) In cases where a package tour is cancelled for reasons other than the flight being cancelled, this Regulation should not apply.

(17) Passengers whose flights are delayed for a specified time should be adequately cared for and should be able to cancel their flights with reimbursement of their tickets or to continue them under satisfactory conditions.

(18) Care for passengers awaiting an alternative or a delayed flight may be limited or declined if the provision of the care would itself cause further delay.

(19) Operating air carriers should meet the special needs of persons with reduced mobility and any persons accompanying them.

(20) Passengers should be fully informed of their rights in the event of denied boarding and of cancellation or long delay of flights, so that they can effectively exercise their rights.

(21) Member States should lay down rules on sanctions applicable to infringements of the provisions of this Regulation and ensure that these sanctions are applied. The sanctions should be effective, proportionate and dissuasive.

(22) Member States should ensure and supervise general compliance by their air carriers with this Regulation and designate an appropriate body to carry out such enforcement tasks. The supervision should not affect the rights of passengers and air carriers to seek legal redress from courts under procedures of national law.

(23) The Commission should analyse the application of this Regulation and should assess in particular the opportunity of extending its scope to all passengers having a contract with a tour operator or with a Community carrier, when departing from a third country airport to an airport in a Member State.

(24) Arrangements for greater cooperation over the use of Gibraltar airport were agreed in London on 2

December 1987 by the Kingdom of Spain and the United Kingdom in a joint declaration by the Ministers of Foreign Affairs of the two countries. Such arrangements have yet to enter into operation.

(25) Regulation (EEC) No 295/91 should accordingly be repealed,

HAVE ADOPTED THIS REGULATION:

Article 1

Subject

1. This Regulation establishes, under the conditions specified herein, minimum rights for passengers when:

a) they are denied boarding against their will;

b) their flight is cancelled;

c) their flight is delayed.

2. Application of this Regulation to Gibraltar airport is understood to be without prejudice to the respective legal positions of the Kingdom of Spain and the United Kingdom with regard to the dispute over sovereignty over the territory in which the airport is situated.

3. Application of this Regulation to Gibraltar airport shall be suspended until the arrangements in the Joint Declaration made by the Foreign Ministers of the Kingdom of Spain and the United Kingdom on 2 December 1987 enter into operation. The Governments of Spain and the United Kingdom will inform the Council of such date of entry into operation.

Article 2

Definitions

For the purposes of this Regulation:

a) "air carrier" means an air transport undertaking with a valid operating licence;

b) "operating air carrier" means an air carrier that performs or intends to perform a flight under a contract with a passenger or on behalf of another person, legal or natural, having a contract with that passenger;

c) "Community carrier" means an air carrier with a valid operating licence granted by a Member State in accordance with the provisions of Council Regulation (EEC) No 2407/92 of 23 July 1992 on licensing of air carriers(5);

d) "tour operator" means, with the exception of an air carrier, an organiser within the meaning of Article 2, point 2, of Council Directive 90/314/EEC of 13 June 1990 on package travel, package holidays and package tours (6);

e) "package" means those services defined in Article 2, point 1, of Directive 90/314/EEC;

f) "ticket" means a valid document giving entitlement to trans-

5 () OJ L 240, 24.8.1992, p. 1.
6 () OJ L 158, 23.6.1990, p. 59.

port, or something equivalent in paperless form, including electronic form, issued or authorised by the air carrier or its authorised agent;

g) "reservation" means the fact that the passenger has a ticket, or other proof, which indicates that the reservation has been accepted and registered by the air carrier or tour operator;

h) "final destination" means the destination on the ticket presented at the check-in counter or, in the case of directly connecting flights, the destination of the last flight; alternative connecting flights available shall not be taken into account if the original planned arrival time is respected;

i) "person with reduced mobility" means any person whose mobility is reduced when using transport because of any physical disability (sensory or locomotory, permanent or temporary), intellectual impairment, age or any other cause of disability, and whose situation needs special attention and adaptation to the person's needs of the services made available to all passengers;

j) "denied boarding" means a refusal to carry passengers on a flight, although they have presented themselves for boarding under the conditions laid down in Article 3(2), except where there are reasonable grounds to deny them boarding, such as reasons of health, safety or security, or inadequate travel documentation;

k) "volunteer" means a person who has presented himself for boarding under the conditions laid down in Article 3(2) and responds positively to the air carrier's call for passengers prepared to surrender their reservation in exchange for benefits.

l) "cancellation" means the non-operation of a flight which was previously planned and on which at least one place was reserved.

Article 3

Scope

1.   This Regulation shall apply:

a)   to passengers departing from an airport located in the territory of a Member State to which the Treaty applies;

b)   to passengers departing from an airport located in a third country to an airport situated in the territory of a Member State to which the Treaty applies, unless they received benefits or compensation and were given assistance in that third country, if the operating air carrier of the flight concerned is a Community carrier.

2.   Paragraph 1 shall apply on the condition that passengers:

a)   have a confirmed reservation on the flight concerned and, except in the case of cancellation referred to in Article 5, present themselves for check-in,

   •   as stipulated and at the time indicated in advance

and in writing (including by electronic means) by the air carrier, the tour operator or an authorised travel agent, or, if no time is indicated,

- not later than 45 minutes before the published departure time; or

b) have been transferred by an air carrier or tour operator from the flight for which they held a reservation to another flight, irrespective of the reason.

3. This Regulation shall not apply to passengers travelling free of charge or at a reduced fare not available directly or indirectly to the public. However, it shall apply to passengers having tickets issued under a frequent flyer programme or other commercial programme by an air carrier or tour operator.

4. This Regulation shall only apply to passengers transported by motorised fixed wing aircraft.

5. This Regulation shall apply to any operating air carrier providing transport to passengers covered by paragraphs 1 and 2. Where an operating air carrier which has no contract with the passenger performs obligations under this Regulation, it shall be regarded as doing so on behalf of the person having a contract with that passenger.

6. This Regulation shall not affect the rights of passengers under Directive 90/314/EEC. This Regulation shall not apply in cases where a package tour is cancelled for reasons other than cancellation of the flight.

Article 4

Denied boarding

1. When an operating air carrier reasonably expects to deny boarding on a flight, it shall first call for volunteers to surrender their reservations in exchange for benefits under conditions to be agreed between the passenger concerned and the operating air carrier. Volunteers shall be assisted in accordance with Article 8, such assistance being additional to the benefits mentioned in this paragraph.

2. If an insufficient number of volunteers comes forward to allow the remaining passengers with reservations to board the flight, the operating air carrier may then deny boarding to passengers against their will.

3. If boarding is denied to passengers against their will, the operating air carrier shall immediately compensate them in accordance with Article 7 and assist them in accordance with Articles 8 and 9.

Article 5

Cancellation

1. In case of cancellation of a flight, the passengers concerned shall:

a) be offered assistance by the operating air carrier in accordance with Article 8; and

b) be offered assistance by the operating air carrier in accordance with Article 9(1)(a) and 9(2), as well as, in event of re-routing when the reasonably expected time of departure of the new flight is at least the day after the departure as it was planned for the cancelled flight, the assistance specified in Article 9(1)(b) and 9(1)(c); and

c) have the right to compensation by the operating air carrier in accordance with Article 7, unless:

    (i)   they are informed of the cancellation at least two weeks before the scheduled time of departure; or

    (ii) they are informed of the cancellation between two weeks and seven days before the scheduled time of departure and are offered re-routing, allowing them to depart no more than two hours before the scheduled time of departure and to reach their final destination less than four hours after the scheduled time of arrival; or

    (iii) they are informed of the cancellation less than seven days before the scheduled time of departure and are offered re-routing, allowing them to depart no more than one hour before the scheduled time of departure and to reach their final destination less than two hours after the scheduled time of arrival.

2. When passengers are informed of the cancellation, an explanation shall be given concerning possible alternative transport.

3. An operating air carrier shall not be obliged to pay compensation in accordance with Article 7, if it can prove that the cancellation is caused by extraordinary circumstances which could not have been avoided even if all reasonable measures had been taken.

4. The burden of proof concerning the questions as to whether and when the passenger has been informed of the cancellation of the flight shall rest with the operating air carrier.

Article 6

Delay

1. When an operating air carrier reasonably expects a flight to be delayed beyond its scheduled time of departure:

a) for two hours or more in the case of flights of 1 500 kilometres or less; or

b) for three hours or more in the case of all intra-Community flights of more than 1 500 kilometres and of all other flights between 1 500 and 3 500 kilometres; or

c) for four hours or more in the case of all flights not falling under (a) or (b),

passengers shall be offered by the operating air carrier:

(i)   the assistance specified in Article 9(1)(a) and 9(2); and

(ii) when the reasonably expected time of departure is at least the day after the time of departure previously announced, the assistance specified in Article 9(1)(b) and 9(1)(c); and

(iii) when the delay is at least five hours, the assistance specified in Article 8(1)(a).

2.   In any event, the assistance shall be offered within the time limits set out above with respect to each distance bracket.

Article 7

Right t. compensation

1.   Where reference is made to this Article, passengers shall receive compensation amounting to:

a)   EUR 250 for all flights of 1 500 kilometres or less;

b)   EUR 400 for all intra-Community flights of more than 1 500 kilometres, and for all other flights between 1 500 and 3 500 kilometres;

c)   EUR 600 for all flights not falling under (a) or (b).

In determining the distance, the basis shall be the last destination at which the denial of boarding or cancellation will delay the passenger's arrival after the scheduled time.

2.   When passengers are offered re-routing to their final destination on an alternative flight pursuant to Article 8, the arrival time of which does not exceed the scheduled arrival time of the flight originally booked

a)   by two hours, in respect of all flights of 1 500 kilometres or less; or

b)   by three hours, in respect of all intra-Community flights of more than 1 500 kilometres and for all other flights between 1 500 and 3 500 kilometres; or

c)   by four hours, in respect of all flights not falling under (a) or (b), the operating air carrier may reduce the compensation provided for in paragraph 1 by 50%.

3.   The compensation referred to in paragraph 1 shall be paid in cash, by electronic bank transfer, bank orders or bank cheques or, with the signed agreement of the passenger, in travel vouchers and/or other services.

4.   The distances given in paragraphs 1 and 2 shall be measured by the great circle route method.

Article 8

Right to reimbursement or re-routing

1   Where reference is made to this Article, passengers shall be offered the choice between:

(a) — reimbursement within seven days, by the means provided for in Article 7(3), of the full cost of the ticket at the price at which it was bought, for the part or parts of the journey not made, and for the part or parts already made if the flight is no longer serving any purpose in relation to the passenger's original travel plan, together with, when relevant,

— a return flight to the first point of departure, at the earliest opportunity;

(b) re-routing, under comparable transport conditions, to their final destination at the earliest opportunity; or

(c) re-routing, under comparable transport conditions, to their final destination at a later date at the passenger's convenience, subject to availability of seats.

2.   Paragraph 1(a) shall also apply to passengers whose flights form part of a package, except for the right to reimbursement where such right arises under Directive 90/314/EEC.

3.   When, in the case where a town, city or region is served by several airports, an operating air carrier offers a passenger a flight to an airport alternative to that for which the booking was made, the operating air carrier shall bear the cost of transferring the passenger from that alternative airport either to that for which the booking was made, or to another close-by destination agreed with the passenger.

Article 9

Right to care

1.   Where reference is made to this Article, passengers shall be offered free of charge:

(a) meals and refreshments in a reasonable relation to the waiting time;

(b) hotel accommodation in cases

- where a stay of one or more nights becomes necessary, or

- where a stay additional to that intended by the passenger becomes necessary;

(c) transport between the airport and place of accommodation (hotel or other).

2.   In addition, passengers shall be offered free of charge two telephone calls, telex or fax messages, or e-mails.

3.   In applying this Article, the operating air carrier shall pay particular attention to the needs of persons with reduced mobility and any persons accompanying them, as well as to the needs of unaccompanied children.

Article 10

Upgrading and downgrading

1.   If an operating air carrier places a passenger in a class higher than that for which the ticket was purchased, it may not request any supplementary payment.

2.   If an operating air carrier places a passenger in a class lower than that for which the ticket was purchased, it shall within seven days, by the means provided for in Article 7(3), reimburse

(a) 30% of the price of the ticket for all flights of 1 500 kilometres or less, or

(b) 50% of the price of the ticket for all intra-Community flights of more than 1 500 kilometres, except flights between the European territory of the Member States and the French overseas departments, and for all other flights between 1 500 and 3 500 kilometres, or

(c) 75% of the price of the ticket for all flights not falling under (a) or (b), including flights between the European territory of the Member States and the French overseas departments.

Article 11

Persons with reduced mobility or special needs

1. Operating air carriers shall give priority to carrying persons with reduced mobility and any persons or certified service dogs accompanying them, as well as unaccompanied children.

2. In cases of denied boarding, cancellation and delays of any length, persons with reduced mobility and any persons accompanying them, as well as unaccompanied children, shall have the right to care in accordance with Article 9 as soon as possible.

Article 12

Further compensation

1. This Regulation shall apply without prejudice to a passenger's rights to further compensation. The compensation granted under this Regulation may be deducted from such compensation.

2. Without prejudice to relevant principles and rules of national law, including case-law, paragraph 1 shall not apply to passengers who have voluntarily surrendered a reservation under Article 4(1).

Article 13

Right of redress

In cases where an operating air carrier pays compensation or meets the other obligations incumbent on it under this Regulation, no provision of this Regulation may be interpreted as restricting its right to seek compensation from any person, including third parties, in accordance with the law applicable. In particular, this Regulation shall in no way restrict the operating air carrier's right to seek reimbursement from a tour operator or another person with whom the operating air carrier has a contract. Similarly, no provision of this Regulation may be interpreted as restricting the right of a tour operator or a third party, other than a passenger, with whom an operating air carrier has a contract, to seek reimbursement or compensation from the operating air carrier in accordance with applicable relevant laws.

Article 14

Obligation to inform passengers of their rights

1. The operating air carrier shall ensure that at check-in a clearly legible notice containing the following text is displayed in a manner clearly visible to passengers: "If you are denied boarding or if your flight is cancelled or delayed for at least two hours, ask at the check-in counter or boarding gate for the text stating your rights, particularly with regard to compensation and assistance."

2. An operating air carrier denying boarding or cancelling a flight shall provide each passenger affected with a written notice setting out the rules for compensation and assistance in line with this Regulation. It shall also provide each passenger affected by a delay of at least two hours with an equivalent notice. The contact details of the national designated body referred to in Article 16 shall also be given to the passenger in written form.

3. In respect of blind and visually impaired persons, the provisions of this Article shall be applied using appropriate alternative means.

Article 15

Exclusion of waiver

1. Obligations vis-à-vis passengers pursuant to this Regulation may not be limited or waived, notably by a derogation or restrictive clause in the contract of carriage.

2. If, nevertheless, such a derogation or restrictive clause is applied in respect of a passenger, or if the passenger is not correctly informed of his rights and for that reason has accepted compensation which is inferior to that provided for in this Regulation, the passenger shall still be entitled to take the necessary proceedings before the competent courts or bodies in order to obtain additional compensation.

Article 16

Infringements

1. Each Member State shall designate a body responsible for the enforcement of this Regulation as regards flights from airports situated on its territory and flights from a third country to such airports. Where appropriate, this body shall take the measures necessary to ensure that the rights of passengers are respected. The Member States shall inform the Commission of the body that has been designated in accordance with this paragraph.

2. Without prejudice to Article 12, each passenger may complain to any body designated under paragraph 1, or to any other competent body designated by a Member State, about an alleged infringement of this Regulation at any airport situated on the territory of a Member State or concerning any flight from a third country to an airport situated on that territory.

3. The sanctions laid down by Member States for infringements of this Regulation shall be effective, proportionate and dissuasive.

Article 17

Report

The Commission shall report to the European Parliament and the Council by 1 January 2007 on the operation and the results of this Regulation, in particular regarding:

- the incidence of denied boarding and of cancellation of flights,

- the possible extension of the scope of this Regulation to passengers having a contract with a Community carrier or holding a flight reservation which forms part of a "package tour" to which Directive 90/314/EEC applies and who depart from a third-country airport to an airport in a Member State, on flights not operated by Community air carriers,

- the possible revision of the amounts of compensation referred to in Article 7(1).

The report shall be accompanied where necessary by legislative proposals.

Article 18

Repeal

Regulation (EEC) No 295/91 shall be repealed.

Article 19

Entry into force

This Regulation shall enter into force on 17 February 2005.

This Regulation shall be binding in its entirety and directly applicable in all Member States.

Done at Strasbourg, 11 February 2004.

For the European Parliament
The President
P.COX

For the Council
The President
M.McDOWELL

INDEX

LEGAL TAXONOMY
FROM SWEET & MAXWELL

This index has been prepared using Sweet and Maxwell's Legal Taxonomy. Main index entries conform to keywords provided by the Legal Taxonomy except where references to specific documents or non-standard terms (denoted by quotation marks) have been included. These keywords provide a means of identifying similar concepts in other Sweet & Maxwell publications and online services to which keywords from the Legal Taxonomy have been applied. Readers may find some minor differences between terms used in the text and those which appear in the index. Suggestions to *sweet&maxwell.taxonomy@thomson.com*